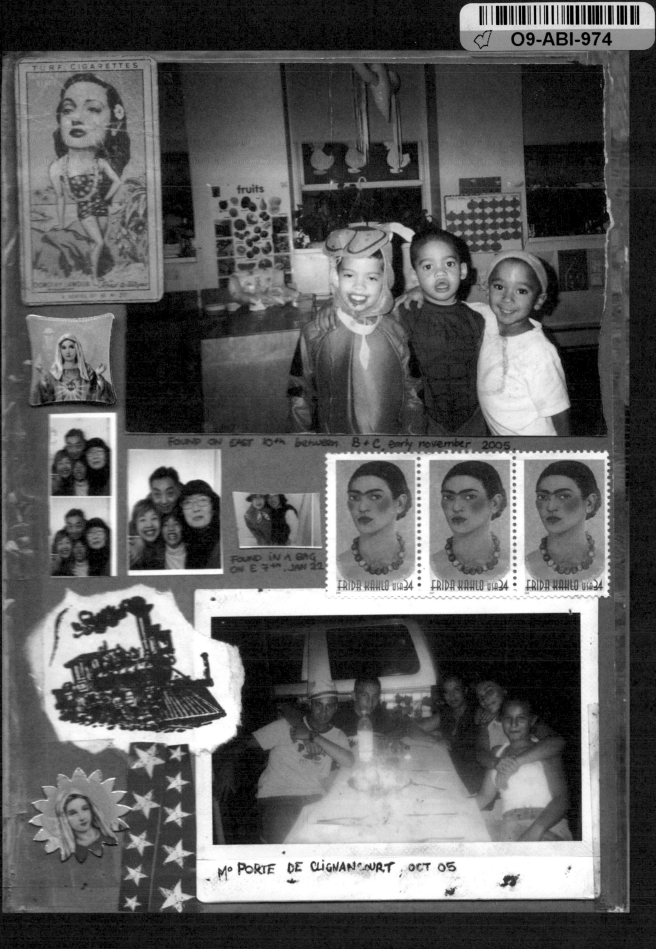

TURF CIGARETTES

fruits

FOUND ON EAST 10th between B + C, early november 2005.

FOUND IN A BAG ON E 7th, JAN 22

FRIDA KAHLO USA 34   FRIDA KAHLO USA 34   FRIDA KAHLO USA 34

M° PORTE DE CLIGNANCOURT, OCT 05

SOPHIE CRUMB: EVOLUTION OF A CRAZY ARTIST

SOPHIE CRUMB: EVOLUTION OF A CRAZY ARTIST

EDITED BY
S., A. & R. CRUMB

W. W. NORTON & COMPANY
NEW YORK LONDON

For information about special discounts for bulk purchases, please contact
W. W. Norton Special Sales at specialsales@wwnorton.com or 800-233-4830

Manufacturing by TWP
Production manager: Devon Zahn
Digital production by Sue Carlson and Alex Price

Library of Congress Cataloging-in-Publication Data

Crumb, Sophie.
Sophie Crumb : evolution of a crazy artist / edited by S., A., & R. Crumb. — 1st ed.
p. cm.
ISBN 978-0-393-07996-8 (hardcover)
1. Crumb, Sophie—Themes, motives. I. Kominsky-Crumb, Aline, 1948–
II. Crumb, R. III. Title.
IV. Title: Evolution of a crazy artist.
NC139.C776A4 2011
741.092—dc22

2010020364

W. W. Norton & Company, Inc.
500 Fifth Avenue, New York, N.Y. 10110
www.wwnorton.com

W. W. Norton & Company Ltd.
Castle House, 75/76 Wells Street, London W1T 3QT

1 2 3 4 5 6 7 8 9 0

Contents

Aline. Drawn from life. May, 2009.

A WORD FROM THE MATERNAL PARENTAL UNIT

I CAN EASILY IMAGINE HOW PEOPLE COULD LOOK AT THIS BOOK SIMPLY AS MORE "CRUMBSPLOITATION"... JUST RIDING ON THE TAIL OF THE SUCCESS OF ROBERT'S BLOCKBUSTER, **GENESIS**. YES, THE SCATHING CRITIQUES ARE OBVIOUS. "OH, THE CRUMBS ARE INDULGING THEMSELVES, PUSHING THEIR CHILD'S WORK ON THEIR LOYAL PUBLIC." SO, TO AVOID FEEDING THIS IDEA, ROBERT AND I ARE KEEPING A LOW PROFILE. NOT WANTING TO USE ROBERT'S FAME TO MOTIVATE YOU, WE ARE COUNTING ON YOU, OUR DISCRIMINATING READERS, TO PERCEIVE THE VALUE OF THIS INTIMATE BODY OF WORK THAT TAKES YOU THROUGH THE SUBTLE BUT DRAMATIC DEVELOPMENT OF A YOUNG ARTIST.

THIS IS A PROJECT WE'D BEEN TALKING ABOUT DOING FOR YEARS, BUT IT TOOK THE ENTHUSIASTIC SUPPORT OF OUR EDITOR, BOB WEIL, TO GET US GOING. THIS BOOK EXISTS PARTLY BECAUSE ROBERT IS A COMPULSIVE ARCHIVIST, AND CAREFULLY SAVED AND DATED THOUSANDS OF SOPHIE'S DRAWINGS. SOPHIE WAS A PROLIFIC ARTIST STARTING AT A VERY EARLY AGE. HOW MUCH OF THIS IS GENETIC AND HOW MUCH IS BEHAVIORAL, I HAVE NO IDEA. ROBERT AND I WERE DRAWING COMICS MORE OR LESS DAILY, SO FOR SOPHIE DRAWING MUST HAVE SEEMED LIKE THE NATURAL THING TO DO. IN CONTRAST, DURING MY ENTIRE CHILDHOOD I NEVER SAW AN ADULT DRAW, EVER, AND YET I DECIDED THAT I WANTED TO BE AN ARTIST WHEN I WAS EIGHT YEARS OLD. I TALKED MY PARENTS INTO LETTING ME TAKE PAINTING CLASSES AND, ON MY OWN, I STARTED COPYING GREAT WORKS OF ART FROM LOW-GRADE ART BOOKS.

SOPHIE NEVER STOPPED DRAWING, NEVER LOST INTEREST. SHE DREW IN A WACKY PERSONAL STYLE AND ALWAYS HAD A STRONG, COMPLETE VISION OF HER OWN UNIVERSE. SHE SURPRISED US AND KEPT US LAUGHING. AT AN EARLY AGE SHE HAD VIVID CONCEPTS OF GOOD AND EVIL (ANGELS AND DEVILS), RICH AND POOR (PRINCESSES AND URCHINS), JOY AND SADNESS, PAIN AND PLEASURE. AND SHE LEARNED HOW TO PLEASE OTHERS WITH HER DRAWINGS.

I'VE SEEN BOOKS ABOUT ART THERAPY THAT SHOW PROGRESSIVE STAGES OF MENTAL ILLNESS, BUT I HAVE NEVER SEEN A BOOK REVEALING PERSONAL EVOLUTION FROM TODDLERHOOD TO ADULTHOOD THROUGH ART... THAT'S RIGHT, FOLKS... IT'S NOT ONLY BECAUSE THESE HAPPEN TO BE THE DRAWINGS OF OUR PRECIOUS LITTLE "GENIUS" THAT THIS IS A UNIQUE AND COMPELLING DOCUMENT!

SO, LIKE, I UNDERSTAND YOUR SKEPTICISM, DUDES, BUT CHECK IT OUT!

— ALINE KOMINSKY-CRUMB, 2010

...AND HERE'S DEAR OLD DAD...

SOPHIE WAS BORN ON SEPTEMBER 27, 1981. SHE WAS A VERY INTENSE, SEETHING LITTLE BEING RIGHT FROM THE BEGINNING. WHATEVER SHE DID, SHE WENT AT IT WITH STRONG FOCUS AND CONCENTRATION, INCLUDING DRAWING. IN NOVEMBER, 1983, WHEN SHE WAS TWO YEARS AND TWO MONTHS OLD, I BEGAN SAVING THE MOST INTERESTING AND EXPRESSIVE OF HER DRAWINGS. SOMETIMES ALINE OR I WOULD SIT AND DRAW WITH HER. I WOULD OFTEN ASK HER WHAT WAS GOING ON IN A DRAWING SHE'D JUST MADE, AND SOMETIMES I WOULD WRITE DOWN AT THE BOTTOM OF THE DRAWING WHAT SHE DESCRIBED TO ME ABOUT IT. THESE EXPLANATIONS ARE PUT IN QUOTES UNDER SOME OF THE EARLY DRAWINGS HERE.

R. CRUMB
BY SOPHIE,
APRIL, 1986

MAKING THE SELECTIONS FOR THIS BOOK, OUT OF THOUSANDS OF SOPHIE'S DRAWINGS, WAS A BIG JOB. WHAT I'D SAVED FROM HER CHILDHOOD WAS A TINY FRACTION OF ALL THE DRAWING SHE DID. STILL, THESE AMOUNTED TO MANY HUNDREDS. BESIDES THESE LOOSE DRAWINGS THERE ARE DOZENS OF SCHOOL NOTEBOOKS AND SKETCHBOOKS. ALINE AND SOPHIE AND I SPENT MANY HOURS SIFTING THROUGH THIS MASSIVE OUTPUT, CHOOSING DRAWINGS WE THOUGHT WOULD REPRESENT THE VARIOUS PHASES SHE'D GONE THROUGH FROM AGE TWO UNTIL NOW. AFTER MANY HARD CHOICES WE STILL ENDED UP WITH TWICE THE PAGE LIMIT SET BY THE PUBLISHER, AND THEN HAD TO MAKE A SECOND, EVEN MORE RUTHLESS SELECTION.

NATURALLY, ALINE AND I ALWAYS THOUGHT THAT SOPHIE WAS AN EXCEPTIONALLY GIFTED ARTIST, BUT THE MAIN POINT OF THIS COMPILATION IS NOT TO SHOW OFF HER TALENT, BUT TO TRACK THE DEVELOPMENT, THE EVOLUTION, OF A GIVEN HUMAN BEING THROUGH THE MEDIUM OF DRAWING, STARTING FROM VERY EARLY CHILDHOOD. THE FACT THAT SHE DREW INCESSANTLY, AND THAT SO MUCH OF HER ARTWORK HAD BEEN SAVED, MAKES POSSIBLE A HIGHLY REVEALING VISUAL RECORD. ONE CAN LOOK AT THIS BOOK AS A SORT OF CLINICAL STUDY, A PSYCHOLOGICAL TEXTBOOK.

THE ORIGINAL IDEA FOR THE TITLE WAS *EVOLUTION OF AN ARTIST: SOPHIE CRUMB*, BUT AFTER SOPHIE SPENT DAYS AND WEEKS LOOKING AT HER OLD CHILDHOOD AND ADOLESCENT ARTWORK, SHE SAID SHE REALIZED THAT SHE WAS ALWAYS "CRAZY", EVEN AS A KID. HENCE THE ALTERATION, AT HER SUGGESTION, OF THE TITLE. I GUESS WITH PARENTS LIKE ALINE AND ME, WHO BOTH COME FROM "TAINTED" FAMILIES, SHE COULDN'T HELP BUT TURN OUT A BIT ...UHH... ECCENTRIC.

— R. CRUMB
JANUARY, 2010

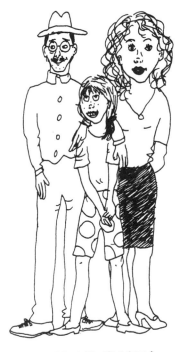

THE CRUMB FAMILY
BY SOPHIE, AUGUST, 1993

EARLY CHILDHOOD 1983 TO 1990 / 2 TO 8 YRS OLD

WAS IT MY PARENTS' OVERLY ATTENTIVE, OVERLY STIMULATING BEHAVIOR THAT MADE ME INTO AN ATTENTION-CRAVING LITTLE SHOW-OFF MONSTER INTENSITY-CASE, OR WAS I BORN THAT WAY? ALL I KNOW IS THAT THEY WERE THE BEST AUDIENCE A KID COULD HAVE; I PROBABLY MADE A LOT OF DRAWINGS JUST TO MAKE MY DAD LAUGH, HE WAS SO INTO IT. I ALSO SPENT HOURS AND HOURS ENTERTAINING MYSELF, FAR OFF IN THE ELABORATE FANTASY WORLD OF AN ONLY CHILD...

I WAS A LITTLE SCREWY, BUT THEN MY FOLKS WEREN'T EXACTLY AVERAGE, AND THEY NEVER LOOKED AT ME FUNNY OR TOLD ME I WAS WEIRD, AND ALWAYS ENCOURAGED MY CREATIVITY, SO I JUST KEPT ON WITH IT...
... AND LOOK AT ME NOW!

Sophie (top), Daddy (bottom left), & Mommy (bottom right). Age 26 months, Nov., 1983.

"A child in her house." Age 27 months, Dec., 1983.

"A snake chasing a girl." Age 2½, May, 1984.

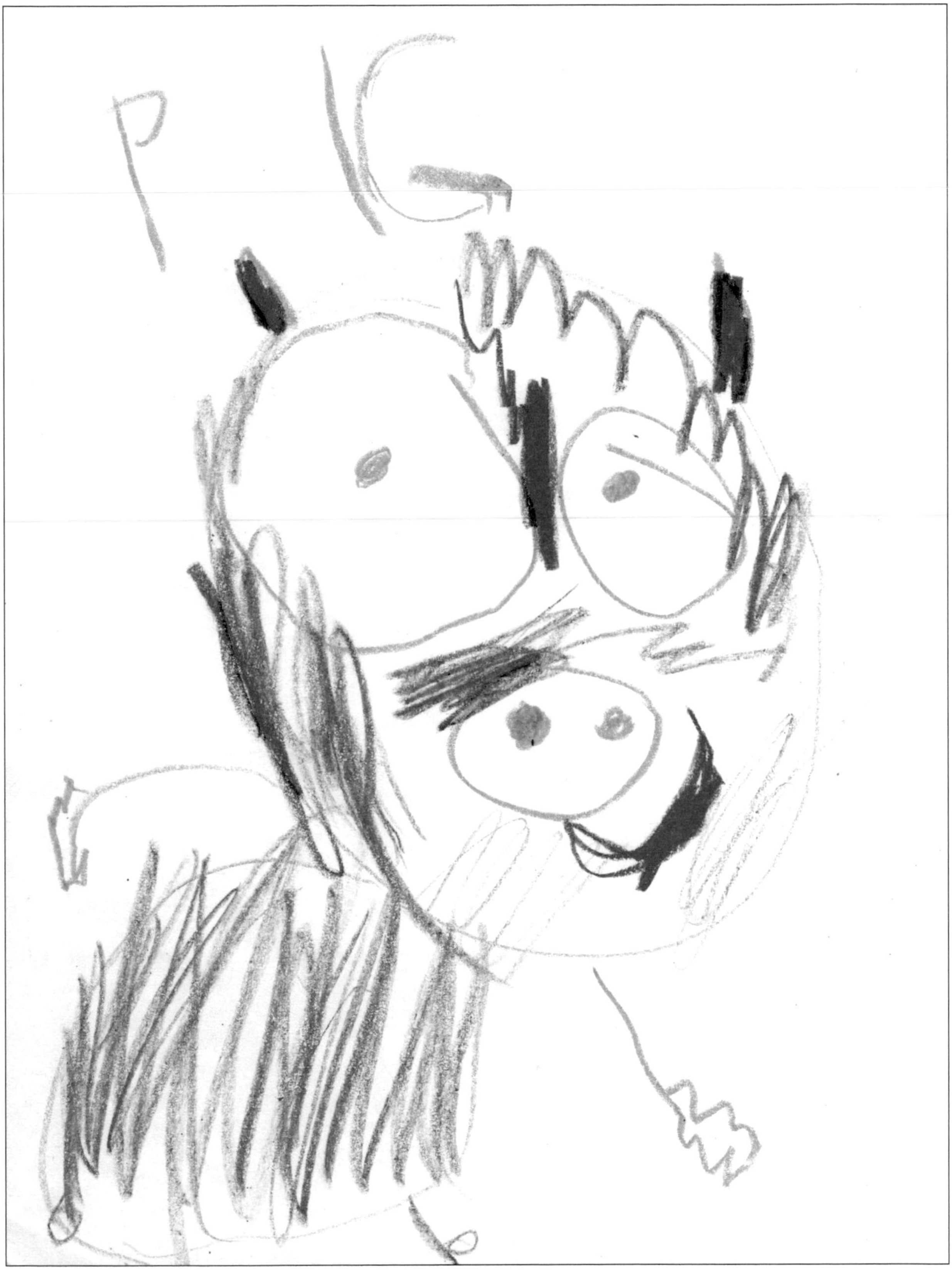
PIG

Age 2½, May, 1984.

Self-portrait. Age 2½, June, 1984.

"A mother picking up her baby's toys." Age 2½, July, 1984.

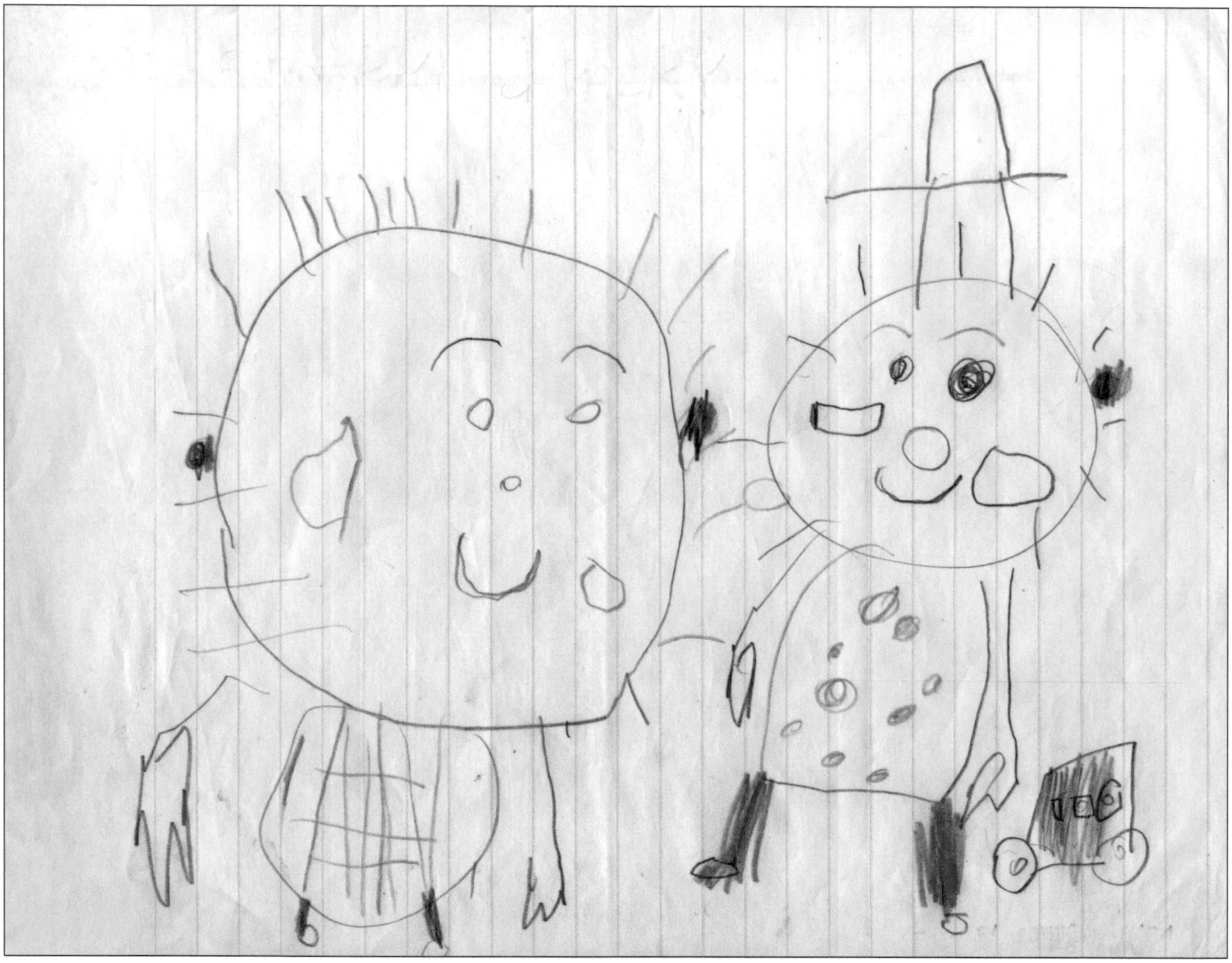

“Packy & Macky.” Age 3, late 1984.

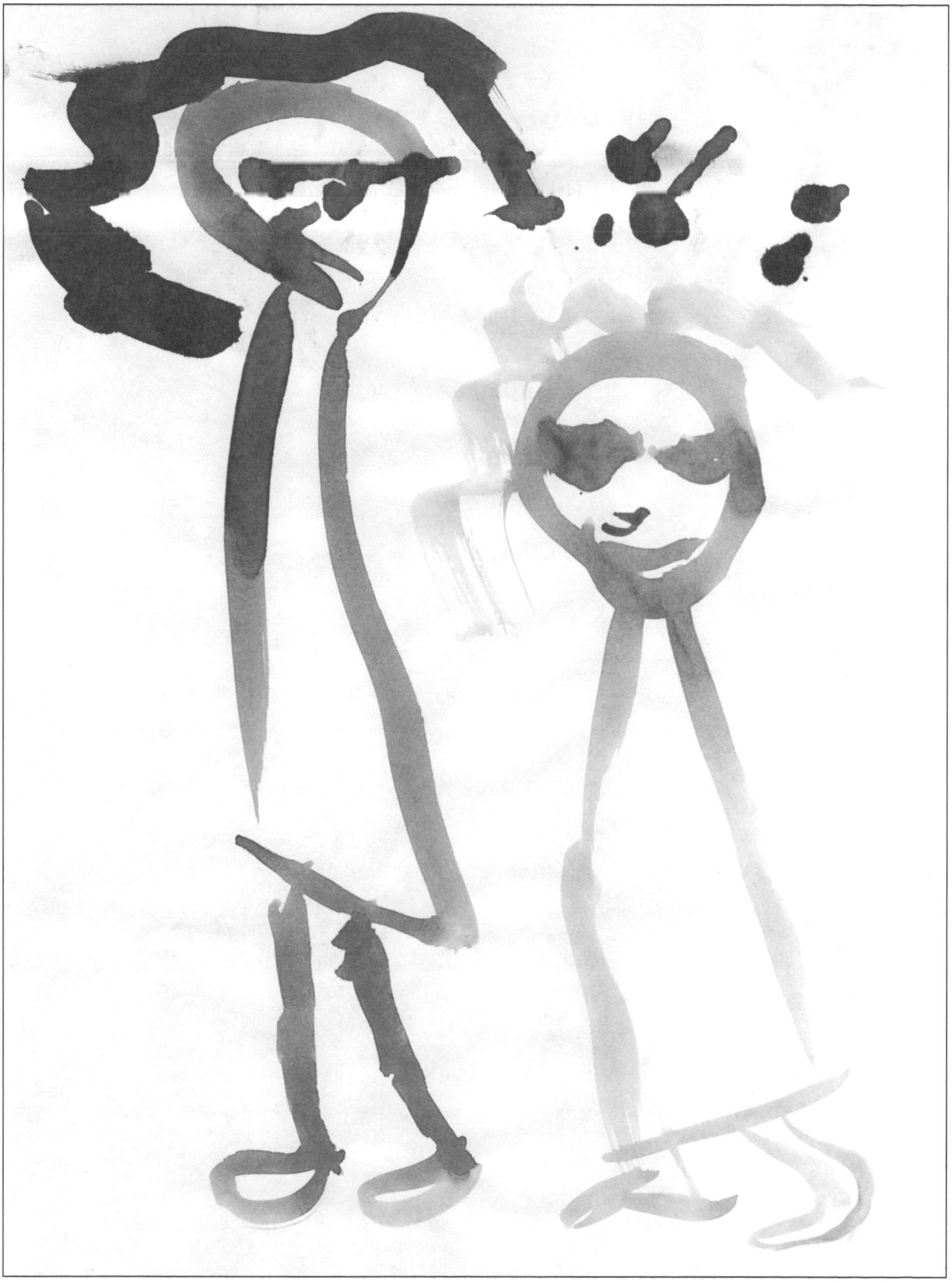

Age 3, Oct., 1984.

One of many family portraits. Age 3, Dec., 1984.

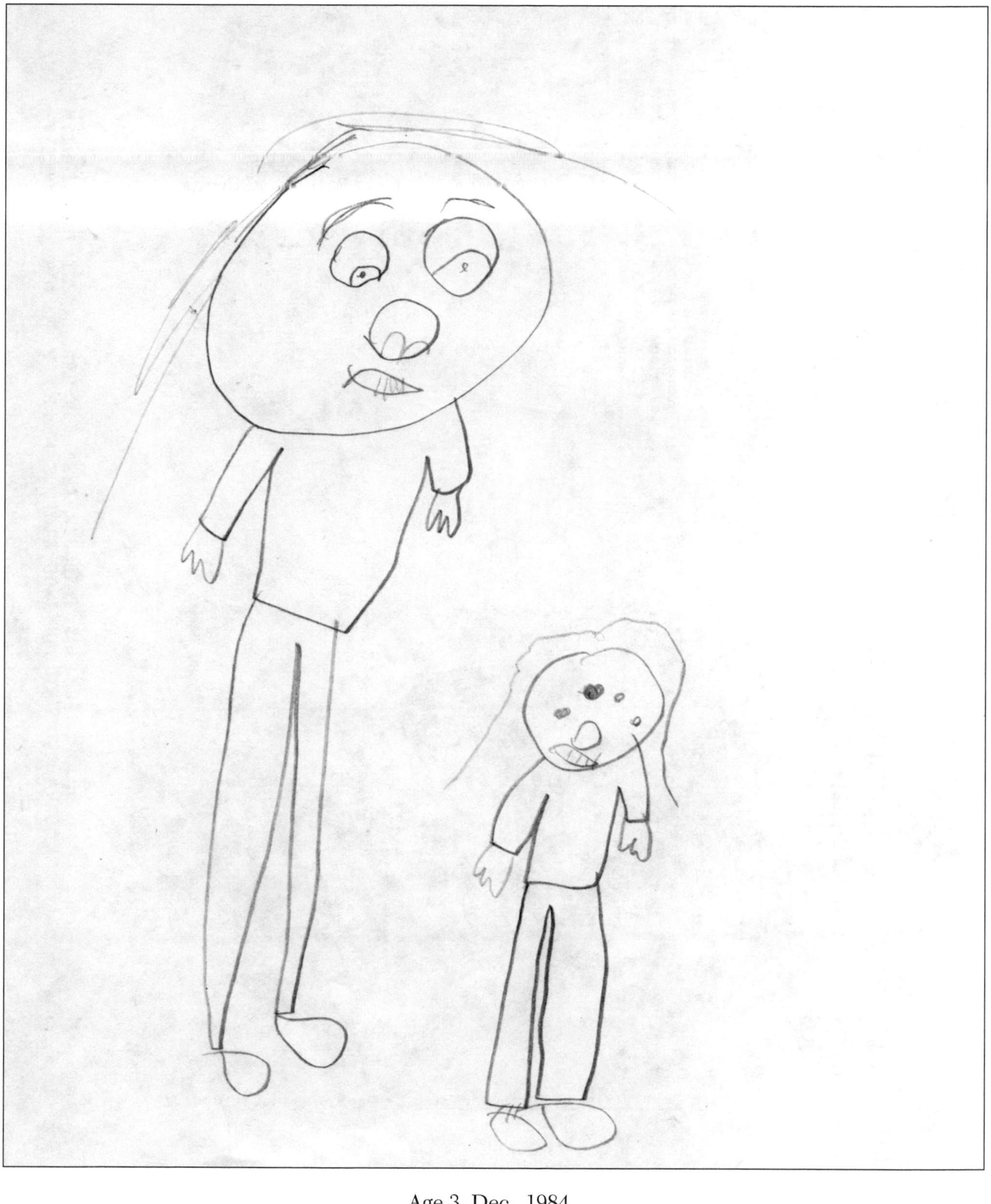

Age 3, Dec., 1984.

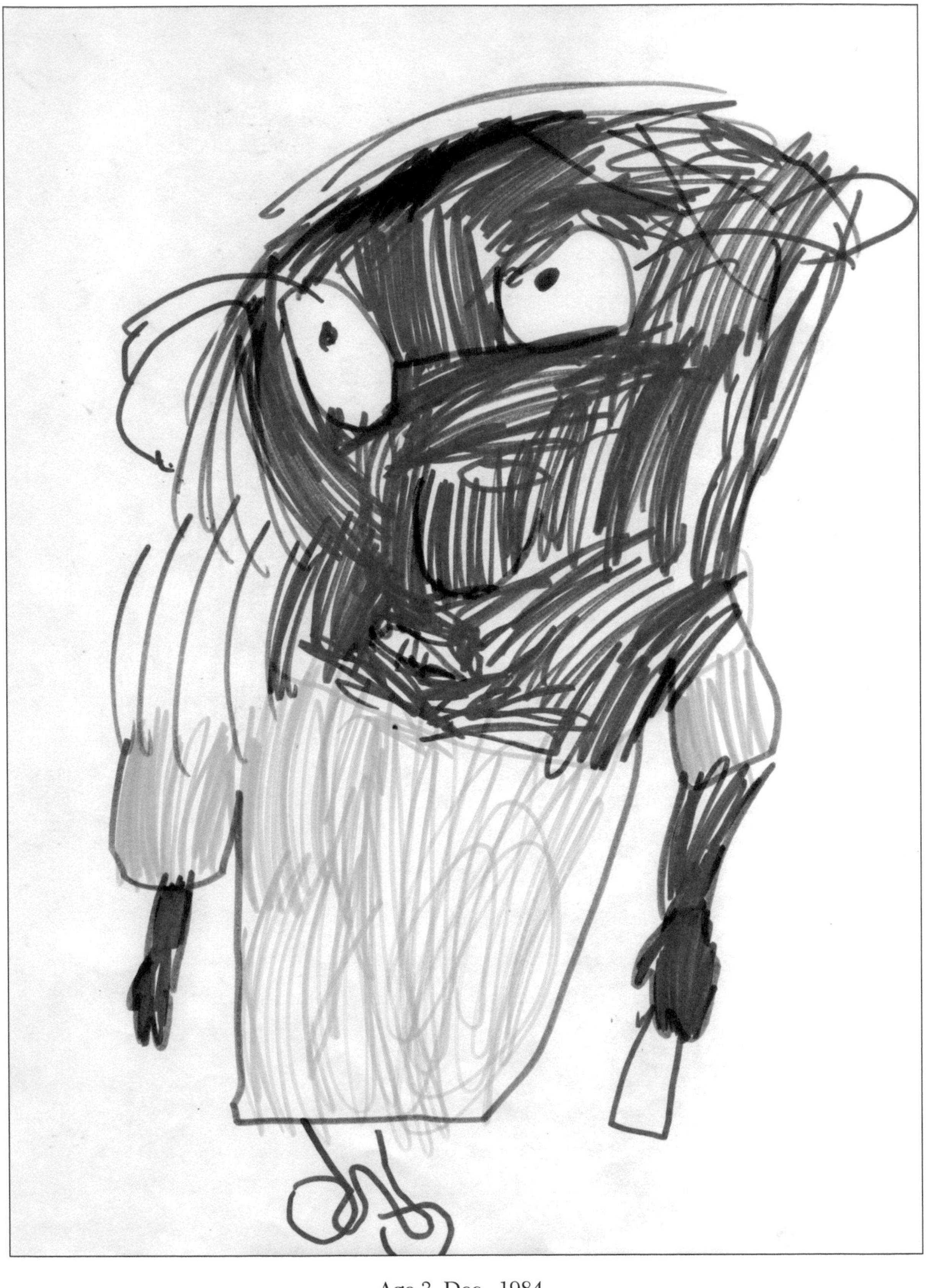

Age 3, Dec., 1984.

First sexually explicit drawing. Age 3, Dec., 1984.

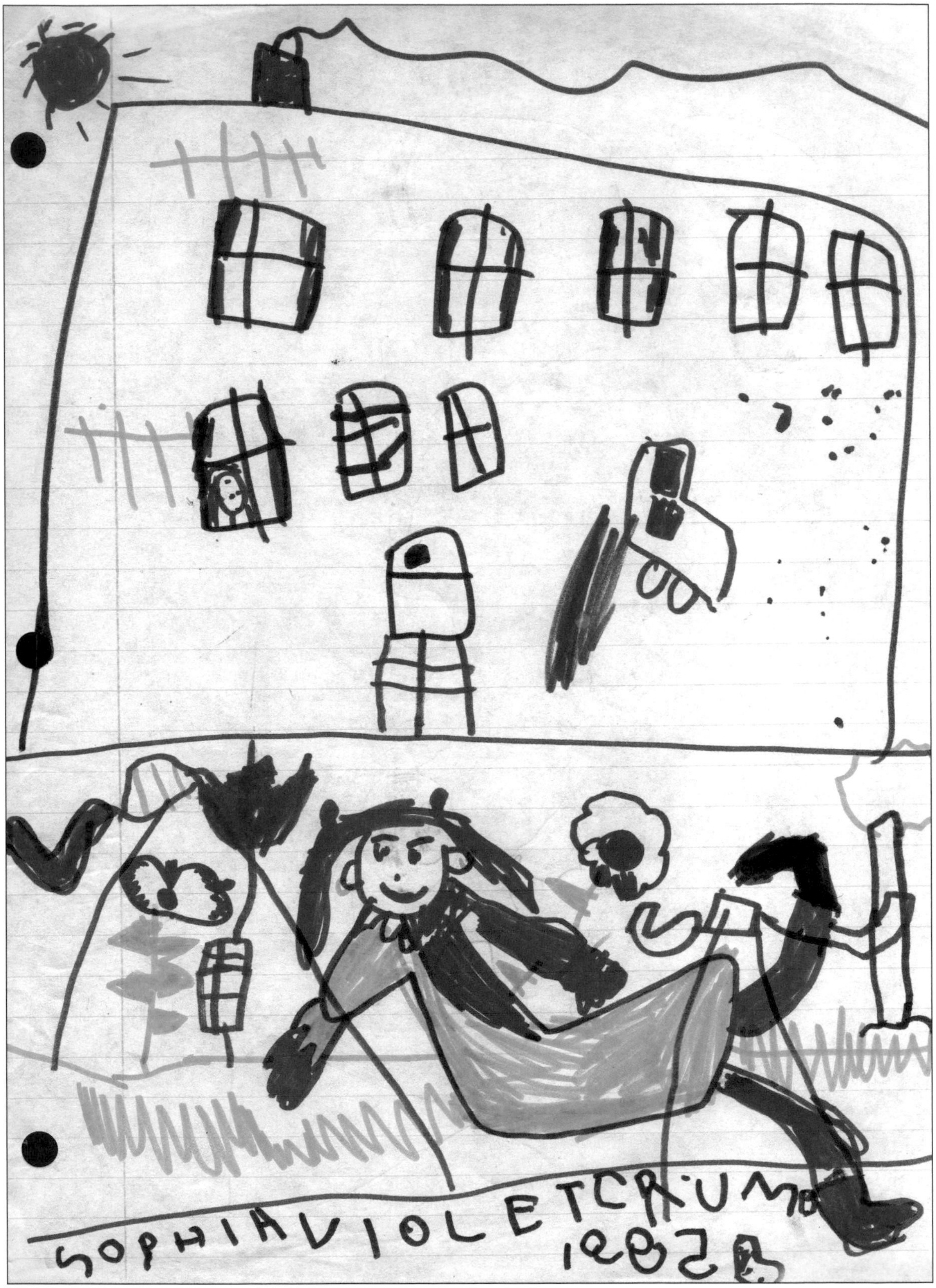
SOPHIAVIOLETCRUMB

Age 3, Jan., 1985.

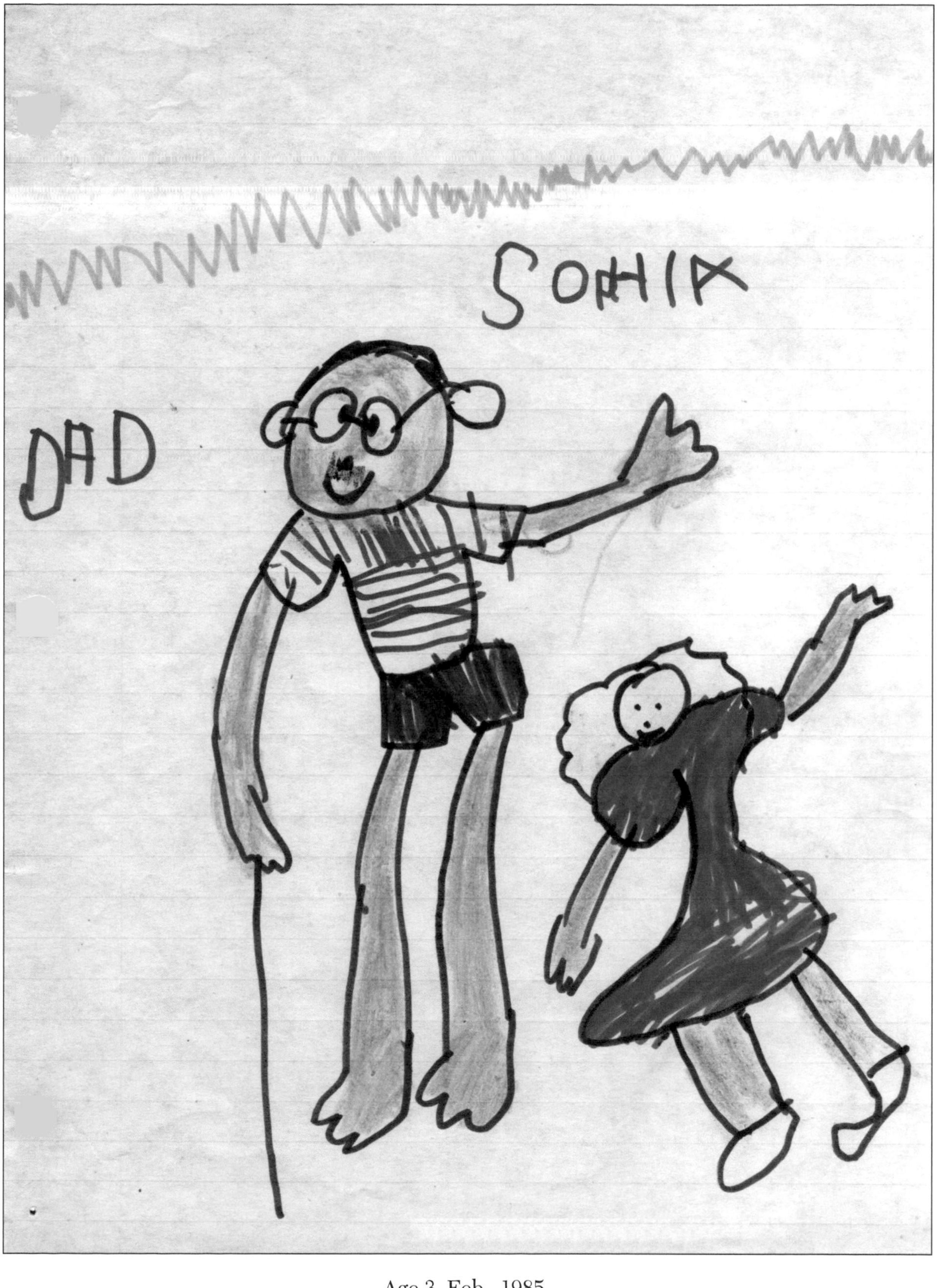
SOPHIA
DAD

Age 3, Feb., 1985.

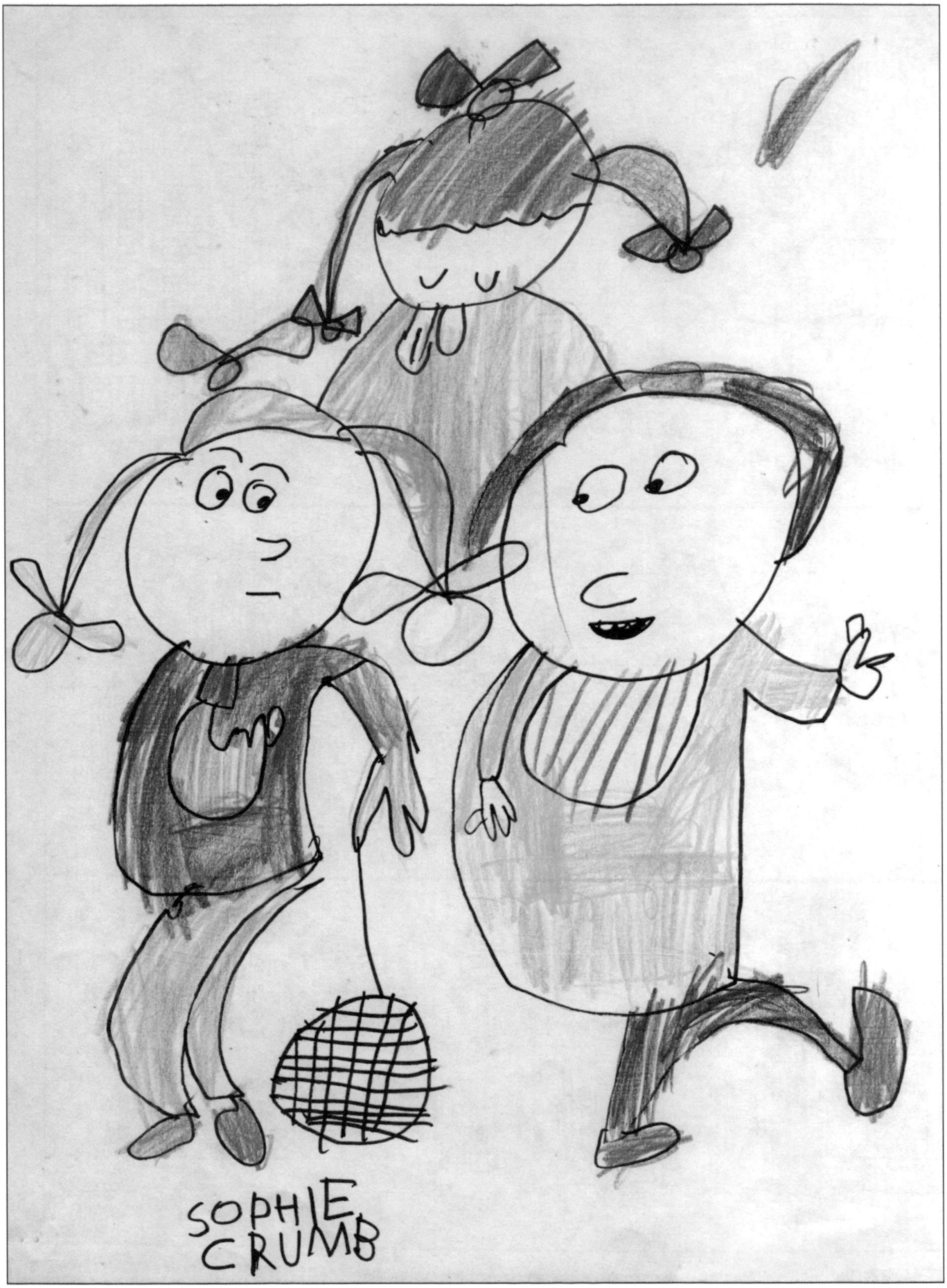
SOPHIE
CRUMB

Age 3, May, 1985.

"A little girl getting into a bathtub from her footstool." Age 3, May, 1985.

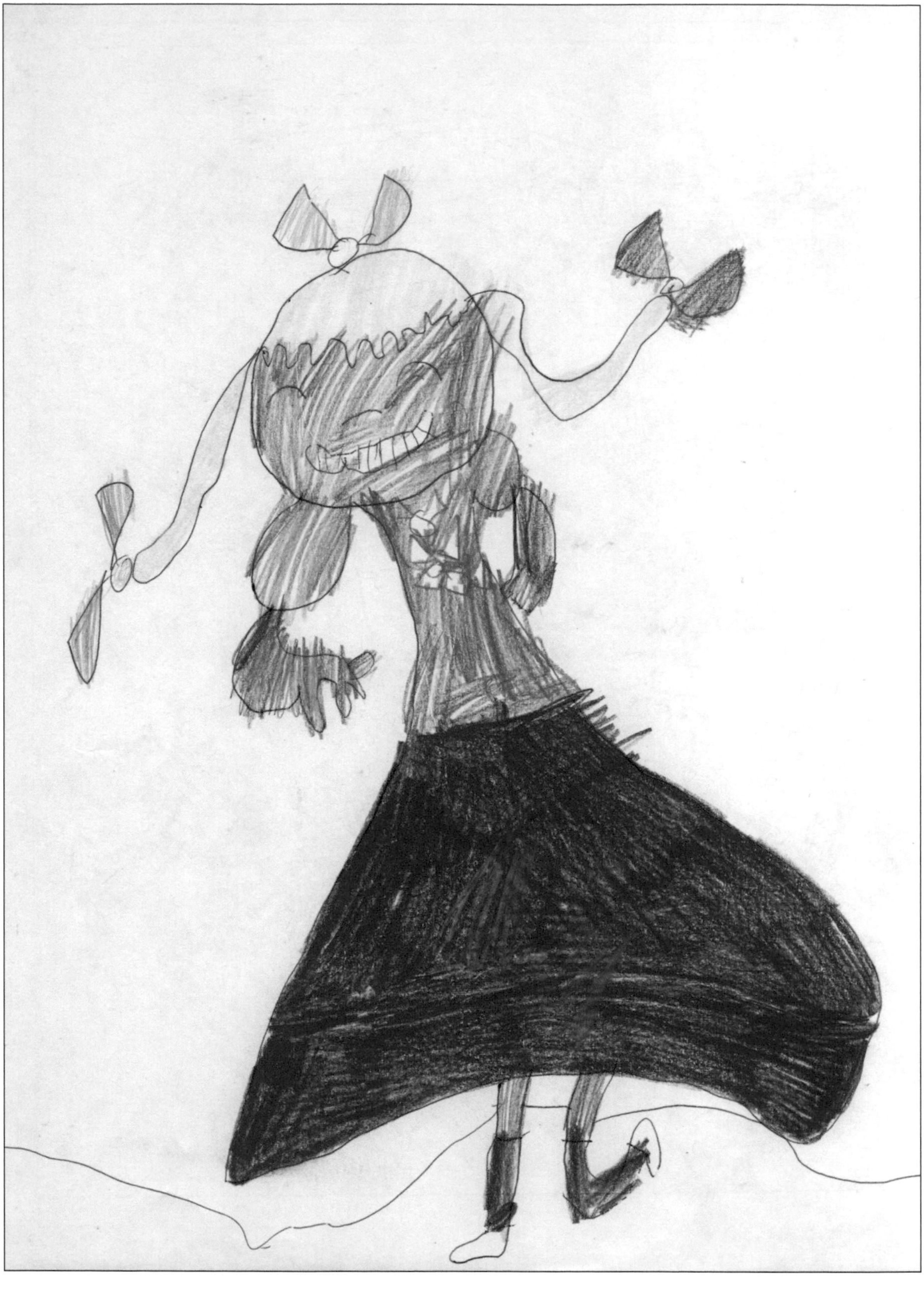

Age 3, May, 1985.

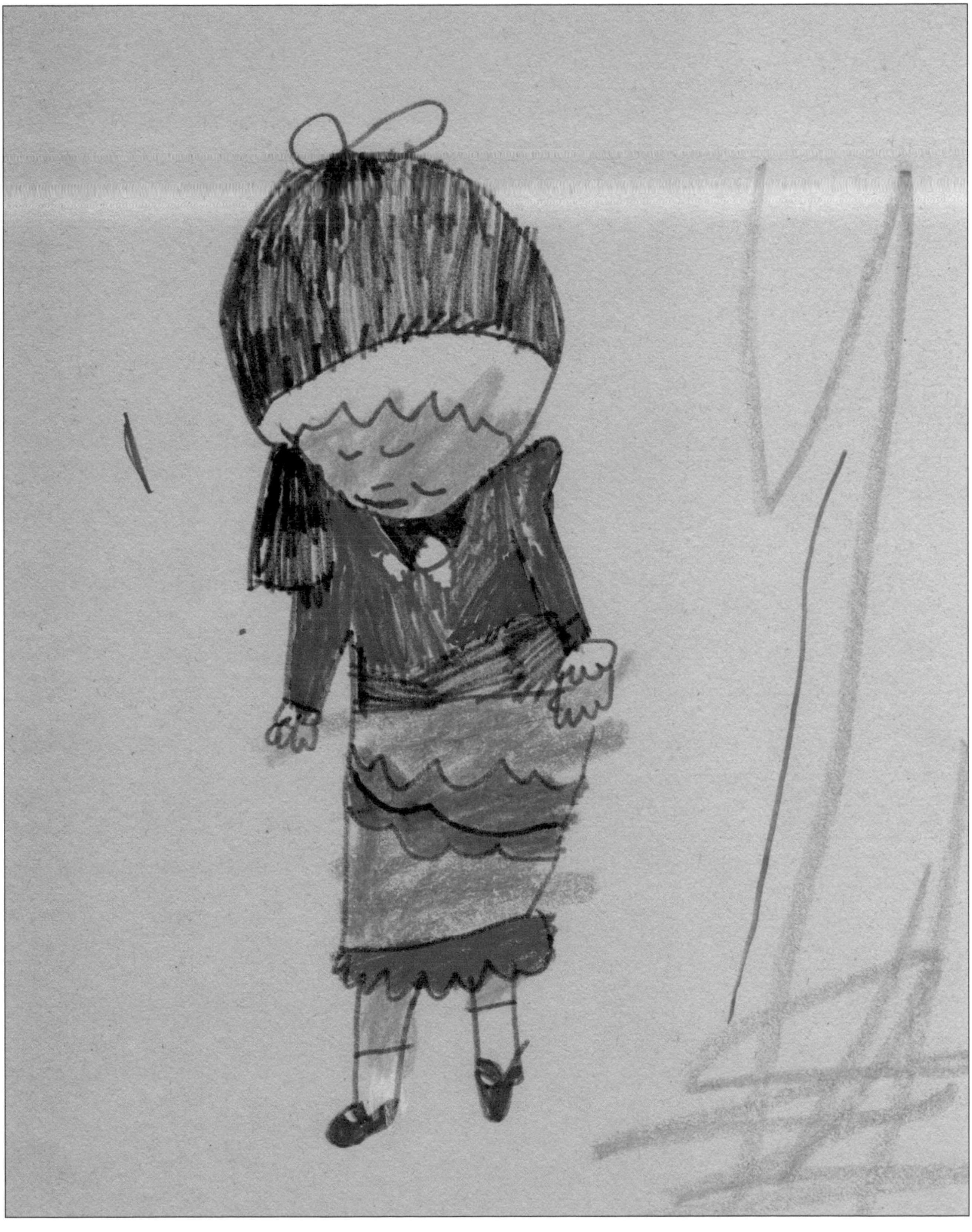

Age 3, Sept., 1985.

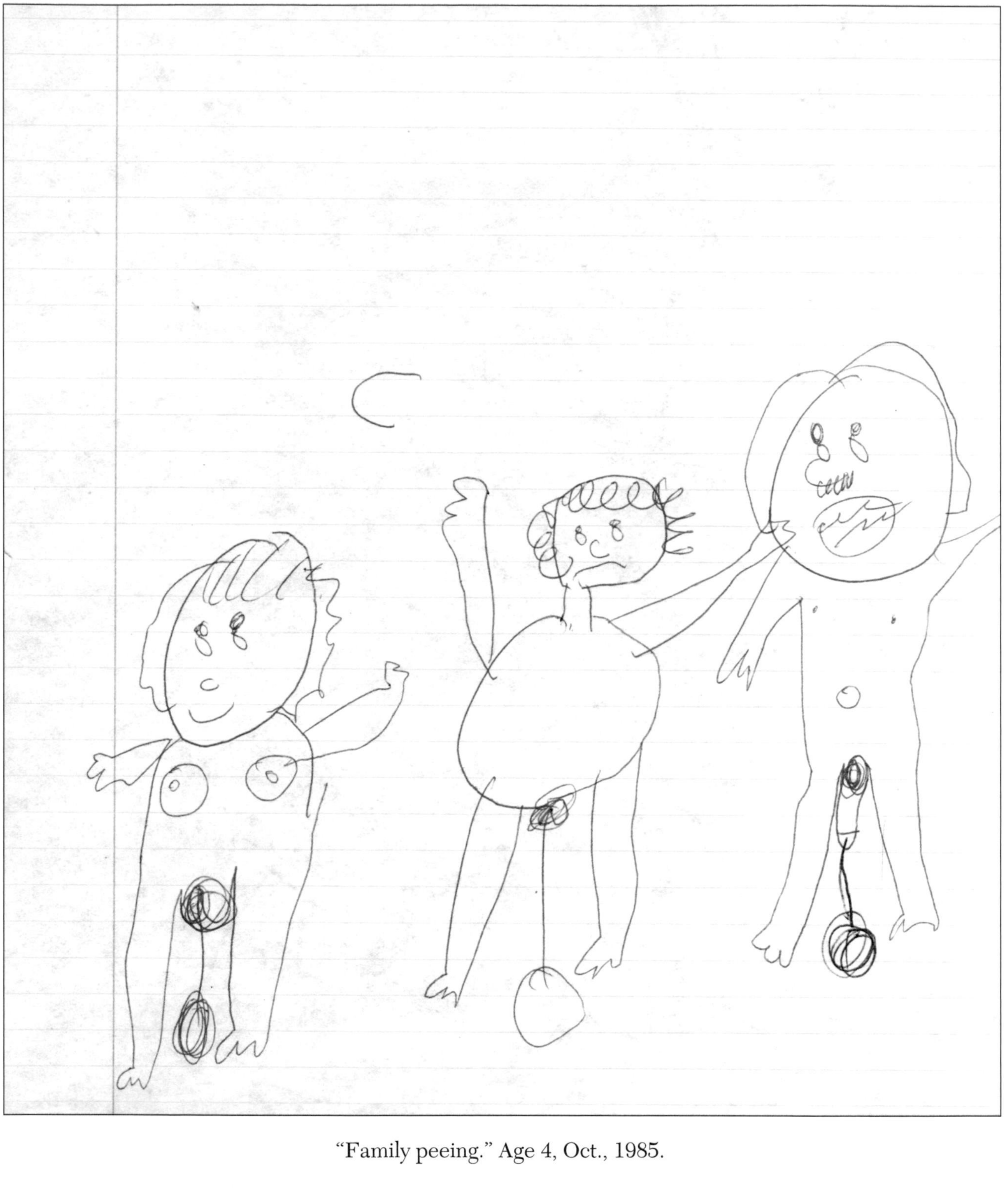

“Family peeing.” Age 4, Oct., 1985.

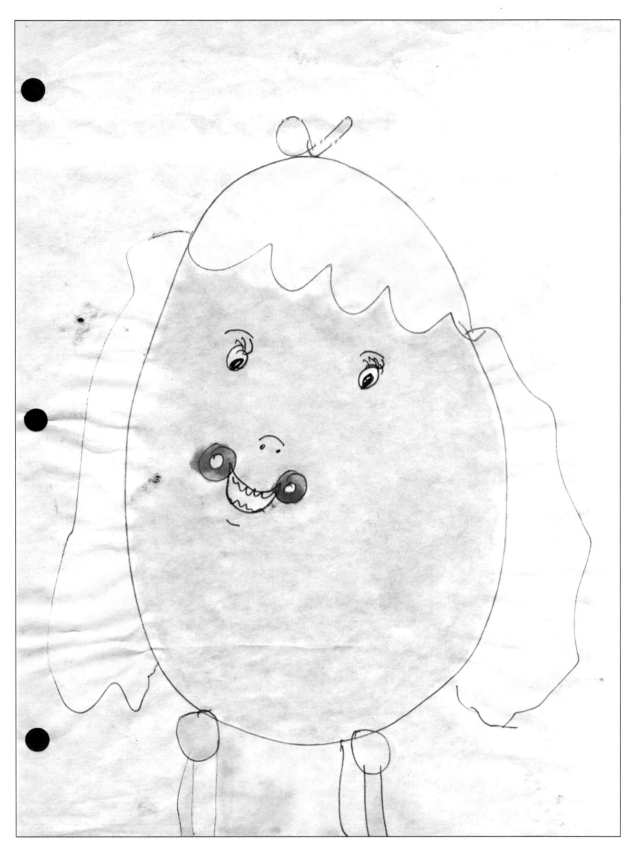

Self-portrait. Age 4, Oct., 1985.

First time in Paris. Age 4, March, 1986.

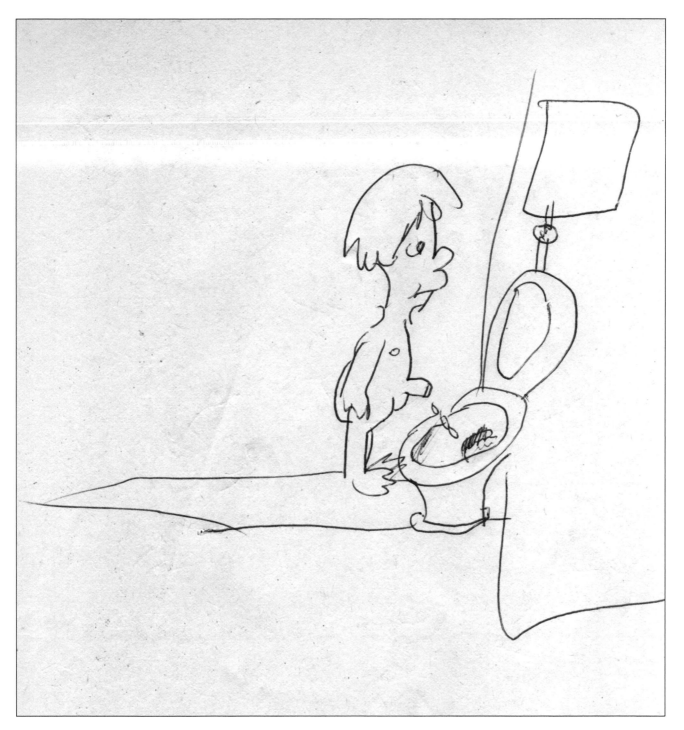

Age 4, April, 1986.

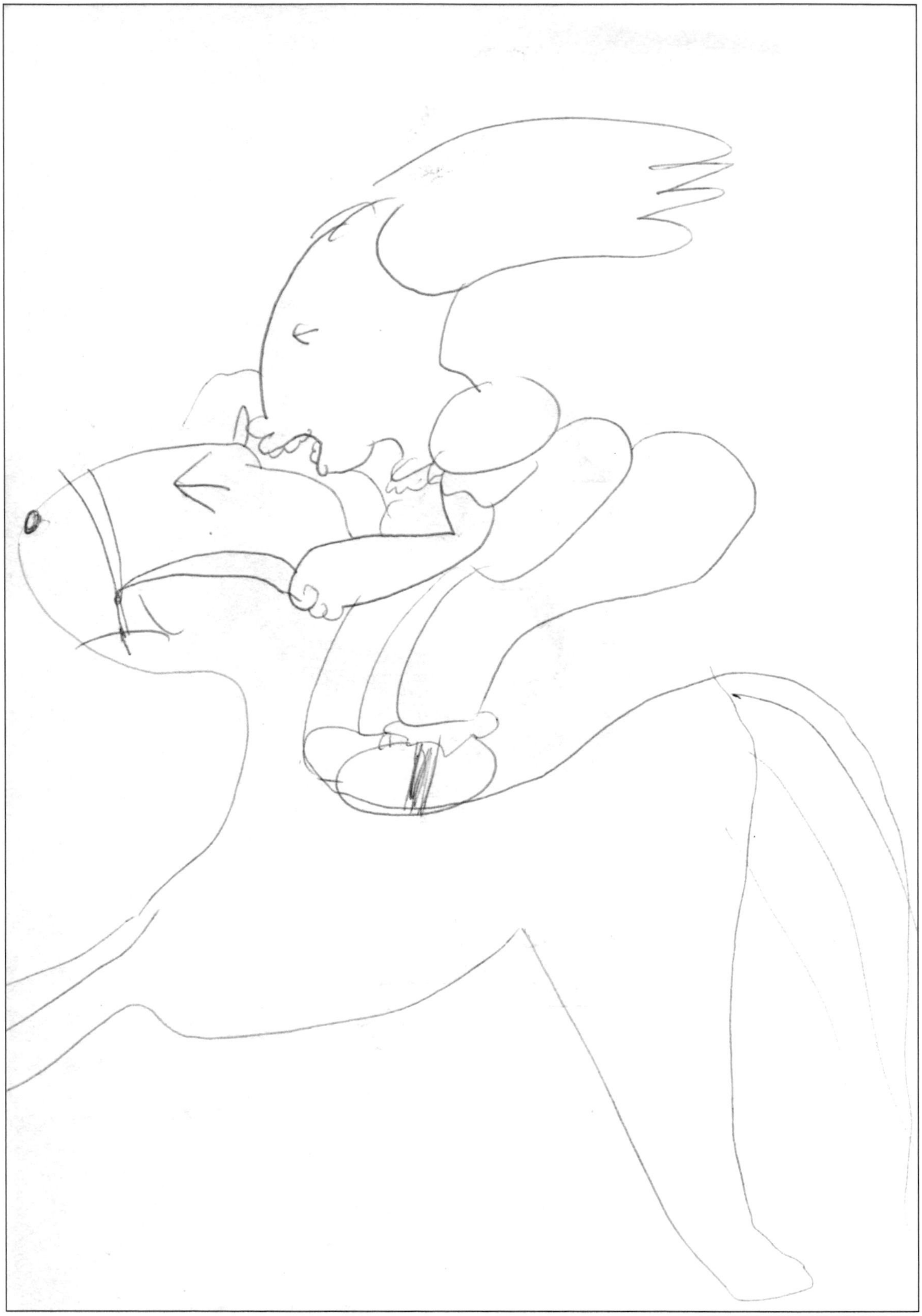

Age 4, spring, 1986.

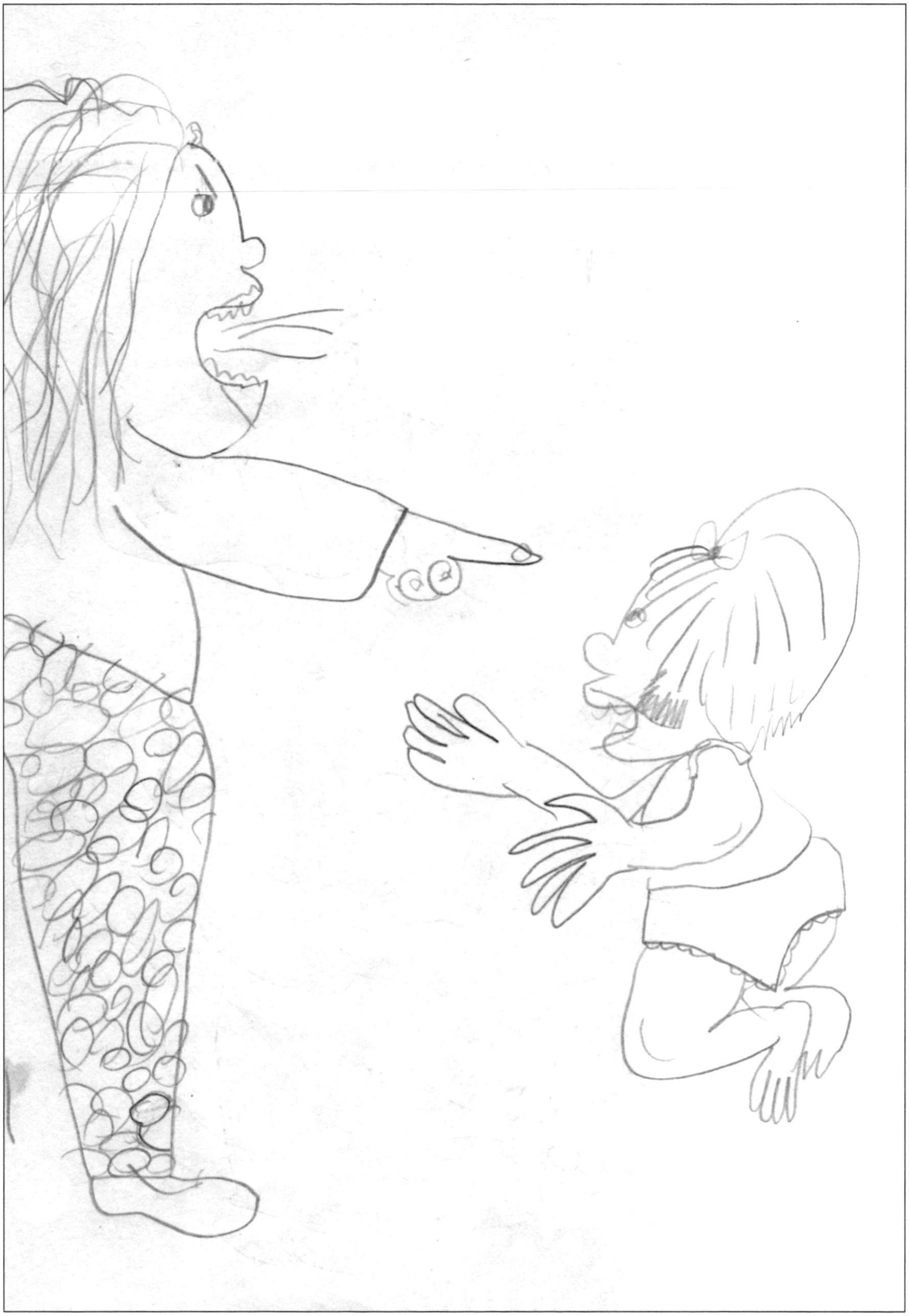

"Get dressed!" Age 4, spring, 1986.

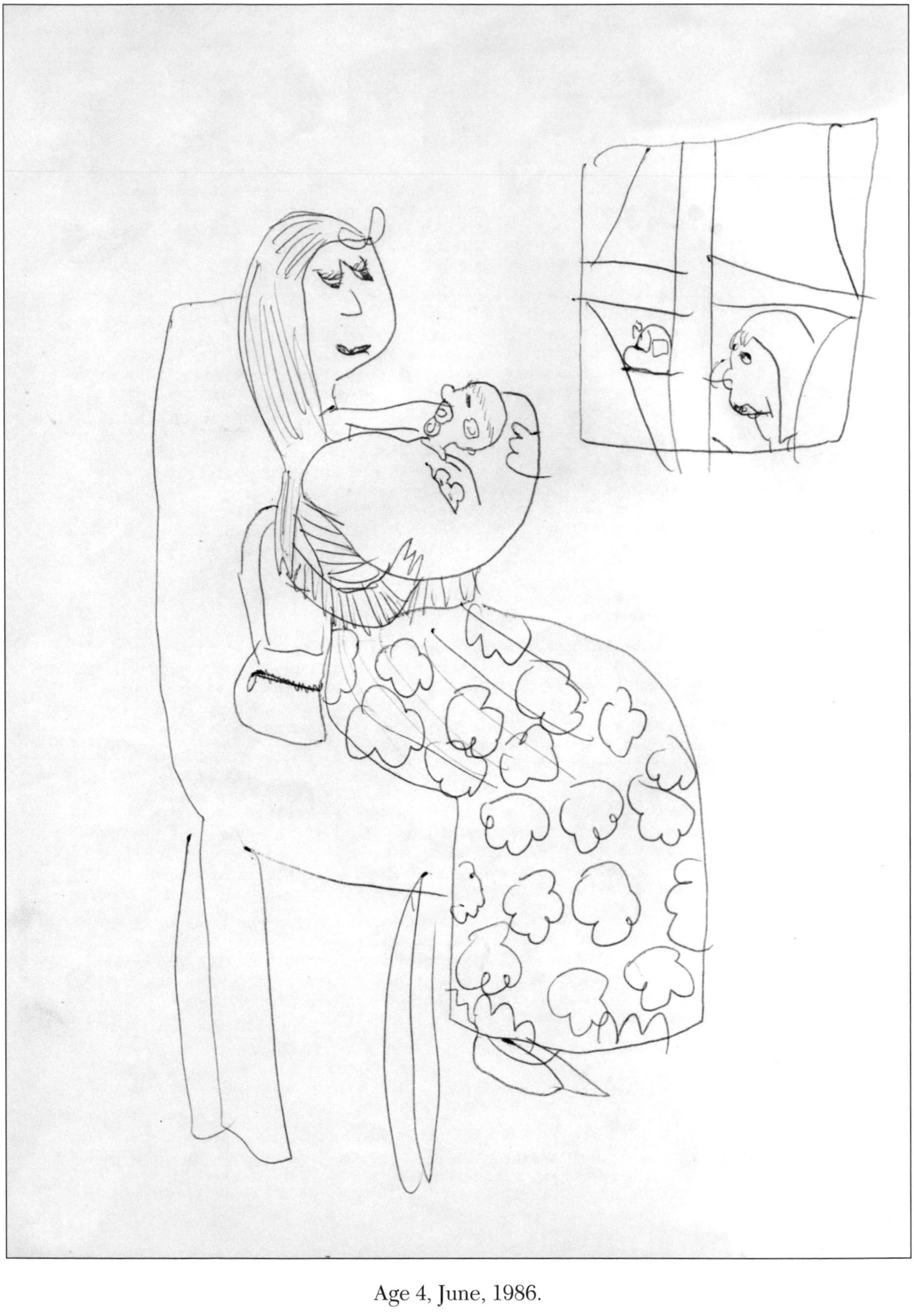

Age 4, June, 1986.

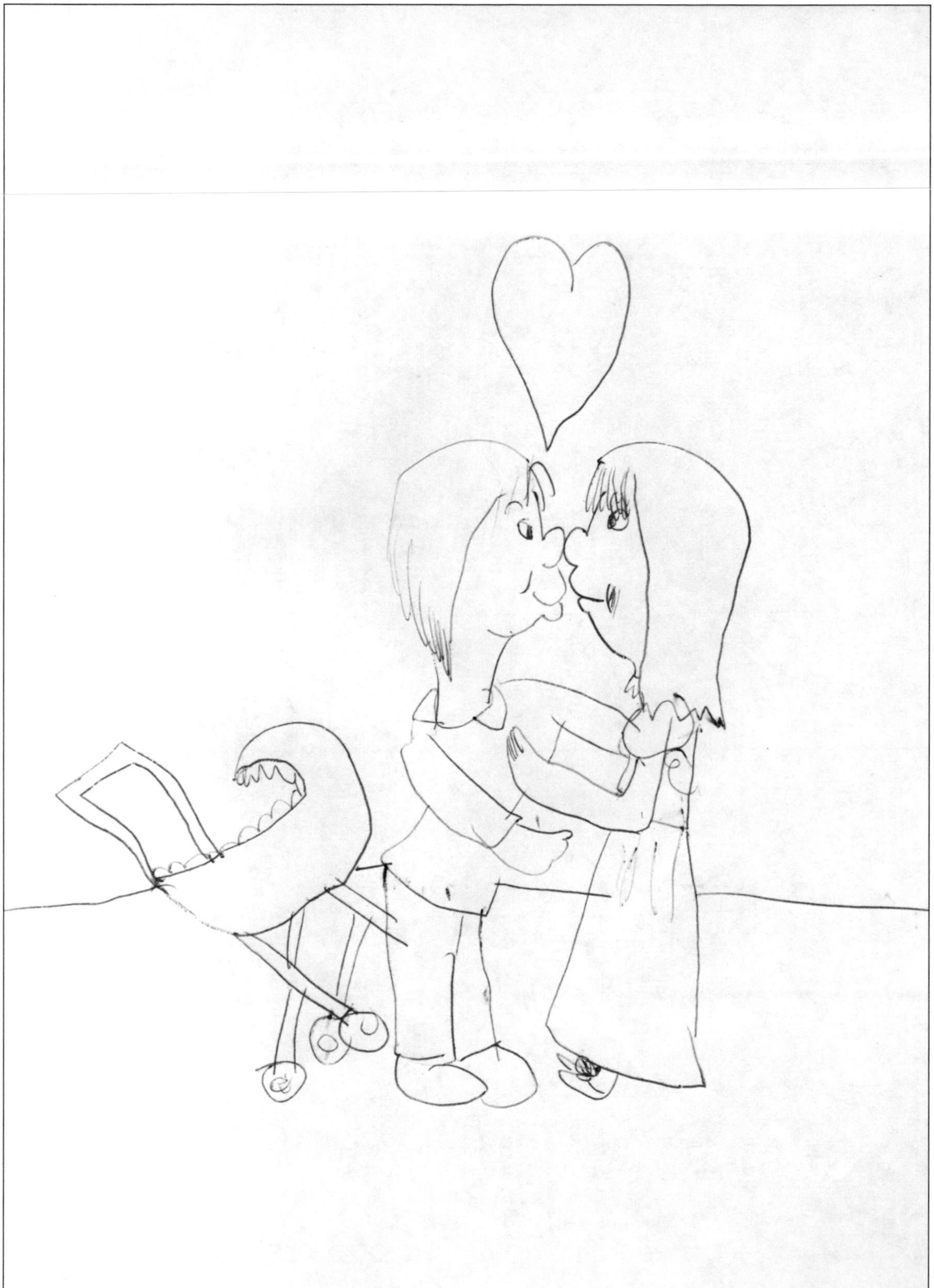

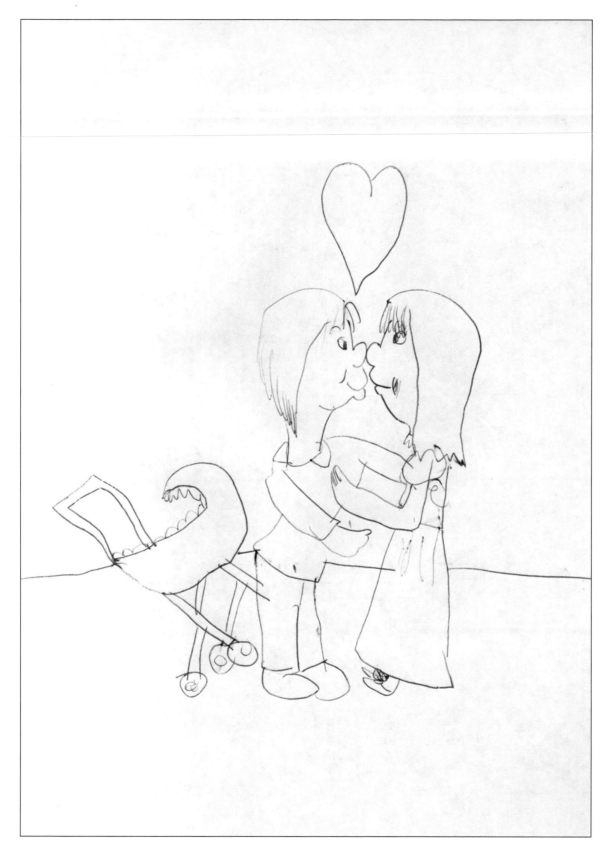

Age 4, June, 1986.

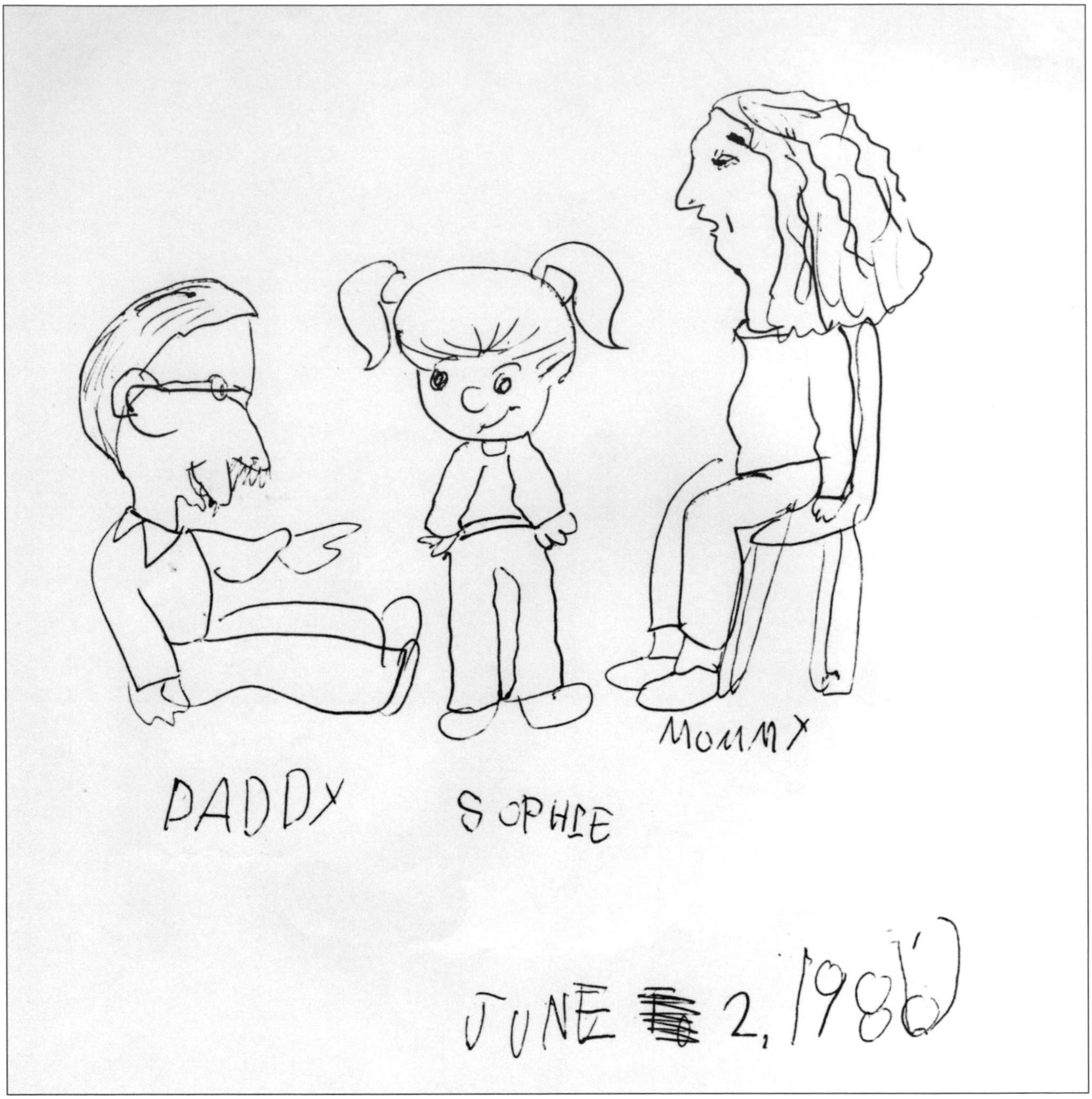
DADDY
SOPHIE
MOMMY
JUNE 2, 1986

Age 4, June, 1986.

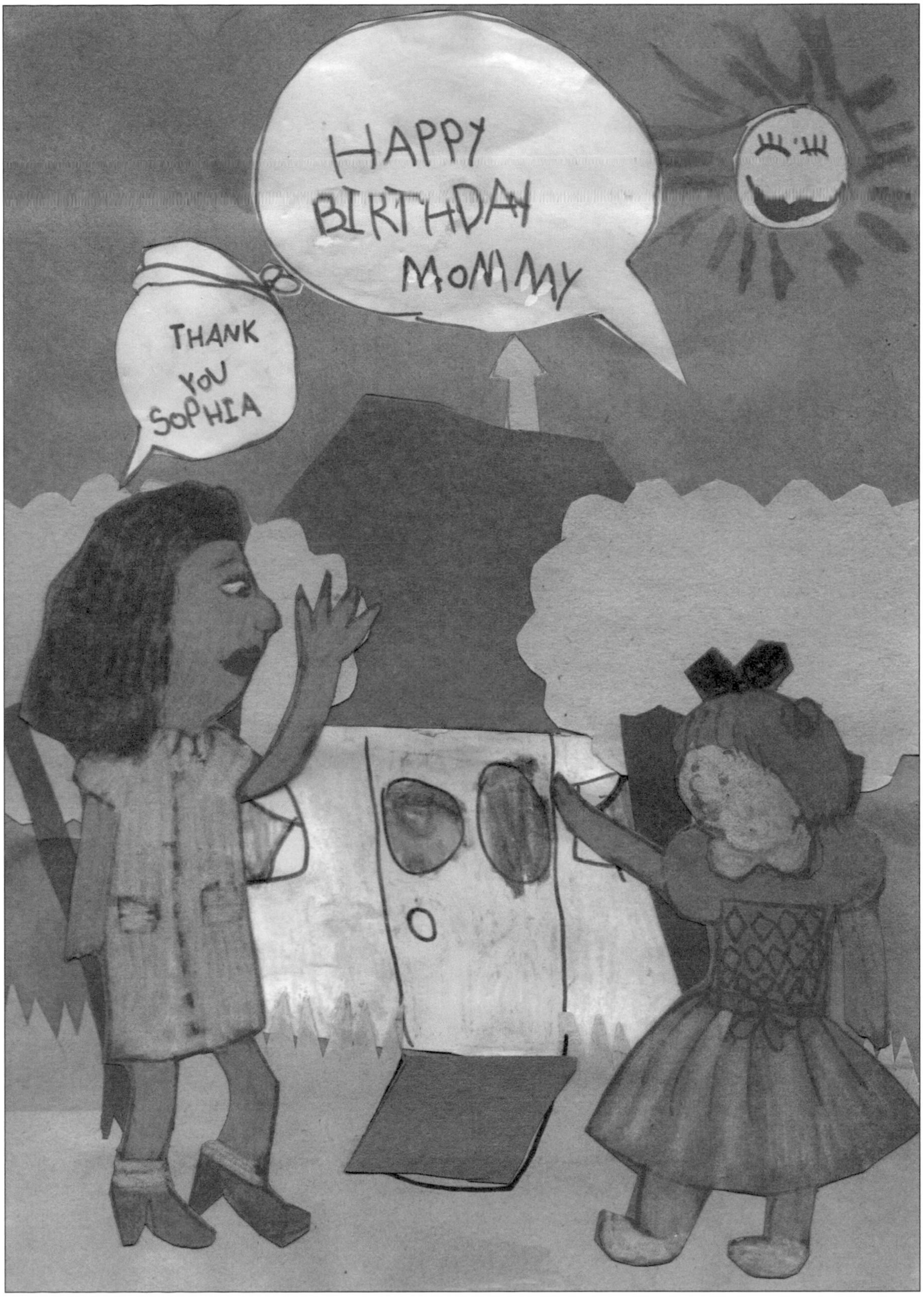
HAPPY BIRTHDAY MOMMY
THANK YOU SOPHIA

Age 4, Aug., 1986.

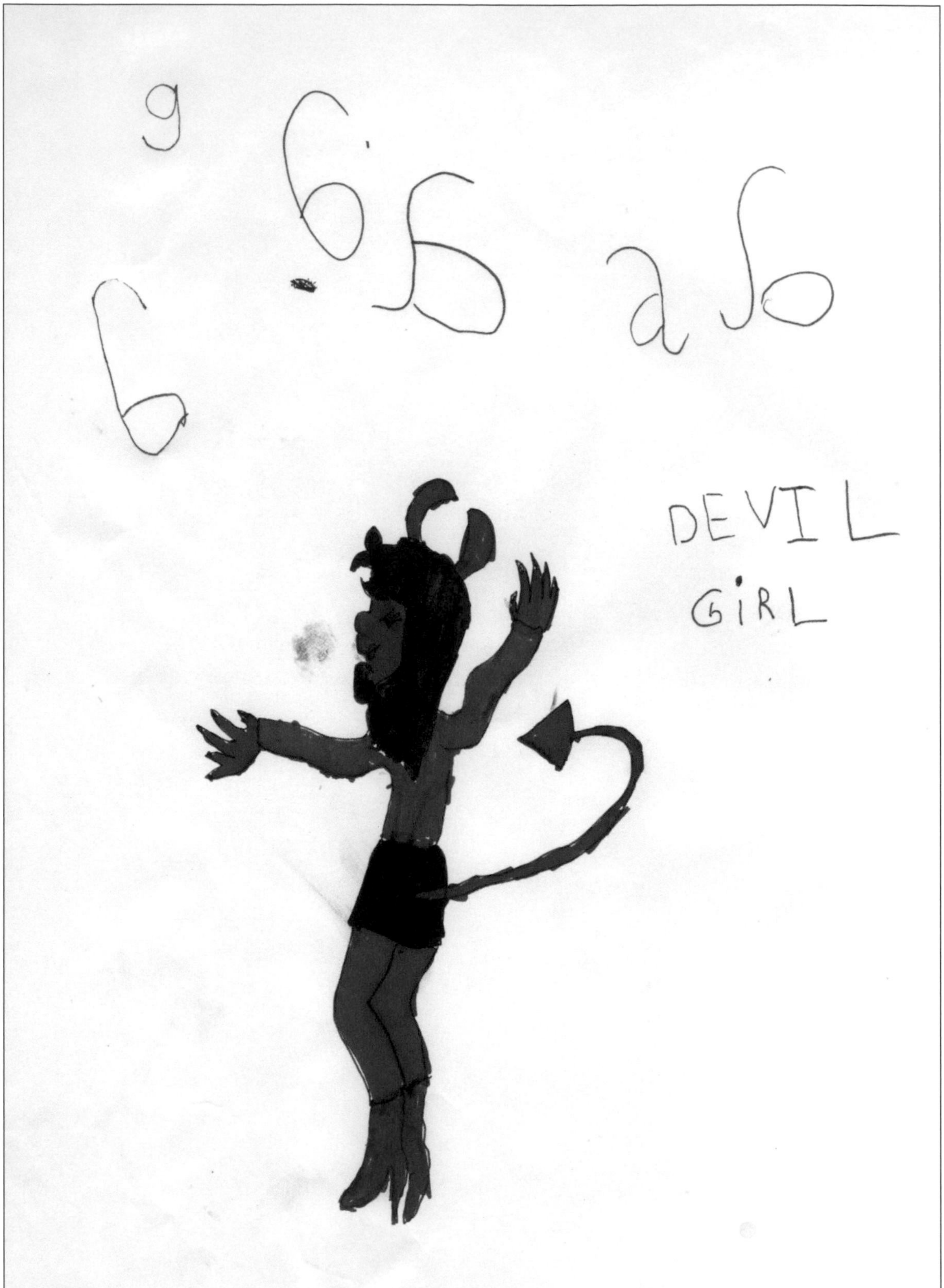
DEVIL
GIRL

Age 5, Nov., 1986.

I asked Sophie what each person was doing and wrote down what she told me.—R. C. Age 5, Dec., 1986.

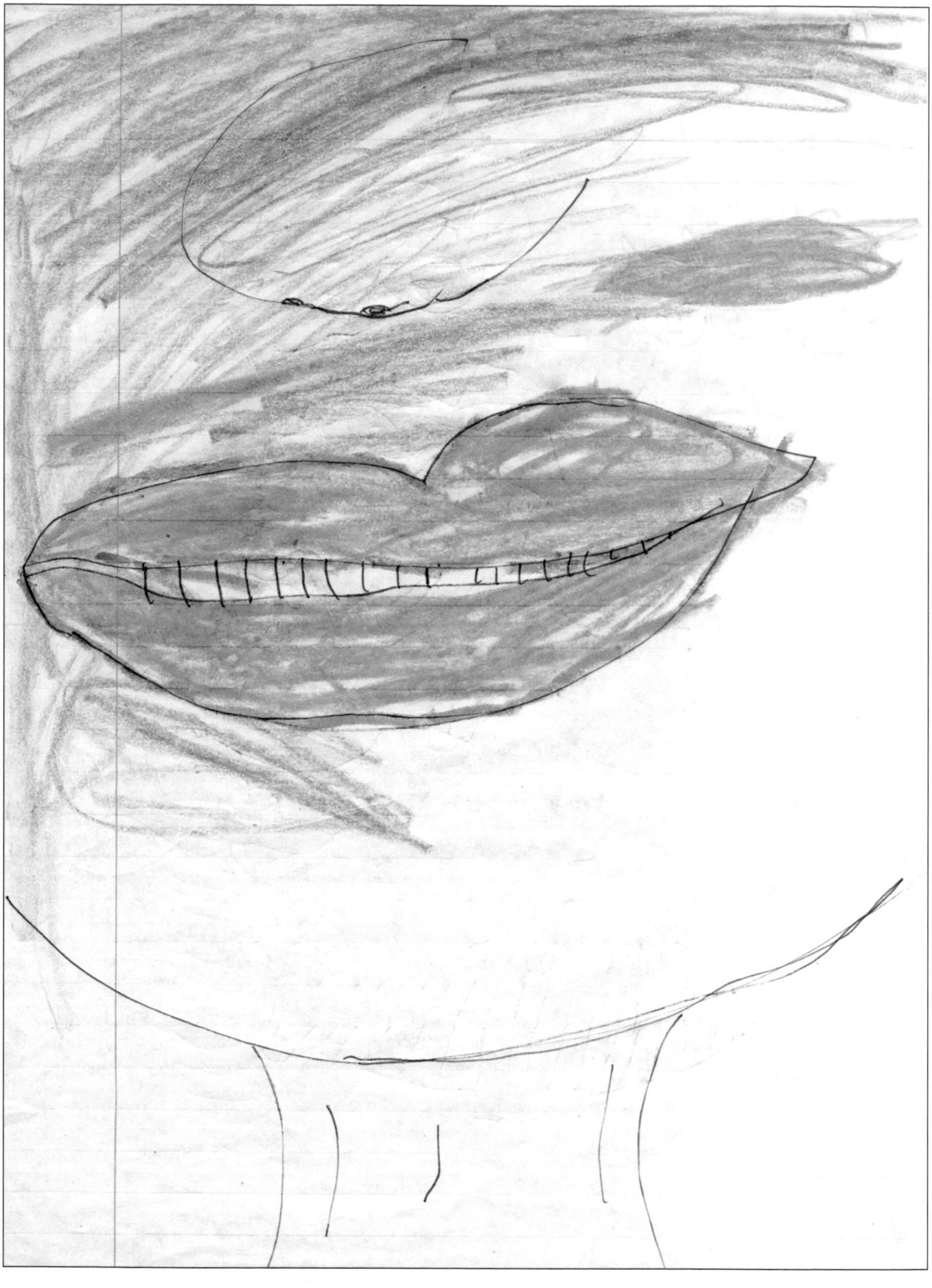

"Grandma." Age 5, Jan., 1987.

Age 5, Jan., 1987.

Age 5, Jan., 1987.

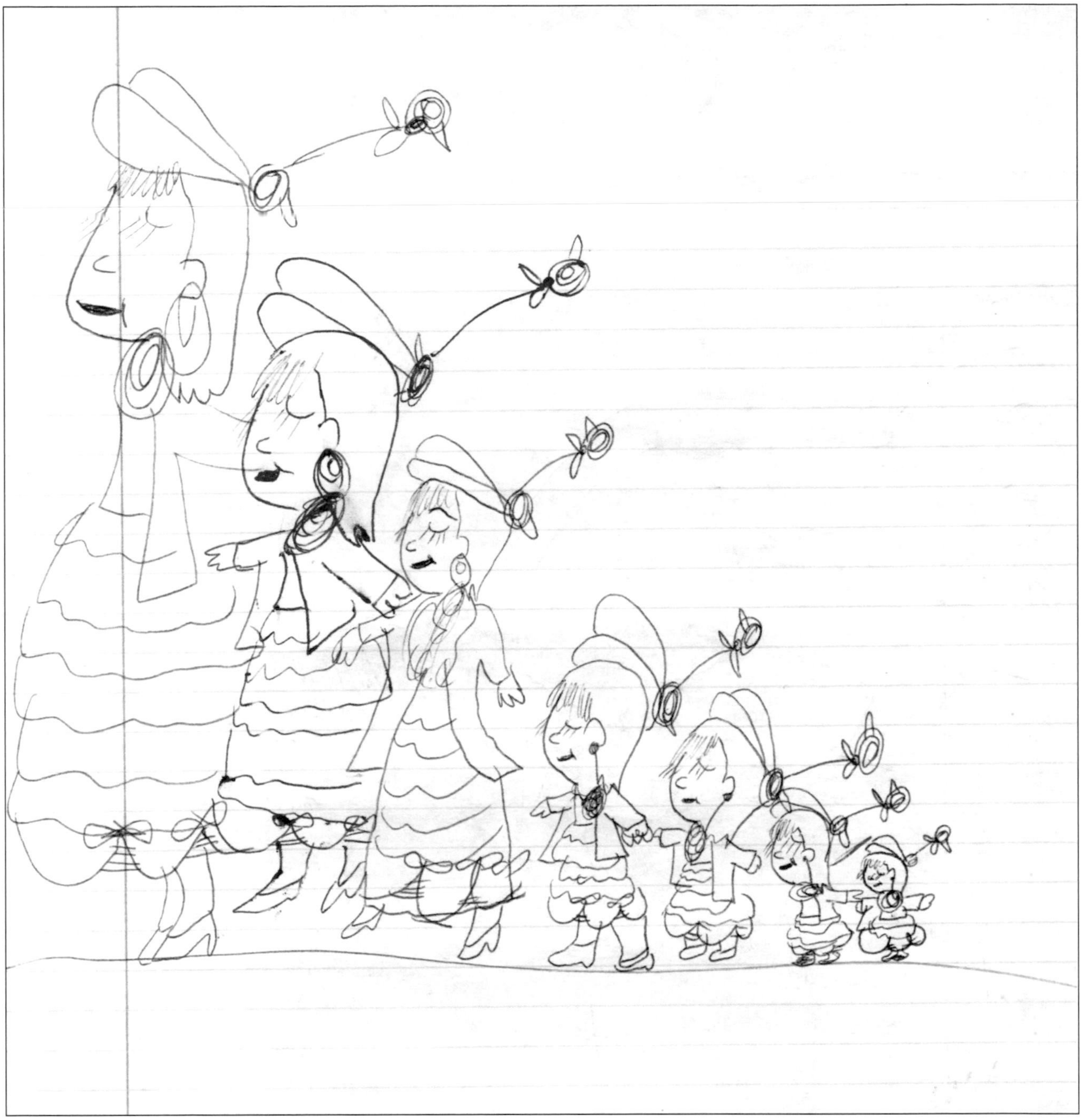

Age 5, Jan., 1987.

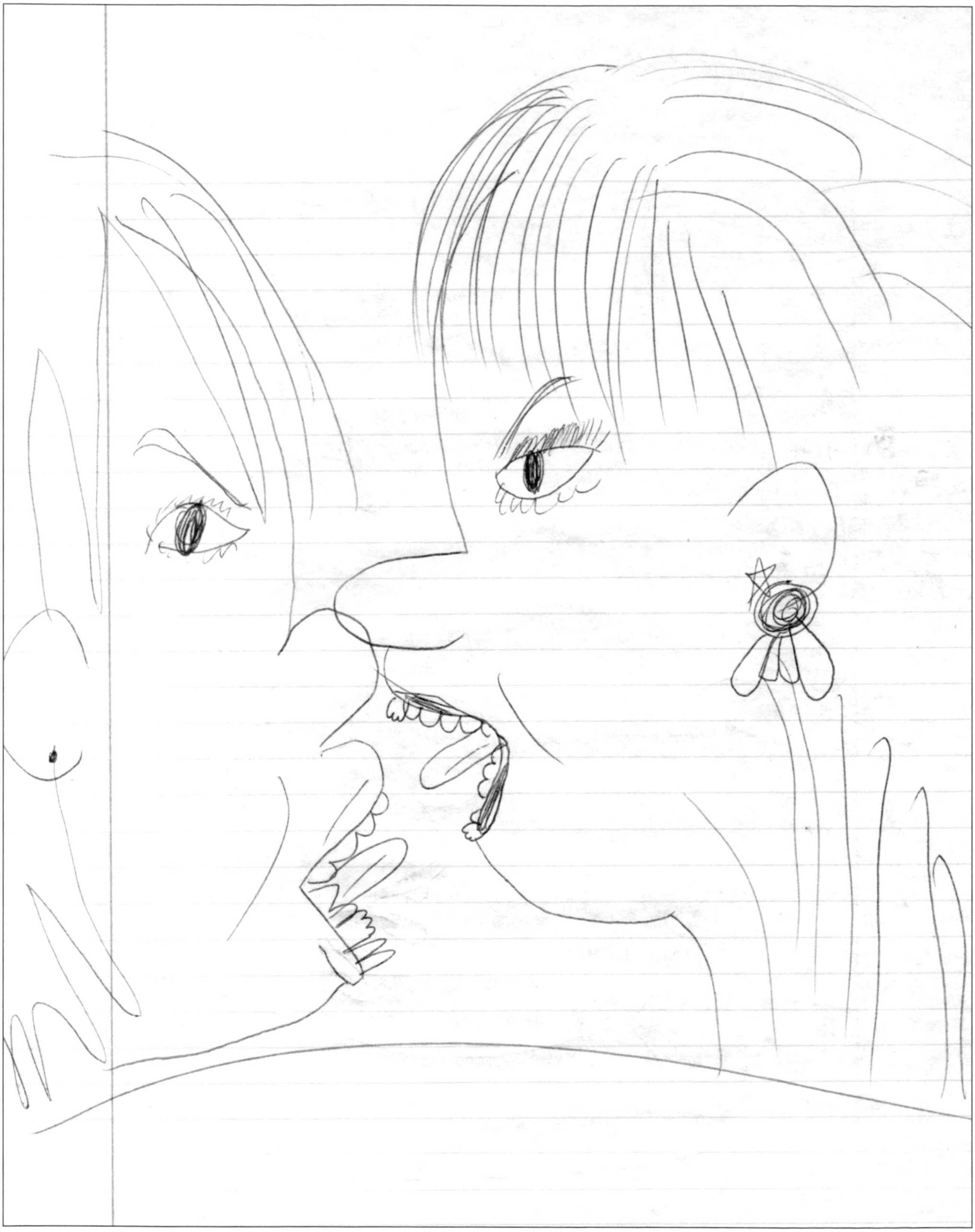

Age 5, Feb., 1987.

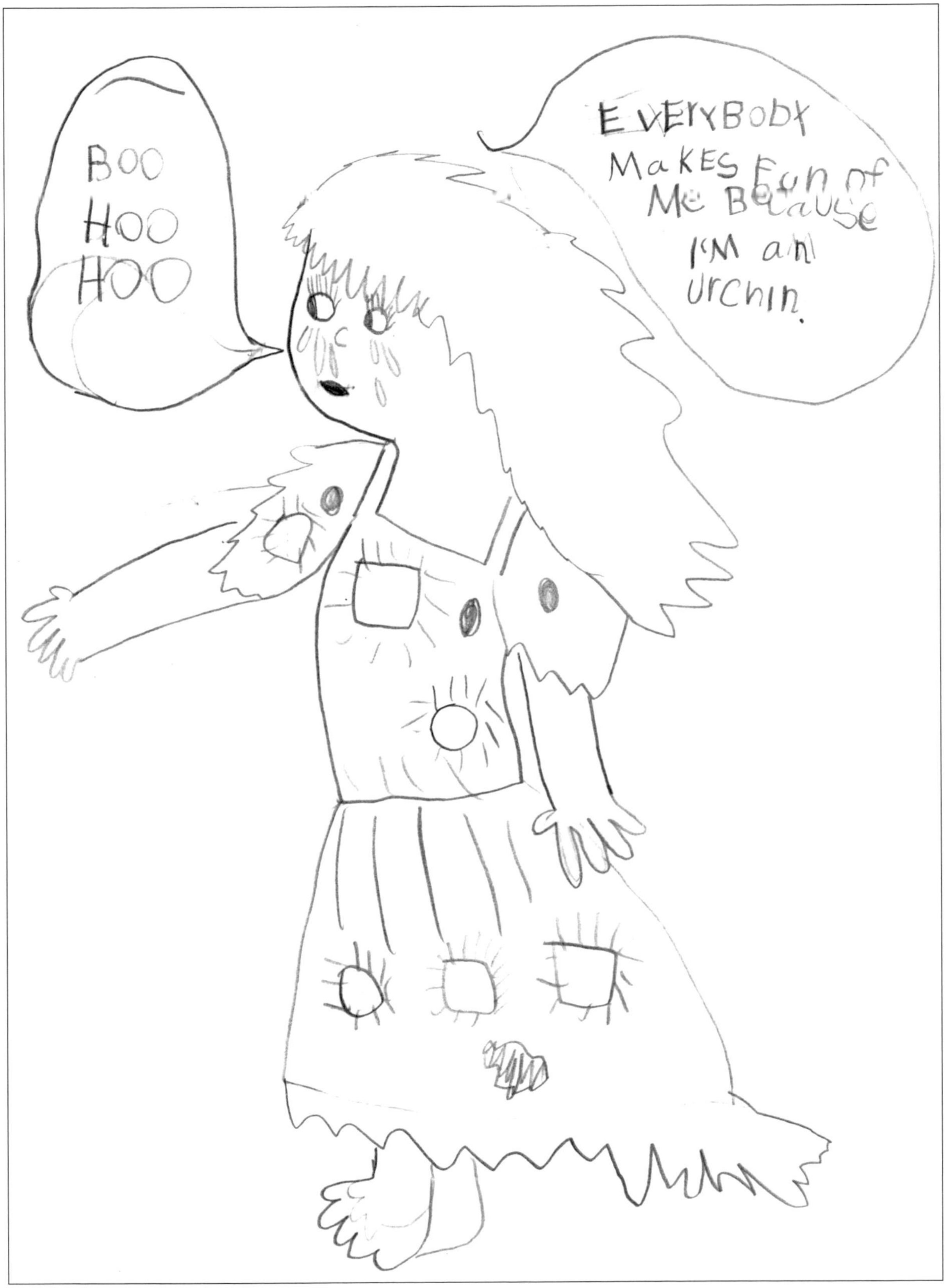
BOO
HOO
HOO
EVERYBODY
MaKES Fun of
Me Because
I'M an
urchin.

Age 5, April, 1987.

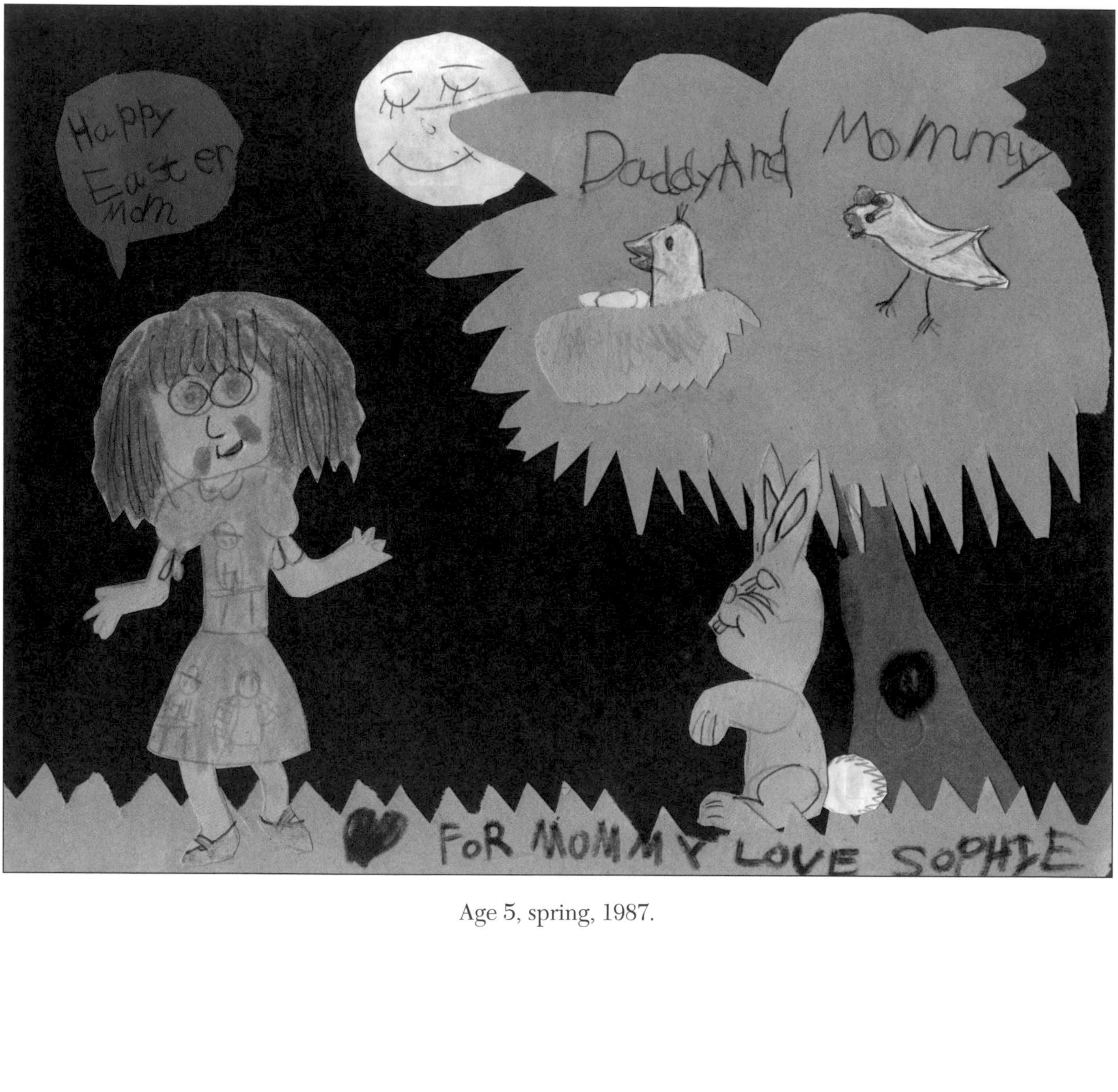
Happy Easter Mom
Daddy And Mommy
FOR MOMMY LOVE SOPHIE

Age 5, spring, 1987.

Portrait of Aline. Drawn from life. Age 5, May, 1987.

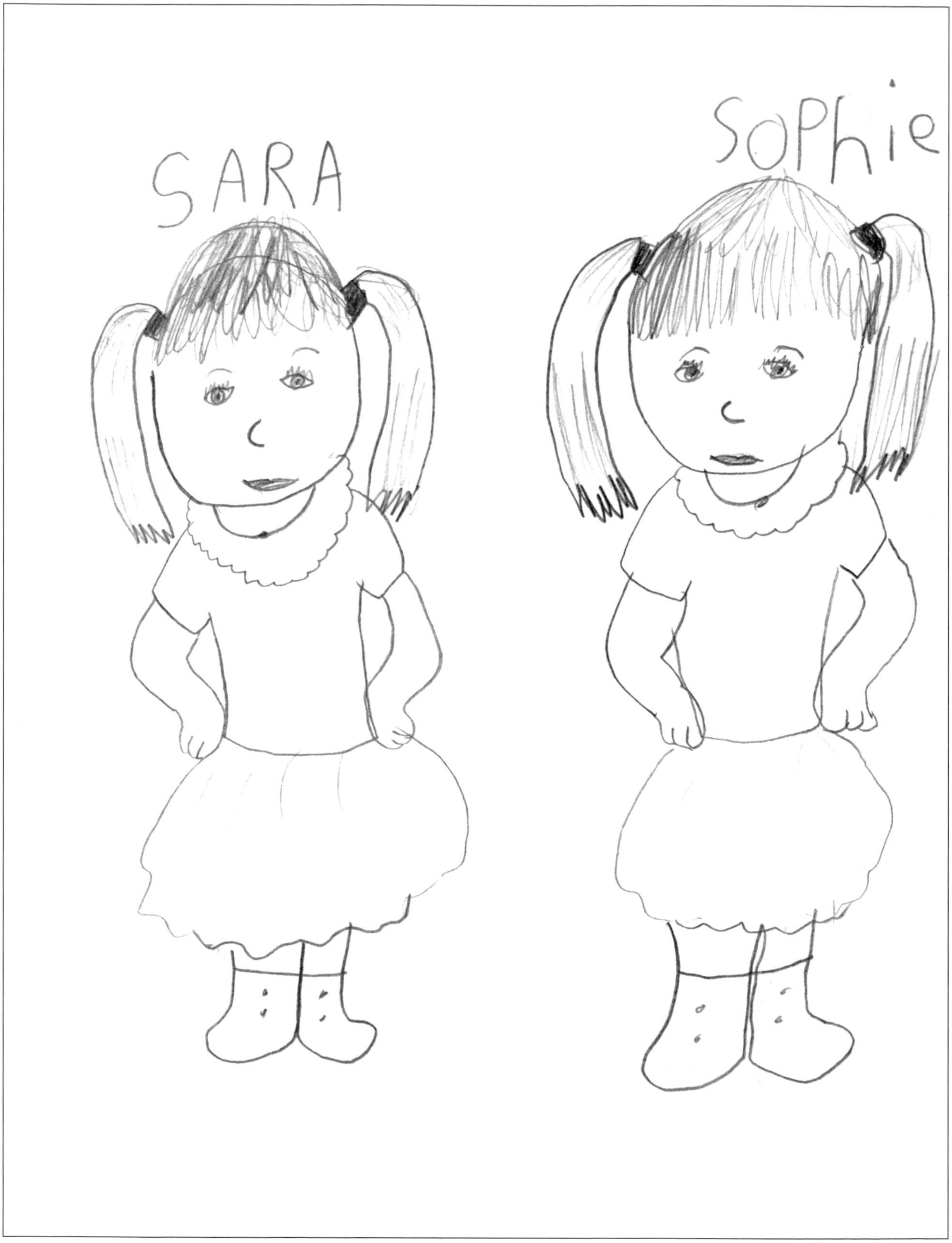
SARA
Sophie

"Twins." Age 5, Aug., 1987.

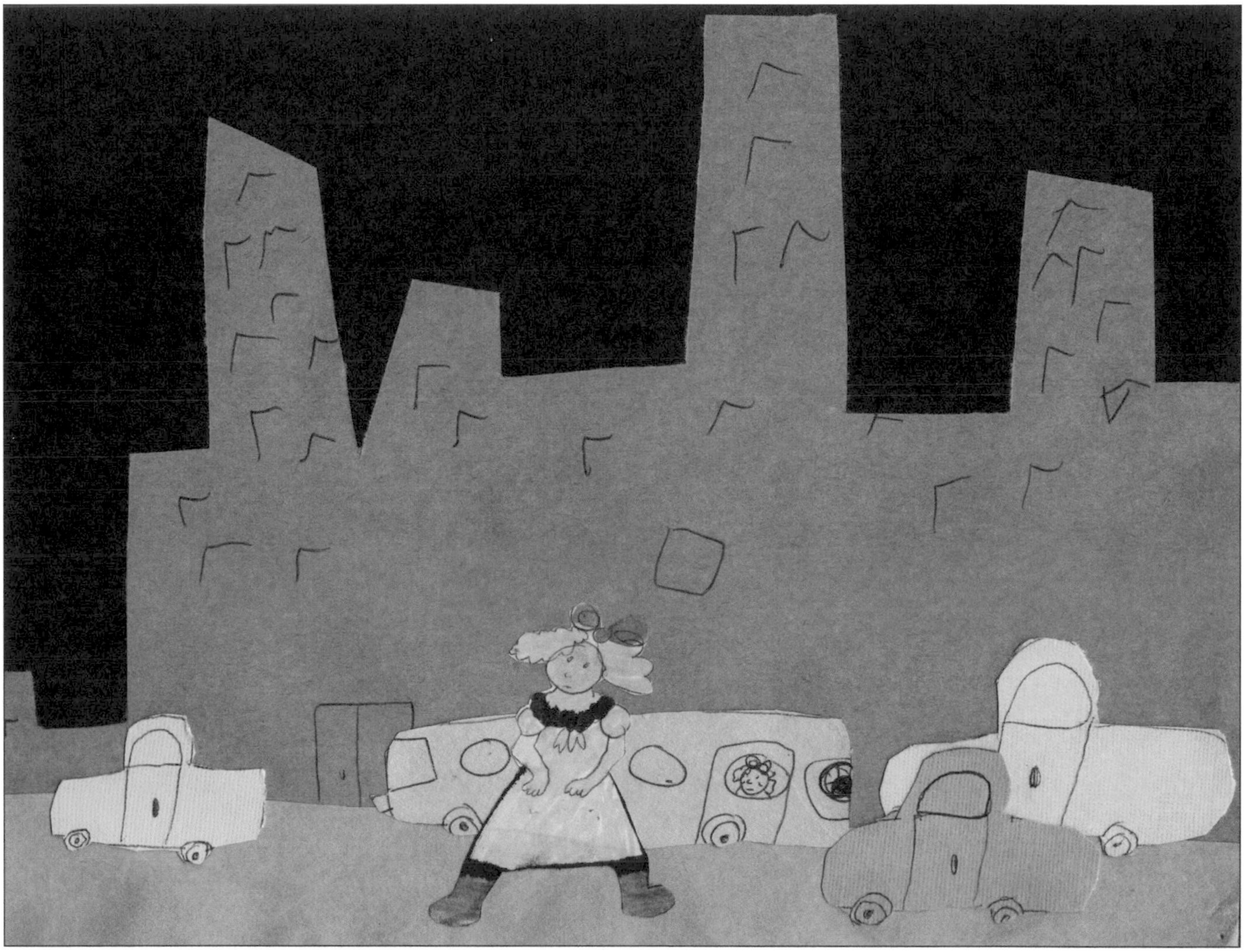

Age 6, Dec., 1987.

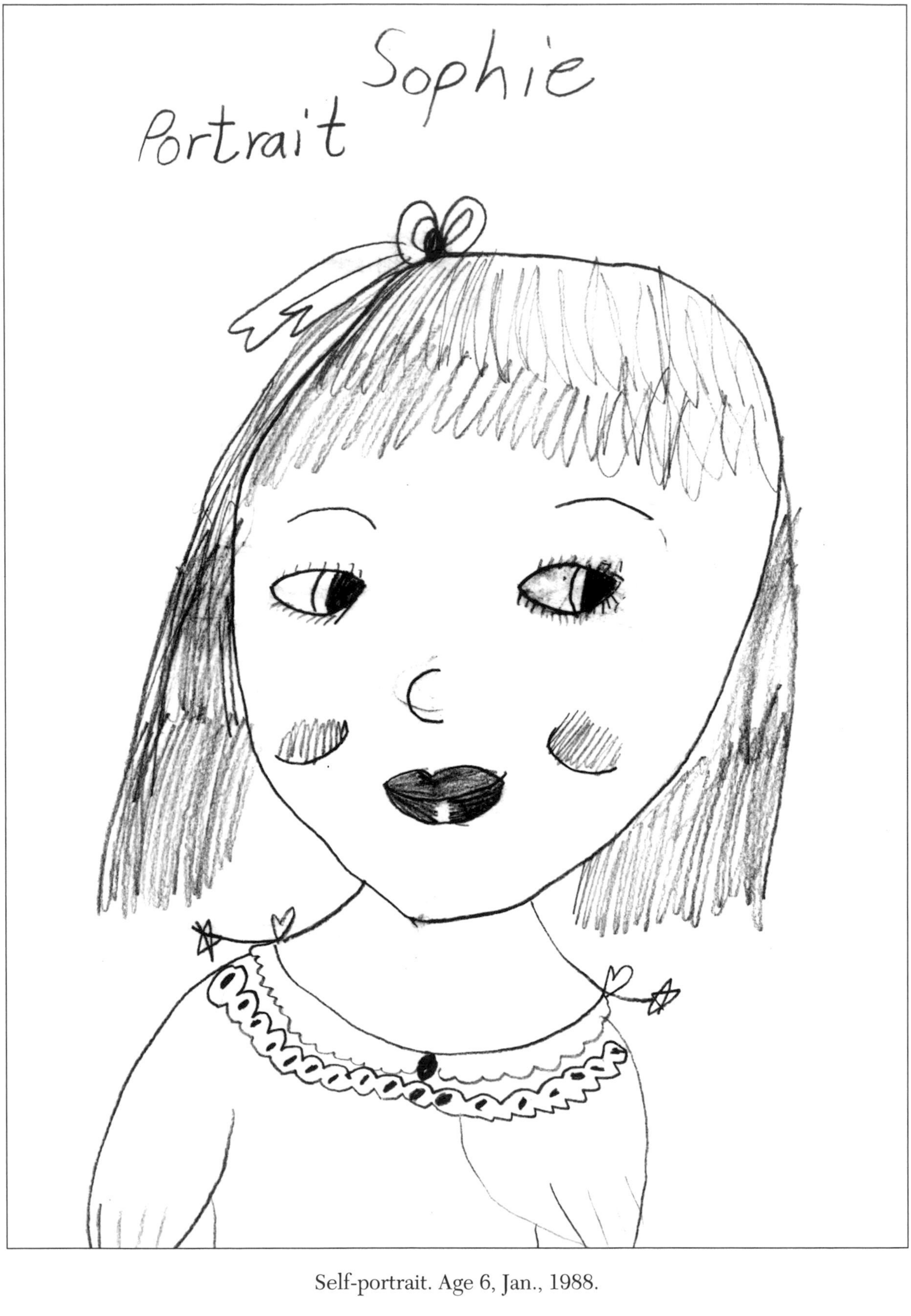
Sophie
Portrait

Self-portrait. Age 6, Jan., 1988.

Sophie hated swimming lessons but loved being underwater. Age 6, spring, 1988.

Inspired by listening to an old recording by The Carter Family. Age 6, April, 1988.

The Three Stooges period. Age 6, spring, 1988.

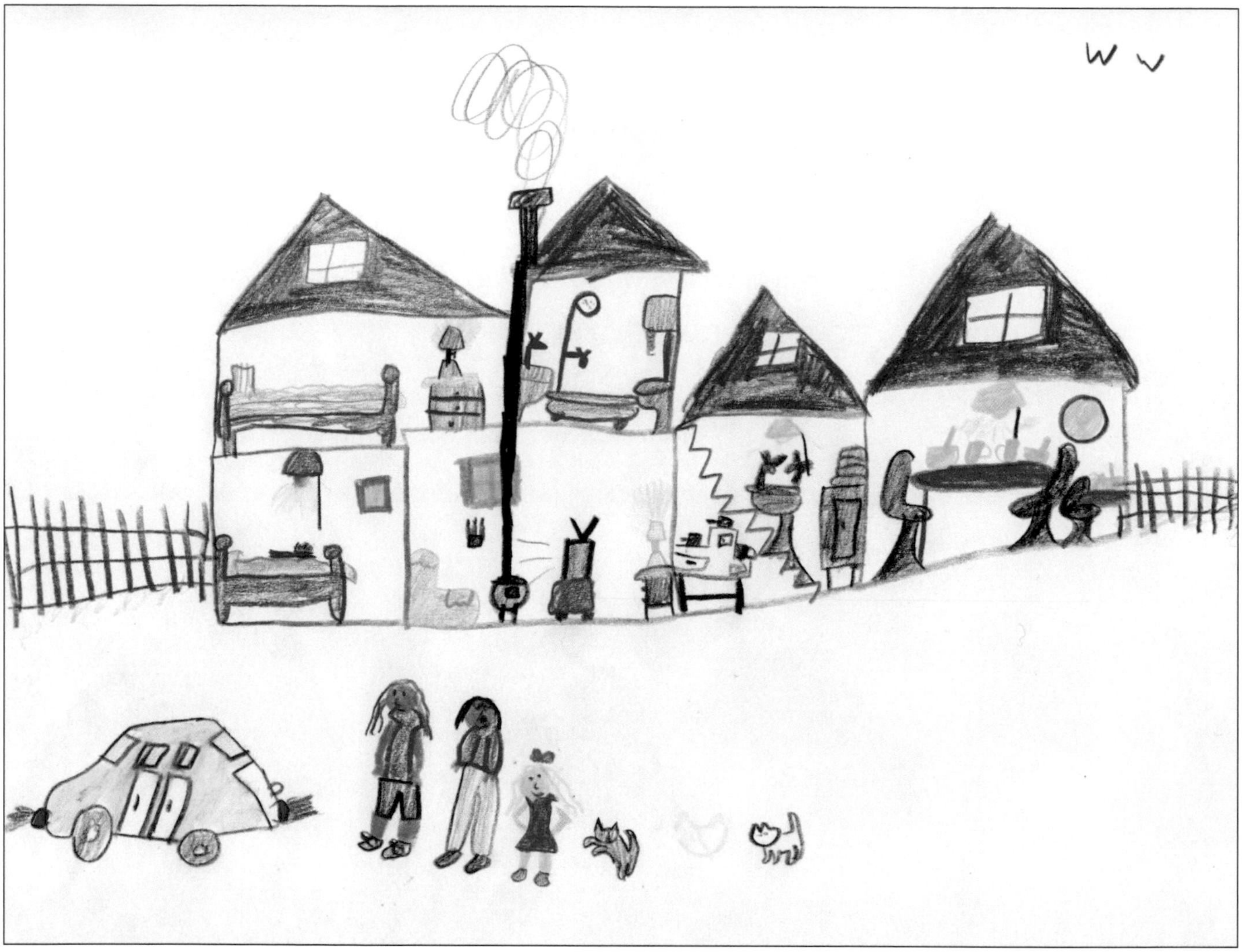
W W

Age 7, Nov., 1988.

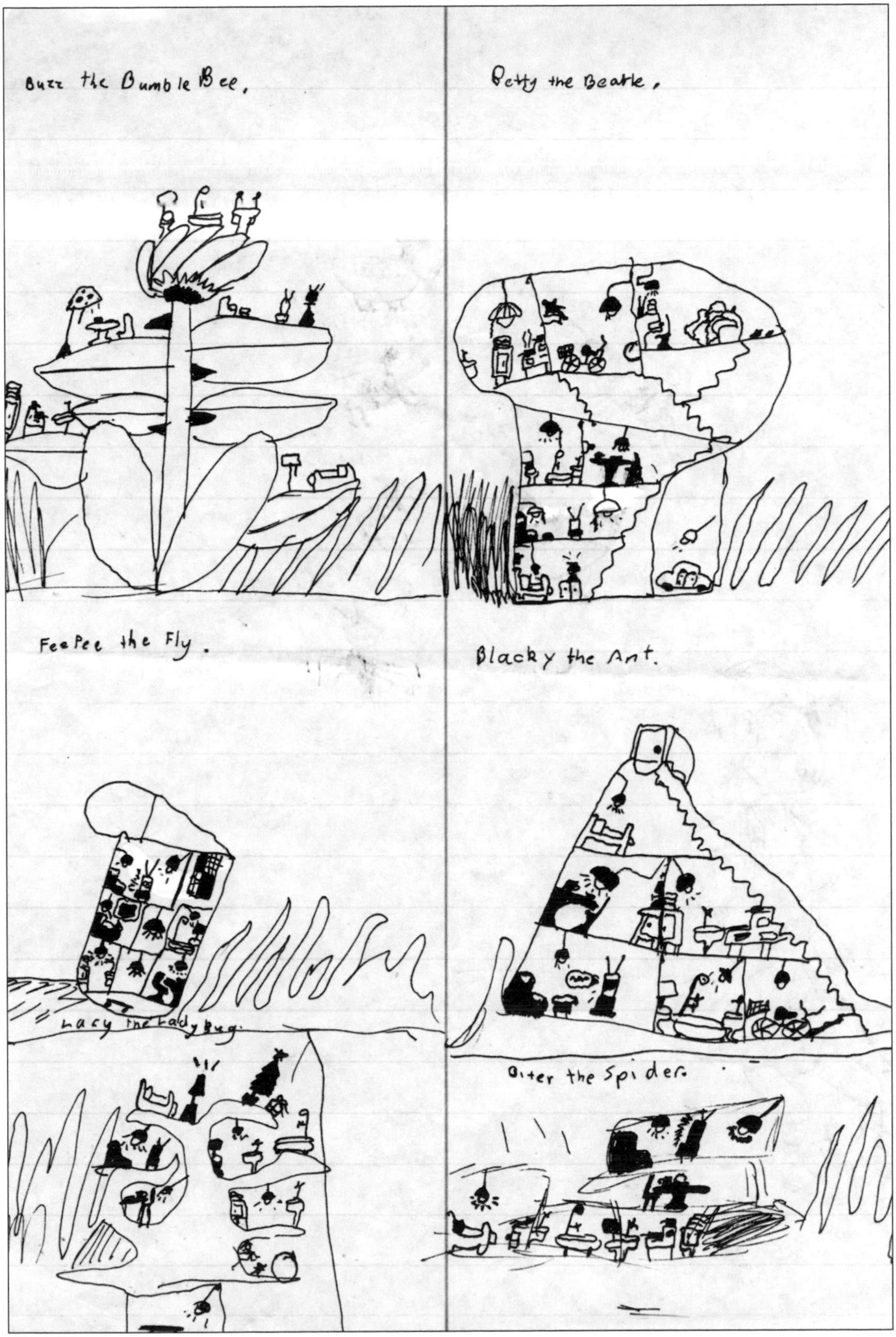
Buzz the Bumble Bee.
Betty the Beatle.
FeePee the Fly.
Blacky the Ant.
Lacy the Lady bug.
Oiter the Spider.

Age 7, Dec., 1988.

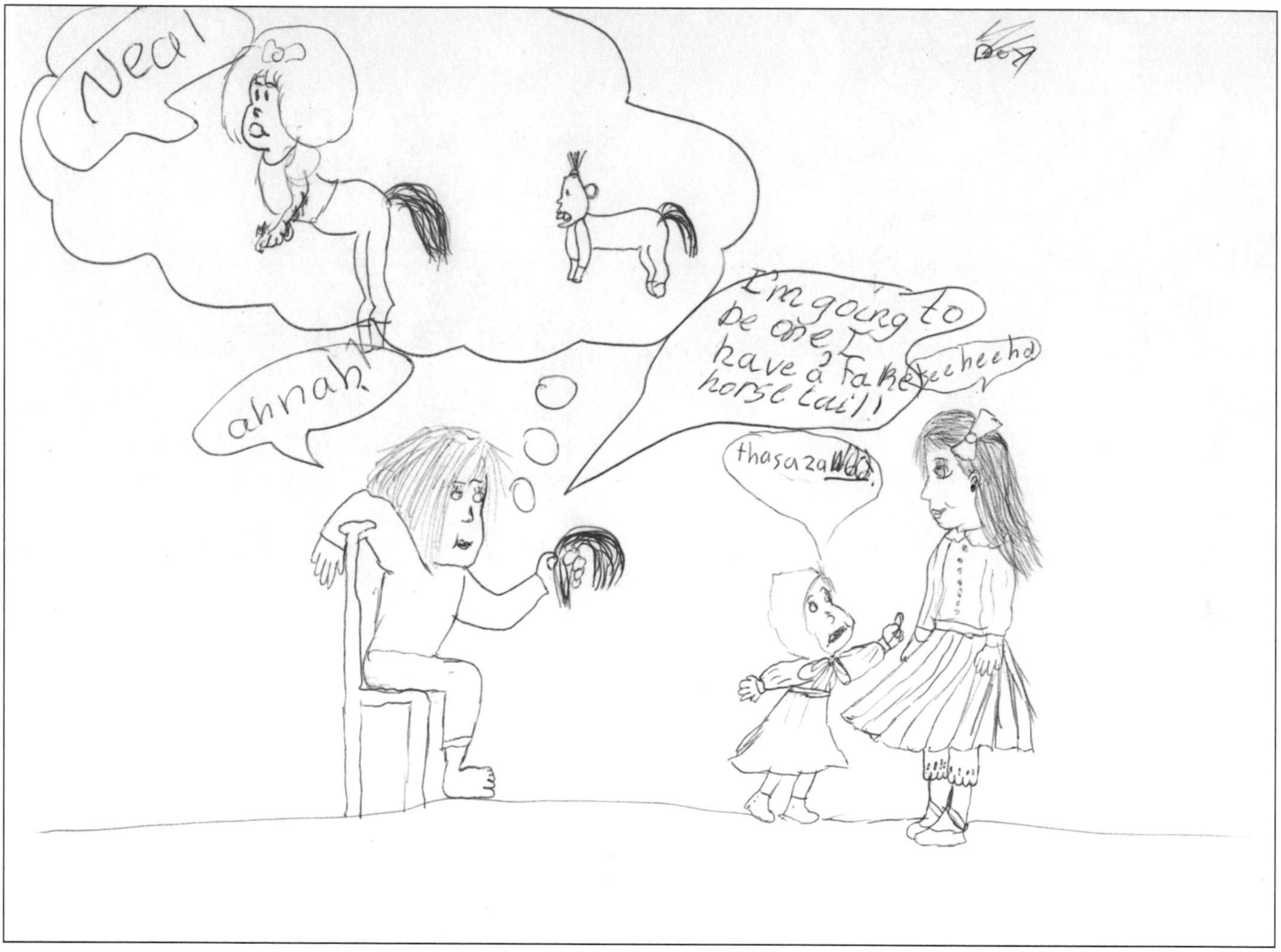
Neal
ahnah!
I'm going to be one I have a fake horse tail!!

Age 7, Dec., 1988.

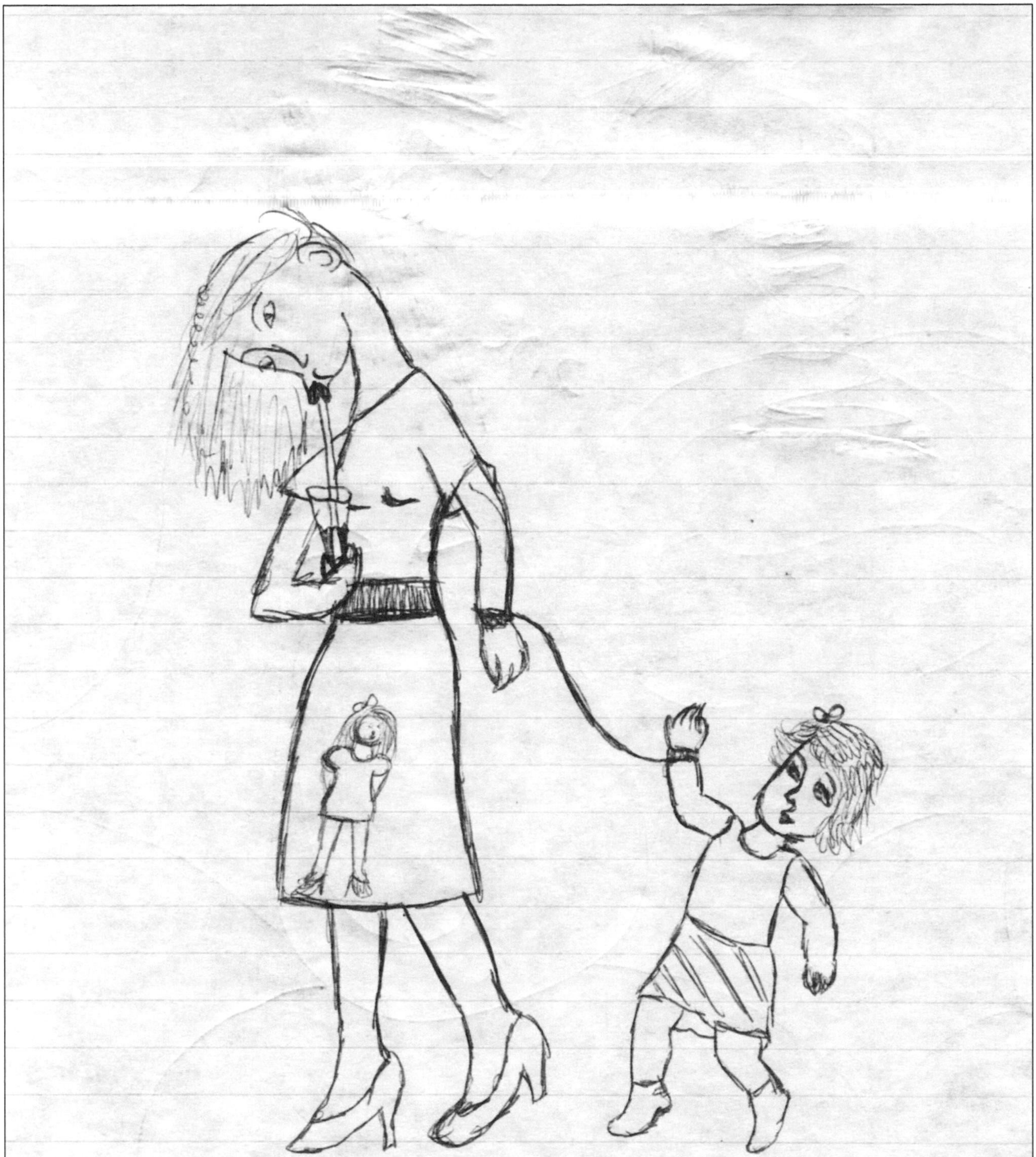

Age 7, early 1989.

Mom as gypsy. Age 7, Feb., 1989.

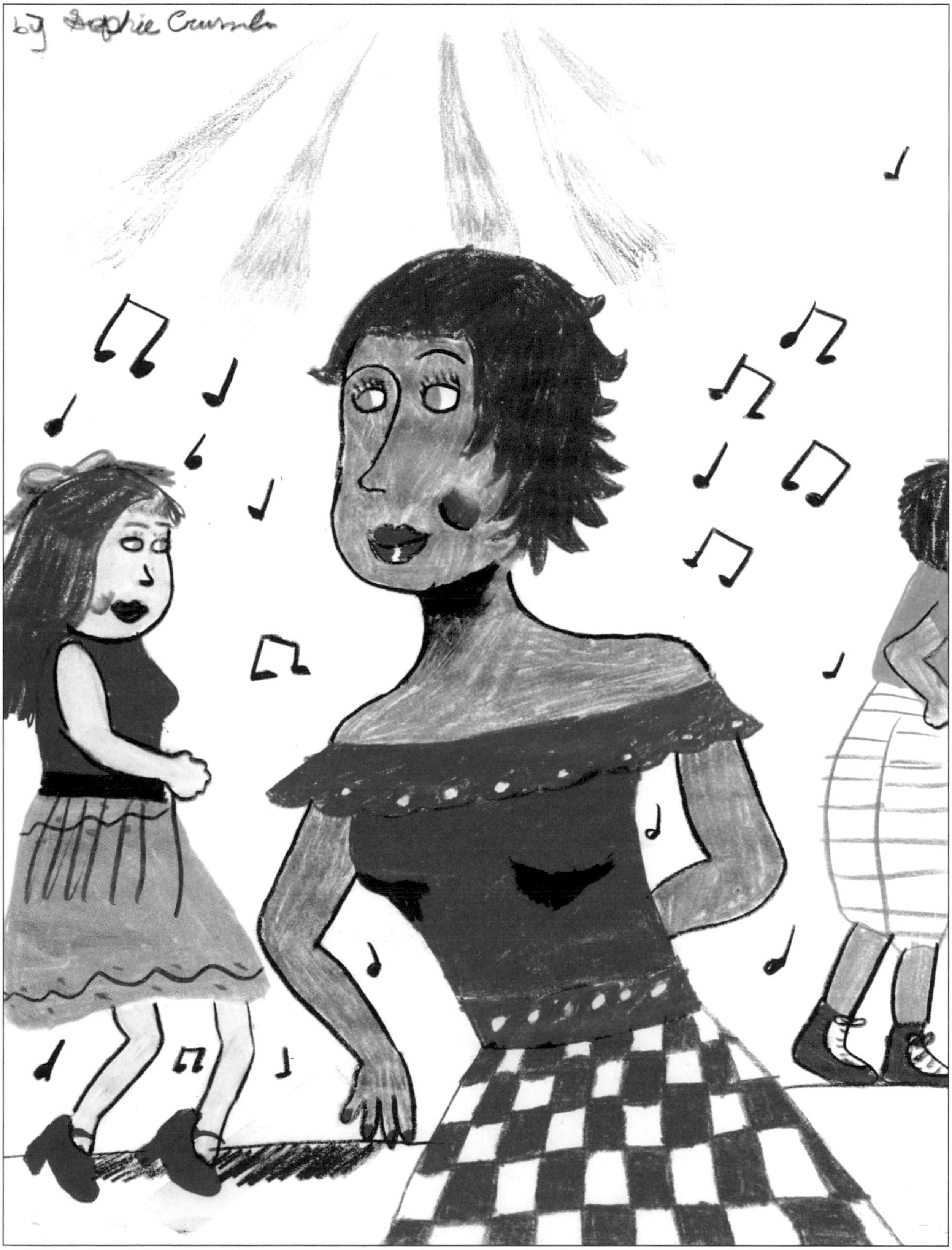
by Sophie Crumb

Age 7, March, 1989.

"A girl dancer and her teacher, Pamela Trokanski." Age 7, April, 1989.

"She turns into a pizza slice." Age 7, summer, 1989.

Age 7, Aug., 1989.

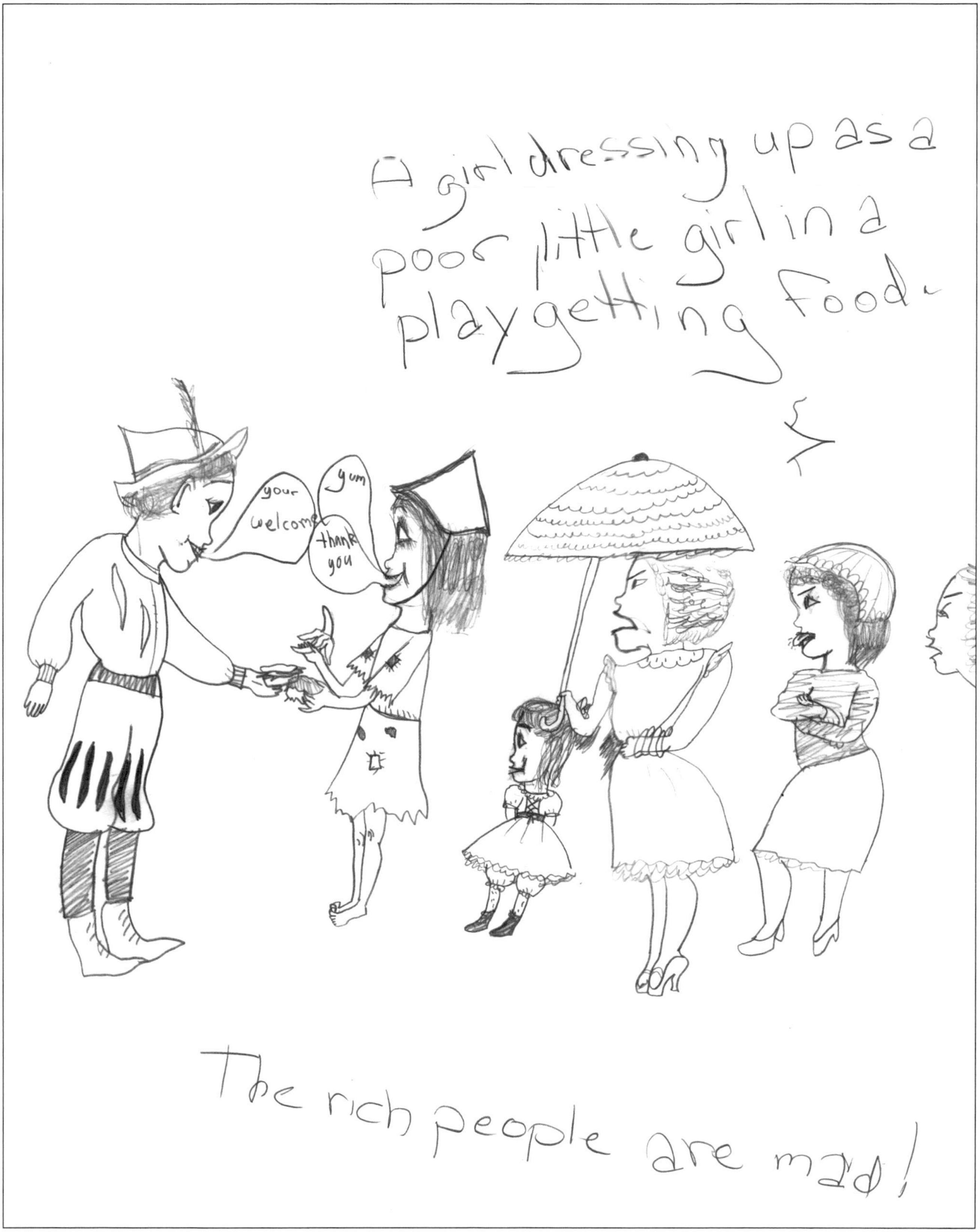
A girl dressing up as a poor little girl in a play getting food.
your welcome
yum
thank you
The rich people are mad!

Age 8, Oct., 1989.

smart/stipid Sophie — based on me!

M the girl who never gets
paid attention to

Is this ironic?? Age 8, Dec., 1989.

Age 8, Jan., 1990.

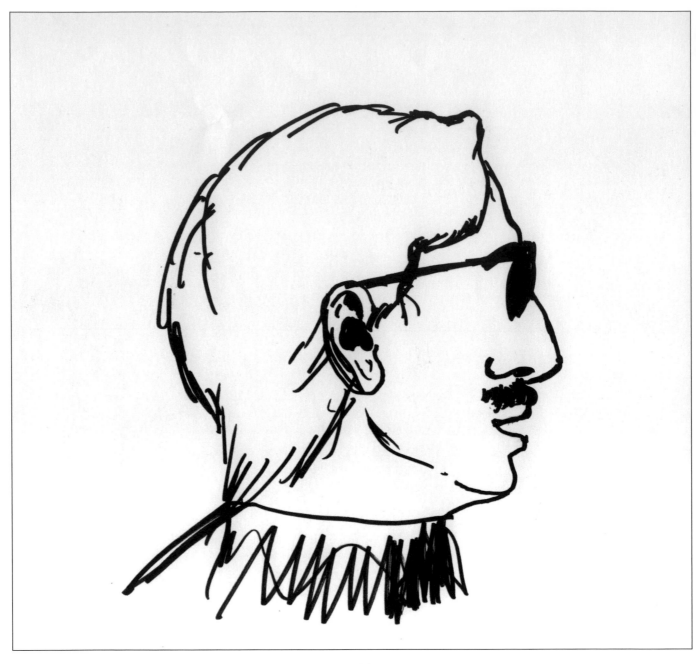

R. Crumb. Drawn from life. Age 8, Jan., 1990.

A man, a plan, a canal, panama

Self-portrait. Age 8, spring, 1990.

TO MY
Mother
ALINE
WHO
REMINDED
ME OF
GYPSIES

Age 8, March, 1990.

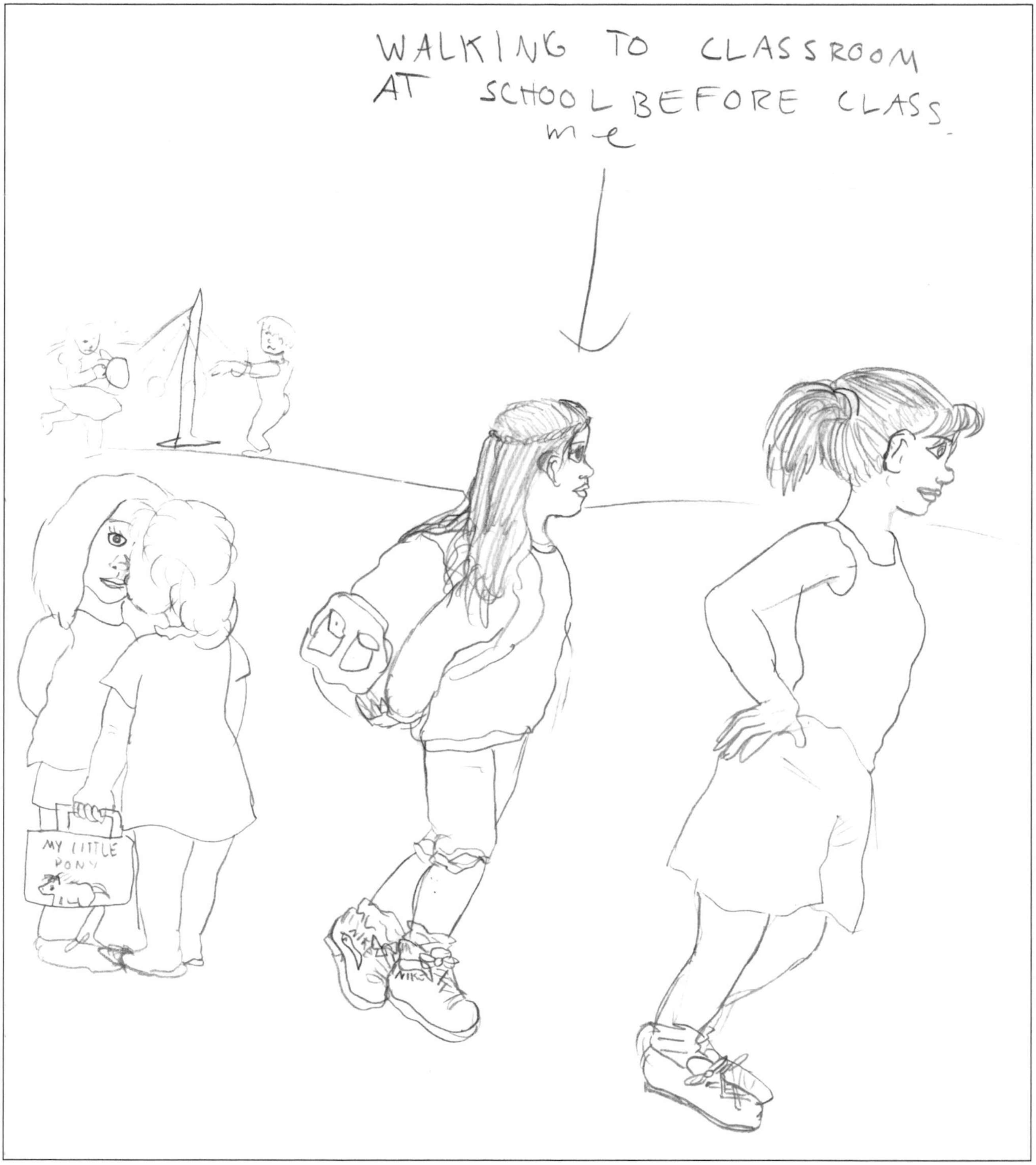
WALKING TO CLASSROOM AT SCHOOL BEFORE CLASS.
me
MY LITTLE PONY

Age 8, March, 1990.

Age 9, Nov., 1990.

EARLY ADOLESCENCE
1990 to 1996 / 8 to 15 yrs old

WE MOVED TO FRANCE WHEN I WAS NINE. THE YEARS THAT FOLLOWED ARE ODDLY DIM AND BLURRY IN MY MIND. BUT I MUST'VE BEEN KILLING TIME AND THE ANGUISH OF A NEW LIFE BY DRAWING BECAUSE THE AMOUNT OF DOODLES AND SKETCHES ARCHIVED BY MY FATHER HURTS ONE'S HEAD TO LOOK THROUGH! NANCY, LITTLE LULU, OLD WALT DISNEY, BETTY BOOP, POPEYE, GOLDEN BOOKS, ETC., ETC., INSPIRED AND OBSESSED ME, THANKS TO A BRAIN WASHING, VINTAGE EDUCATION.

PUBERTY MADE ME BECOME SELF-CONS-CIOUS, AND I TRIED TO CONFORM, TO FIT THE COOL STANDARD EVEN THOUGH I NEVER SUCCEEDED IN THAT BRANCH. SKETCHBOOKS WERE ALWAYS WITH ME, AND BECAME ILLUSTRATED DIARIES FULL OF TEENAGE ANGST.

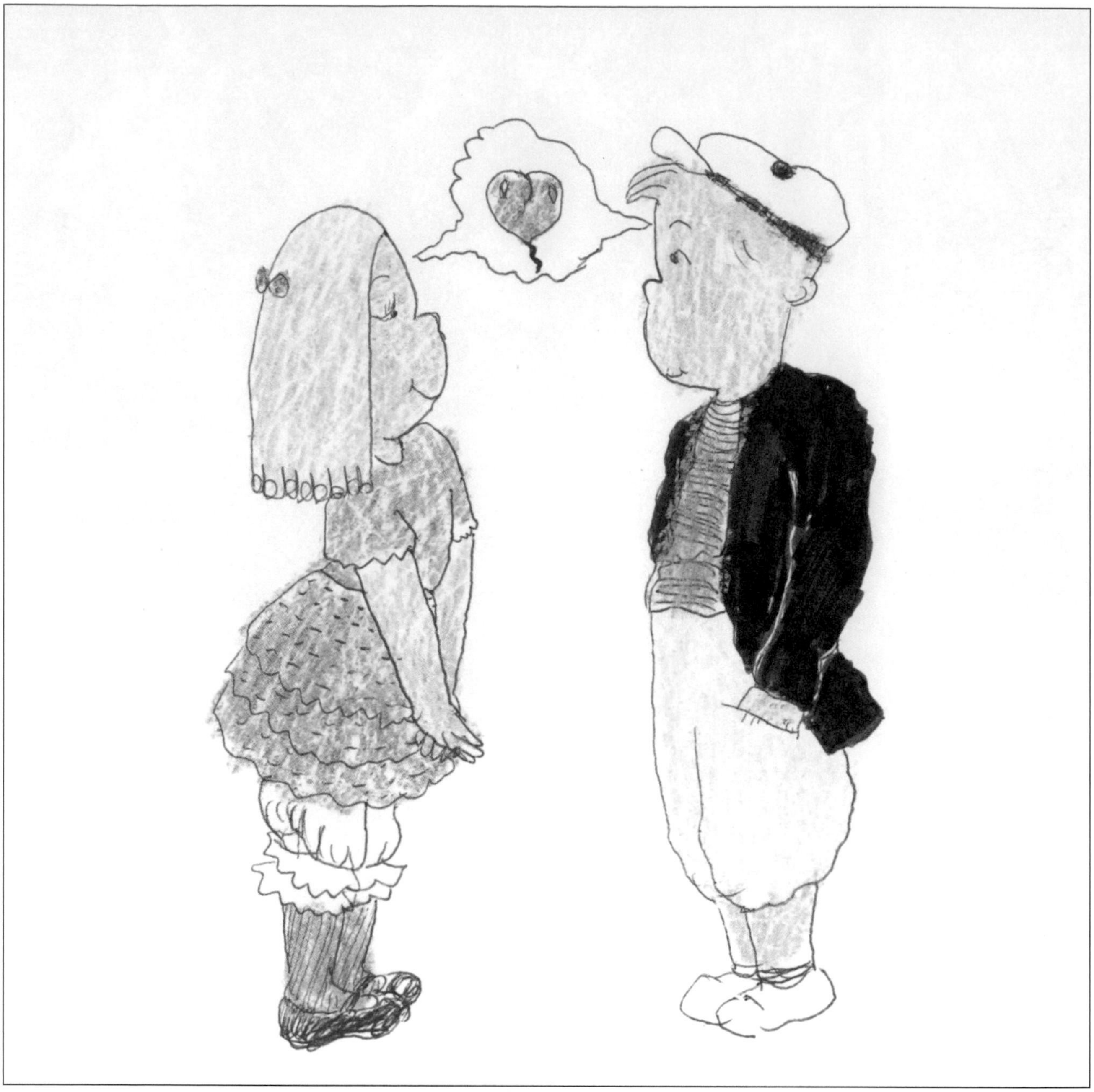

Age 9, Jan., 1991.

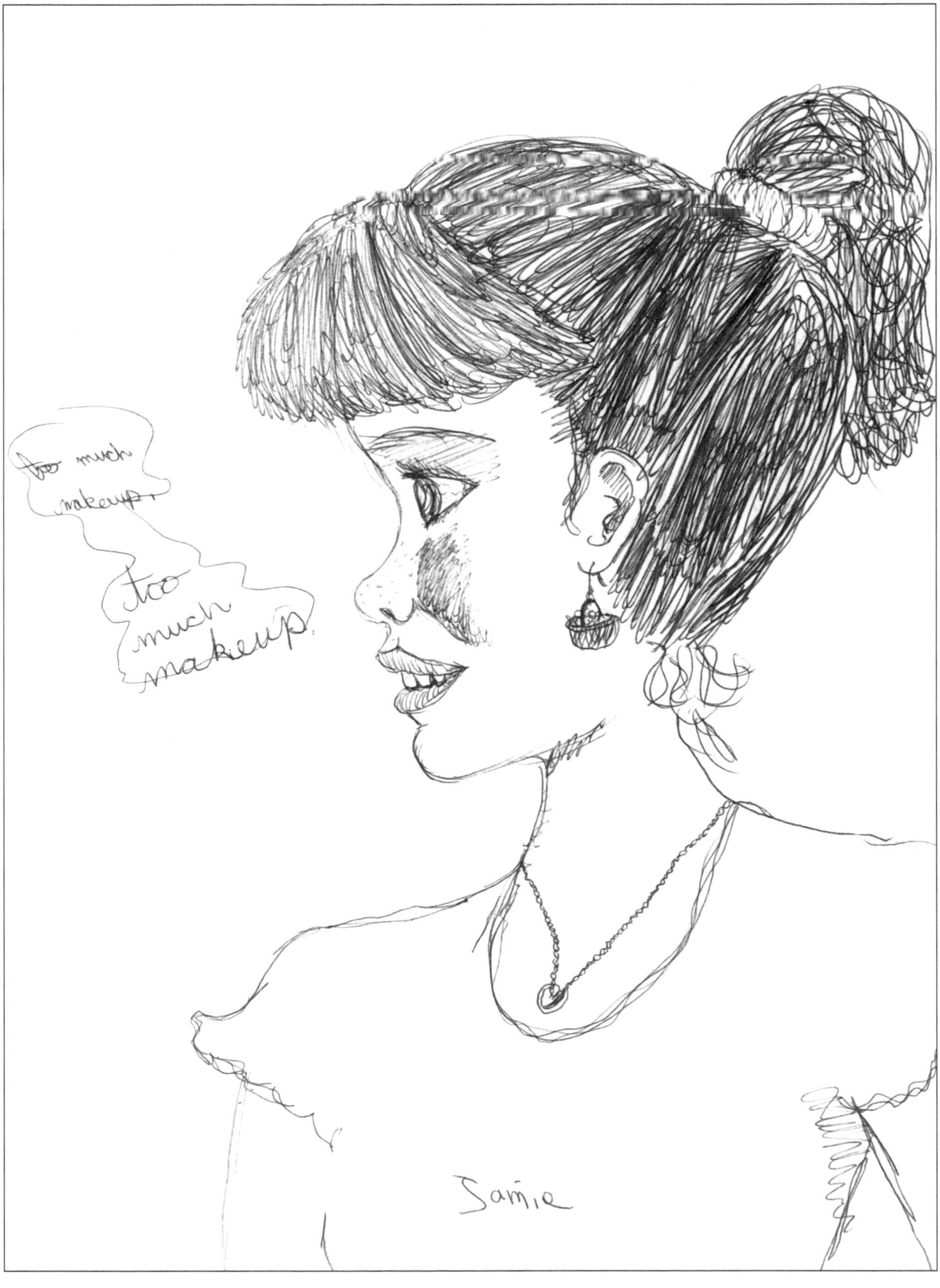
~~too~~ much makeup.
too much makeup.
Samie

Age 9, spring, 1991.

Sophie's "gang" in fourth grade, just before moving to France. Age 9, spring, 1991.

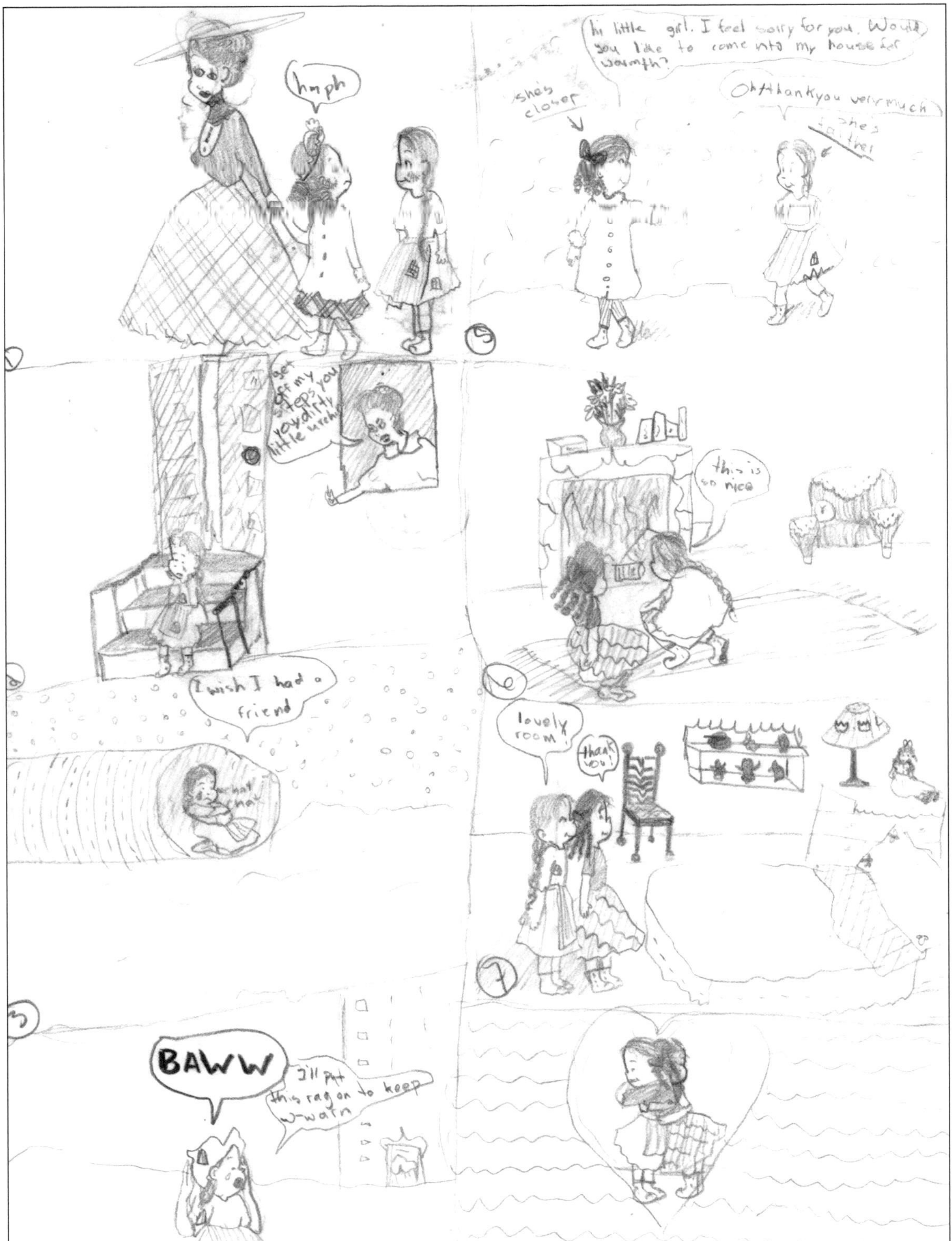
hmph
get off my steps you you dirty little urchin
I wish I had a friend
BAWW
I'll put this rag on to keep w-warm
hi little girl. I feel sorry for you. Would you like to come into my house for warmth?
she's closer
Oh thank you very much
she's farther
this is so nice
lovely room!
thank you!
THE END

Age 9, April, 1991.

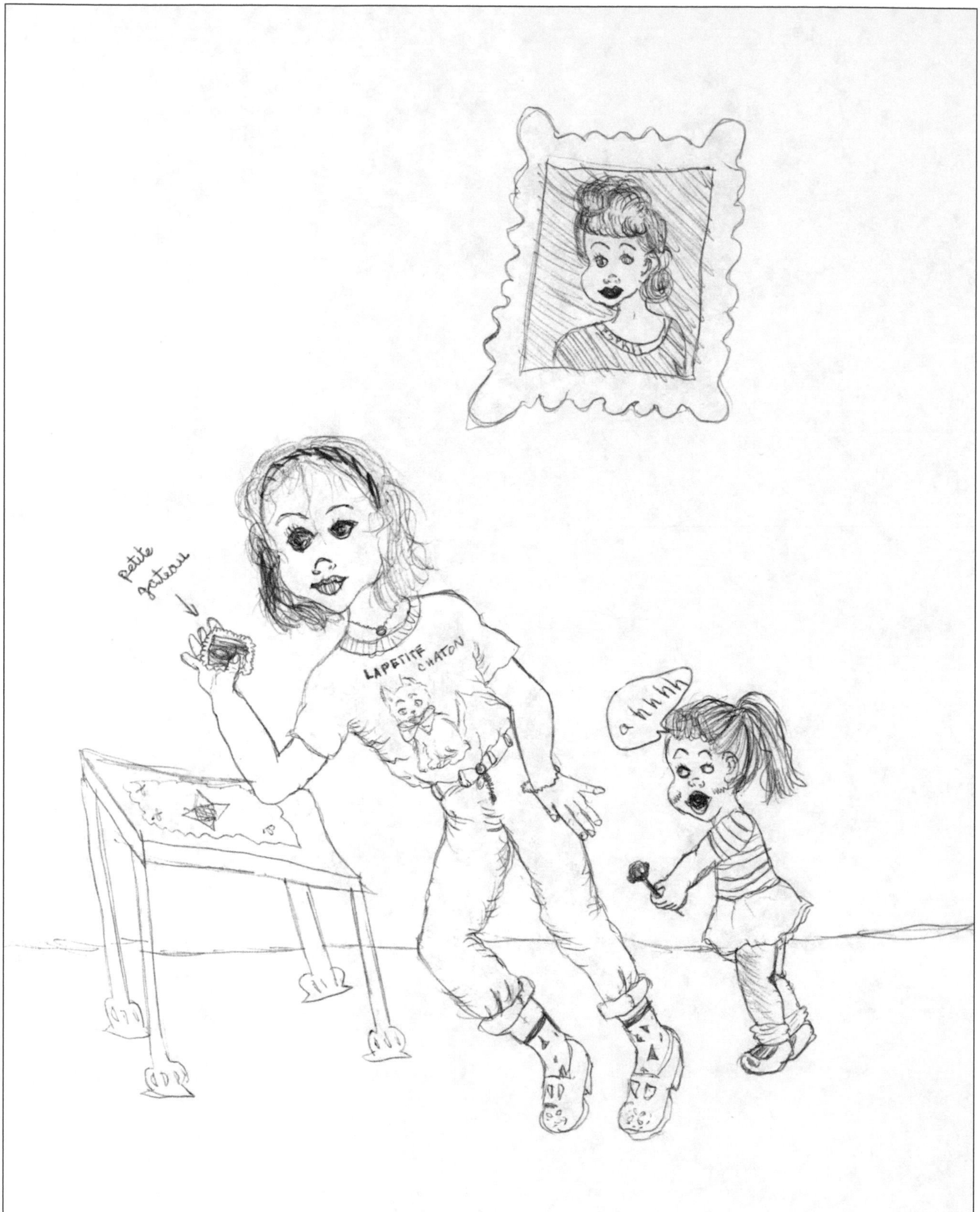
petite gateau
LA PETITE CHATON
ahhhh

Age 9, spring, 1991.

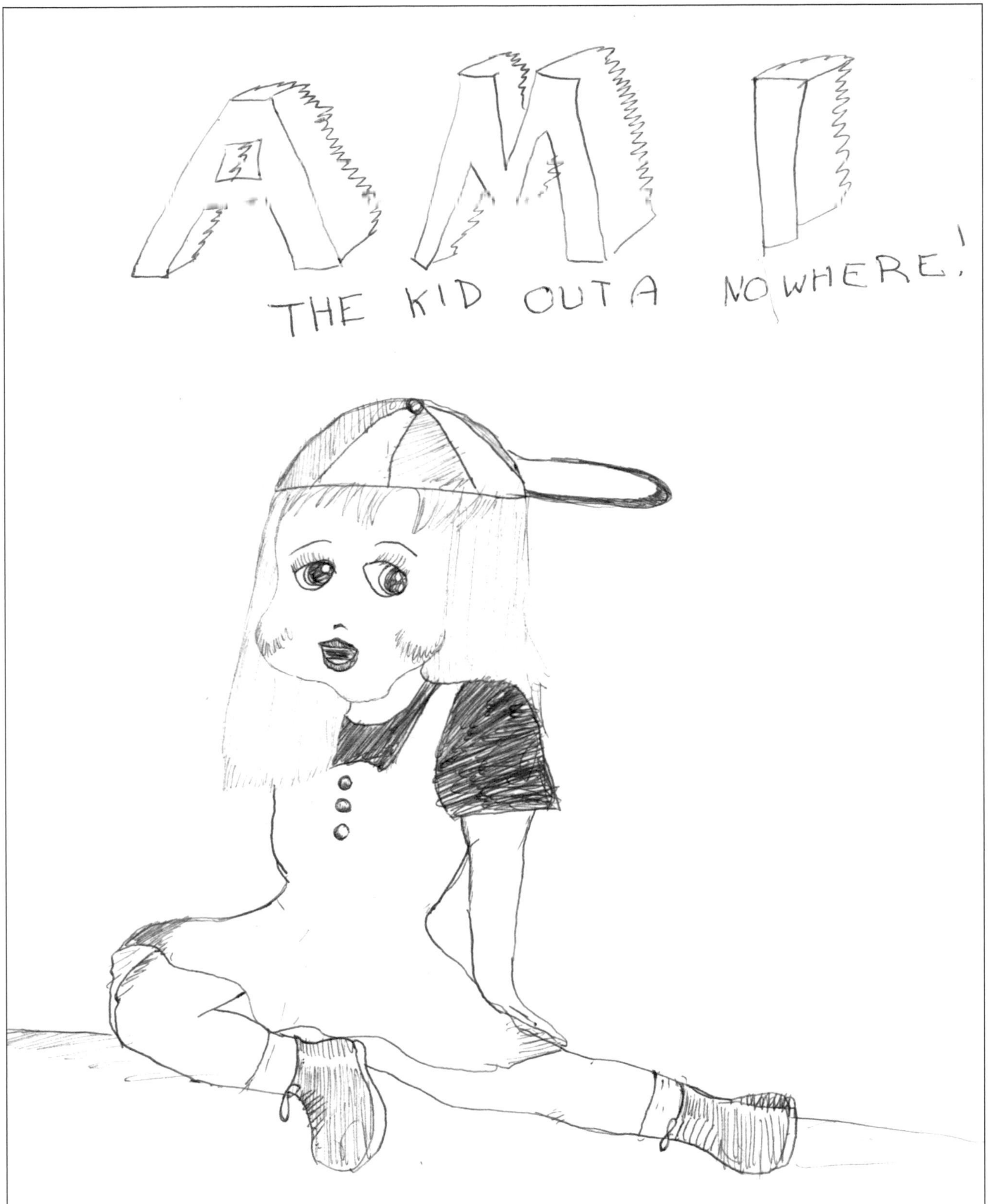
AMI
THE KID OUTA NOWHERE!

Age 9, July, 1991.

Self-portrait. Drawn from a photograph. Age 9, Aug., 1991.

"I wanna look like that one," says Sophie, pointing to the one on the left. "The fat one is me," she says, pointing to the one in the middle. "The one on the right is Julie Gagner."

Sophie at school in Sauve. Agathe helps her with the lessons.

Age 9, Sept., 1991.

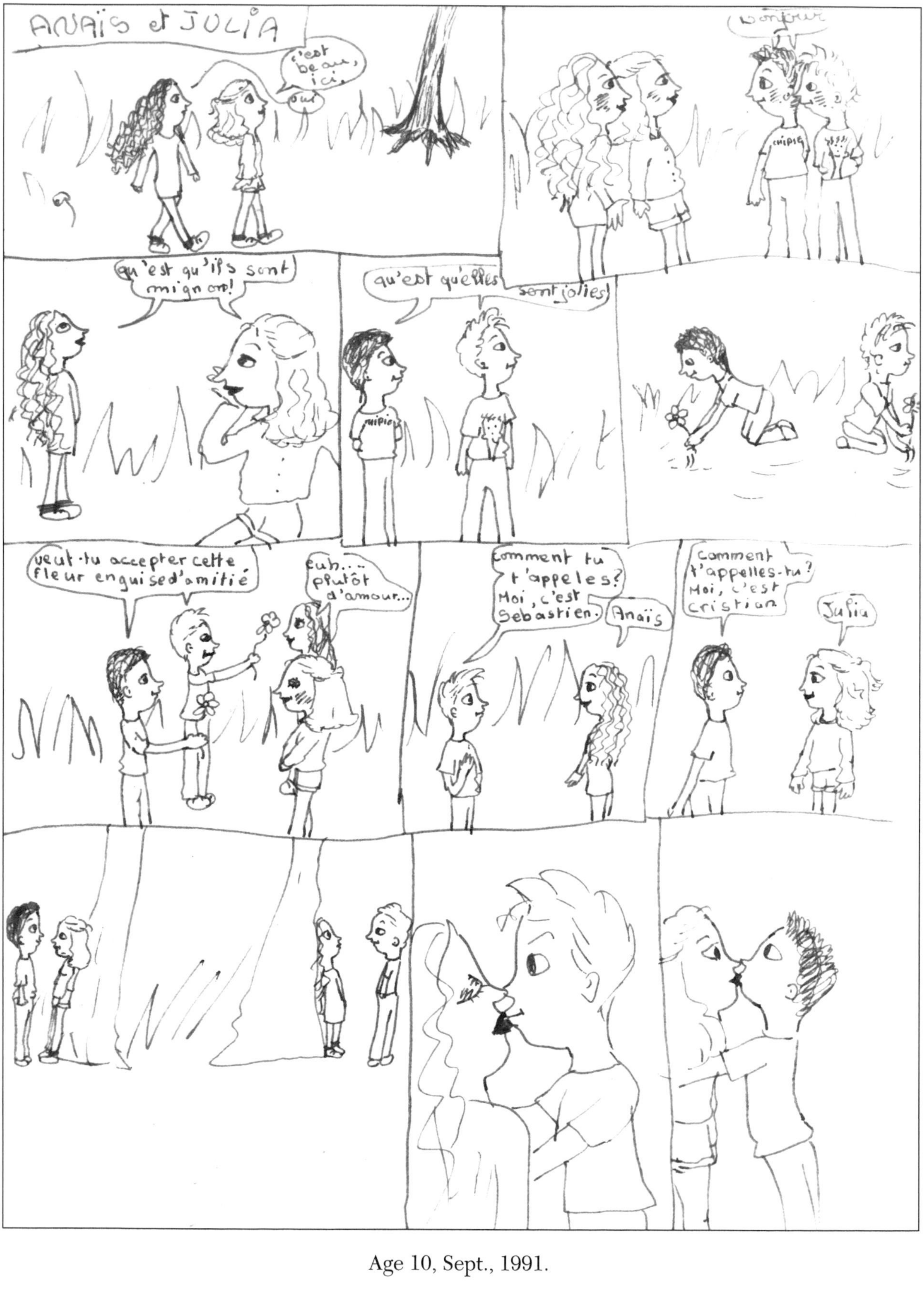
ANAÏS et JULIA
c'est beau, ici.
oui
Bonjour
qu'est qu'ils sont mignon!
qu'est qu'elles sont jolies!
veut-tu accepter cette fleur enguise d'amitié
euh... plutôt d'amour...
comment tu t'appeles? Moi, c'est Sebastien.
Anaïs
comment t'appelles-tu? Moi, c'est cristian
Julia

Age 10, Sept., 1991.

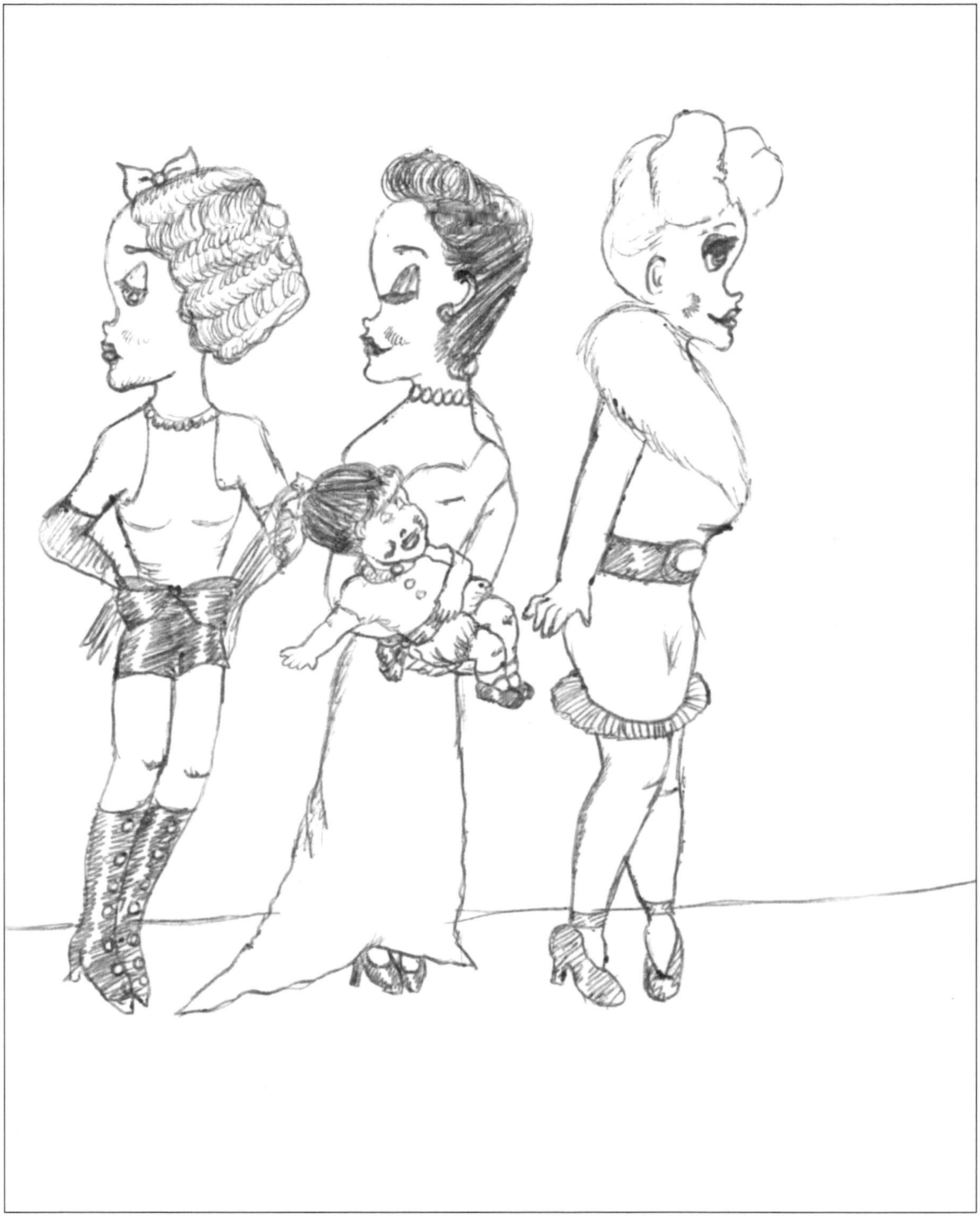

Age 10, late 1991.

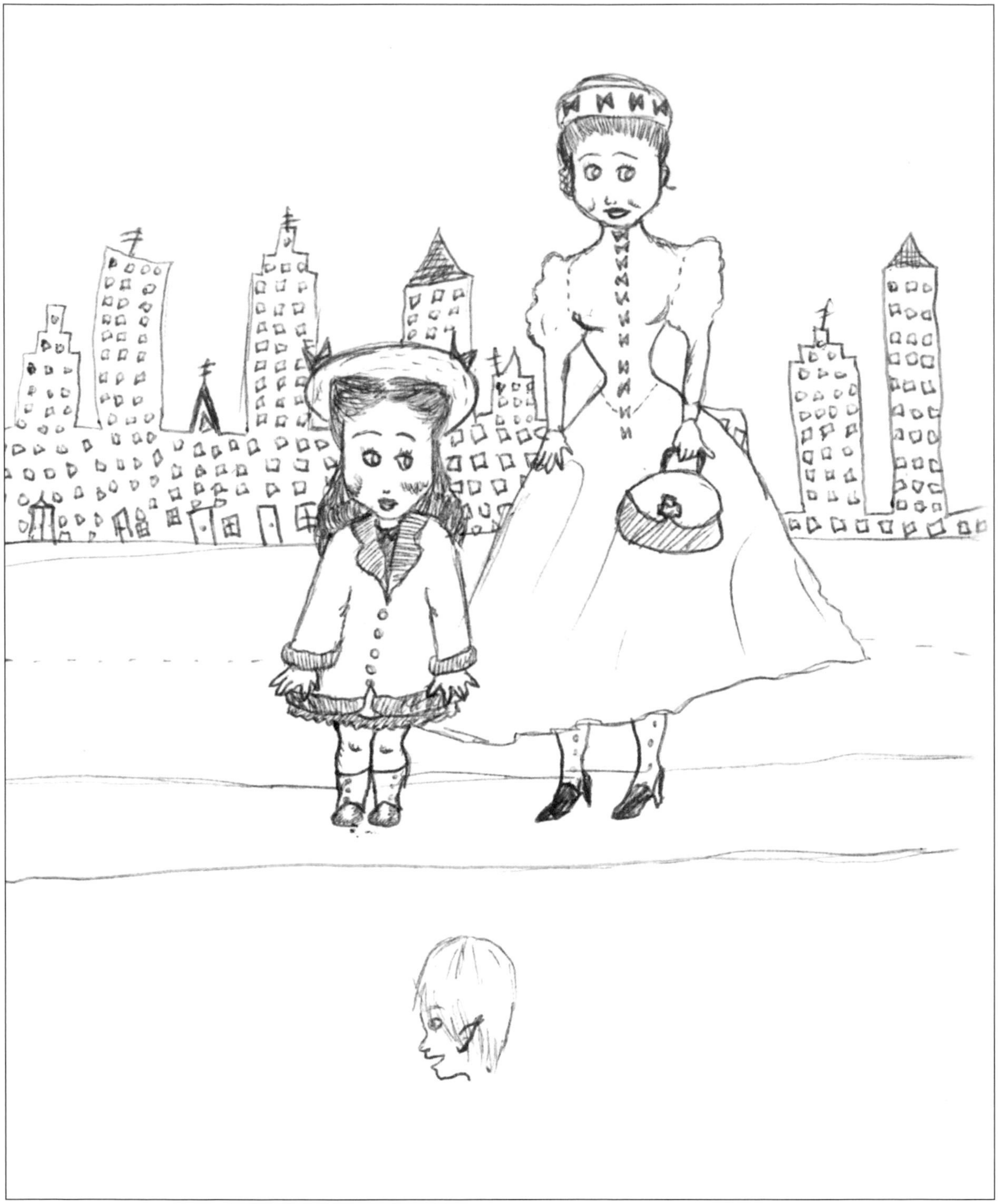

Age 10, late 1991.

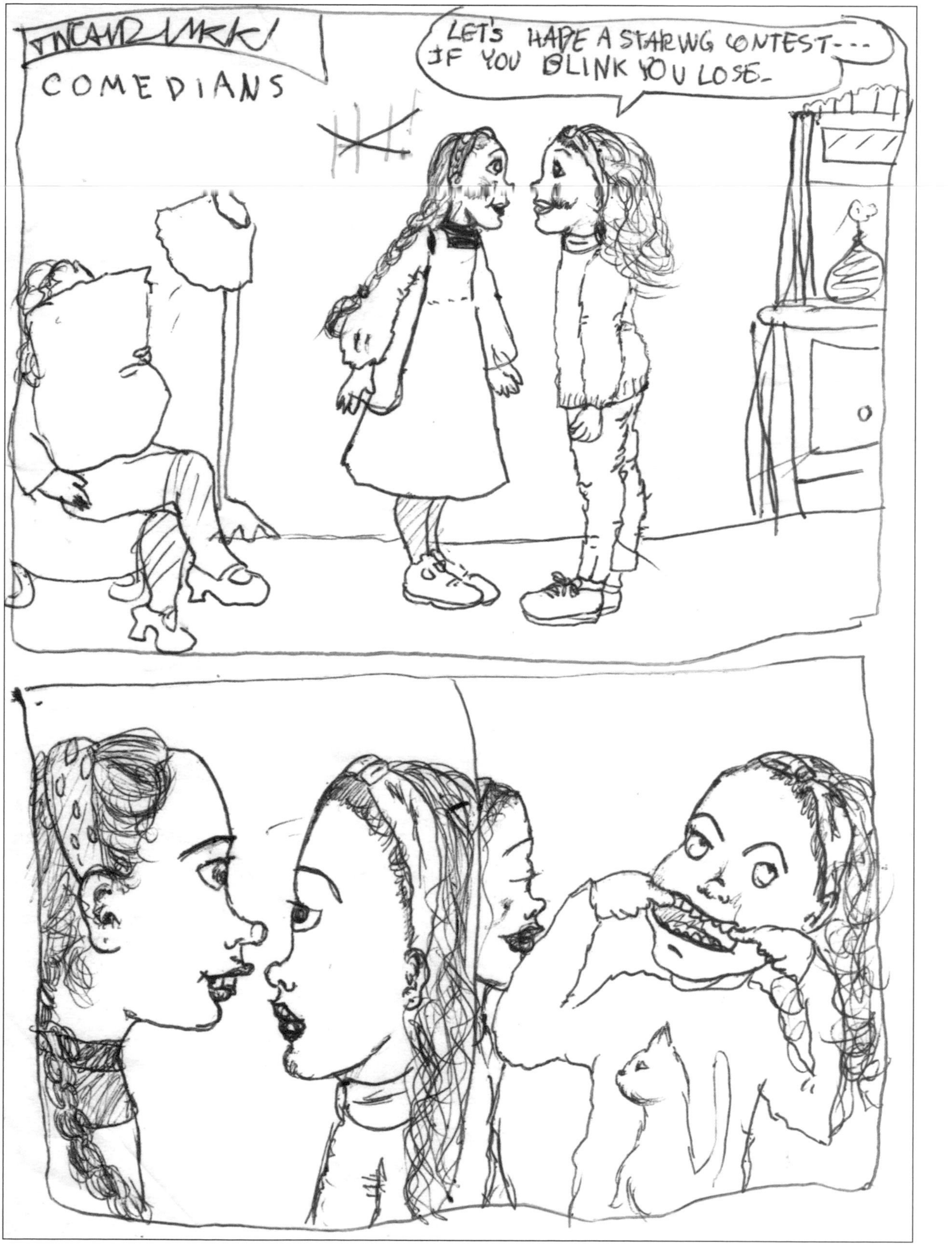
COMEDIANS
LET'S HAPE A STARWG CONTEST--- IF YOU BLINK YOU LOSE-

Age 10, Jan., 1992.

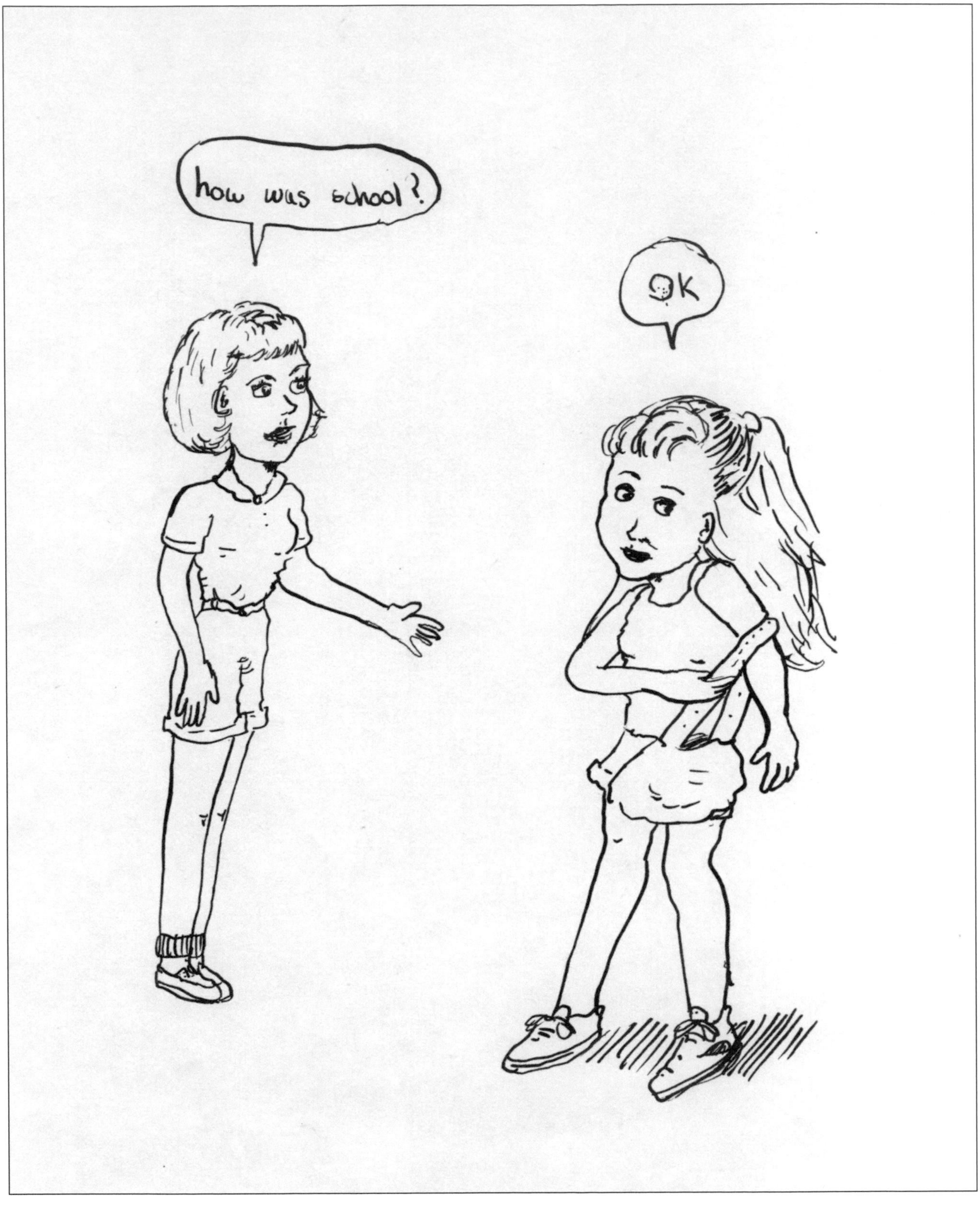
how was school?
OK

Age 10, Jan., 1992.

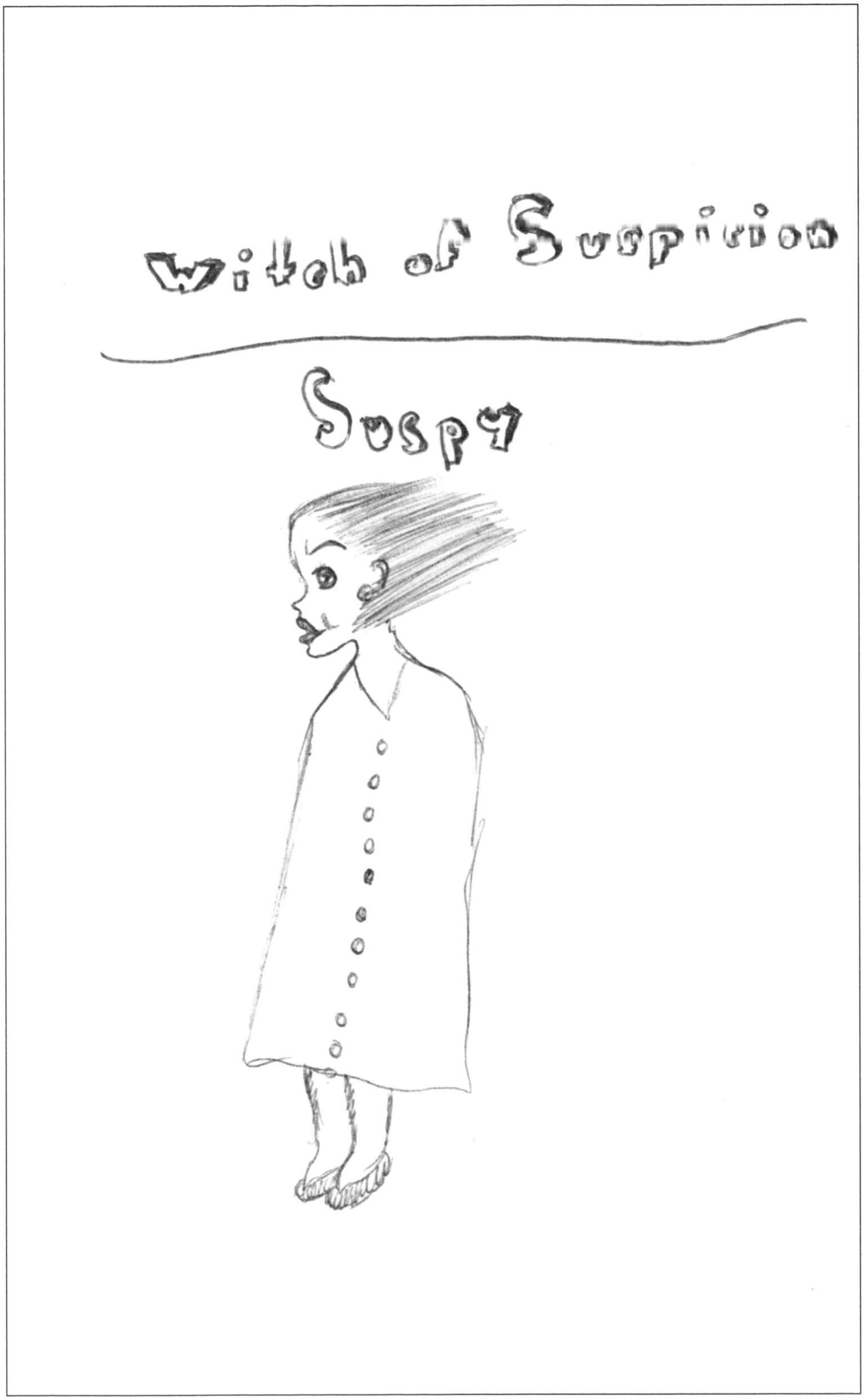
Witch of Suspicion
Suspy

Age 10, early 1992.

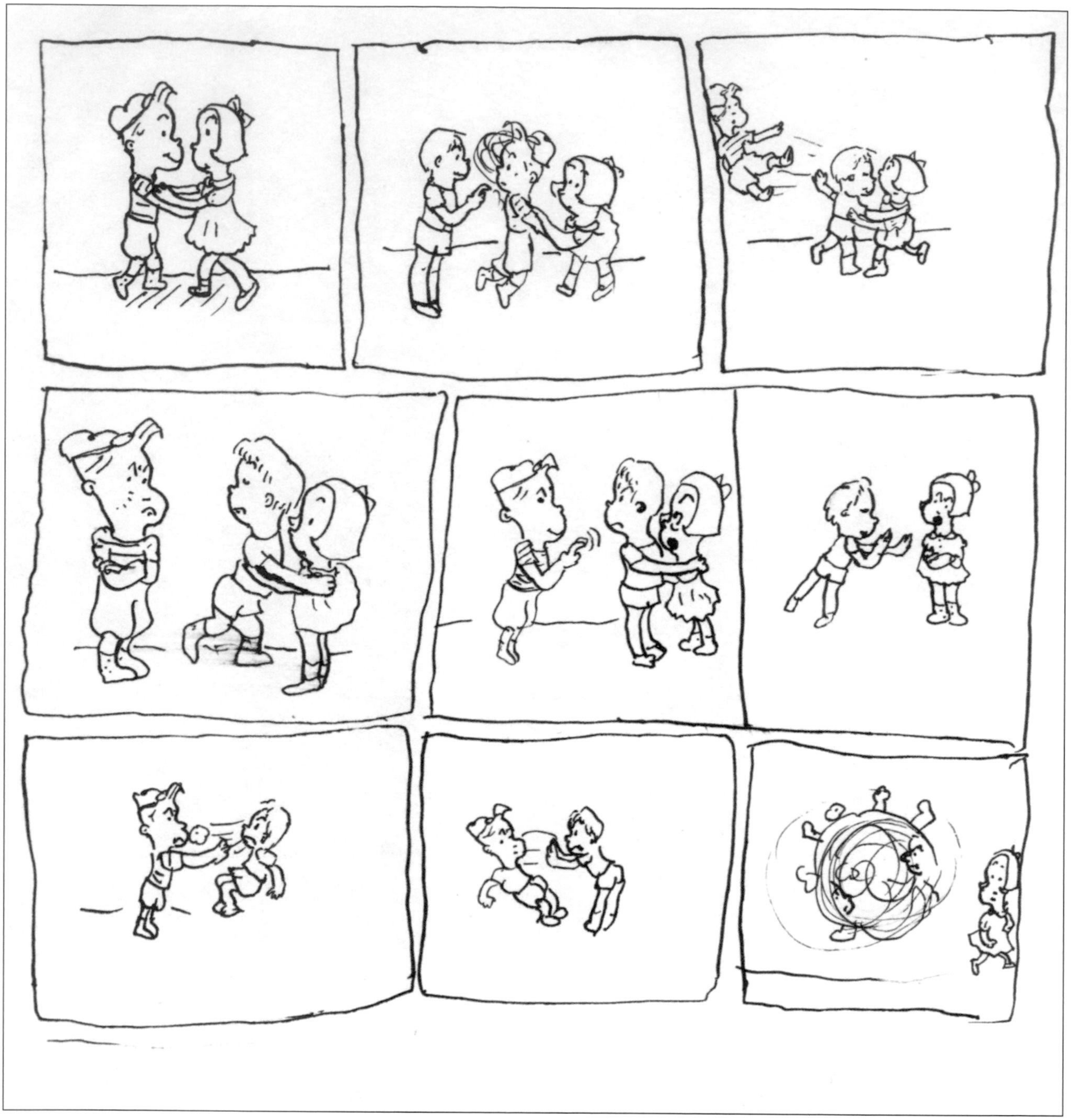

Age 10, Feb., 1992.

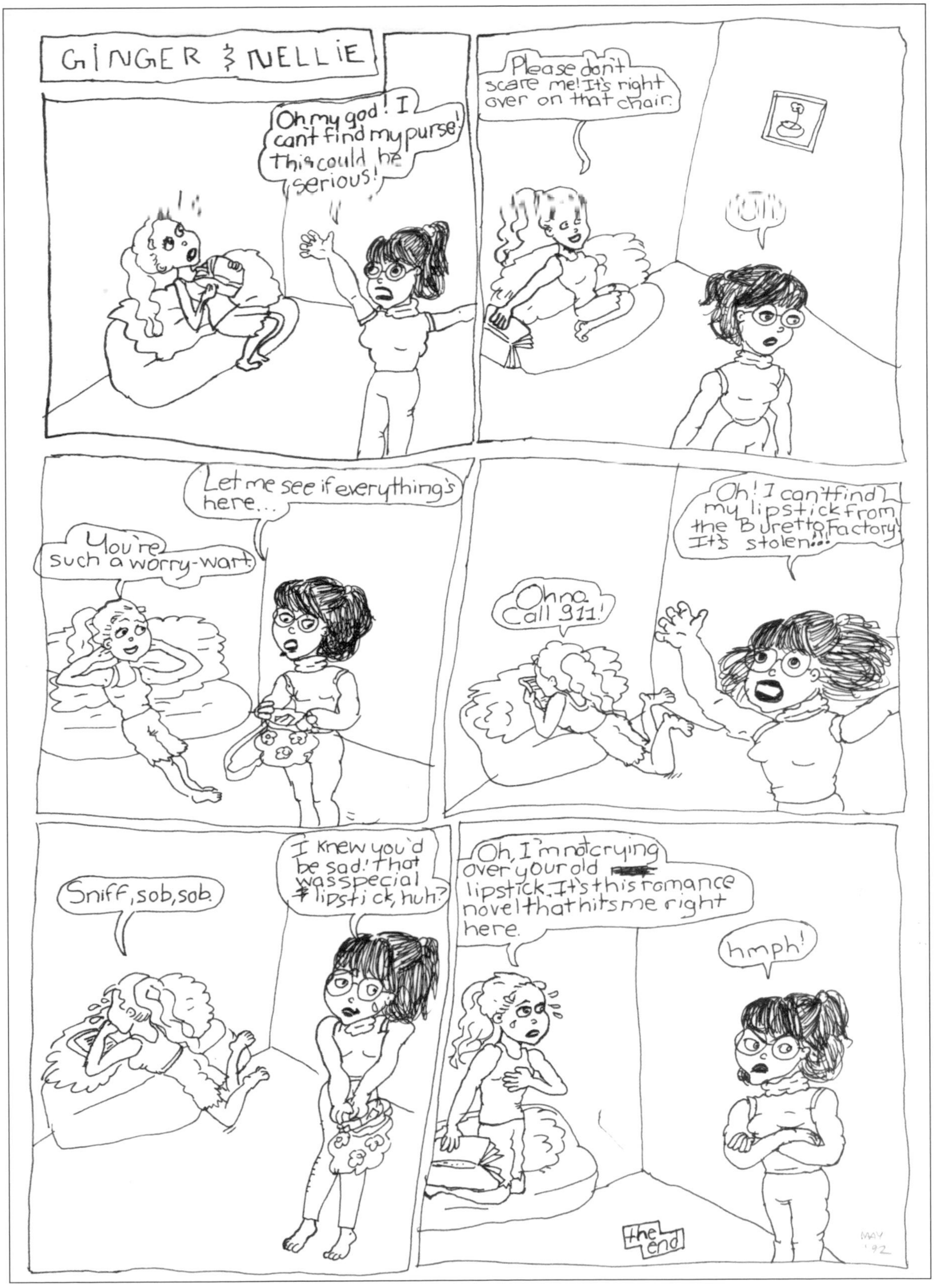
GINGER & NELLIE
Oh my god! I can't find my purse! this could be serious!
Please don't scare me! It's right over on that chair.
Let me see if everything's here...
You're such a worry-wart.
Oh! I can't find my lipstick from the Buretto Factory! It's stolen!!!
Oh no. Call 911!
Sniff, sob, sob.
I knew you'd be sad! that was special & lipstick, huh?
Oh, I'm not crying over your old [redacted] lipstick. It's this romance novel that hits me right here.
hmph!
the end
MAY '92

Age 10, May, 1992.

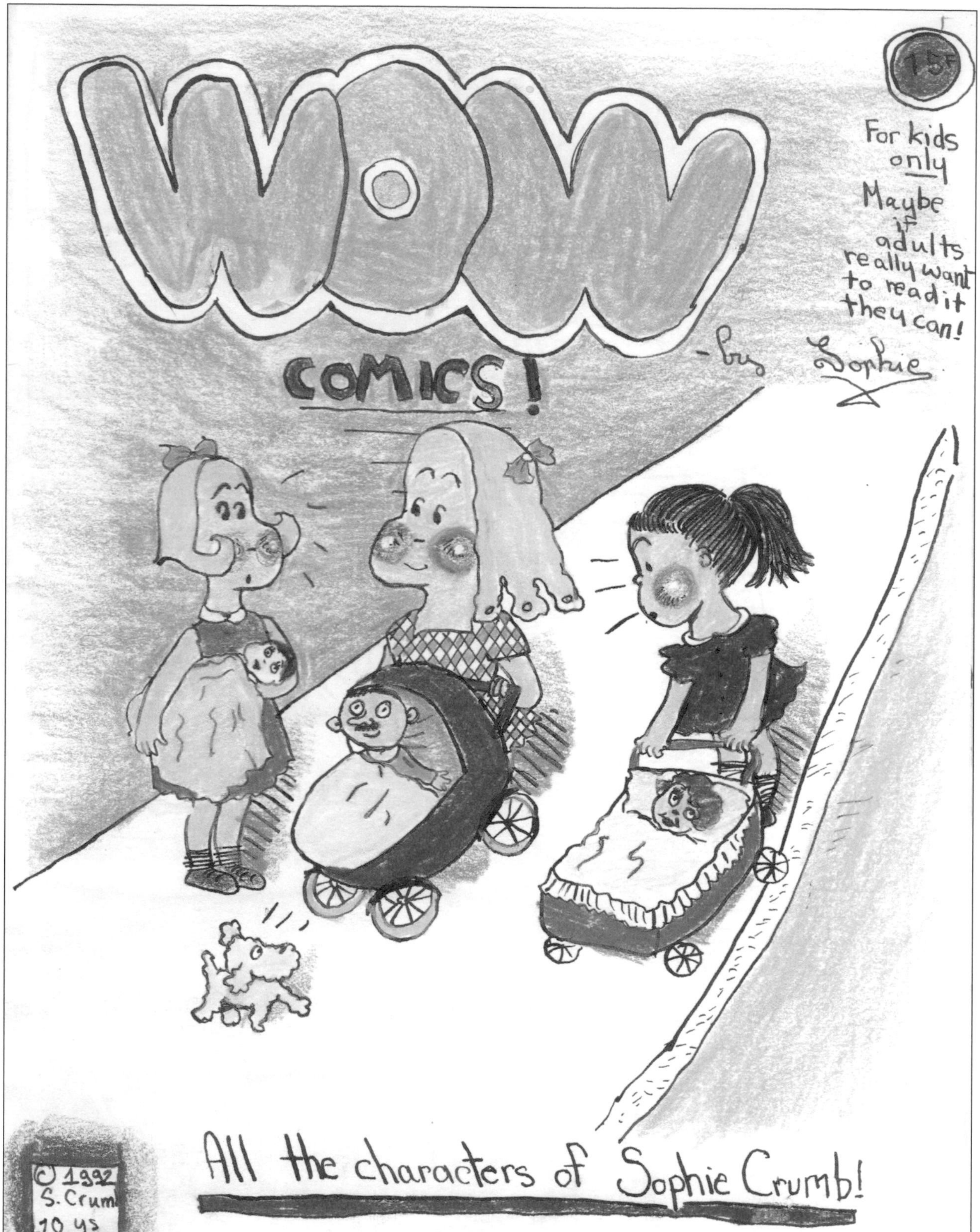
WOW
COMICS!
-by Sophie
15¢
For kids only Maybe if adults really want to read it they can!
All the characters of Sophie Crumb!
© 1992 S. Crumb 10 ys

Age 10, mid-1992.

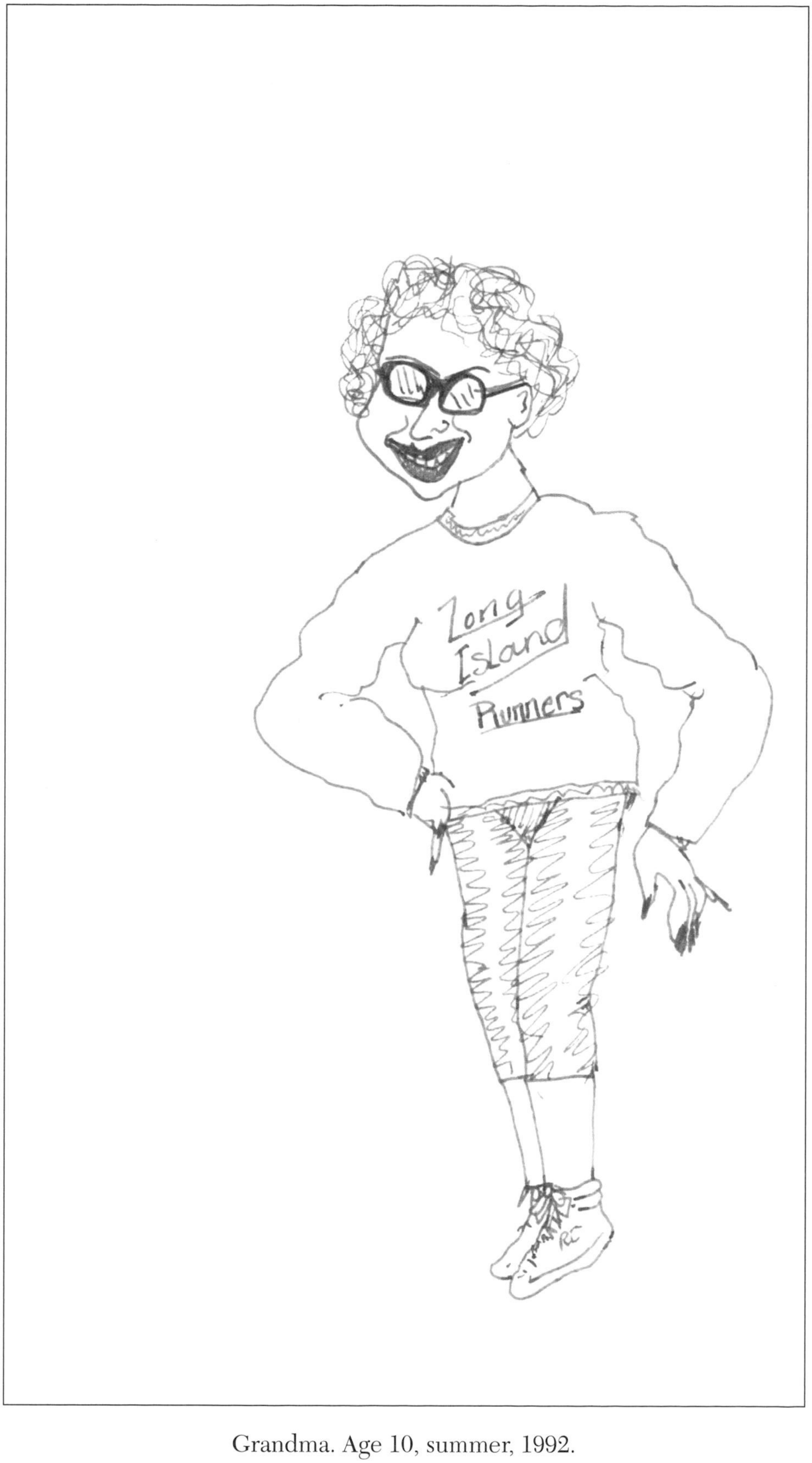
Long
Island
Runners
RC

Grandma. Age 10, summer, 1992.

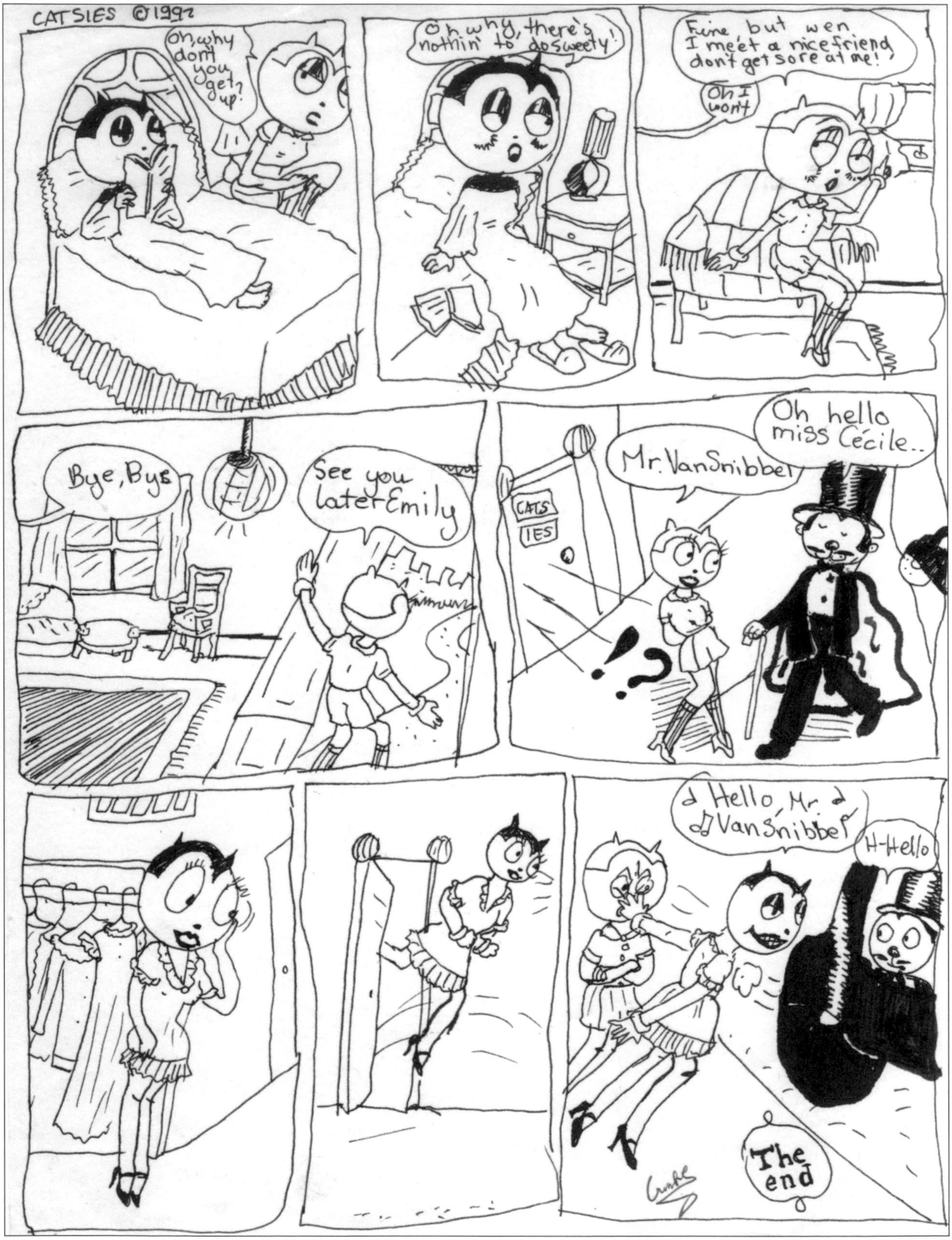
CATSIES ©1992
Oh, why dont you get up.
Oh why, there's nothin' to do sweety!
Fine, but wen I meet a nice friend don't get sore at me!
Oh I won't
Bye, Bye
See you later Emily
CATS IES
Mr. VanSnibbel
Oh hello miss Cécile...
!?
Hello, Mr. VanSnibbel
H-Hello
The end

Age 10, 1992.

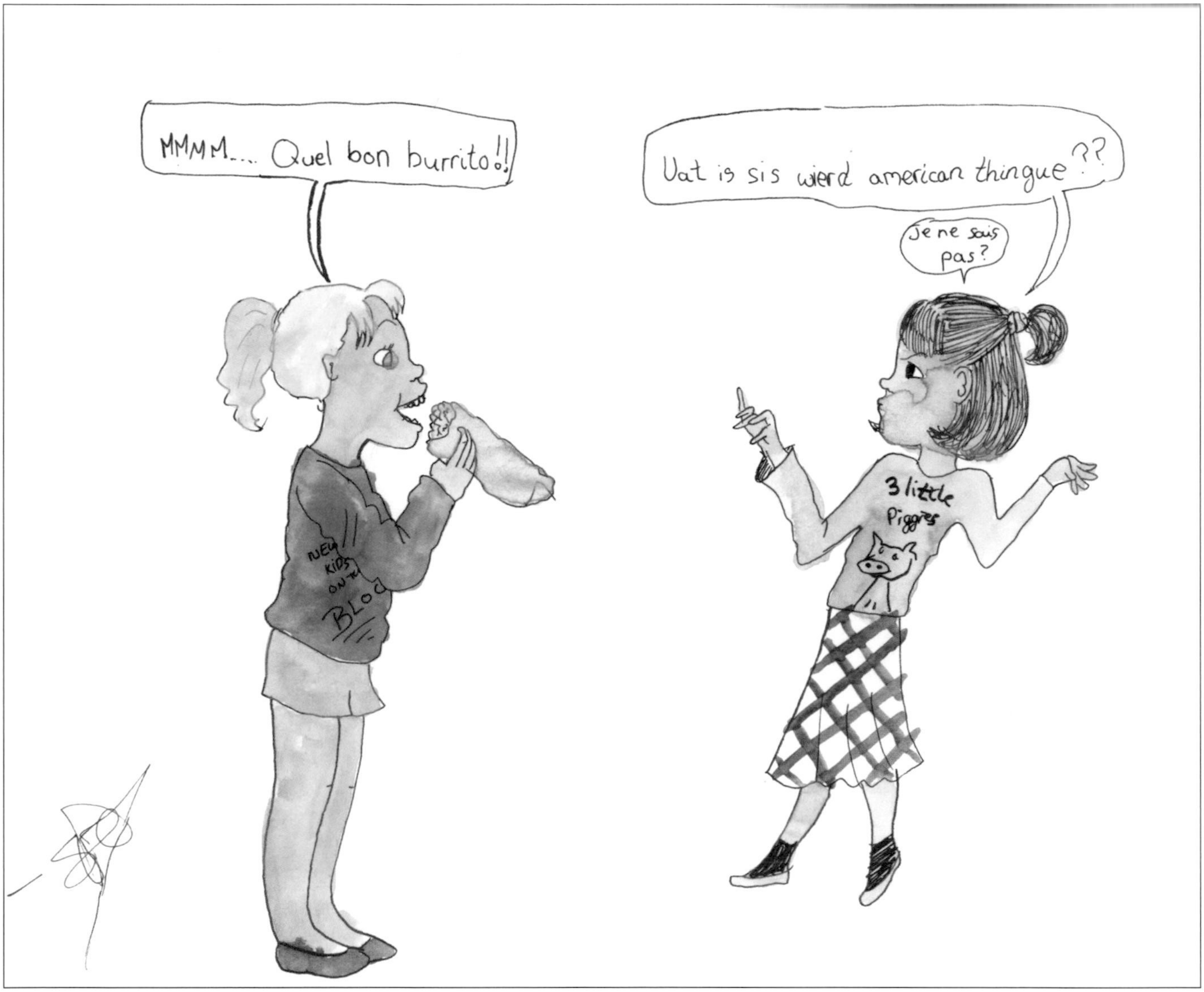
MMMM.... Quel bon burrito!!
Vat is sis wierd american thingue??
Je ne sais pas?
NEW KIDS ON THE BLOC
3 little Piggies

Age 11, Nov., 1992.

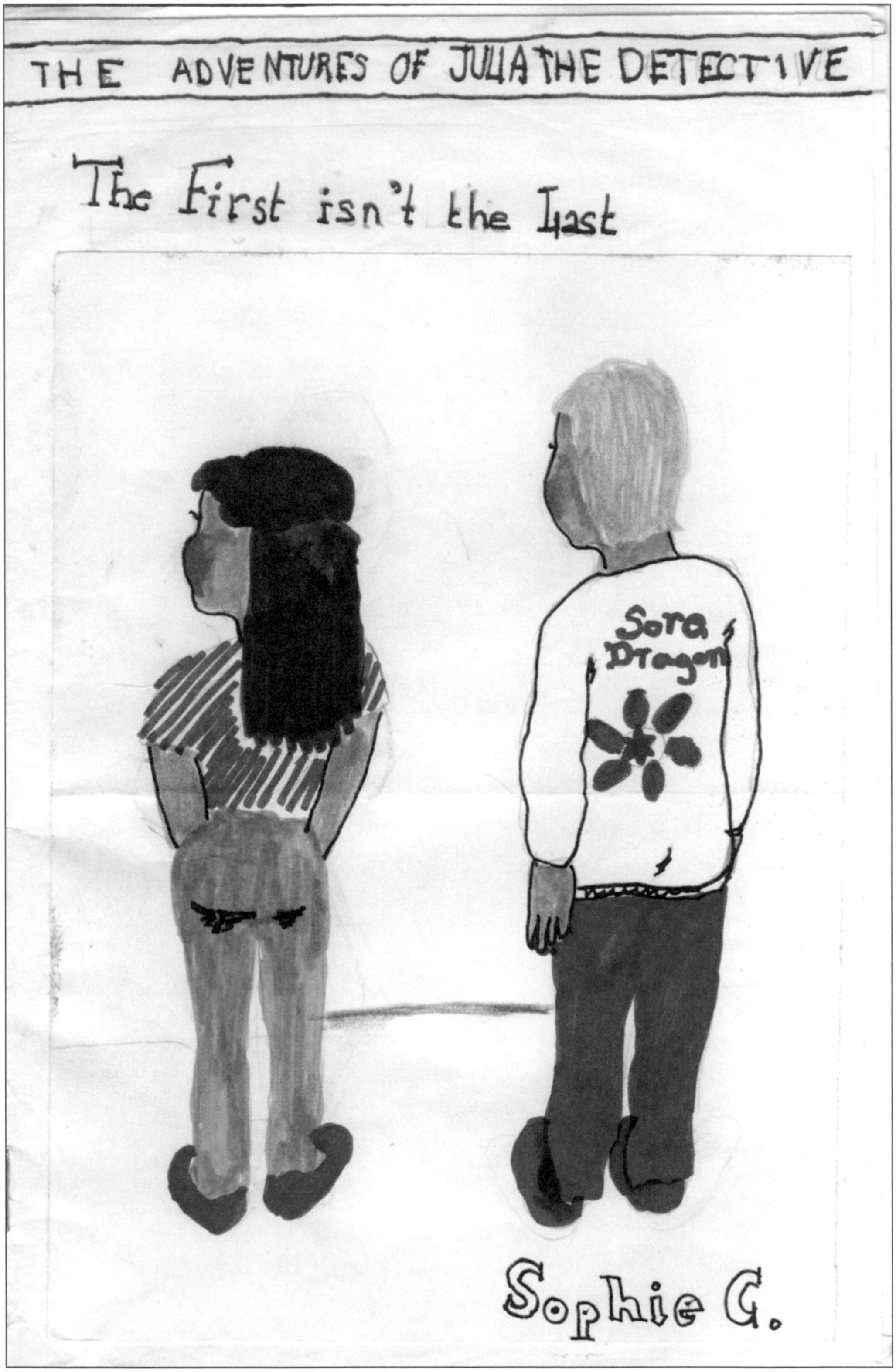
THE ADVENTURES OF JULIA THE DETECTIVE
The First isn't the Last
Sora Dragon
Sophie G.

Age 11, mid-1993.

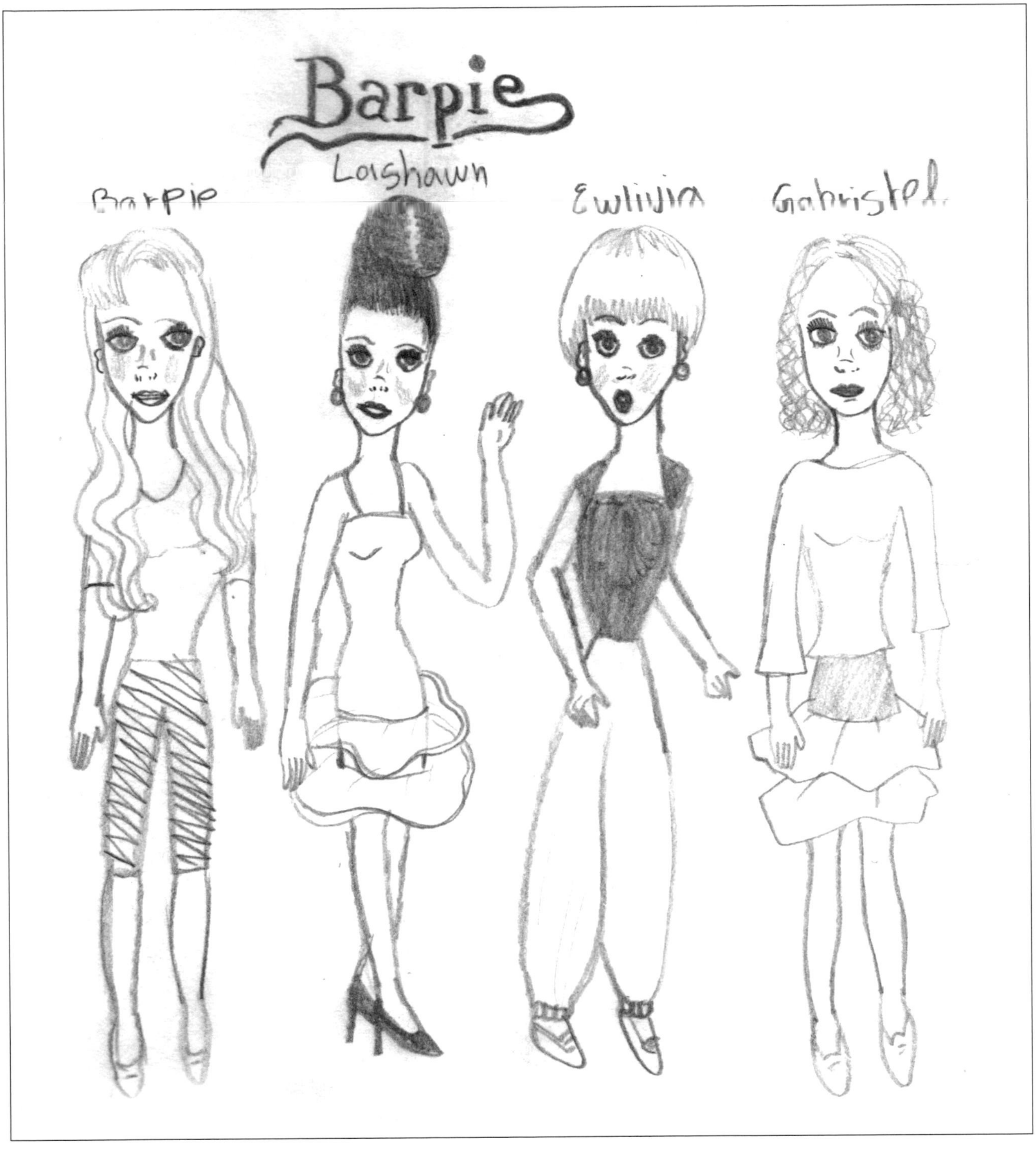
Barpie
Laishawn
Barpie
Gabristel

Age 11, Aug., 1993.

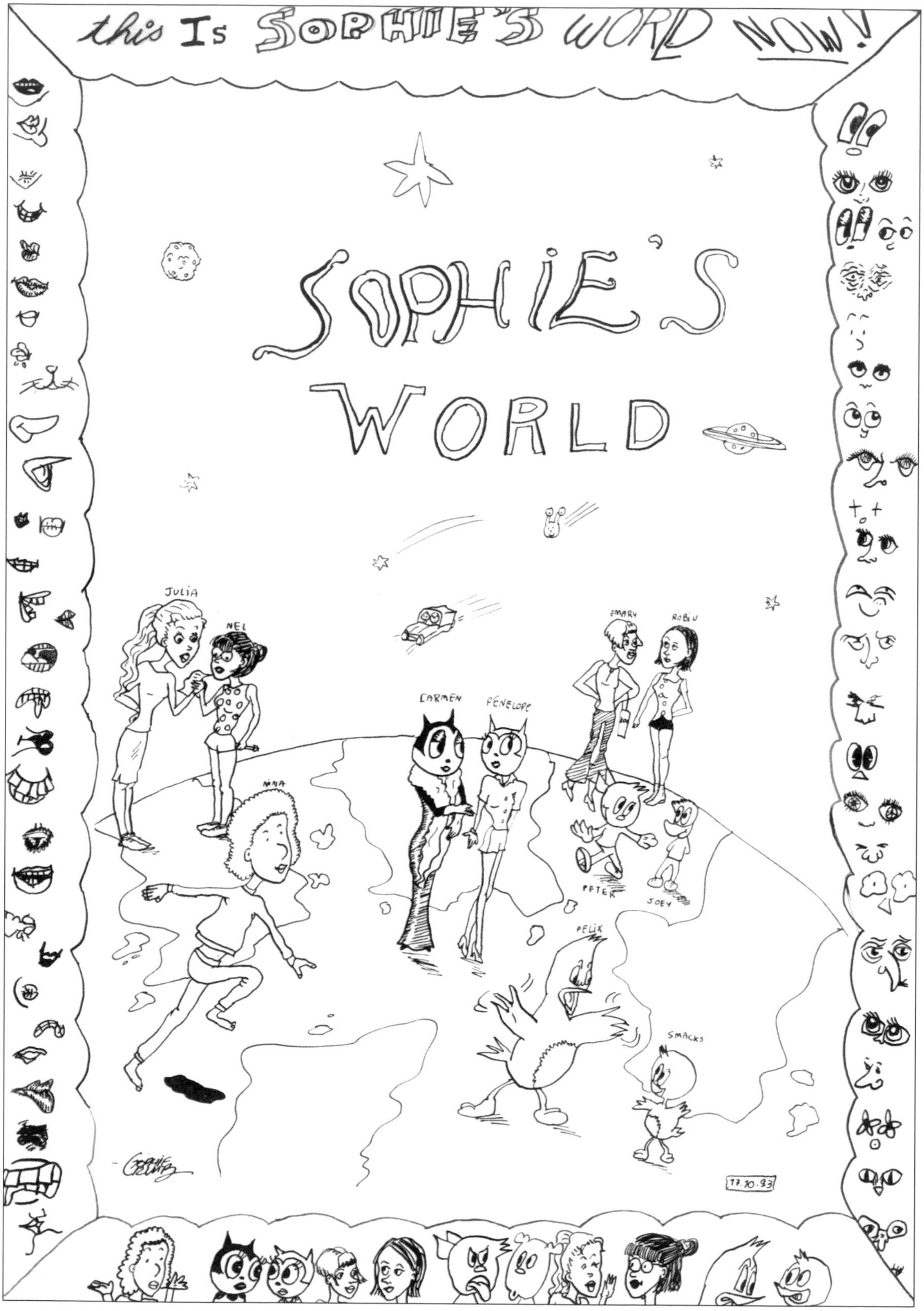
this Is SOPHIE'S WORLD NOW!
SOPHIE'S WORLD
JULIA
NEL
EMARY
ROBIN
CARMEN
PENELOPE
NINA
PETER
JOEY
FELIX
SMACKS
17.10.93

Age 12, Oct., 1993.

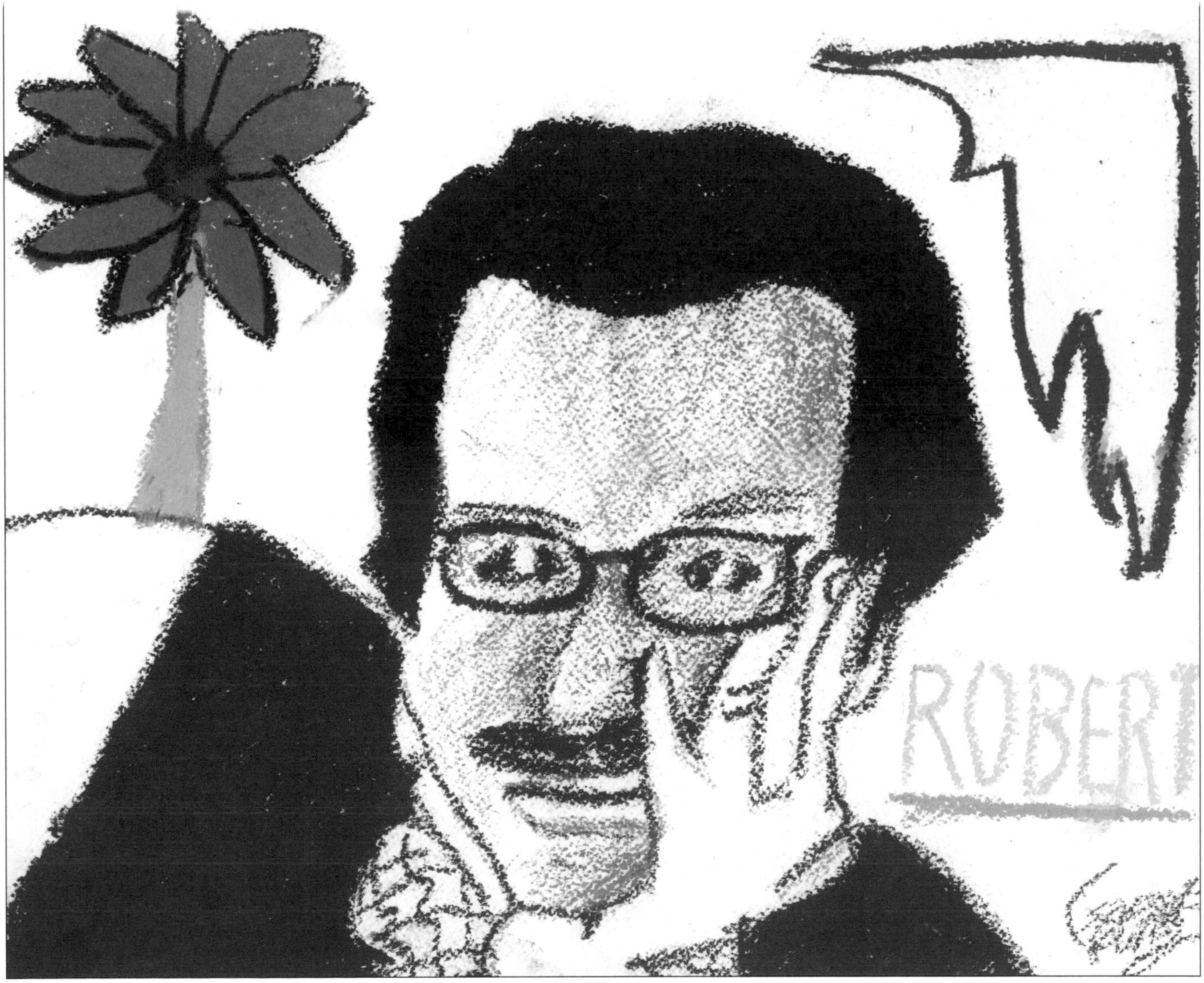
ROBERT

Age 12, late 1993.

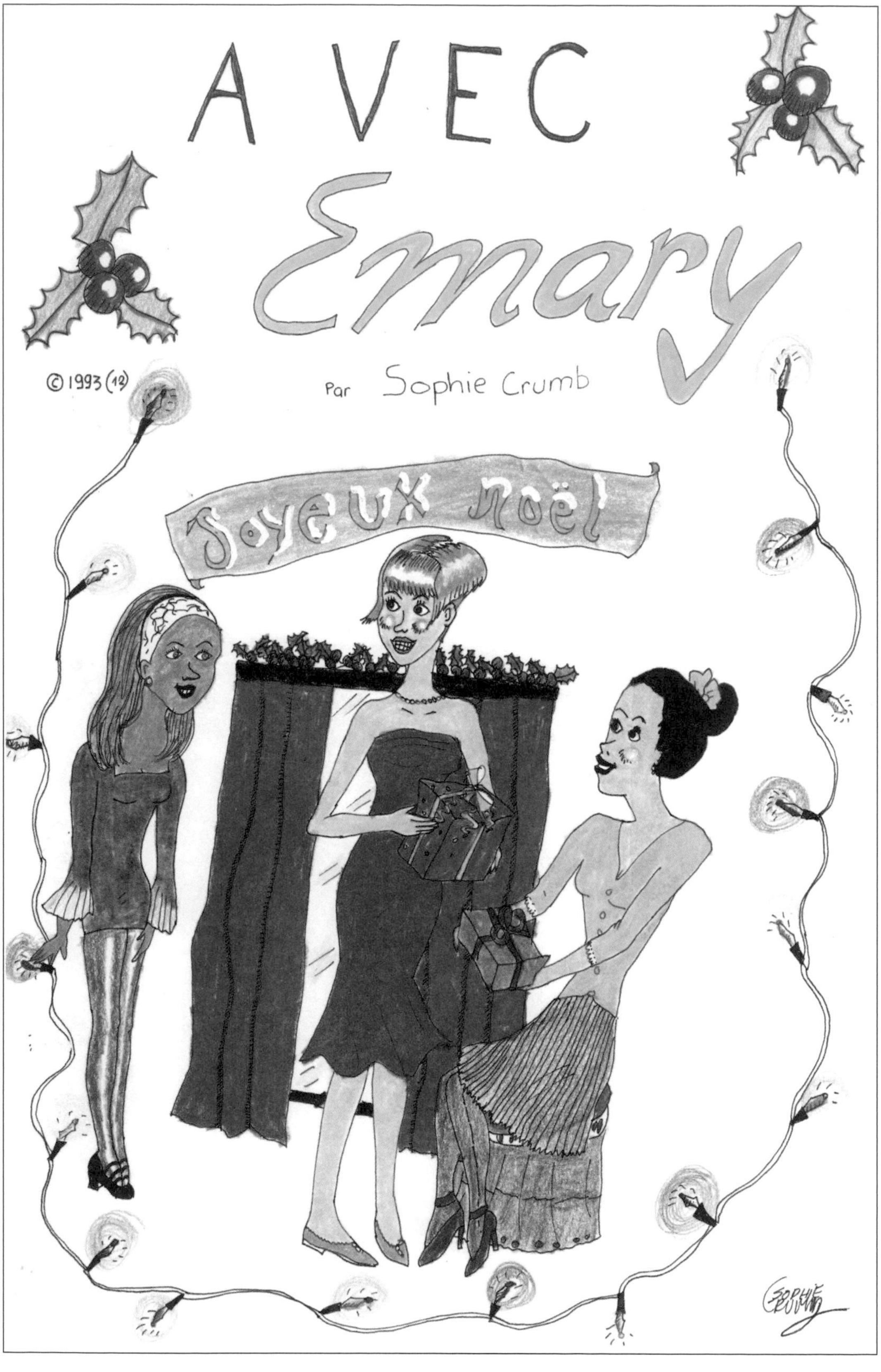
A VEC
Emary
©1993 (12)
Par Sophie Crumb
Joyeux noël

Age 12, Dec., 1993.

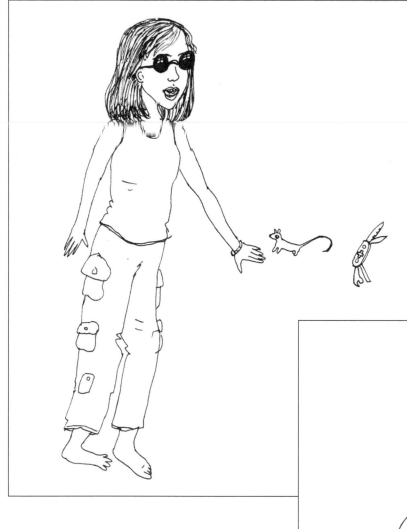

The things Sophie wants: army pants, Swiss pocket knife, a rat. (She got them all!)

Sophie with her video camera.

Age 12, Feb., 1994.

NO!!!

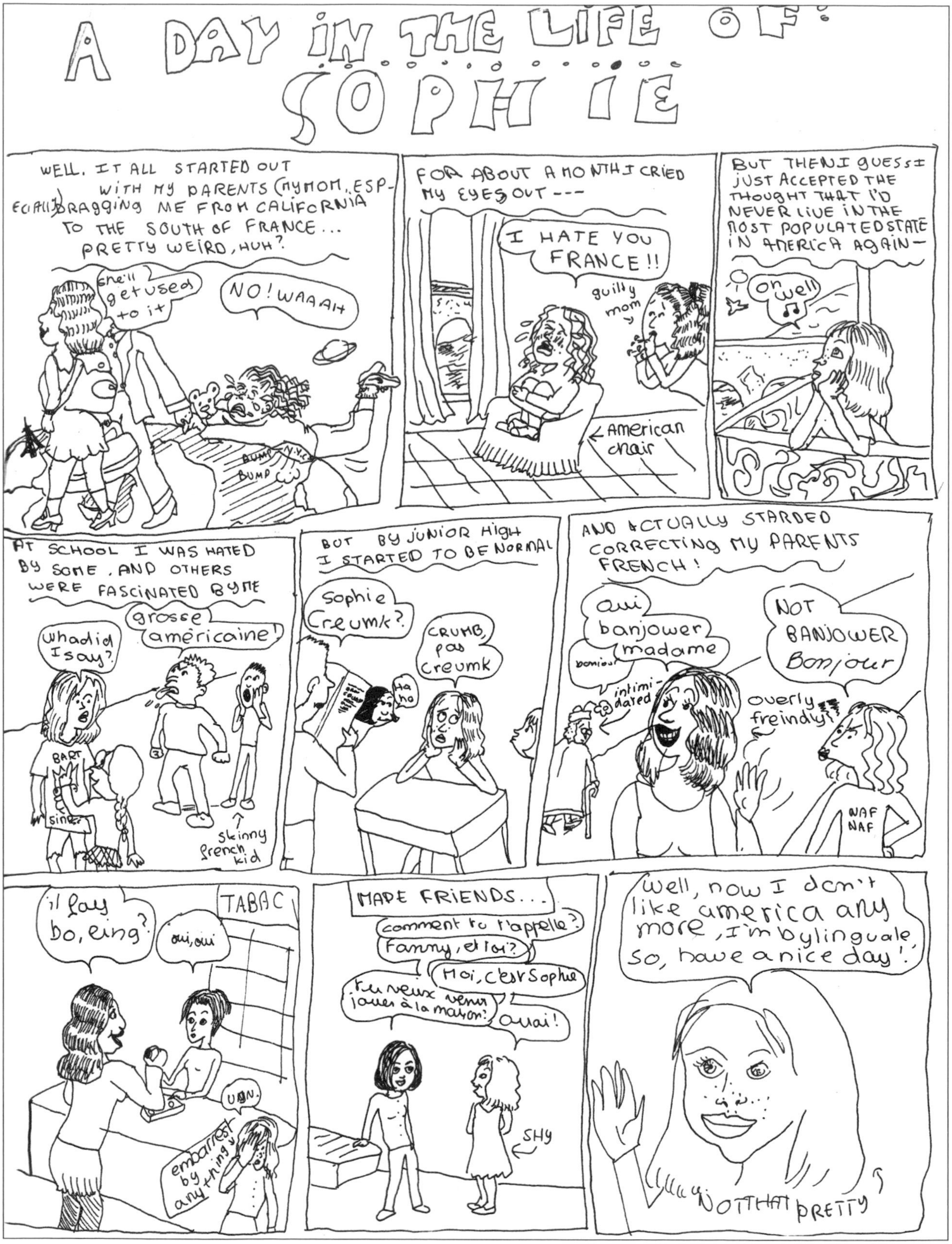
A DAY IN THE LIFE OF: SOPHIE
WELL, IT ALL STARTED OUT WITH MY PARENTS (MY MOM, ESPECIALLY) DRAGGING ME FROM CALIFORNIA TO THE SOUTH OF FRANCE... PRETTY WEIRD, HUH?
She'll get used to it
NO! WAAAAH
BUMP BUMP
N.Y.C.
FOR ABOUT A MONTH I CRIED MY EYES OUT---
I HATE YOU FRANCE!!
guilty mom
American chair
BUT THEN I GUESS I JUST ACCEPTED THE THOUGHT THAT I'D NEVER LIVE IN THE MOST POPULATED STATE IN AMERICA AGAIN—
oh well
AT SCHOOL I WAS HATED BY SOME, AND OTHERS WERE FASCINATED BY ME
grosse américaine!
whadid I say?
BART
skinny french kid
BUT BY JUNIOR HIGH I STARTED TO BE NORMAL
Sophie Creumk?
CRUMB, pas Creumk
ha ho
AND ACTUALLY STARDED CORRECTING MY PARENTS FRENCH!
oui banjower madame
bonjour
intimidated
NOT BANJOWER Bonjour
overly freindly
NAF NAF
il fay bo, eing?
oui, oui
TABAC
UHN.
embarrest by anything
MADE FRIENDS...
comment tu t'appelle?
Fanny, et toi?
Moi, c'est Sophie
tu veux venir jouer à la maison?
Ouai!
SHY
Well, now I don't like america any more, I'm bylinguale so, have a nice day!
NOT THAT PRETTY

Age 12, early 1994.

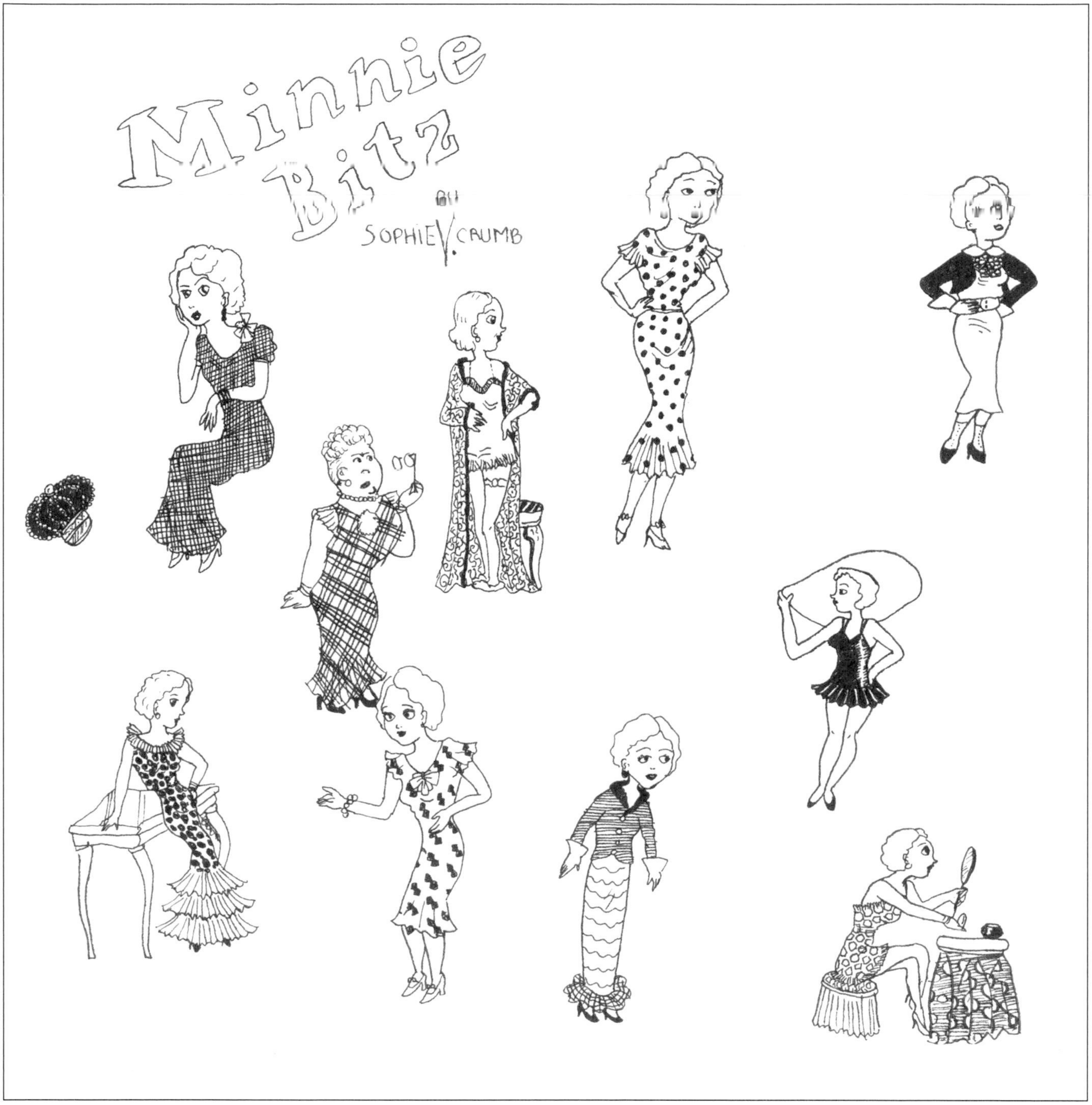
Minnie Bitz
By
SOPHIE V. CRUMB

Age 12, early 1994.

the person with no **torso**!?

she hasn't let go!
She has to get revenge!
The person who cut her
in half is still alive
while the rest of her
body is in a glass
cabinet!

She has
adventures...

and fun!

Age 12, summer, 1994.

"Cinderella and her two sisters." Age 12, late summer, 1994.

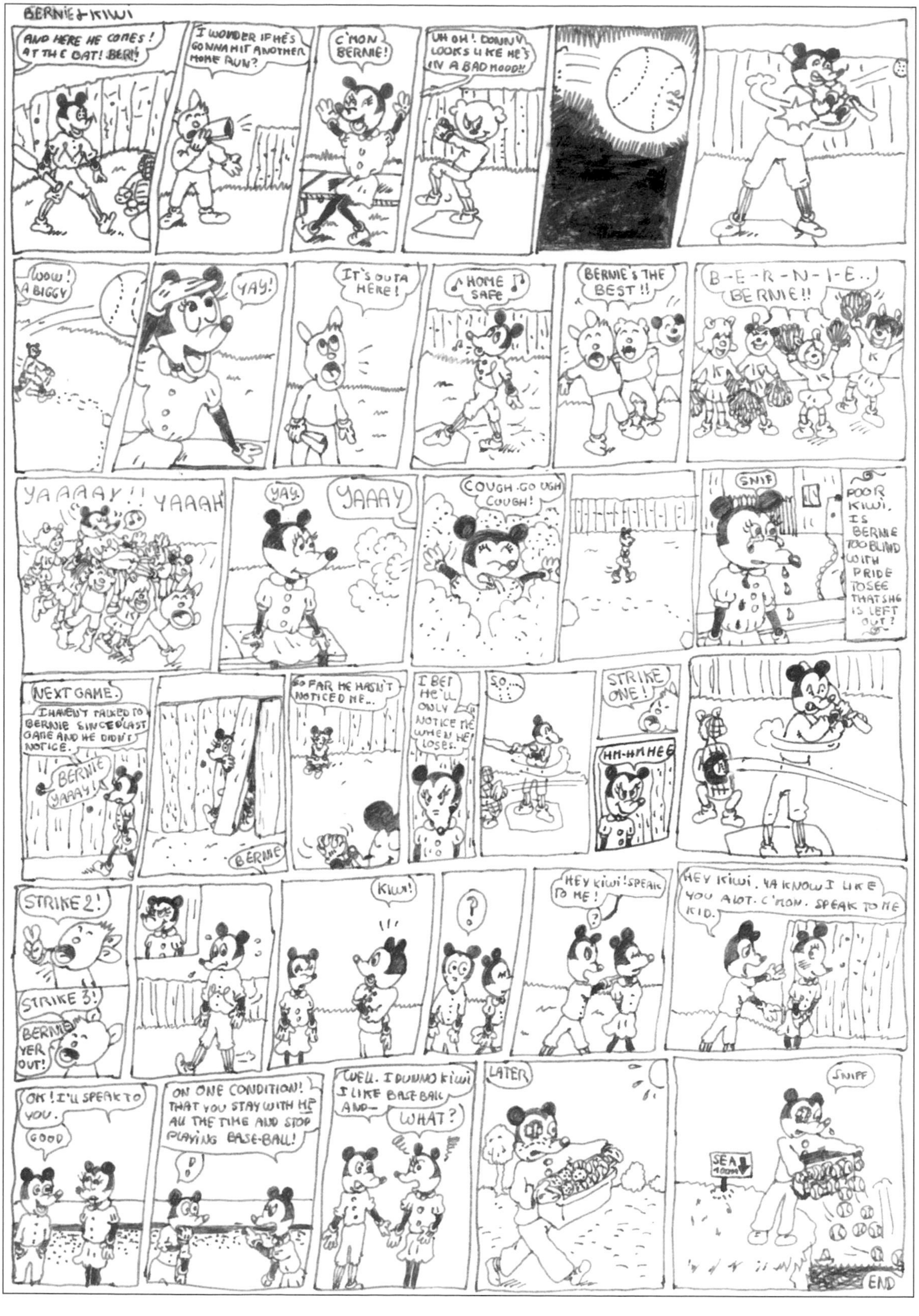

BERNIE & KIWI
AND HERE HE COMES! AT THE BAT! BER!!
I WONDER IF HE'S GONNA HIT ANOTHER HOME RUN?
C'MON BERNIE!
UH OH! DONNY LOOKS LIKE HE'S IN A BAD MOOD!!
WOW! A BIGGY
YAY!
IT'S OUTA HERE!
HOME SAFE
BERNIE'S THE BEST!!
B-E-R-N-I-E.. BERNIE!!
YAAAAY!! YAAAH
YAY
YAAAY
COUGH. COUGH COUGH!
SNIF
POOR KIWI. IS BERNIE TOO BLIND WITH PRIDE TO SEE THAT SHE IS LEFT OUT?
NEXT GAME.
I HAVEN'T TALKED TO BERNIE SINCE LAST GAME AND HE DIDN'T NOTICE.
BERNIE YAAAY!
BERNIE
SO FAR HE HASN'T NOTICED ME..
I BET HE'LL ONLY NOTICE ME WHEN HE LOSES.
SO...
STRIKE ONE!
HM-HM HEE
STRIKE 2!
STRIKE 3!
BERNIE YER OUT!
KIWI!
?
HEY KIWI! SPEAK TO ME!
?
HEY KIWI. YA KNOW I LIKE YOU ALOT. C'MON. SPEAK TO ME KID.
OK! I'LL SPEAK TO YOU.
GOOD
ON ONE CONDITION! THAT YOU STAY WITH ME ALL THE TIME AND STOP PLAYING BASE-BALL!
WELL. I DUNNO KIWI I LIKE BASE BALL AND—
WHAT?
LATER
SNIFF
SEA
END

Age 13, late 1994.

Sophie didn't like that her mother smoked cigarettes. Age 13, Jan., 1995.

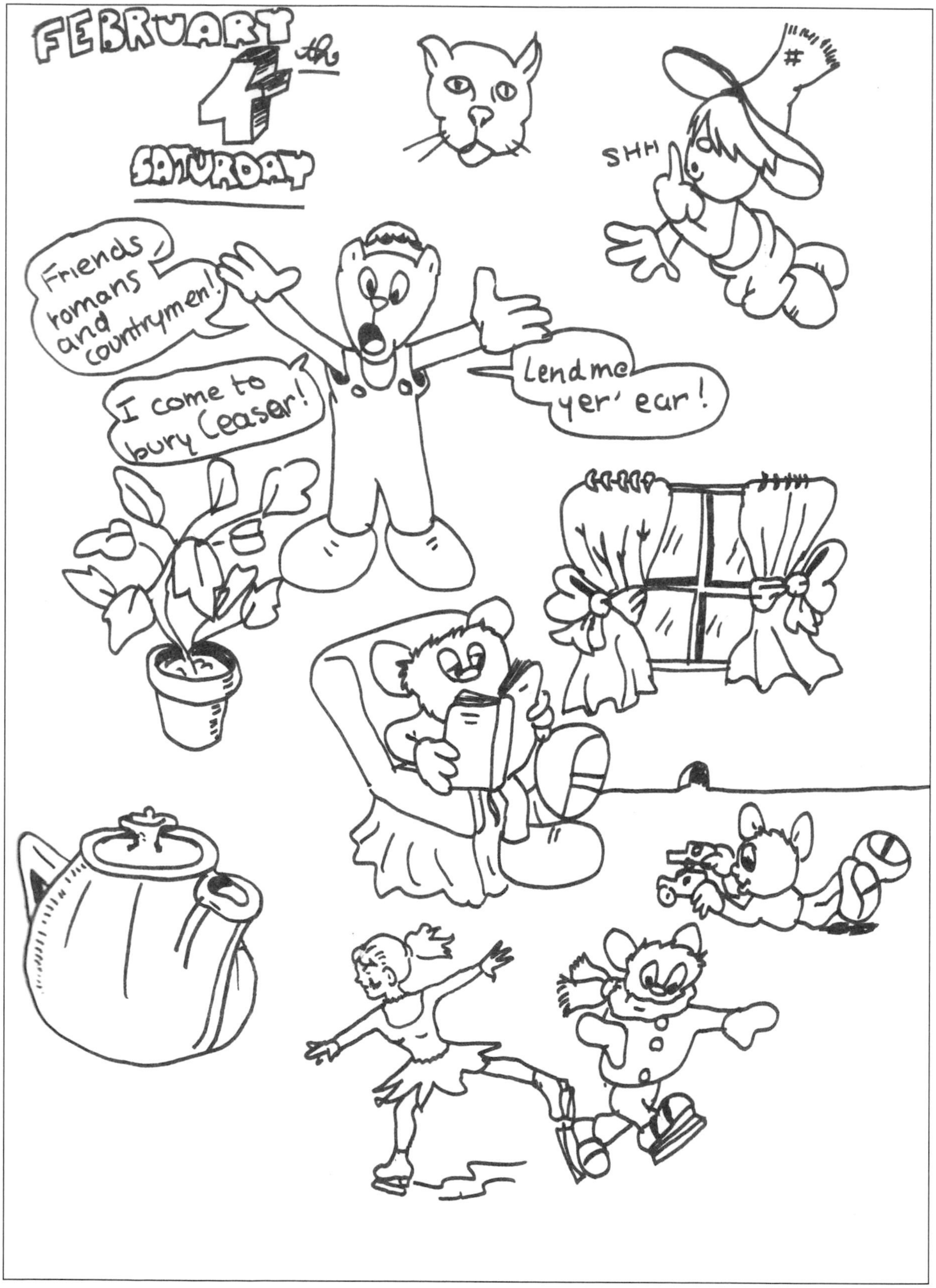
FEBRUARY
4th
SATURDAY
SHH
Friends romans and countrymen!
Lend me yer' ear!
I come to bury Ceaser!

Age 13, Feb., 1995.

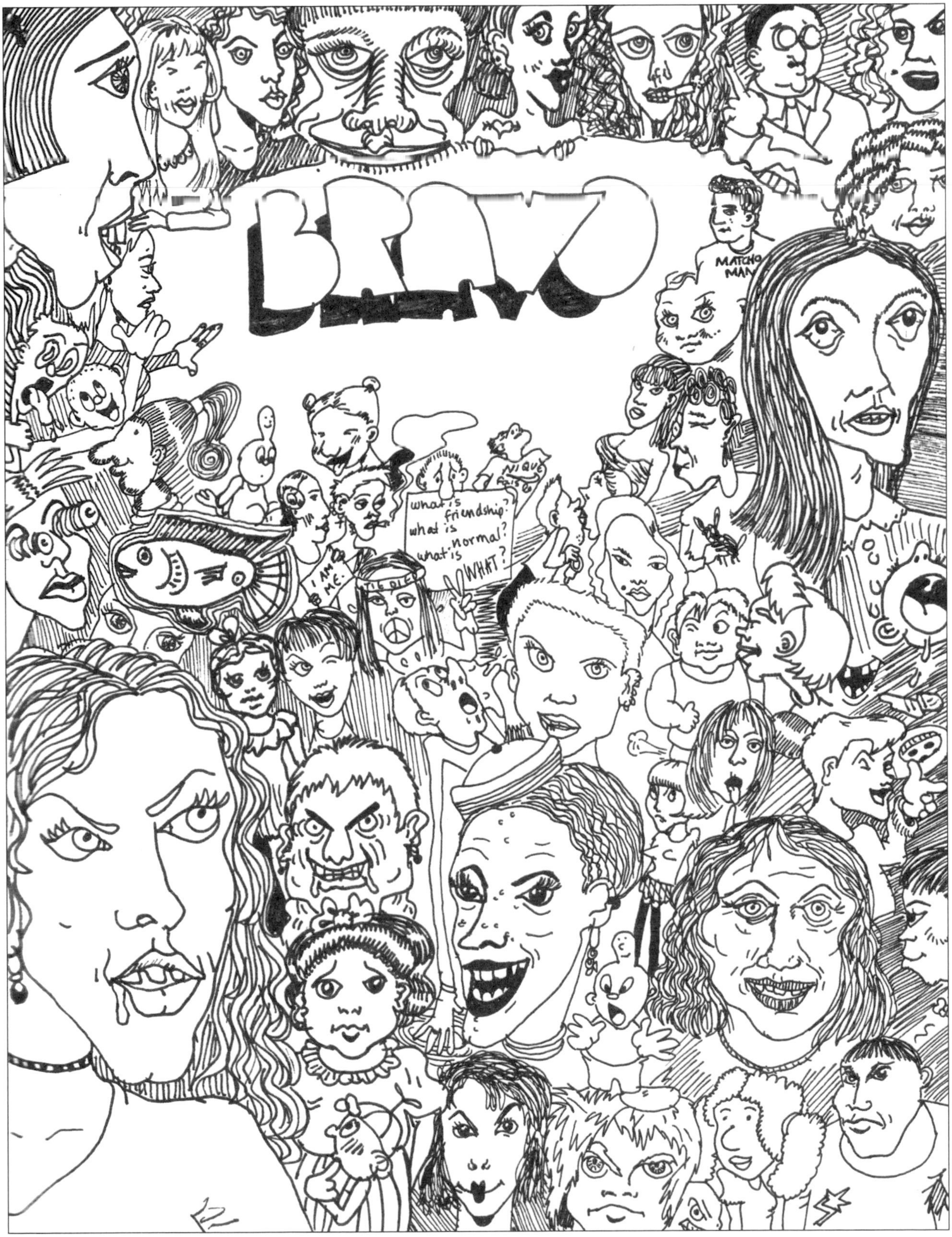
BRAVO
MATCHO MAN
what is friendship?
what is normal?
what is WHAT?
I AM ME.
TIE DIE
NIQUE

Age 13, March, 1995.

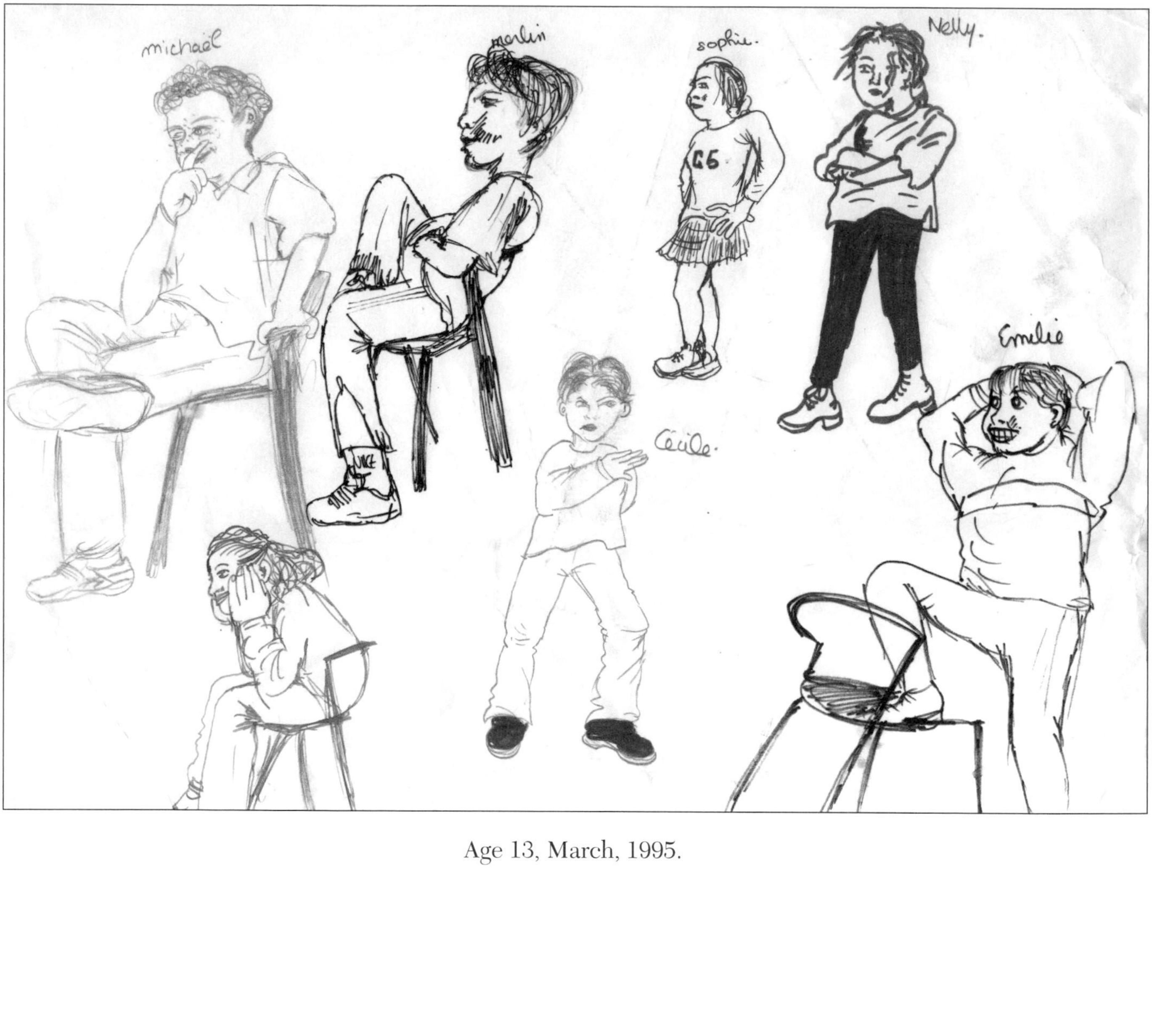
michael
sophie.
Nelly.
Emelie
Cécile.

Age 13, March, 1995.

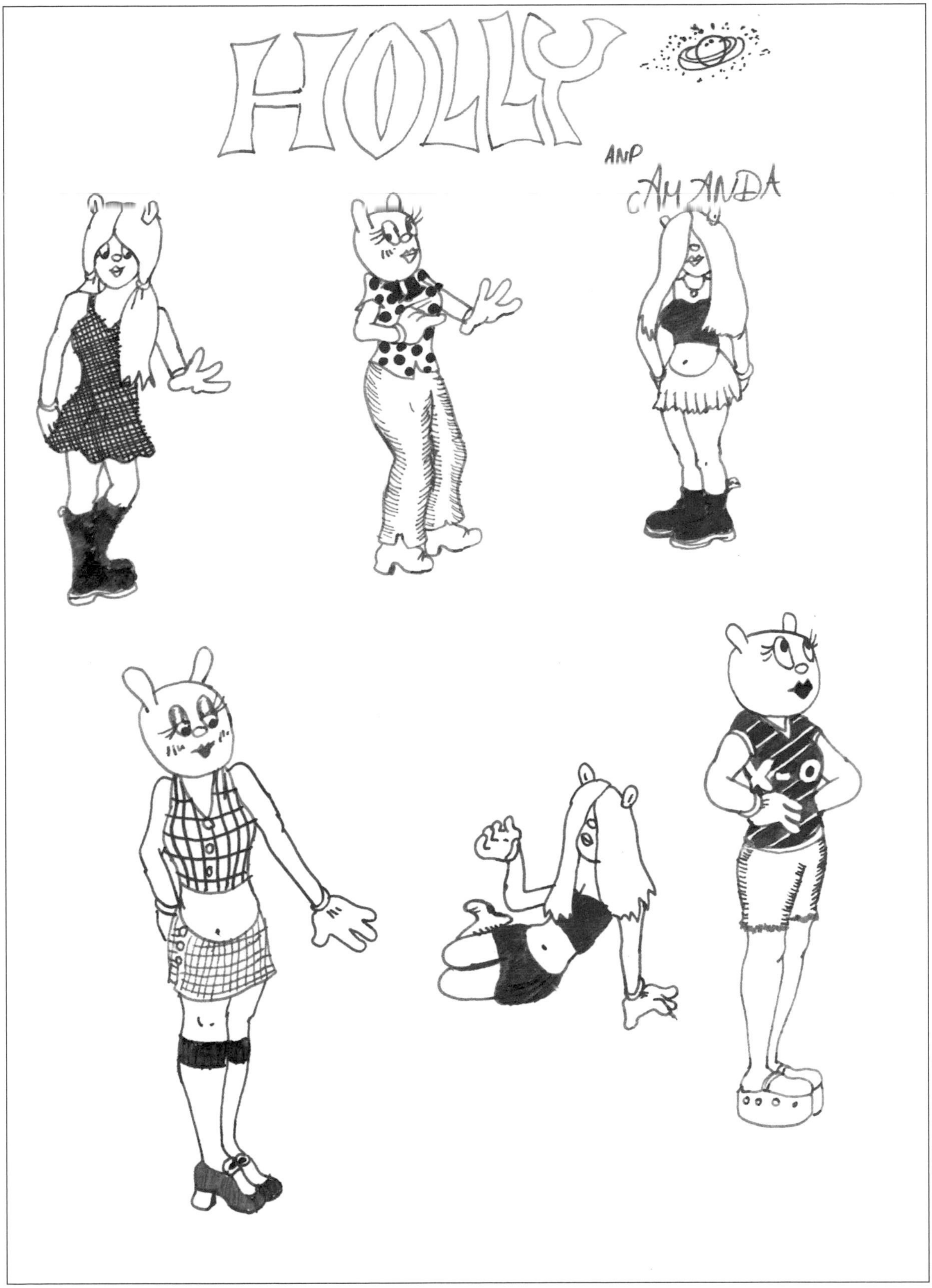
HOLLY
AND
AMANDA
X-O

Age 13, April, 1995.

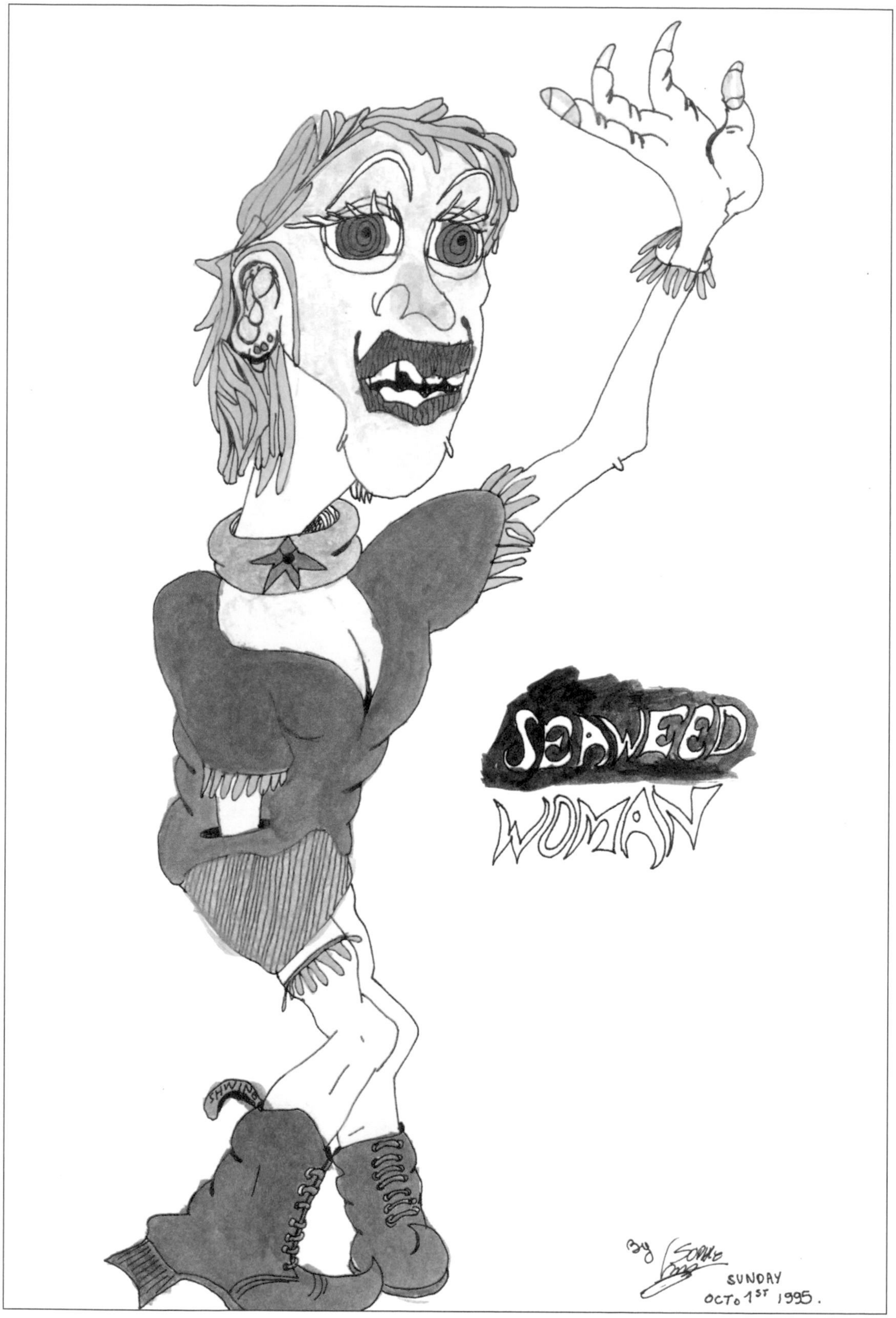
SEAWEED
WOMAN
SHWING
By
SUNDAY
OCT. 1ST 1995.

Age 14, Oct., 1995.

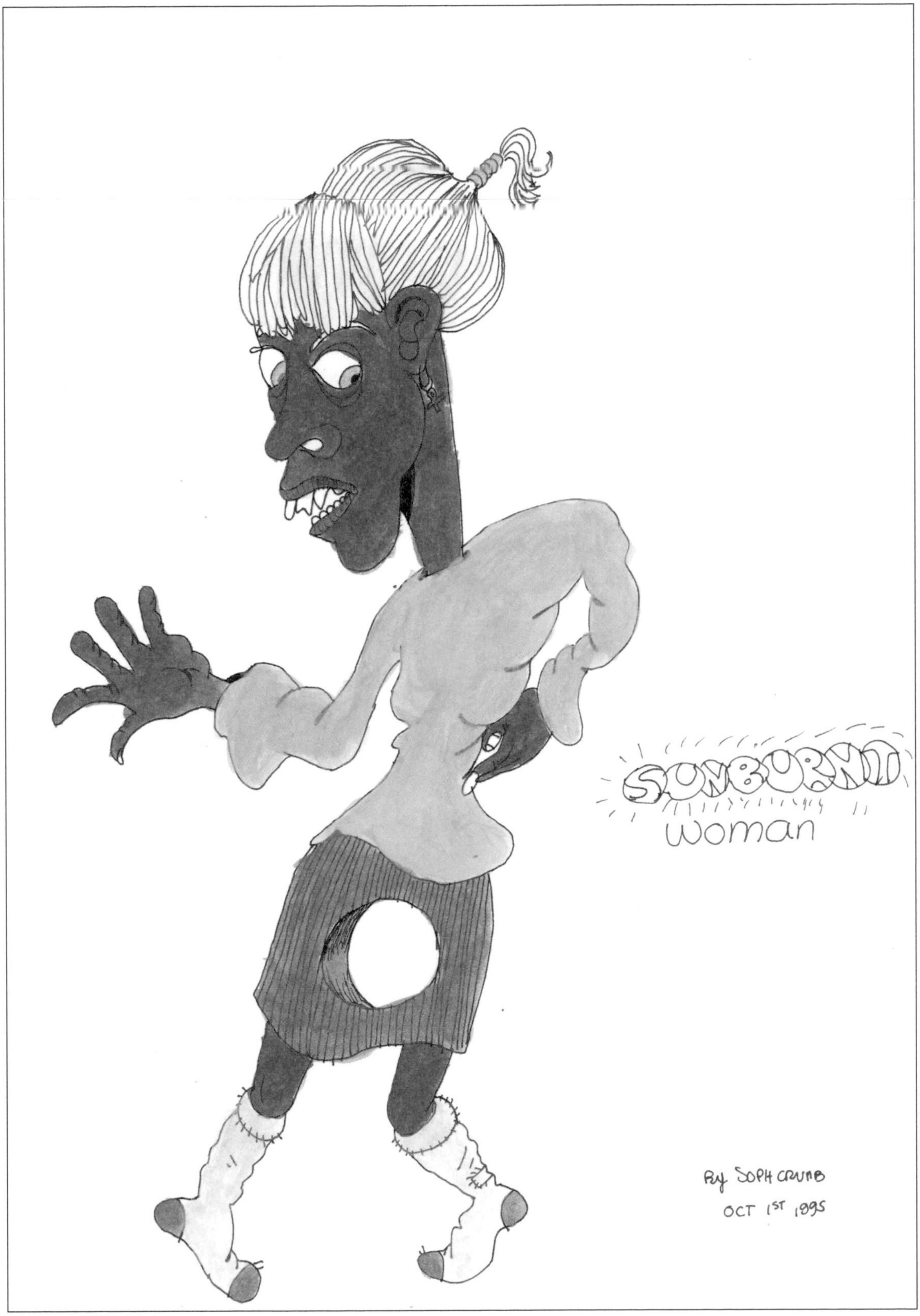
SUNBURNT
woman
By SOPH CRUMB
OCT 1ST 1995

Age 14, Oct., 1995.

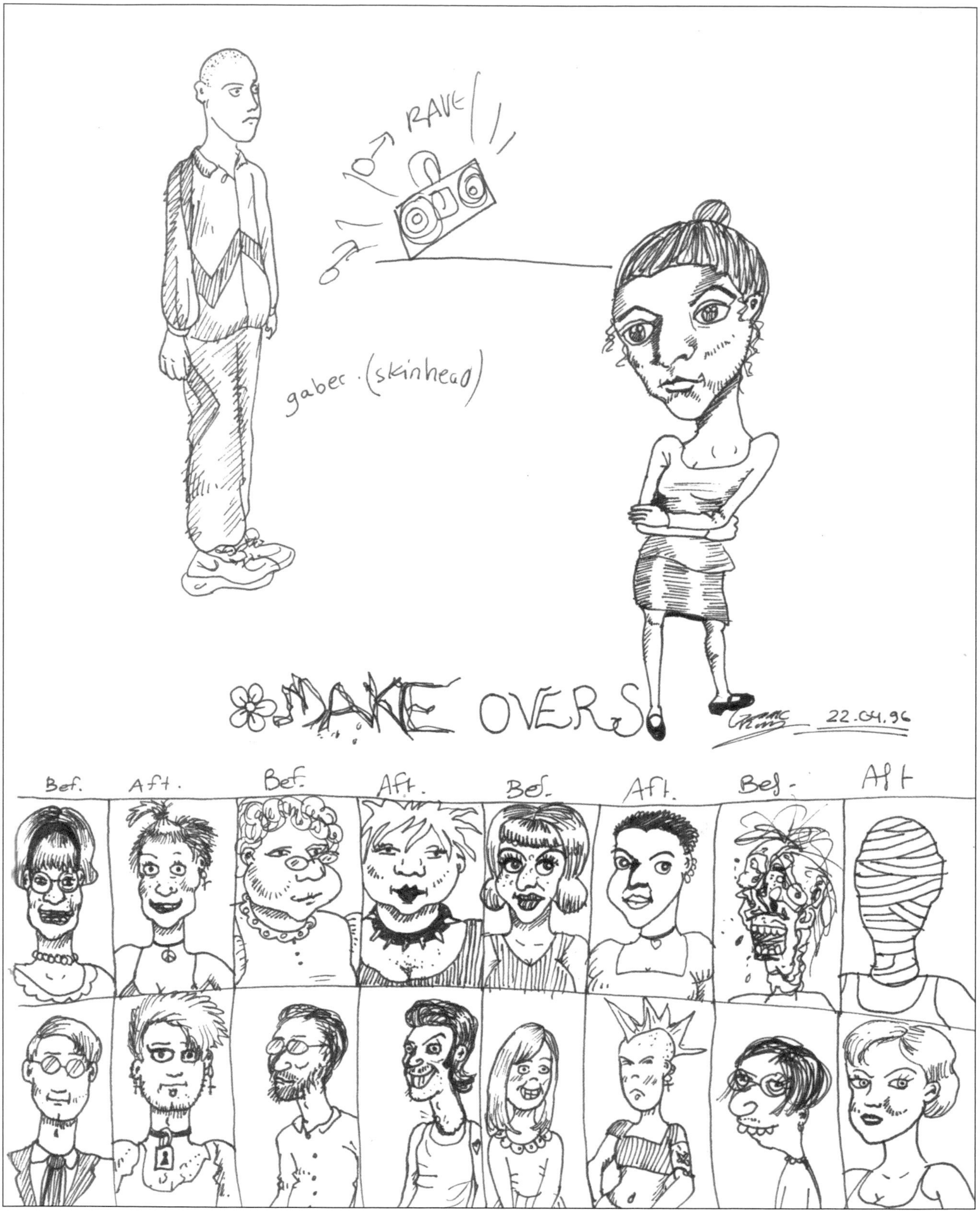
RAVE
gaber (skinhead)
MAKE OVERS
22.04.96
Bef.
Aft.
Bef.
Aft.
Bef.
Aft.
Bef.
Aft

Age 14, April, 1996.

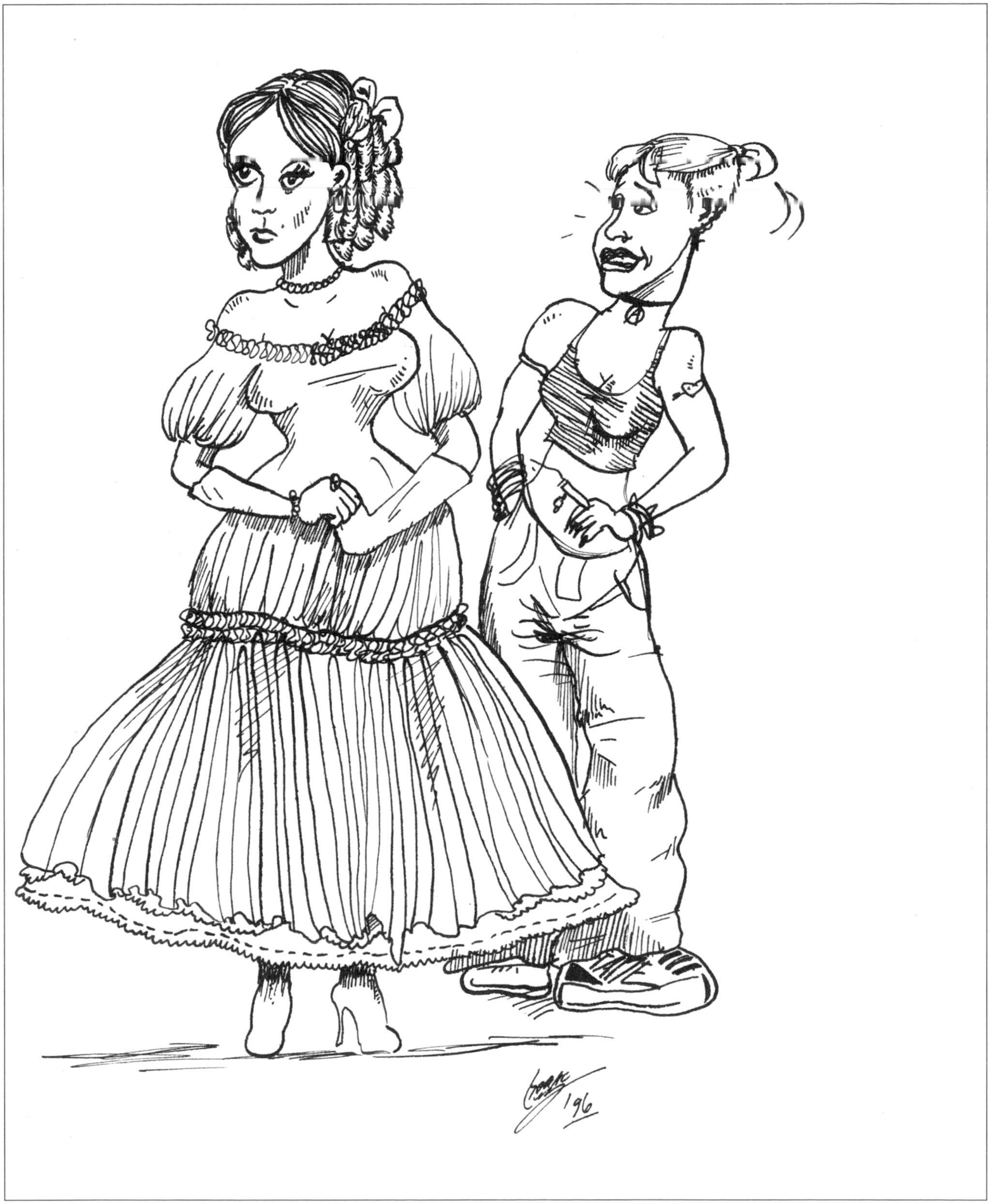

Age 14, July, 1996.

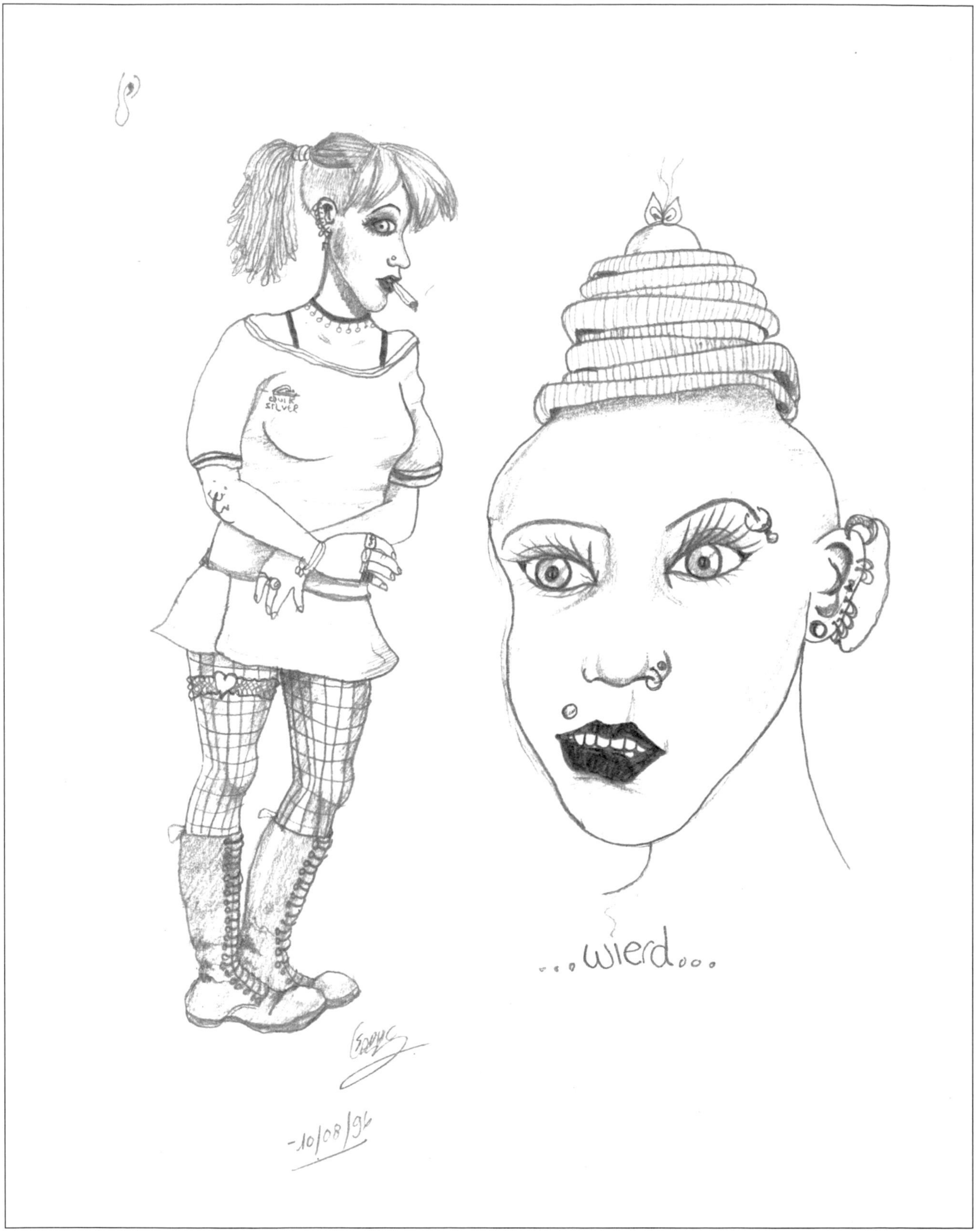
QUIK SILVER
...wierd...
-10/08/96

Age 14, Aug., 1996.

LATE ADOLESCENCE
1996 to 2000 / 15 to 19 YRS OLD

DURING THESE YEARS, MY FATHER'S INCREASING FAME STARTED TO LOOM OVER ME, AS I SLOWLY REALIZED IT WAS MY FATE TO FOREVER BE COMPARED TO "THE LEGEND" IF I KEPT ON DRAWING.

IT WAS A HEAVY THING, TRYING TO FIND A STYLE, AN ARTISTIC IDENTITY OF MY OWN. IMPATIENT AND FRUSTRATED, I HAD A HARD TIME FINISHING A COMIC. I FOUND REFUGE IN TEENAGE LIFE: HASH, BEER, BOYS, DRAMA, HIGH SCHOOL DORMS AND GRUNGY BONGO PARTIES FILLED MY DAYS AND MY SKETCH-BOOKS. I FELT A NEED TO RECORD TIME, AFRAID OF FORGETTING IT ALL.

I TOOK ART IN SCHOOL AND LOVED LIFE DRAWING AND ART HISTORY BUT WAS SKEPTICAL OF THE BADLY TAUGHT, PRETENTIOUS CONTEMPORARY ART CURRICULUM.

STILL, ART CLASS AND ENGLISH CLASS ARE WHAT GOT ME THROUGH HIGH SCHOOL WITHOUT FLUNKING, AS I SPENT MOST CLASS TIME DOODLING AND DAYDREAMING...

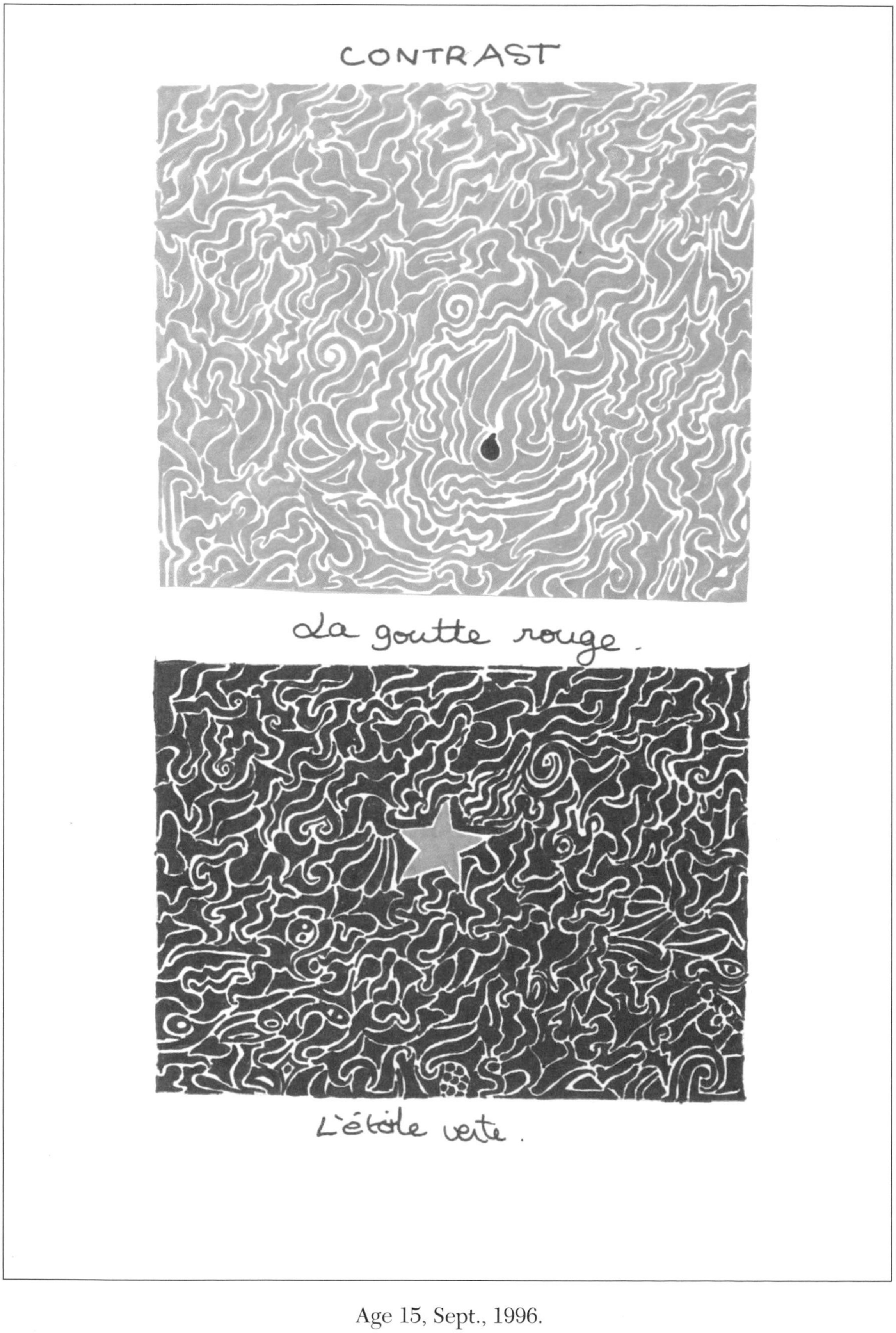
CONTRAST
La goutte rouge.
L'étoile verte.

Age 15, Sept., 1996.

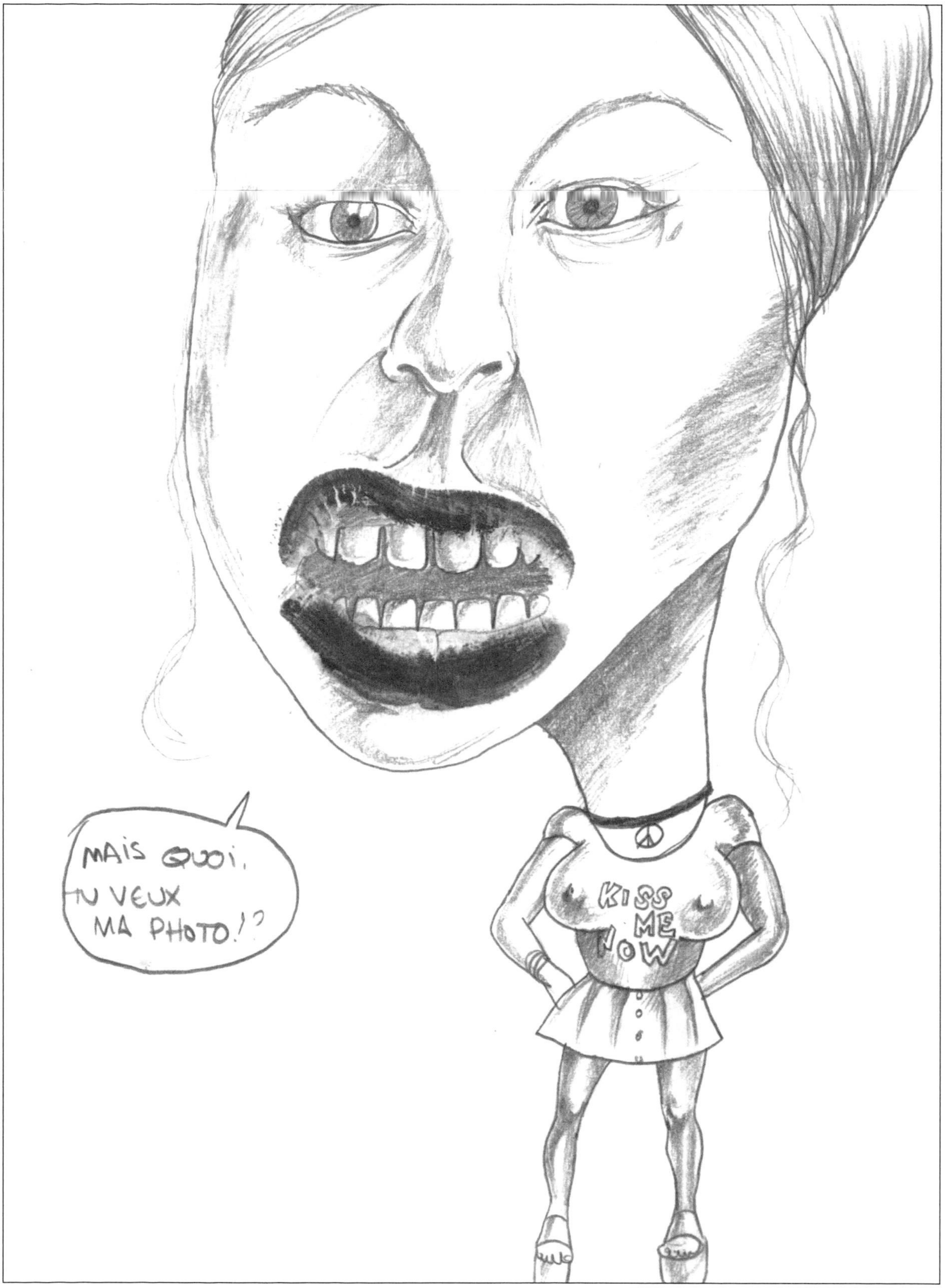
MAIS QUOI, TU VEUX MA PHOTO!?
KISS ME NOW

Age 15, May, 1997.

Sophie's best friend, Cecile. Drawn from life in art class. Age 15, June, 1997.

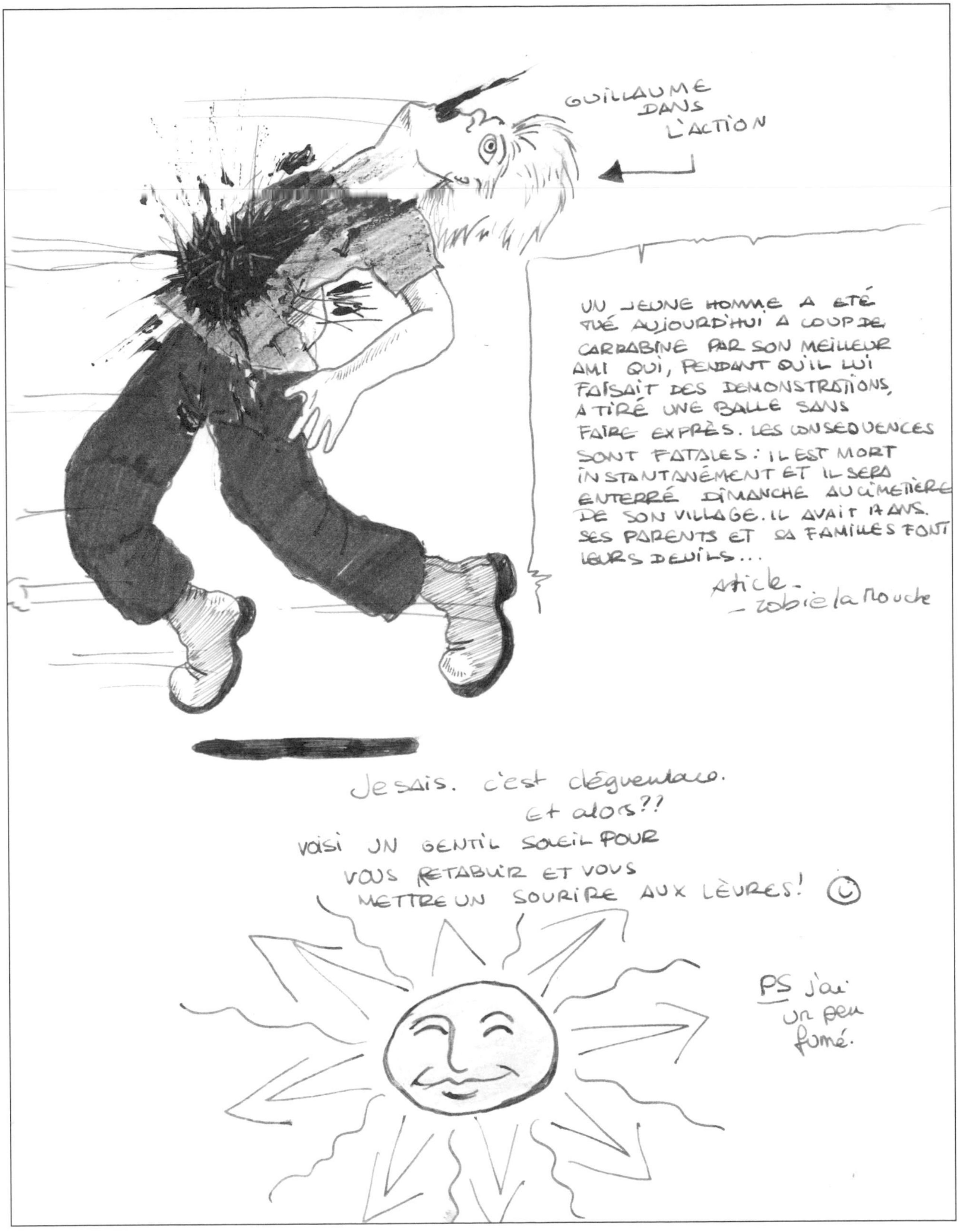
GUILLAUME DANS L'ACTION
UN JEUNE HOMME A ÉTÉ TUÉ AUJOURD'HUI A COUP DE CARRABINE PAR SON MEILLEUR AMI QUI, PENDANT QU'IL LUI FAISAIT DES DEMONSTRATIONS, A TIRÉ UNE BALLE SANS FAIRE EXPRÈS. LES CONSEQUENCES SONT FATALES: IL EST MORT INSTANTANÉMENT ET IL SERA ENTERRÉ DIMANCHE AU CIMETIÈRE DE SON VILLAGE. IL AVAIT 17 ANS. SES PARENTS ET SA FAMILLES FONT LEURS DEUILS...
Article - Zobie la Mouche
Je sais. c'est dégueulasse. et alors??
voisi UN GENTIL SOLEIL POUR VOUS RETABLIR ET VOUS METTRE UN SOURIRE AUX LÈVRES! ☺
PS J'ai un peu fumé.

Age 16, Oct., 1997.

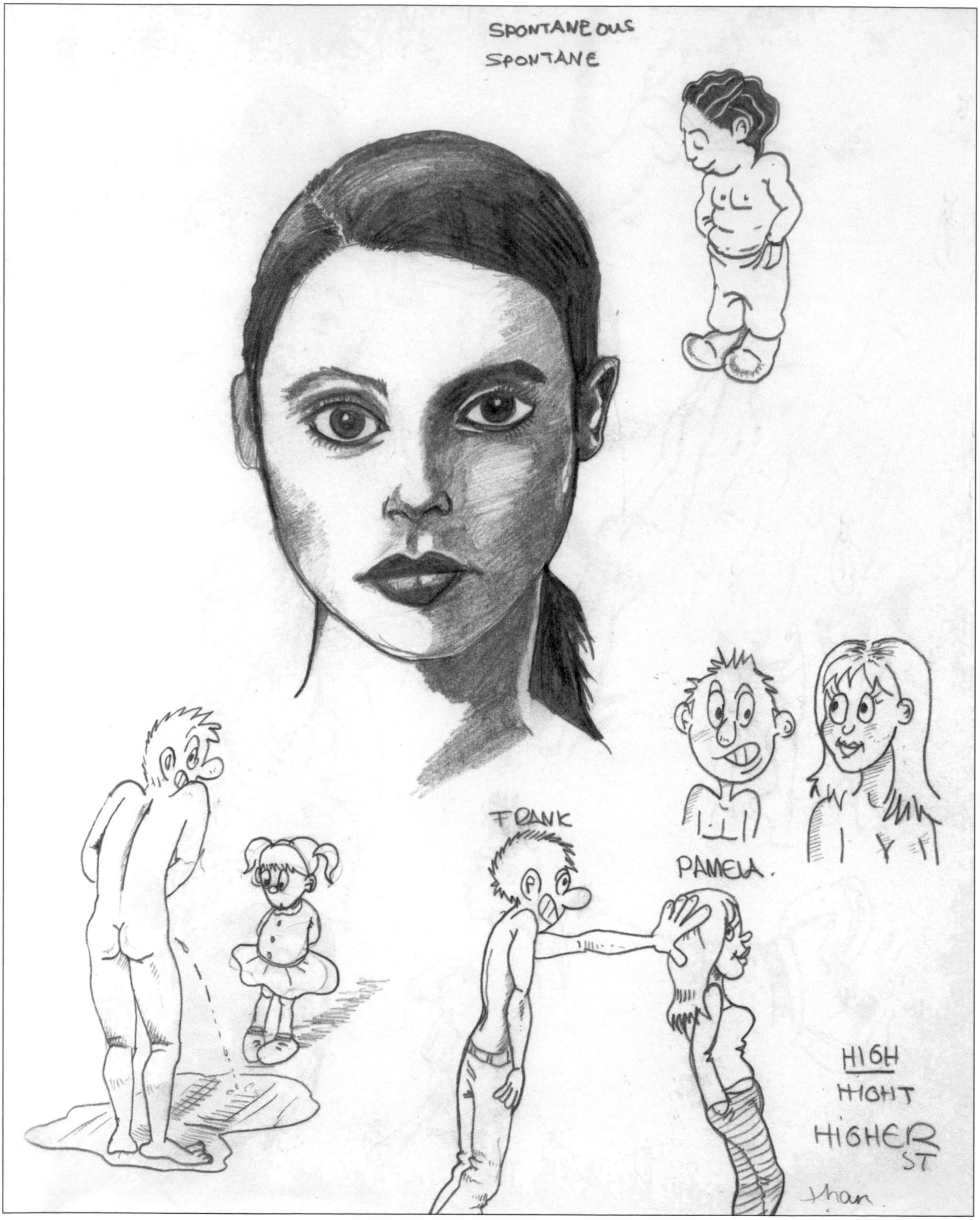
SPONTANEOUS
SPONTANE
FRANK
PAMELA.
HIGH
HIGHT
HIGHER
ST

Age 16, Nov., 1997.

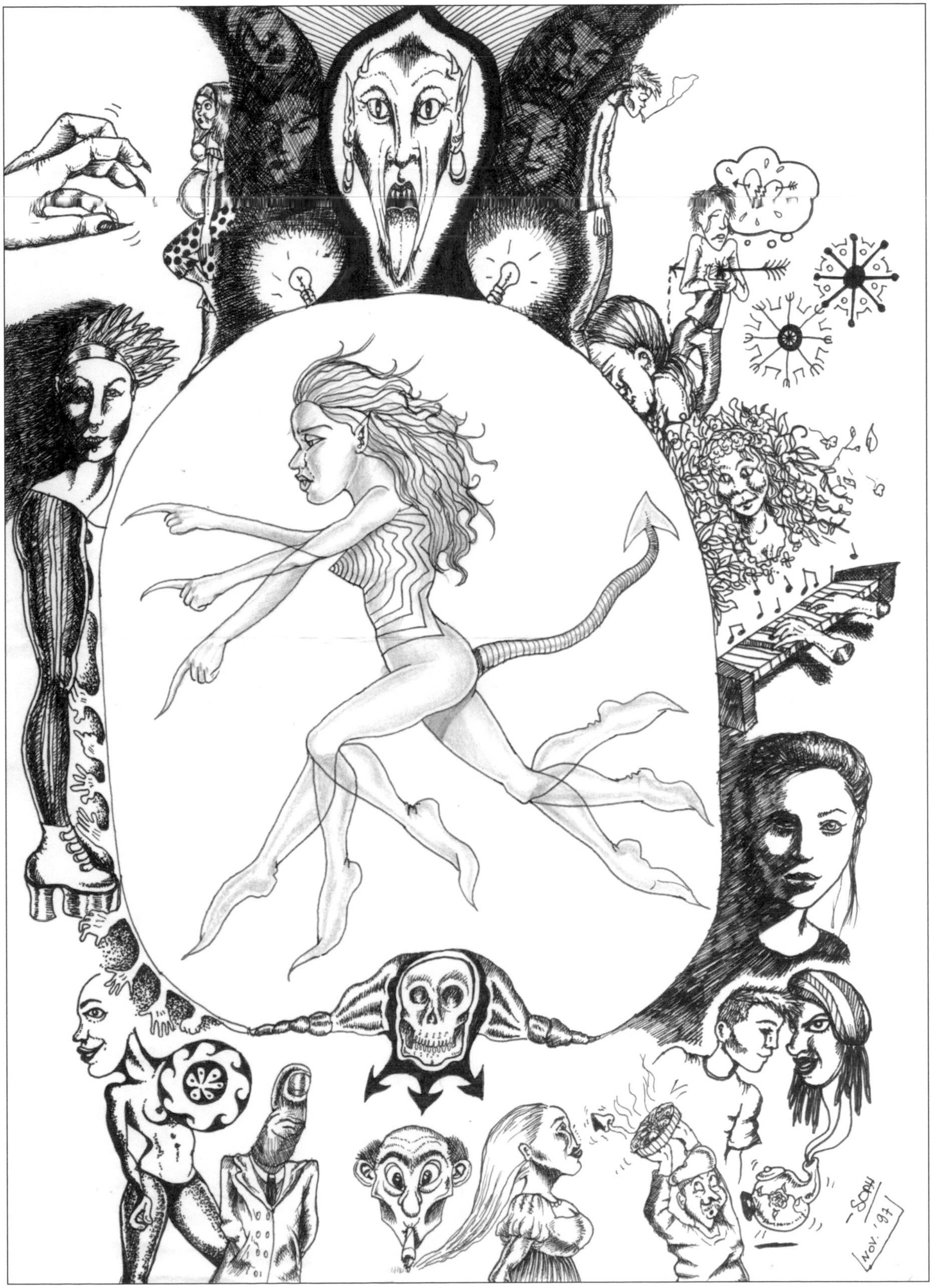
-SOPH
NOV. '97

Age 16, Nov., 1997.

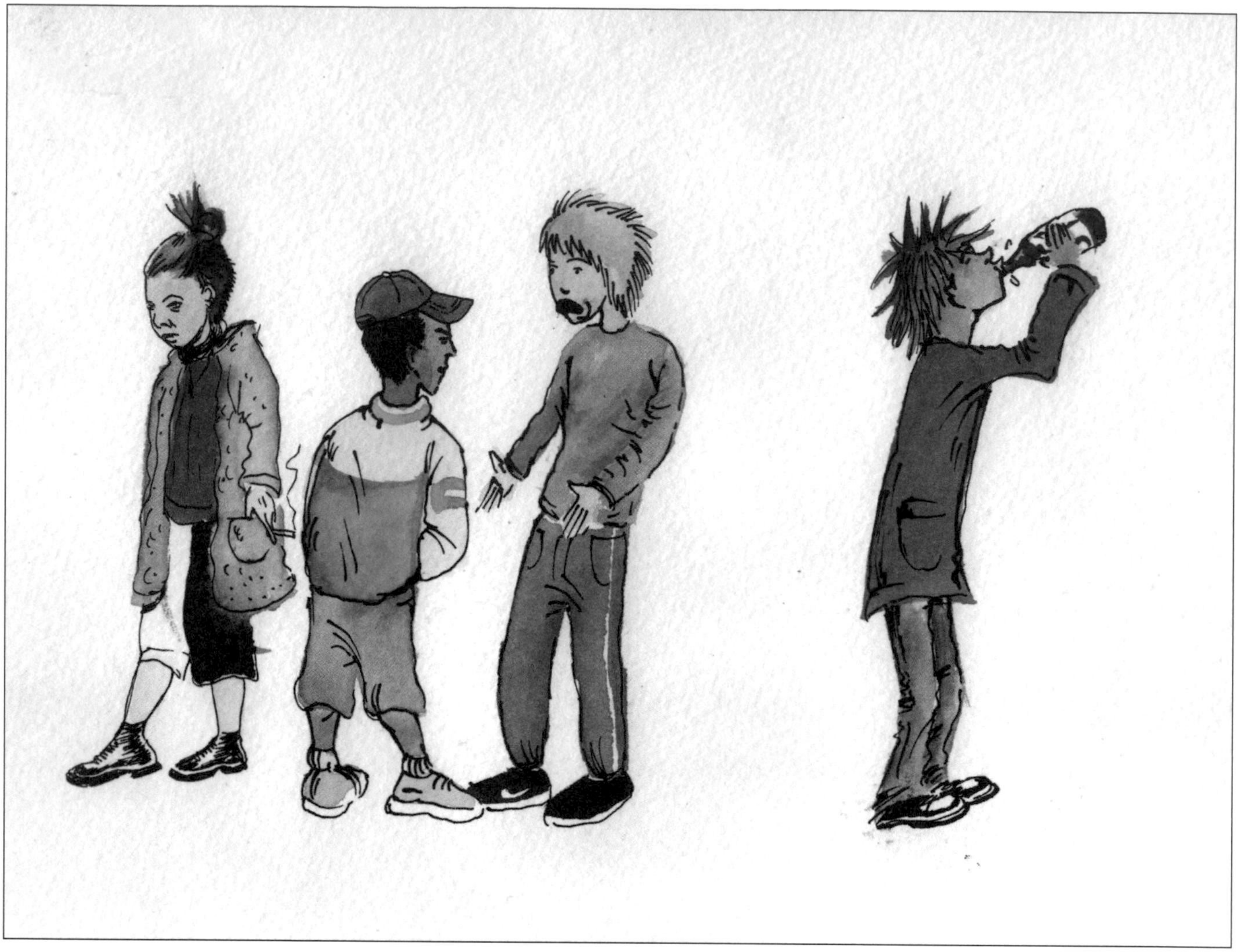

Age 16, 1998.

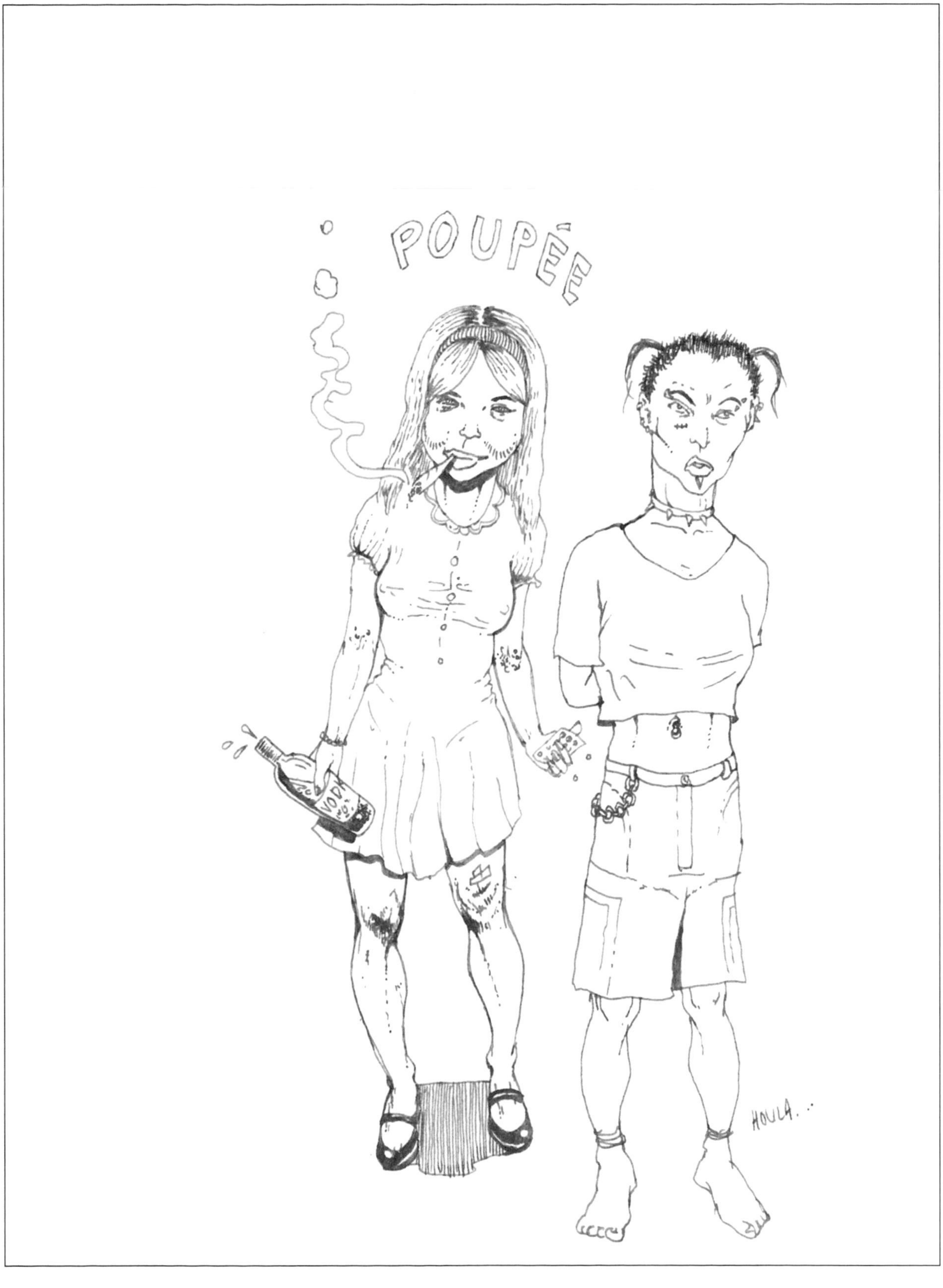
POUPÉE
HOULA. . .

Age 16, 1998.

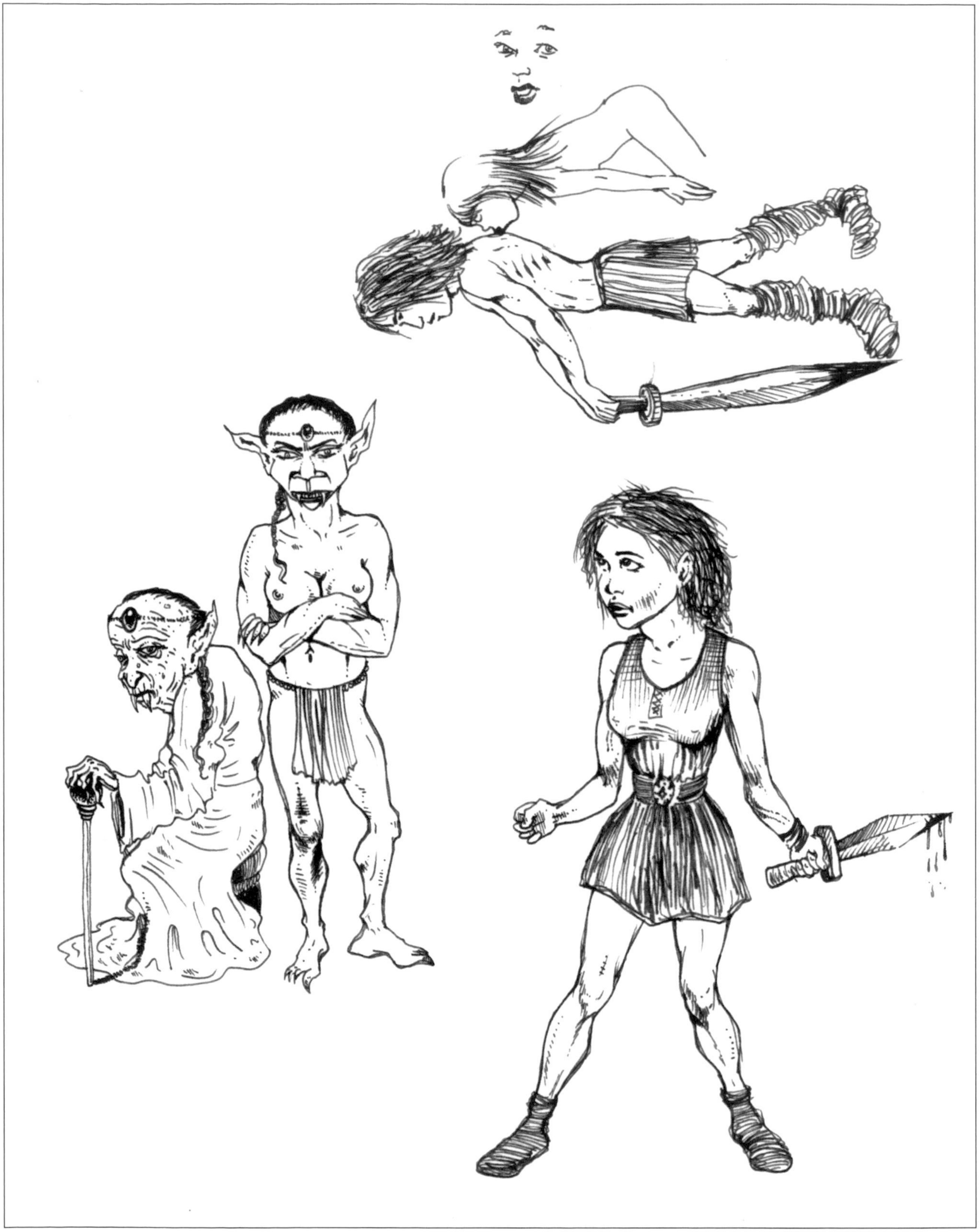

Age 16, 1998.

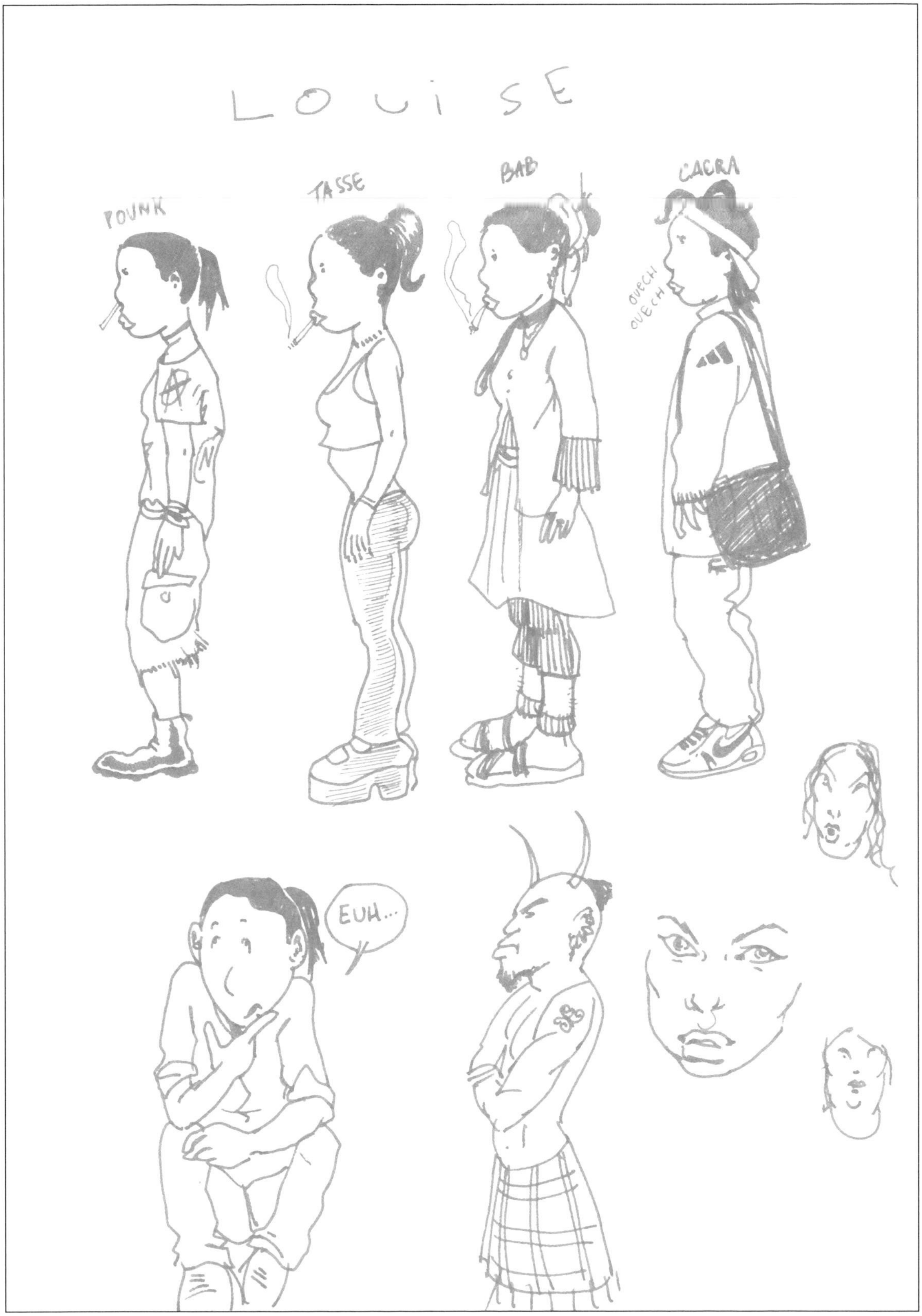
LOUISE
POUNK
TASSE
BAB
CAGRA
OUECH OUECH
EUH...

Age 16, 1998.

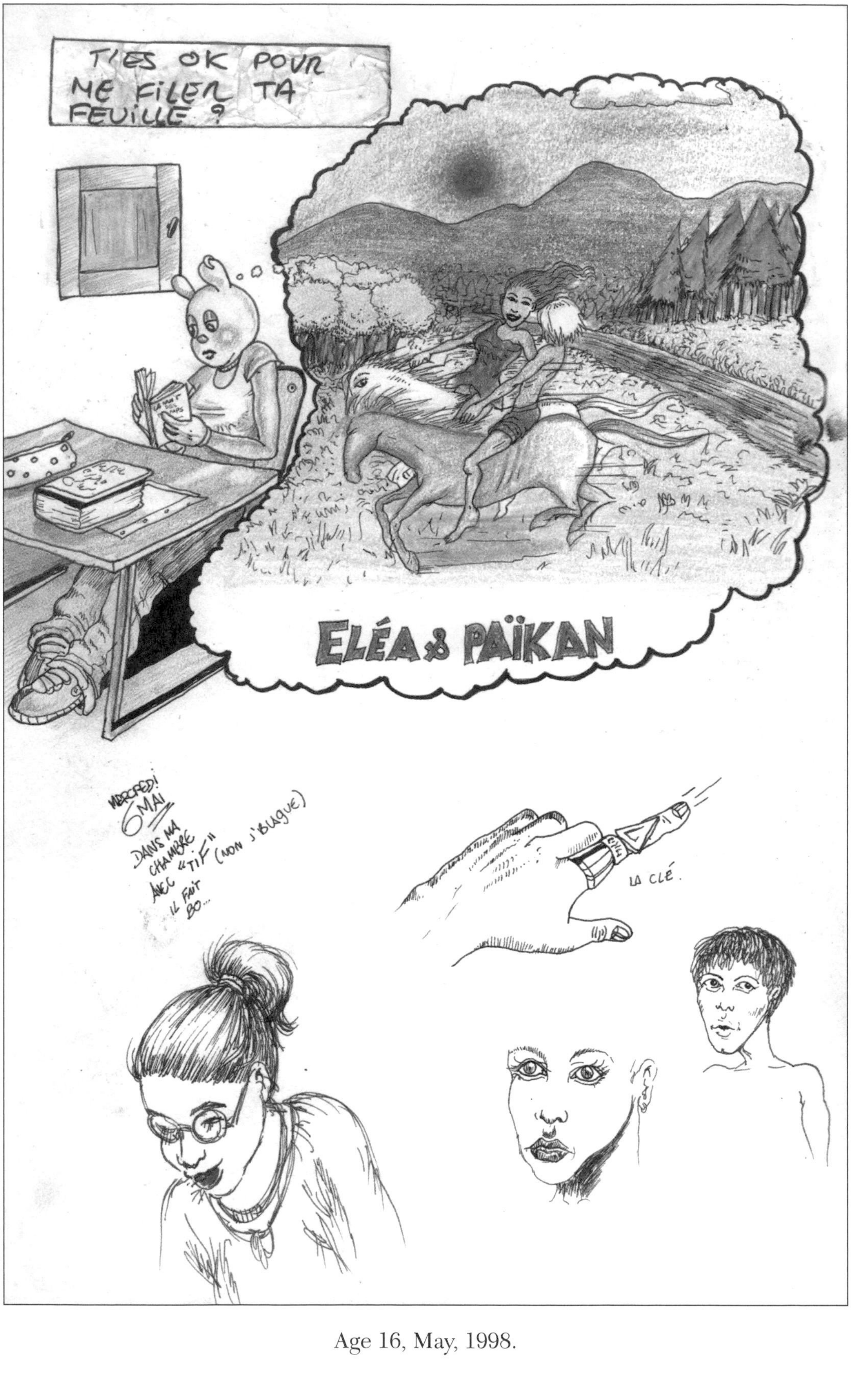
T'ES OK POUR ME FILER TA FEUILLE ?
ELÉA & PAÏKAN
MERCREDI 6 MAI
DANS MA CHAMBRE AVEC "TIF" (NON J'BLAGUE)
IL FAIT BO...
LA CLÉ.

Age 16, May, 1998.

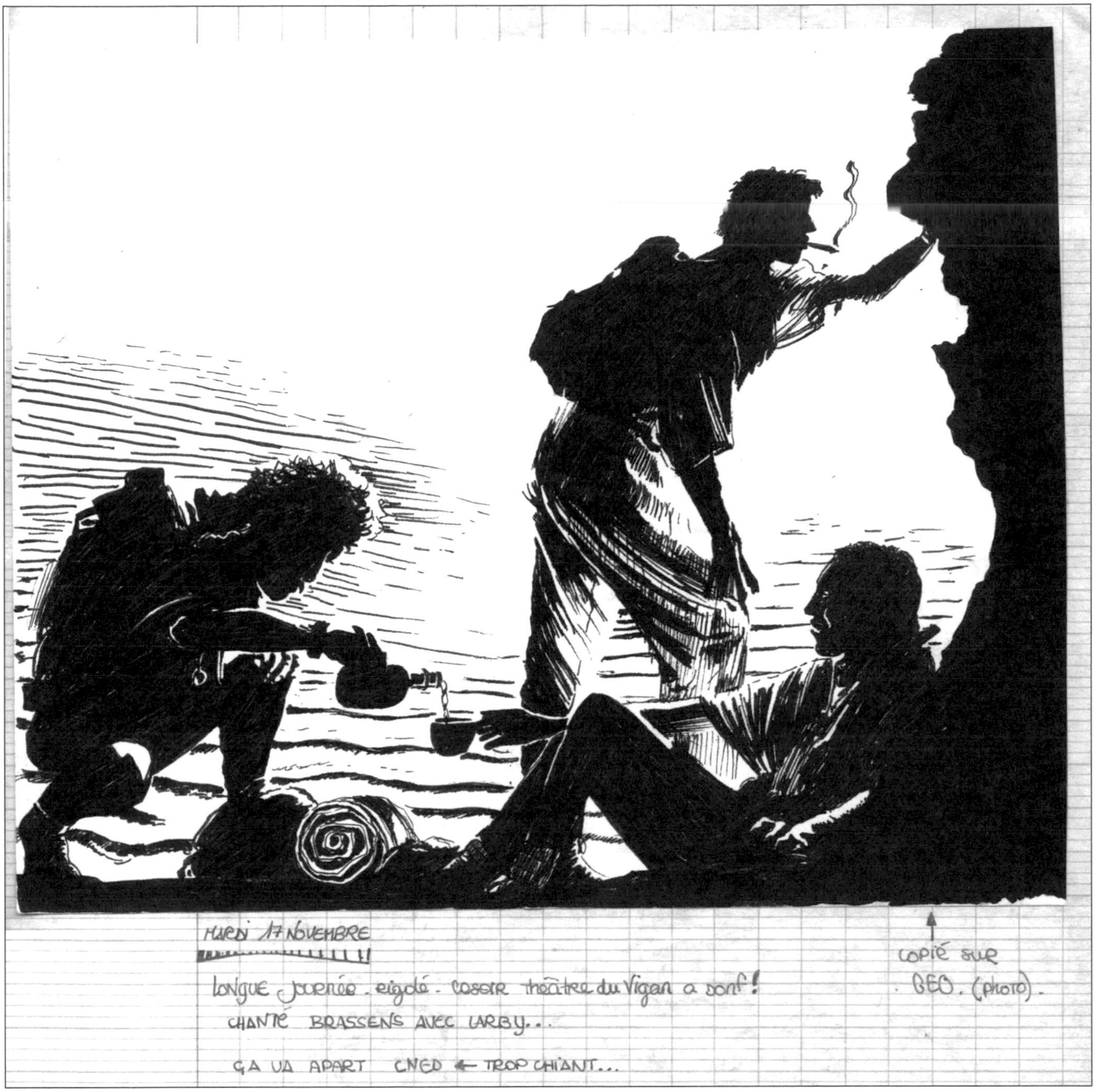
MARDI 17 NOVEMBRE
longue journée. rigolé. soirée théâtre du Vigan a donf!
CHANTÉ BRASSENS AVEC LARBY...
ÇA VA APART CNED ← TROP CHIANT...
COPIÉ SUR
. BEO. (photo).

Age 17, Nov., 1998.

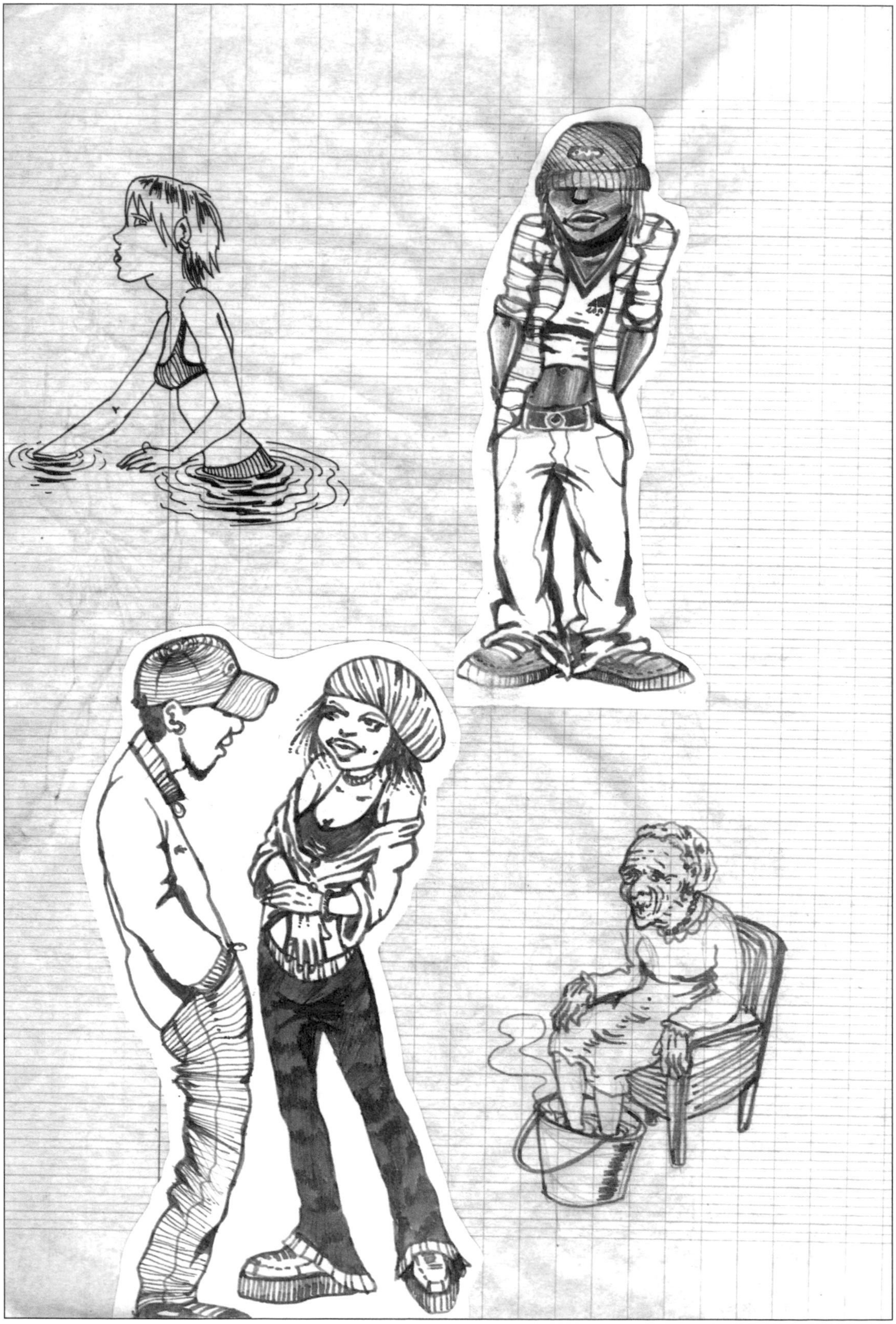

Age 17, Nov.–Dec., 1998.

Age 17, 1999.

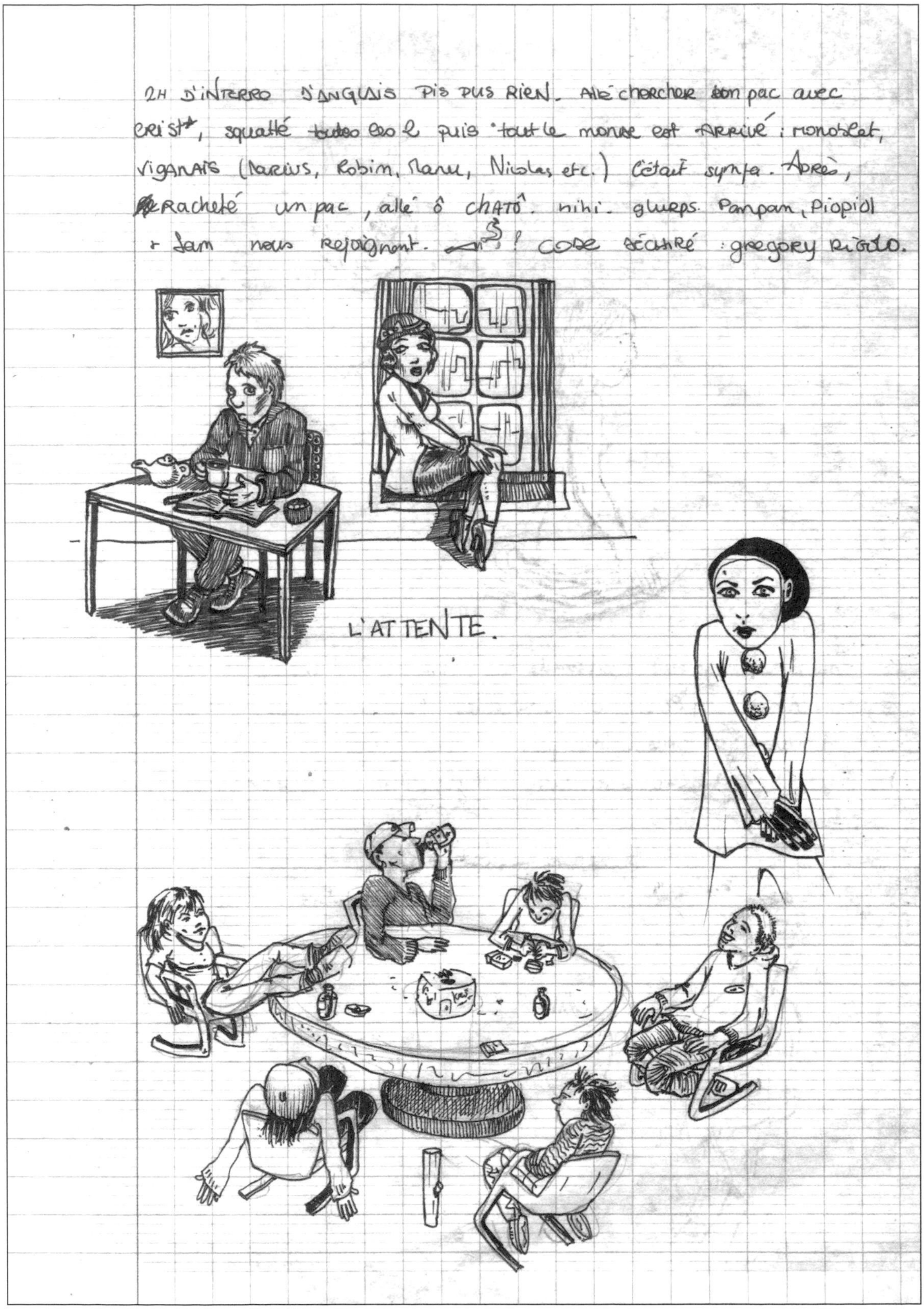

Age 17, Nov., Dec., 1998.

Age 17, early 1999.

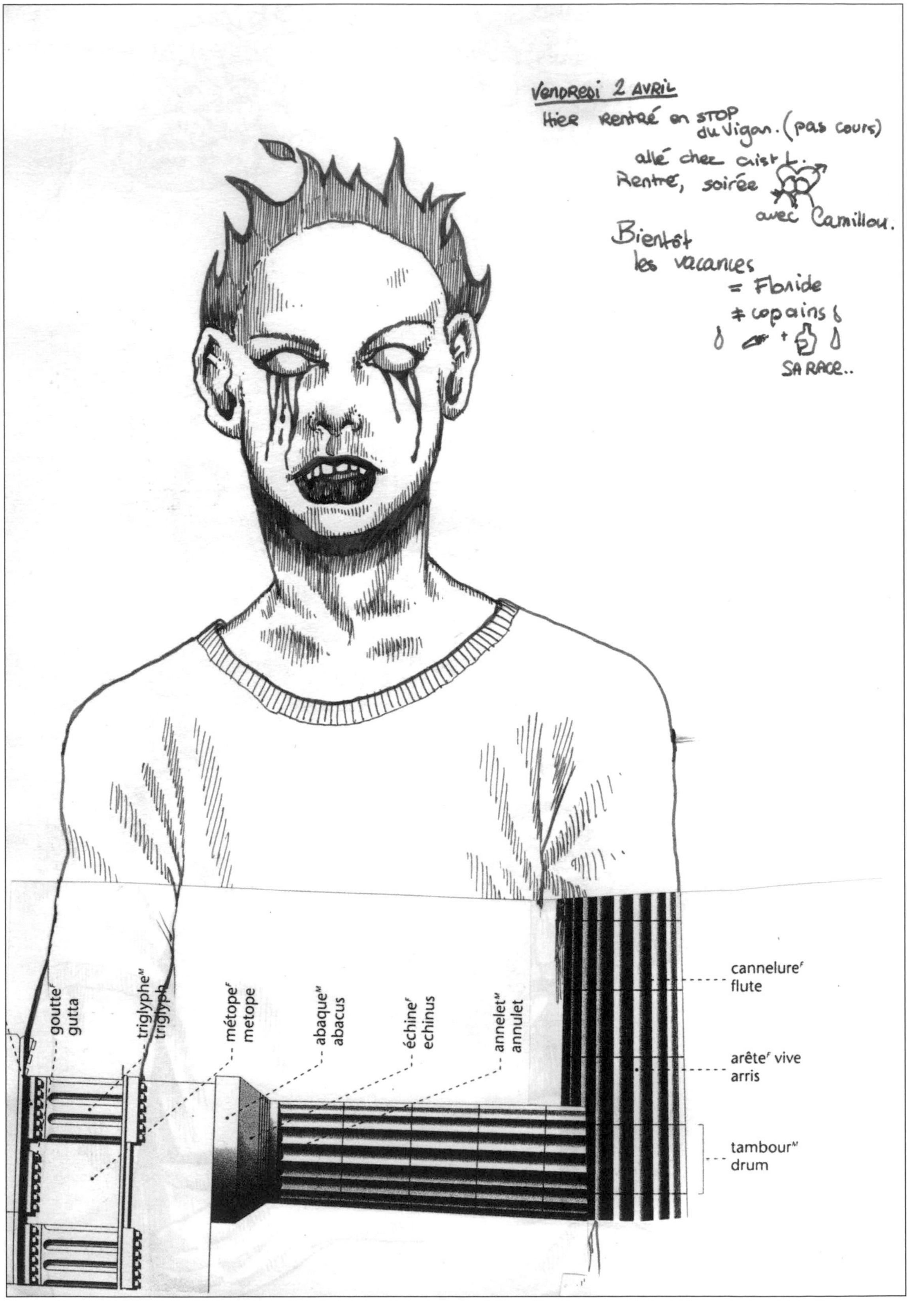
Vendredi 2 AVRIL
Hier rentré en stop du Vigan. (pas cours)
allé chez Crist L.
Rentré, soirée
avec Camillou.
Bientôt les vacances
= Floride
≠ copains
SA RACE..
goutte gutta
triglyphe triglyph
métope metope
abaque abacus
échine echinus
annelet annulet
cannelure flute
arête vive arris
tambour drum

Age 17, April, 1999.

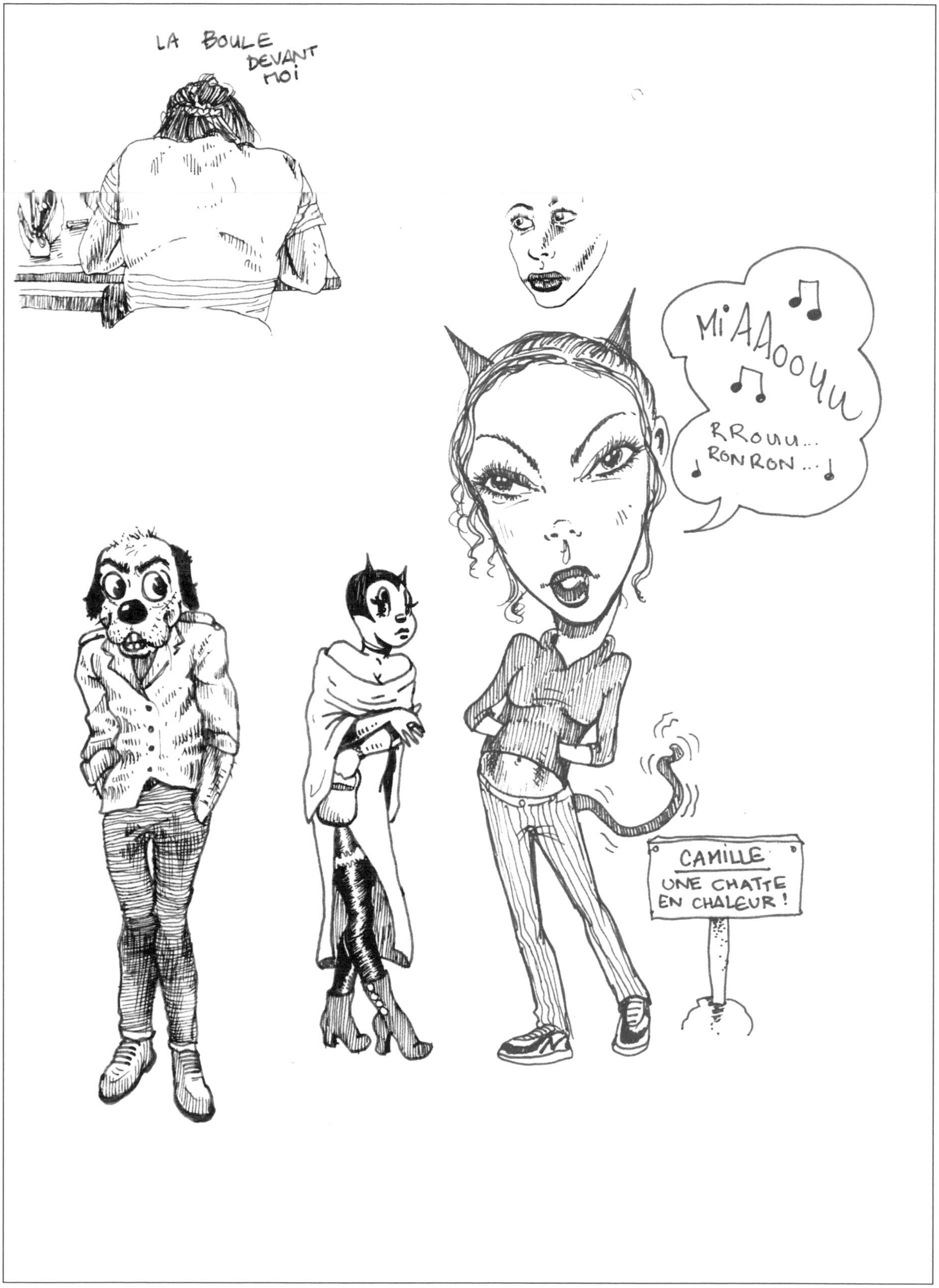
LA BOULE DEVANT MOI
MiAAAooyu
RRouuu... RONRON...
CAMILLE
UNE CHATTE EN CHALEUR!

Age 17, April, 1999.

09 · 08 · '99

"A gypsy on the beach in Corsica." Drawn from life. Age 17, Aug., 1999.

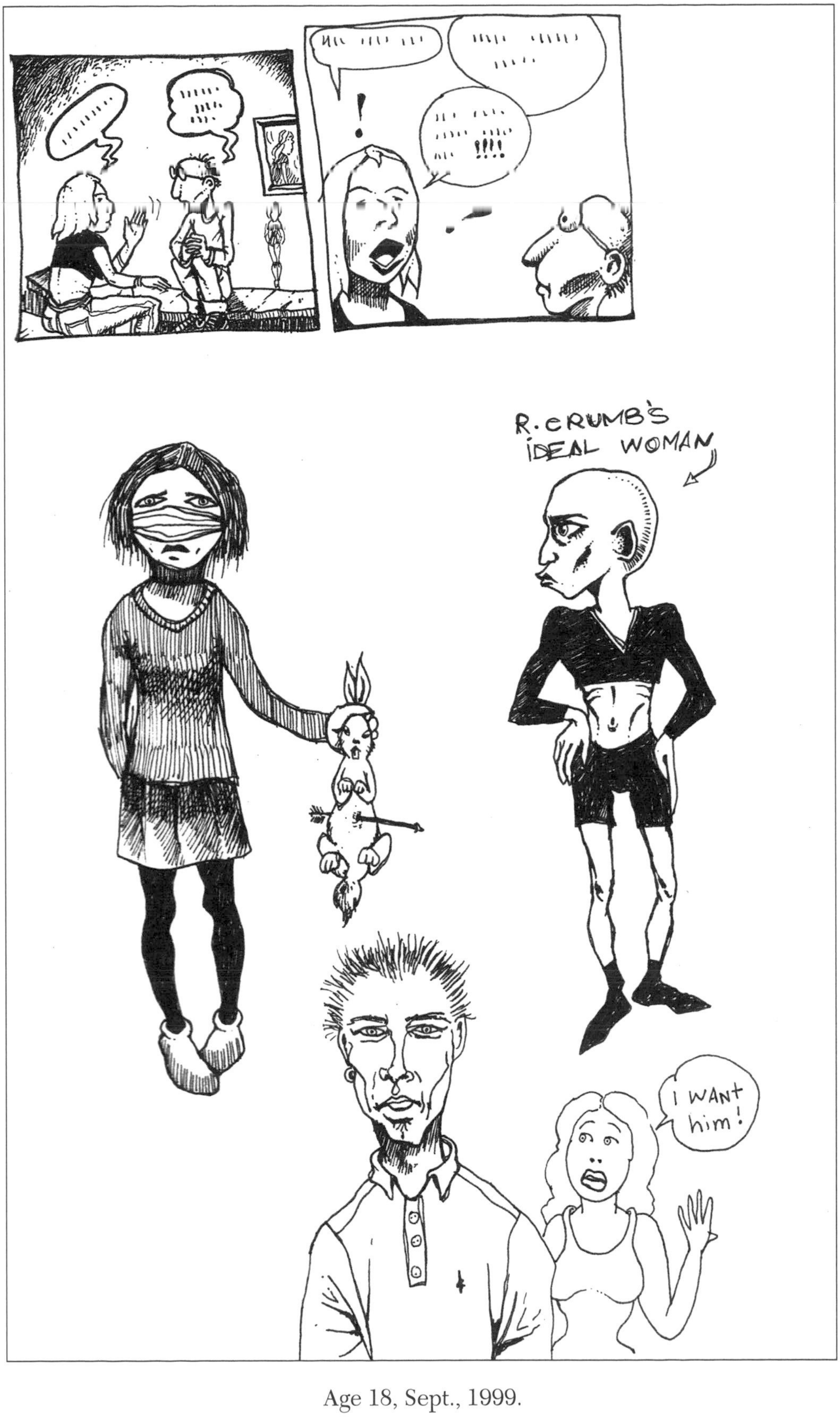
R. CRUMB'S
IDEAL WOMAN
I WANT
him!

Age 18, Sept., 1999.

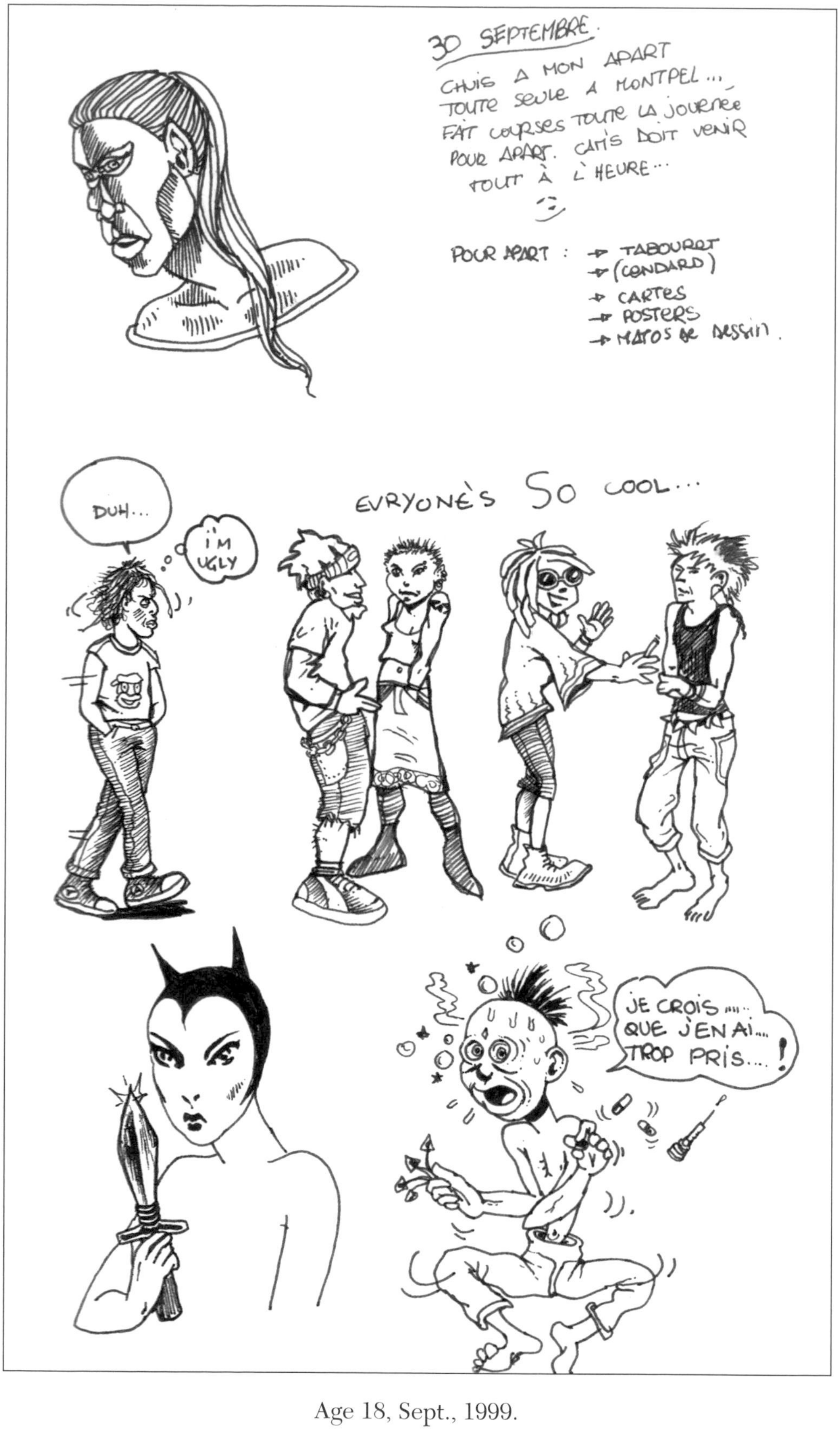
30 SEPTEMBRE.
CHUIS A MON APART
TOUTE SEULE A MONTPEL...
FAIT COURSES TOUTE LA JOURNEE
POUR APART. CATIS DOIT VENIR
TOUT À L'HEURE...
POUR APART : → TABOURET
→ (CONDARD)
→ CARTES
→ POSTERS
→ MATOS DE DESSIN.
DUH...
I'M UGLY
EVRYONE'S SO COOL...
JE CROIS... QUE J'EN AI... TROP PRIS...!

Age 18, Sept., 1999.

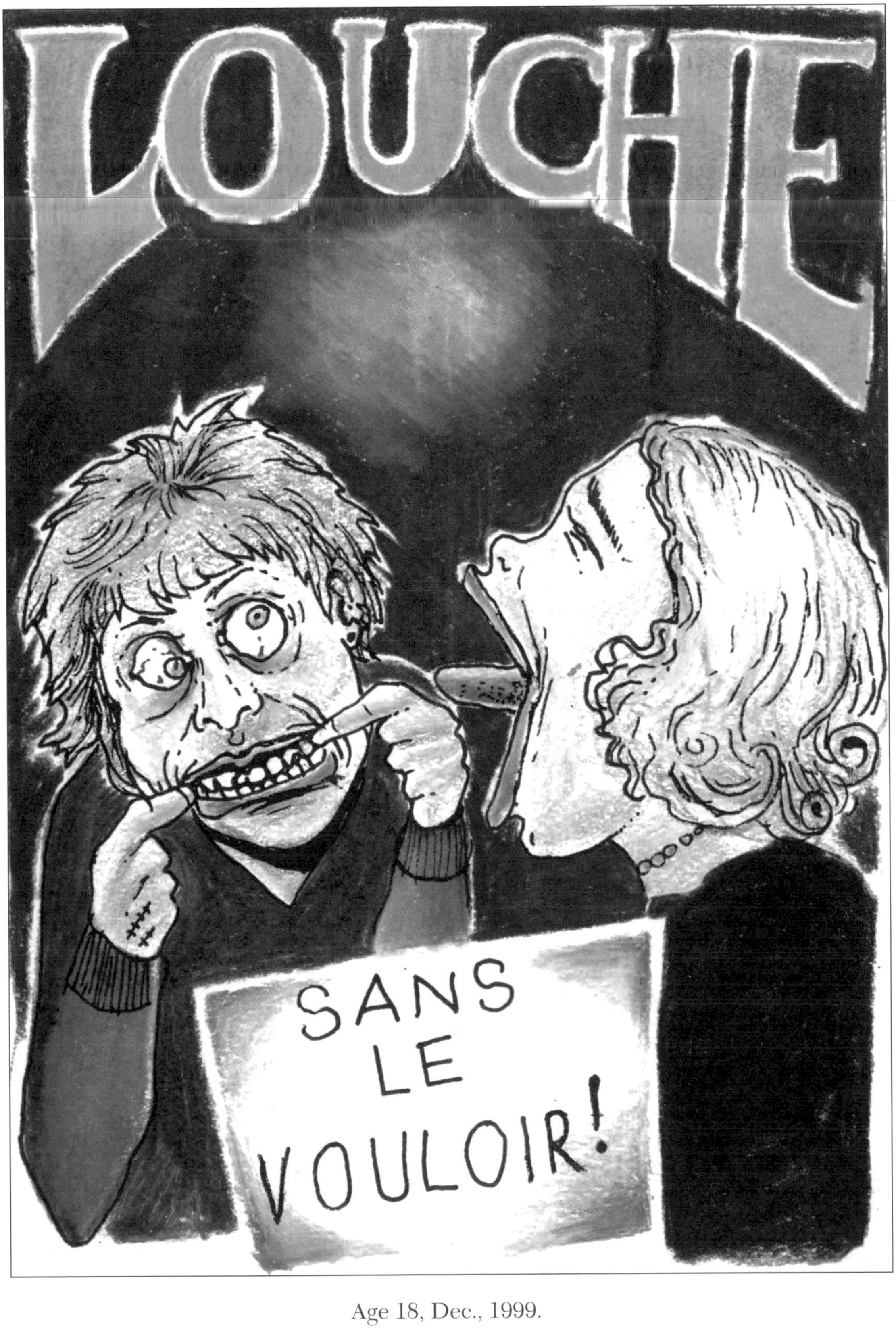
LOUCHE
SANS LE VOULOIR!

Age 18, Dec., 1999.

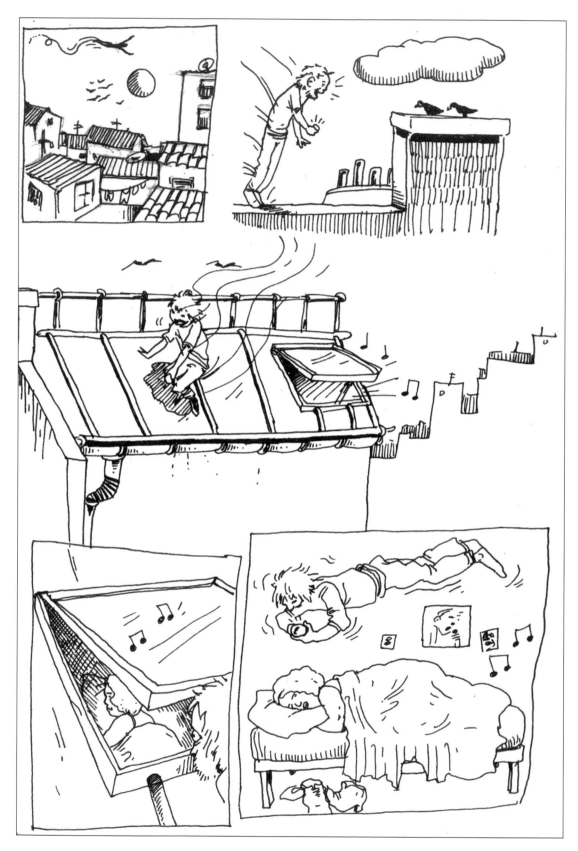

Age 18, Dec., 1999.

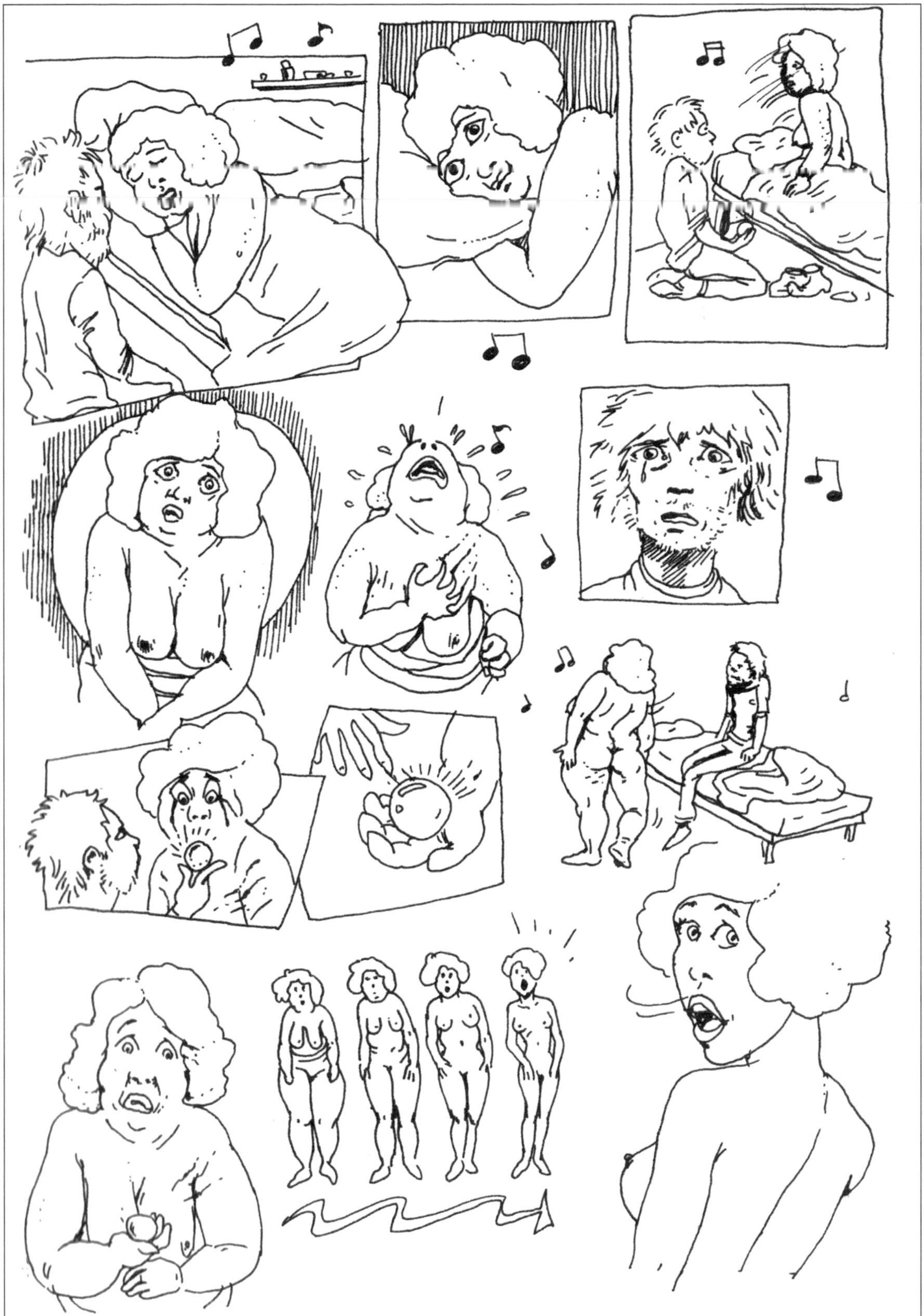

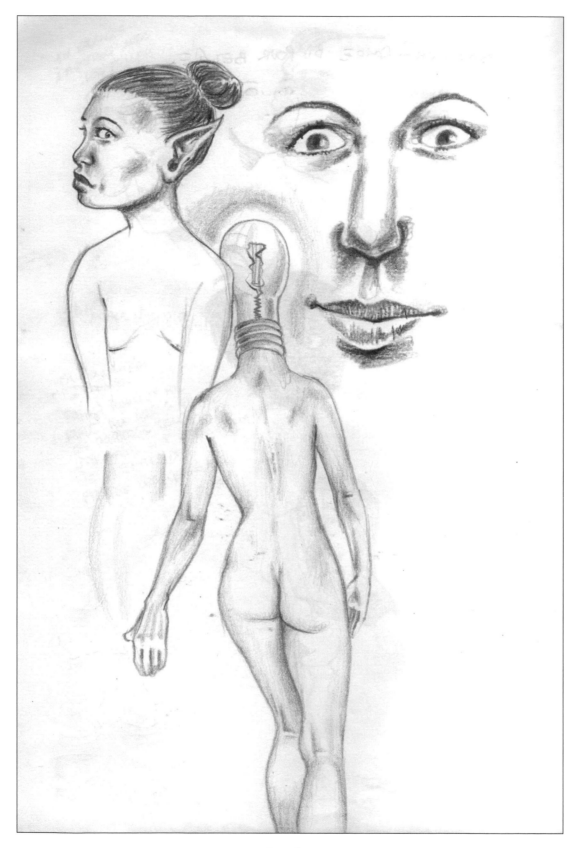

Age 18, Feb., 2000.

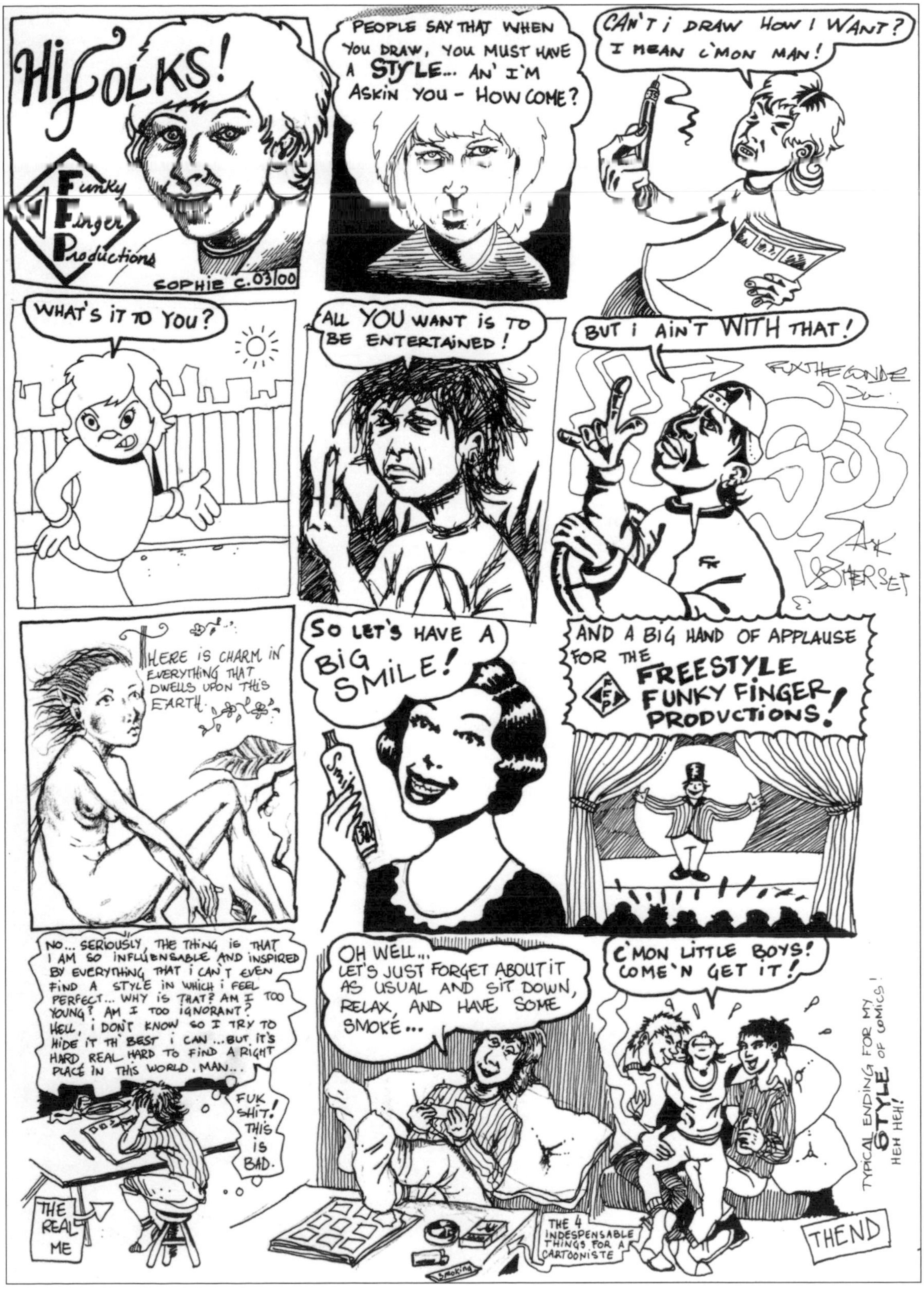

HI FOLKS!
Funky Finger Productions
SOPHIE C. 03/00
PEOPLE SAY THAT WHEN YOU DRAW, YOU MUST HAVE A STYLE... AN' I'M ASKIN YOU - HOW COME?
CAN'T i DRAW HOW I WANT? I MEAN C'MON MAN!
WHAT'S IT TO YOU?
ALL YOU WANT is TO BE ENTERTAINED!
BUT i AIN'T WITH THAT!
THERE is CHARM IN EVERYTHING THAT DWELLS UPON THIS EARTH.
SO LET'S HAVE A BIG SMILE!
AND A BIG HAND OF APPLAUSE FOR THE FREESTYLE FUNKY FINGER PRODUCTIONS!
NO... SERIOUSLY, THE THING is THAT I AM SO INFLUENSABLE AND INSPIRED BY EVERYTHING THAT i CAN'T EVEN FIND A STYLE IN WHICH i FEEL PERFECT... WHY is THAT? AM I TOO YOUNG? AM I TOO iGNORANT? HELL, i DON'T KNOW SO I TRY TO HIDE IT TH' BEST i CAN ...BUT IT'S HARD, REAL HARD TO FIND A RIGHT PLACE IN THIS WORLD, MAN...
FUK SHIT! THIS is BAD.
THE REAL ME
OH WELL... LET'S JUST FORGET ABOUT IT AS USUAL AND SIT DOWN, RELAX, AND HAVE SOME SMOKE...
THE 4 INDESPENSABLE THINGS FOR A CARTOONISTE
C'MON LITTLE BOYS! COME 'N GET IT!
TYPICAL ENDING FOR MY STYLE OF COMICS! HEH HEH!
THEND

Age 18, March, 2000.

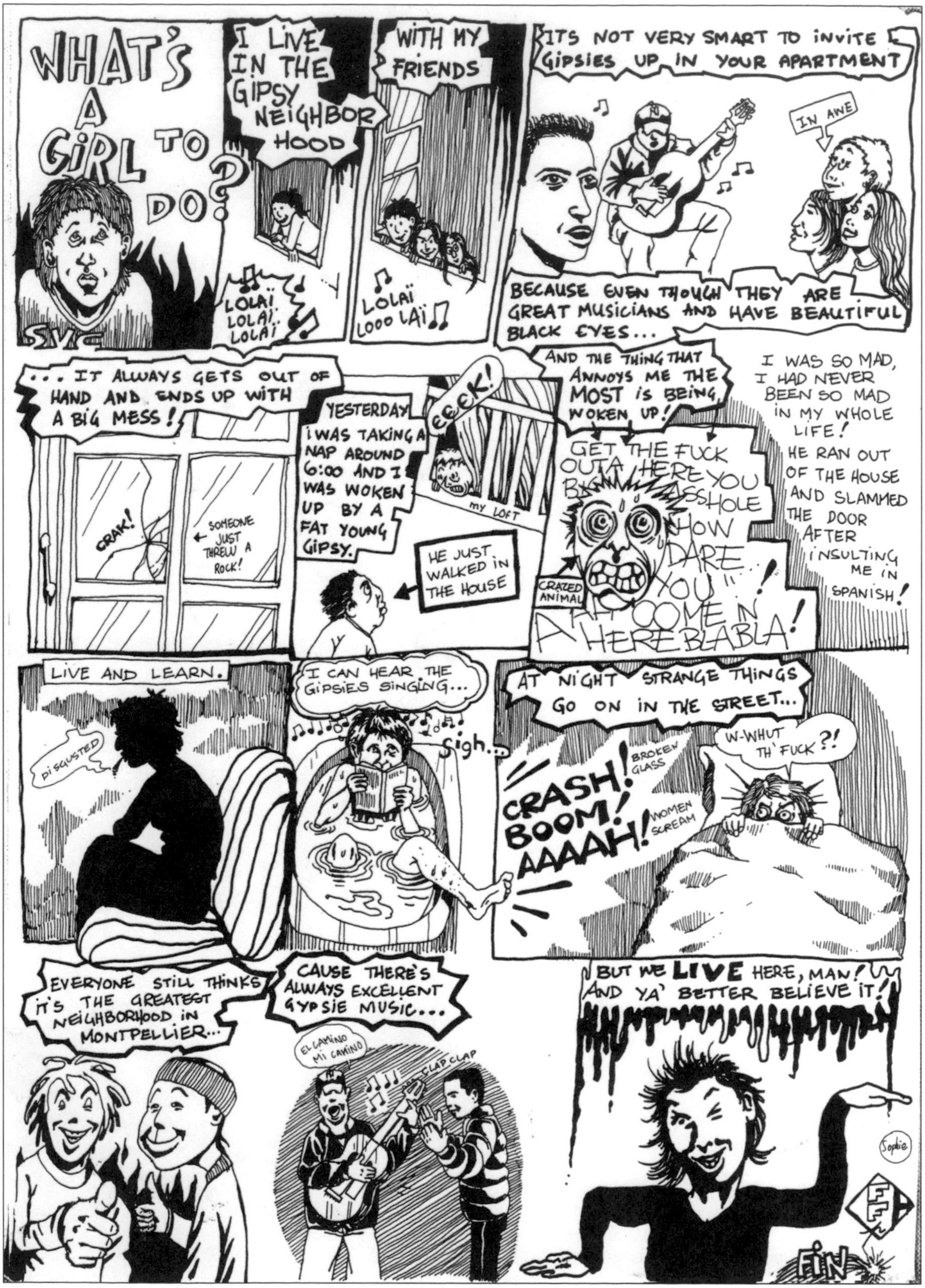
WHAT'S A GIRL TO DO?
I LIVE IN THE GIPSY NEIGHBORHOOD
LOLAÏ LOLAÏ LOLAÏ
WITH MY FRIENDS
LOLAÏ LOOO LAÏ
ITS NOT VERY SMART TO INVITE GIPSIES UP IN YOUR APARTMENT
IN AWE
BECAUSE EVEN THOUGH THEY ARE GREAT MUSICIANS AND HAVE BEAUTIFUL BLACK EYES...
... IT ALWAYS GETS OUT OF HAND AND ENDS UP WITH A BIG MESS!
CRAK!
← SOMEONE JUST THREW A ROCK!
YESTERDAY I WAS TAKING A NAP AROUND 6:00 AND I WAS WOKEN UP BY A FAT YOUNG GIPSY.
EEEK!
MY LOFT
HE JUST WALKED IN THE HOUSE
AND THE THING THAT ANNOYS ME THE MOST IS BEING WOKEN UP!
GET THE FUCK OUTA HERE YOU BIG ASSHOLE HOW DARE YOU ... COME IN HERE BLABLA!
CRAZED ANIMAL
I WAS SO MAD, I HAD NEVER BEEN SO MAD IN MY WHOLE LIFE!
HE RAN OUT OF THE HOUSE AND SLAMMED THE DOOR AFTER INSULTING ME IN SPANISH!
LIVE AND LEARN.
DISGUSTED
I CAN HEAR THE GIPSIES SINGING...
SIGH...
AT NIGHT STRANGE THINGS GO ON IN THE STREET...
CRASH! BOOM! AAAAH!
BROKEN GLASS
WOMEN SCREAM
W-WHUT TH' FUCK?!
EVERYONE STILL THINKS IT'S THE GREATEST NEIGHBORHOOD IN MONTPELLIER...
CAUSE THERE'S ALWAYS EXCELLENT GYPSIE MUSIC...
EL CAMINO MI CAMINO
CLAP CLAP
BUT WE LIVE HERE, MAN! AND YA' BETTER BELIEVE IT!
Sophie
FIN

Age 18, March, 2000.

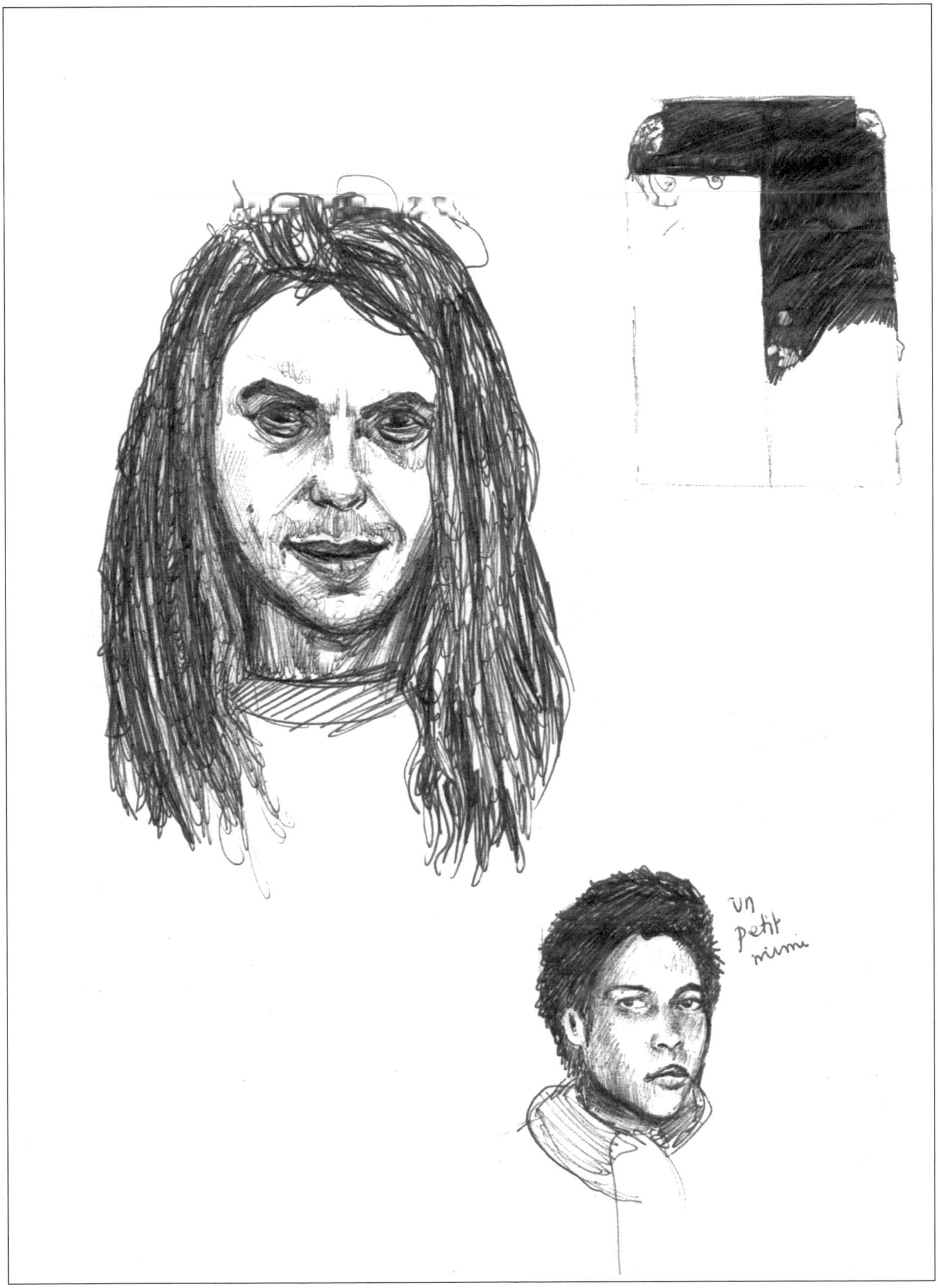
un petit mimi

Age 18, April, 2000.

ST ROCH

Buildings in Montpellier. Drawn from life. Age 18, April, 2000.

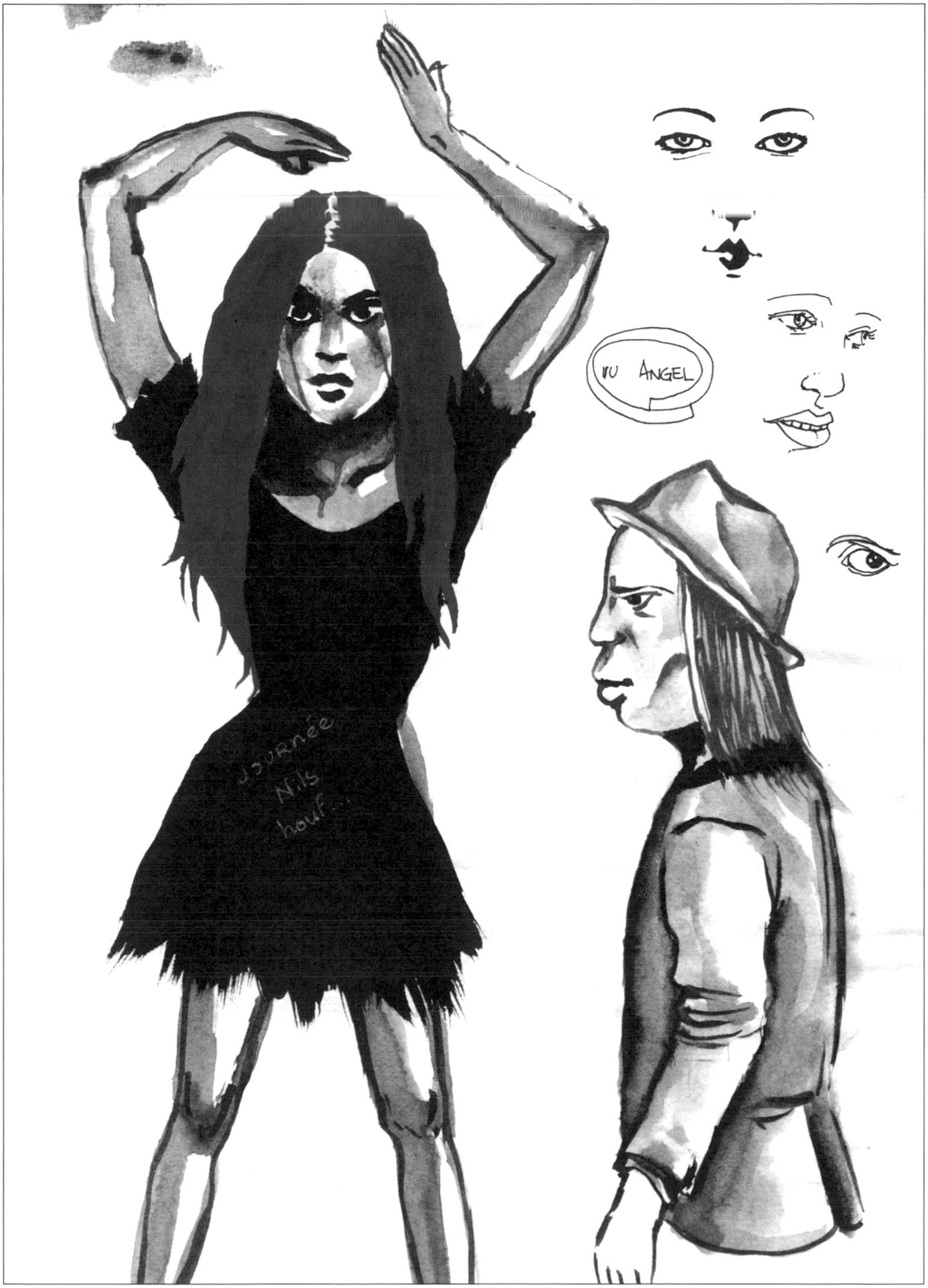
vu Angel
Journée
Nils
houf...

Age 18, April, 2000.

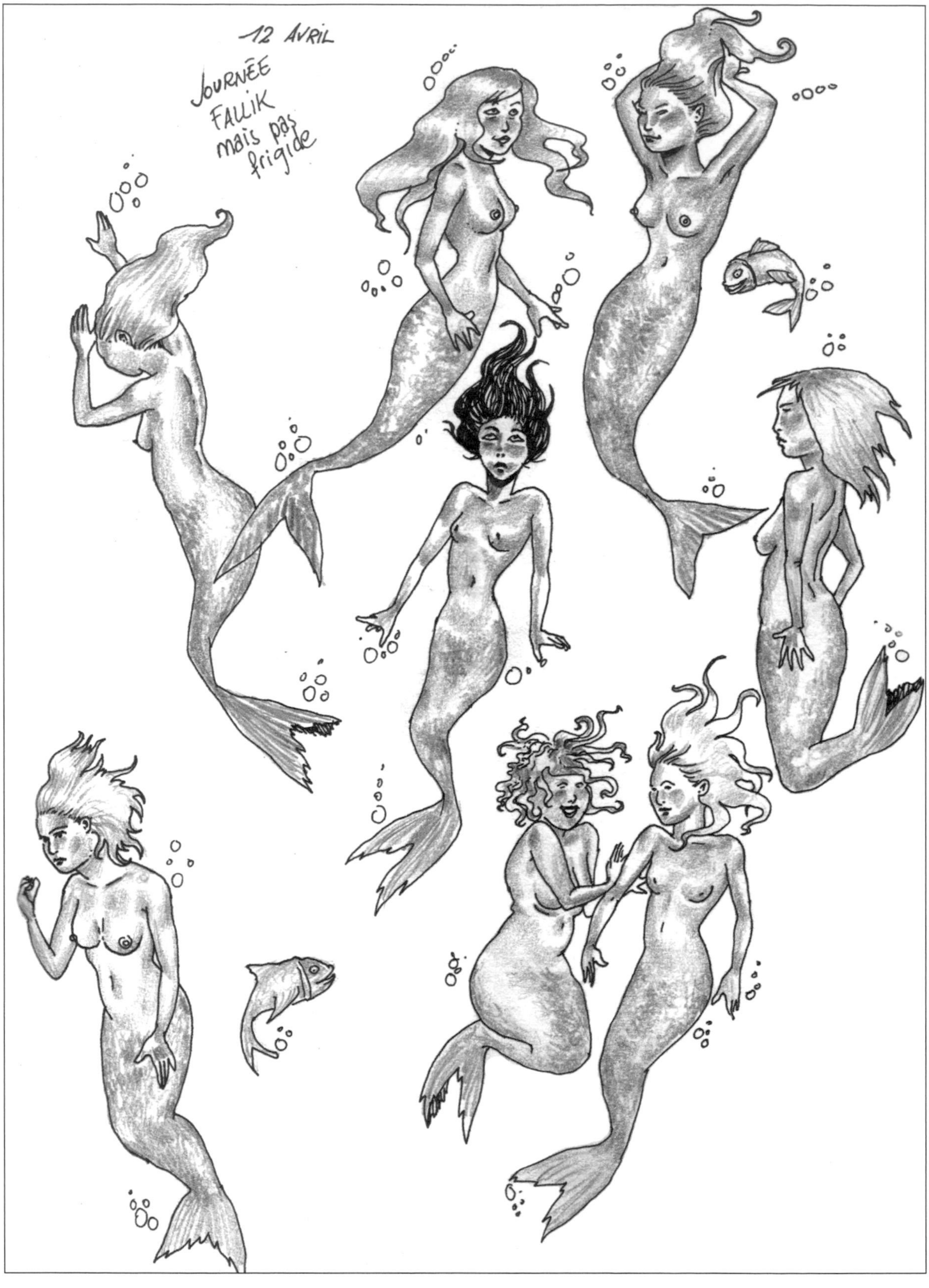
12 AVRIL
JOURNÉE
FALLIK
mais pas
frigide

Age 18, April, 2000.

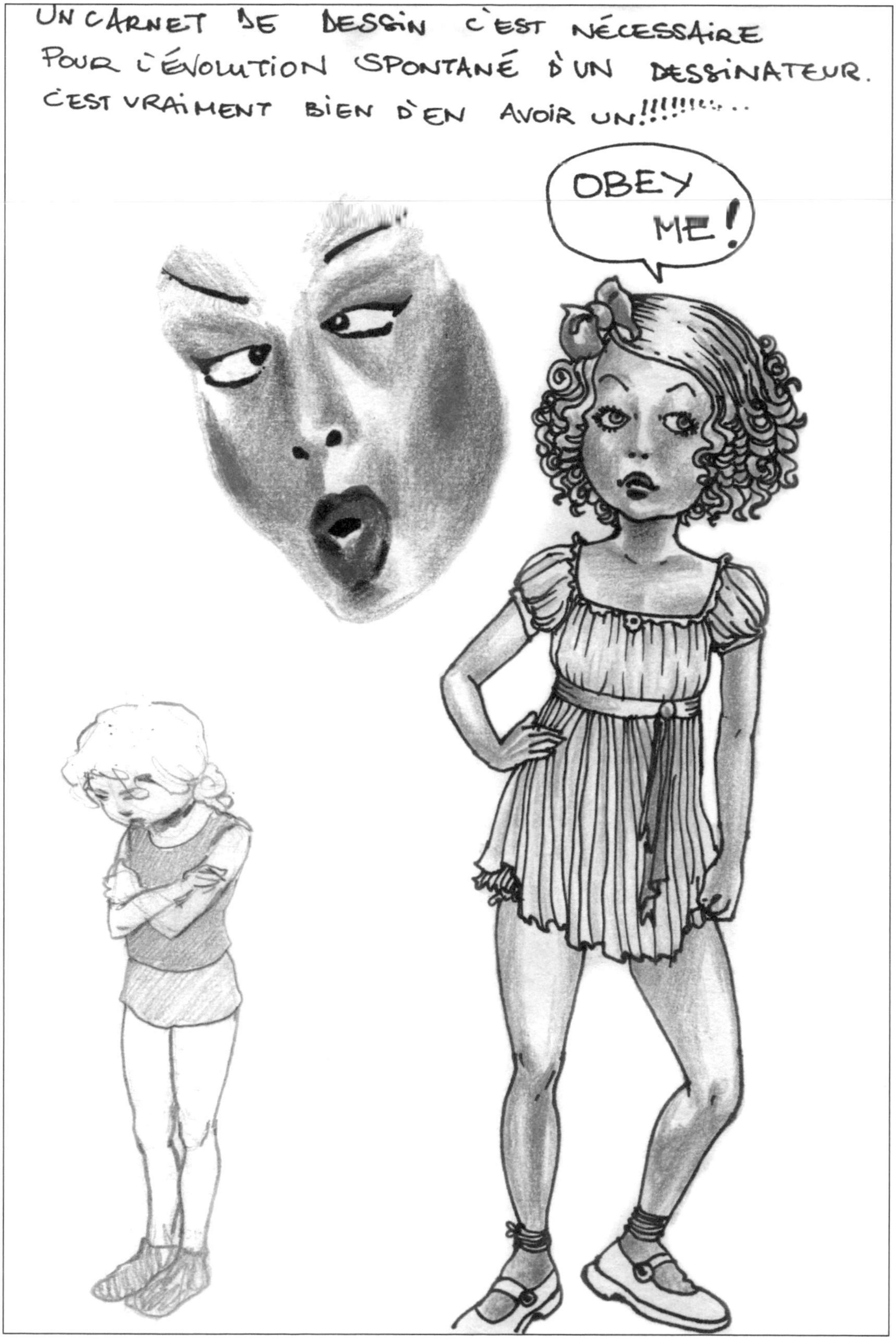
UN CARNET DE DESSIN C'EST NÉCESSAIRE POUR L'ÉVOLUTION SPONTANÉ D'UN DESSINATEUR. C'EST VRAIMENT BIEN D'EN AVOIR UN!!!!!!...
OBEY ME!

Age 18, May, 2000.

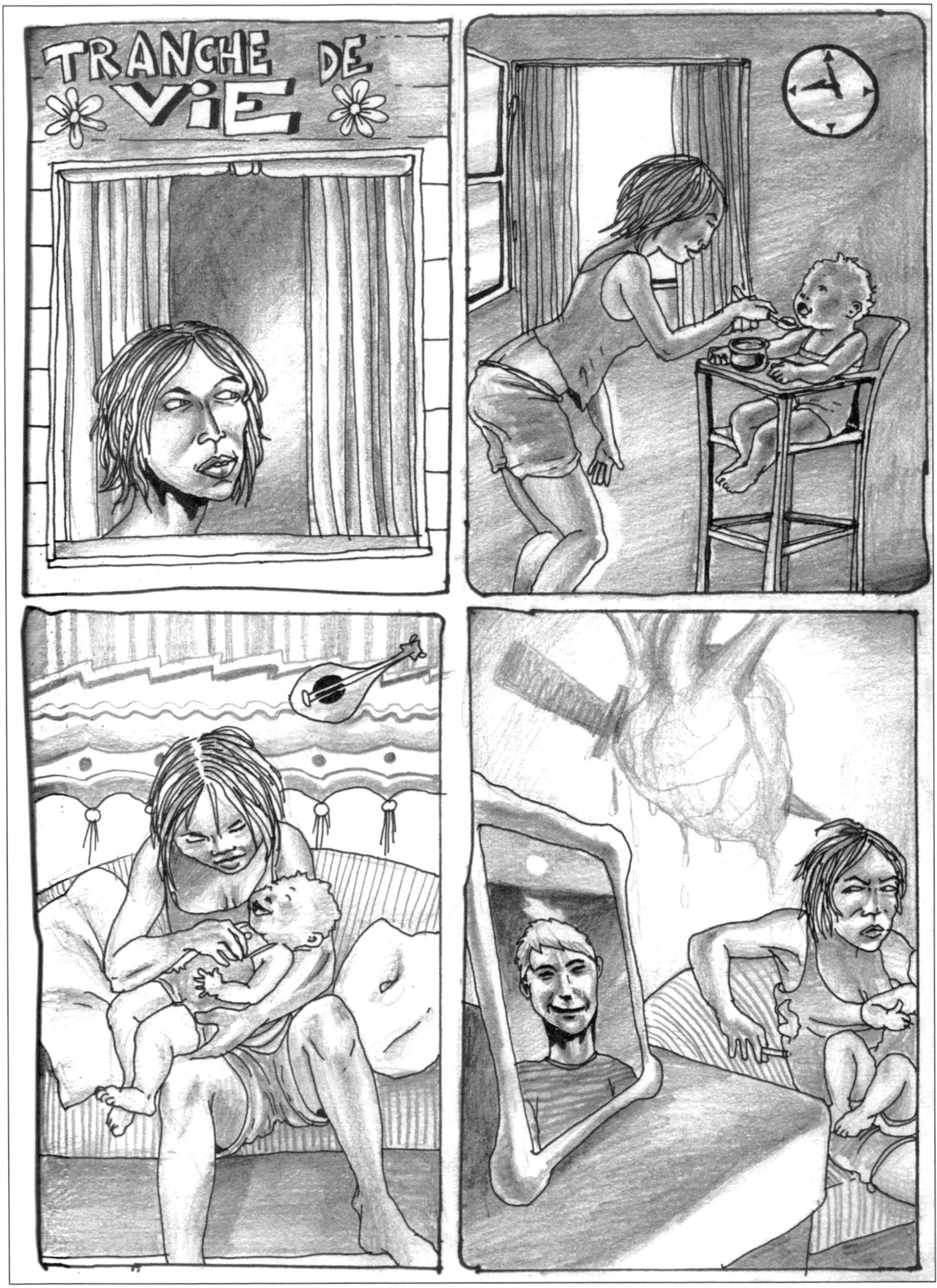
TRANCHE DE VIE

Age 18, May, 2000.

Drawn from life. Age 18, June, 2000.

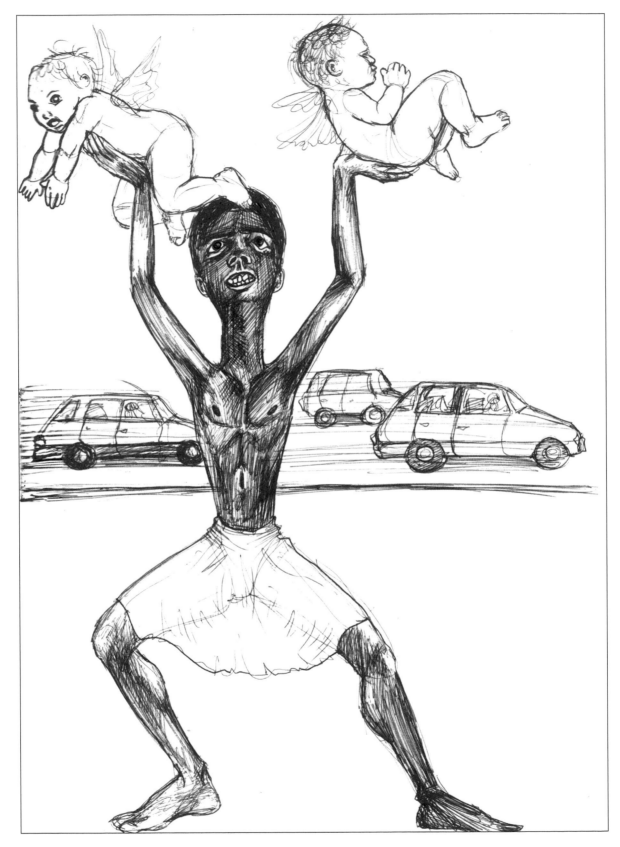

Age 18, Aug., 2000.

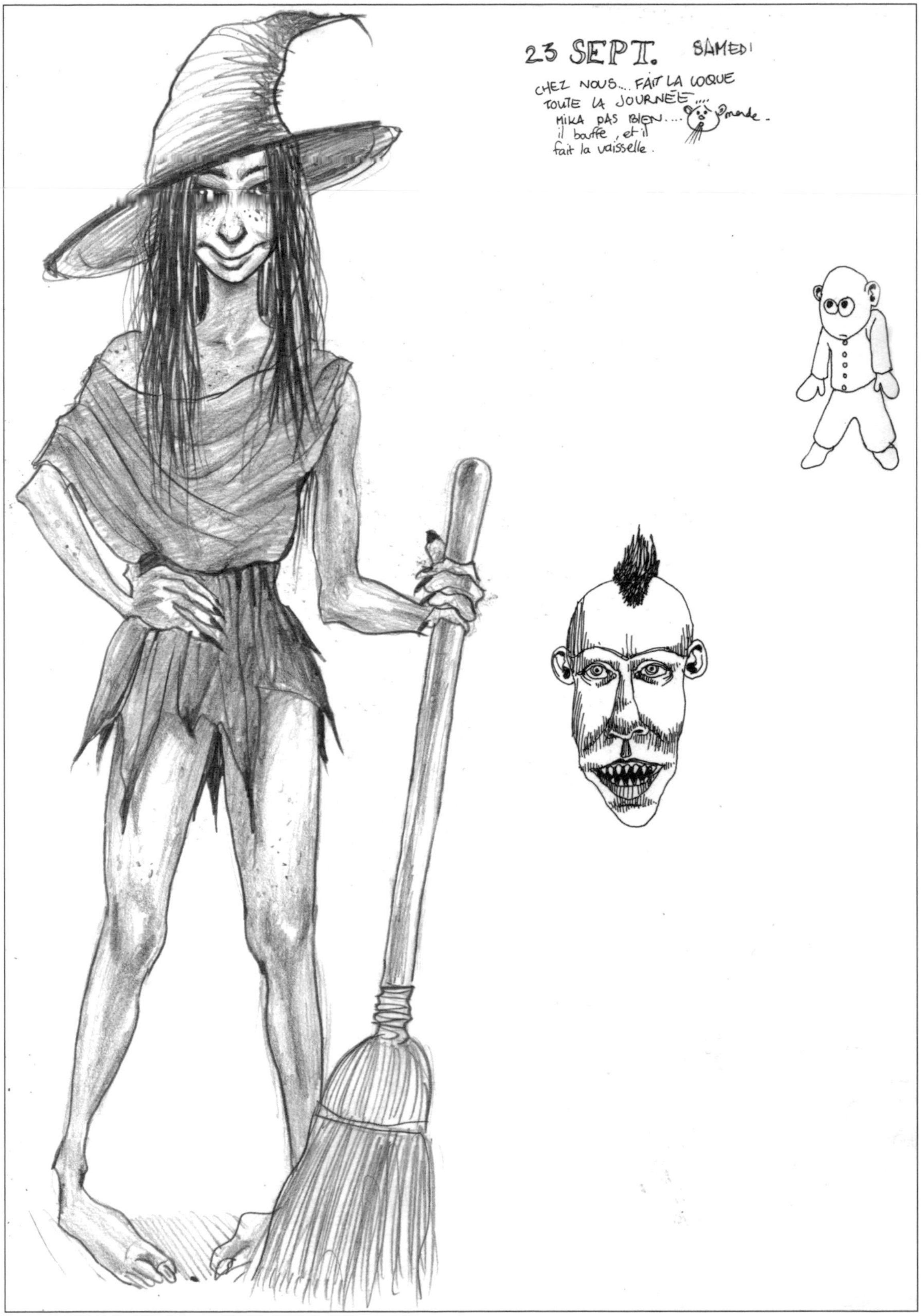
23 SEPT. SAMEDI
CHEZ NOUS.... FAIT LA LOQUE
TOUTE LA JOURNÉE....
MIKA PAS BIEN....
merde.
il bouffe, et il
fait la vaisselle.

Age 18, Sept., 2000.

OUT IN THE WORLD 2000 TO 2003 / 19 TO 22 YRS OLD

PARIS! BIG CITY LIFE! FREEDOM!
WEIRD MOROCCAN WAITER BOY FRIENDS AND
CIRCUS SCHOOL; BEING A PSEUDO ENGLISH TEA-
CHER FOR FANCY PARISIAN COMPANIES WHERE
SUBURBAN SECRETARIES WOULD RANT ABOUT
THEIR UNHAPPY MARRIAGES IN BAD ENGLISH;
LIVING IN BAD NEIGHBORHOODS AND EXPLORING
DIVE BARS AND THE STREETS OF PARIS ON BIKE
AT NIGHT; MEETING ARTISTS AND MUSICIANS,
GOOD AND (MOSTLY) BAD... THE BUZZING LIFE
THAT SURROUNDED ME WAS EXHILARATING AND
STIMULATING.

　　But ART-MAKING WAS STILL A CONFUSING
ISSUE. WORRYING ABOUT WHAT OTHERS WOULD
THINK, FEELING UNWORTHY AS ROYAL HEIRESS
OF "THE LEGEND", TOYED WITH MY SPONTANEITY.
I DID MANAGE TO FINISH A COMIC OR TWO AND
EVEN PUBLISH SOME. BUT MY SKETCHBOOKS
WERE THE PLACE I HAD THE MOST FUN, NOT
HAVING TO WORRY ABOUT ALL THAT. IT
WASN'T "WORK", AND I DREW FREELY,
LETTING IT ALL SPILL OUT...

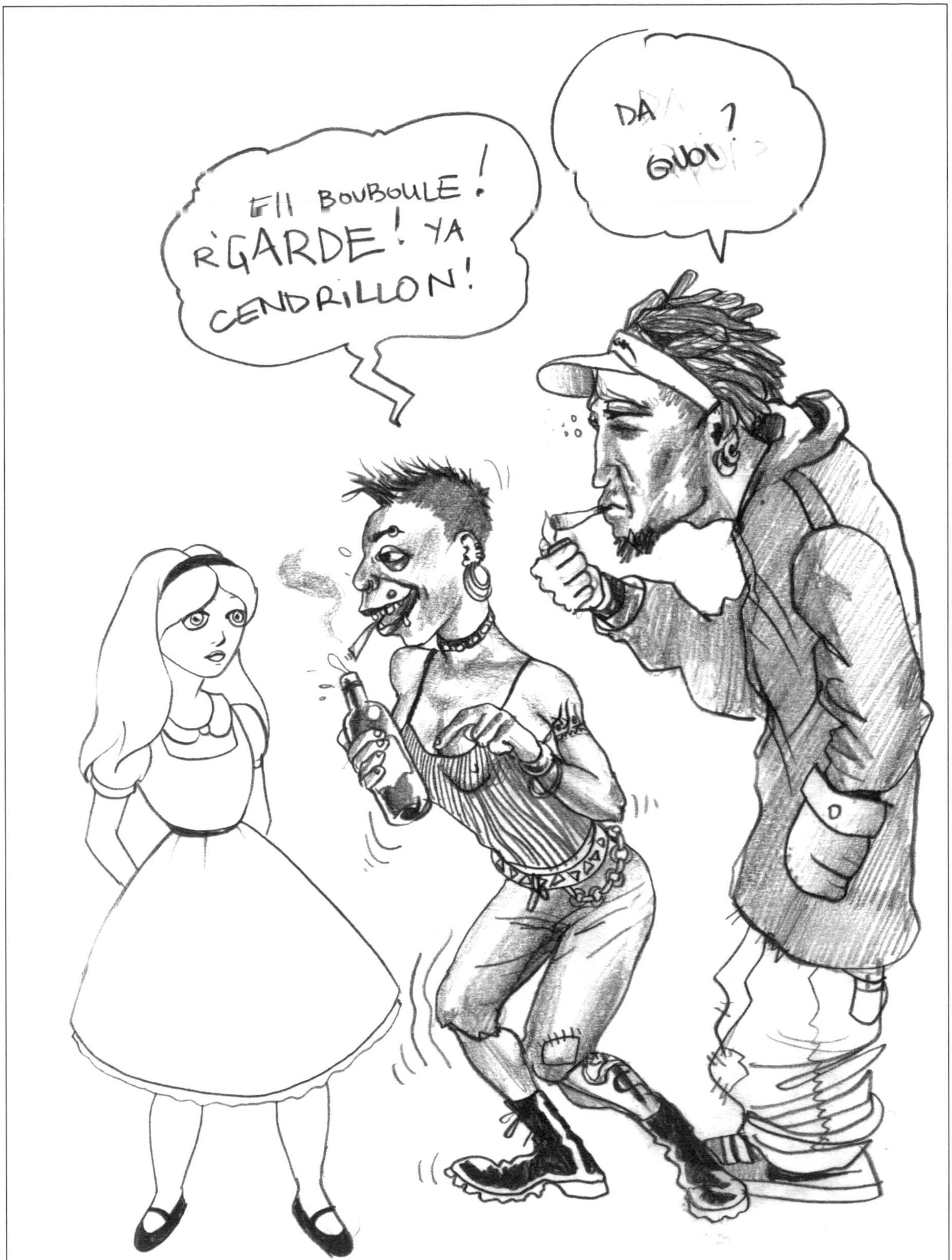
EH BOUBOULE! R'GARDE! YA CENDRILLON!
DA ?
QUOI

Age 19, Nov., 2000.

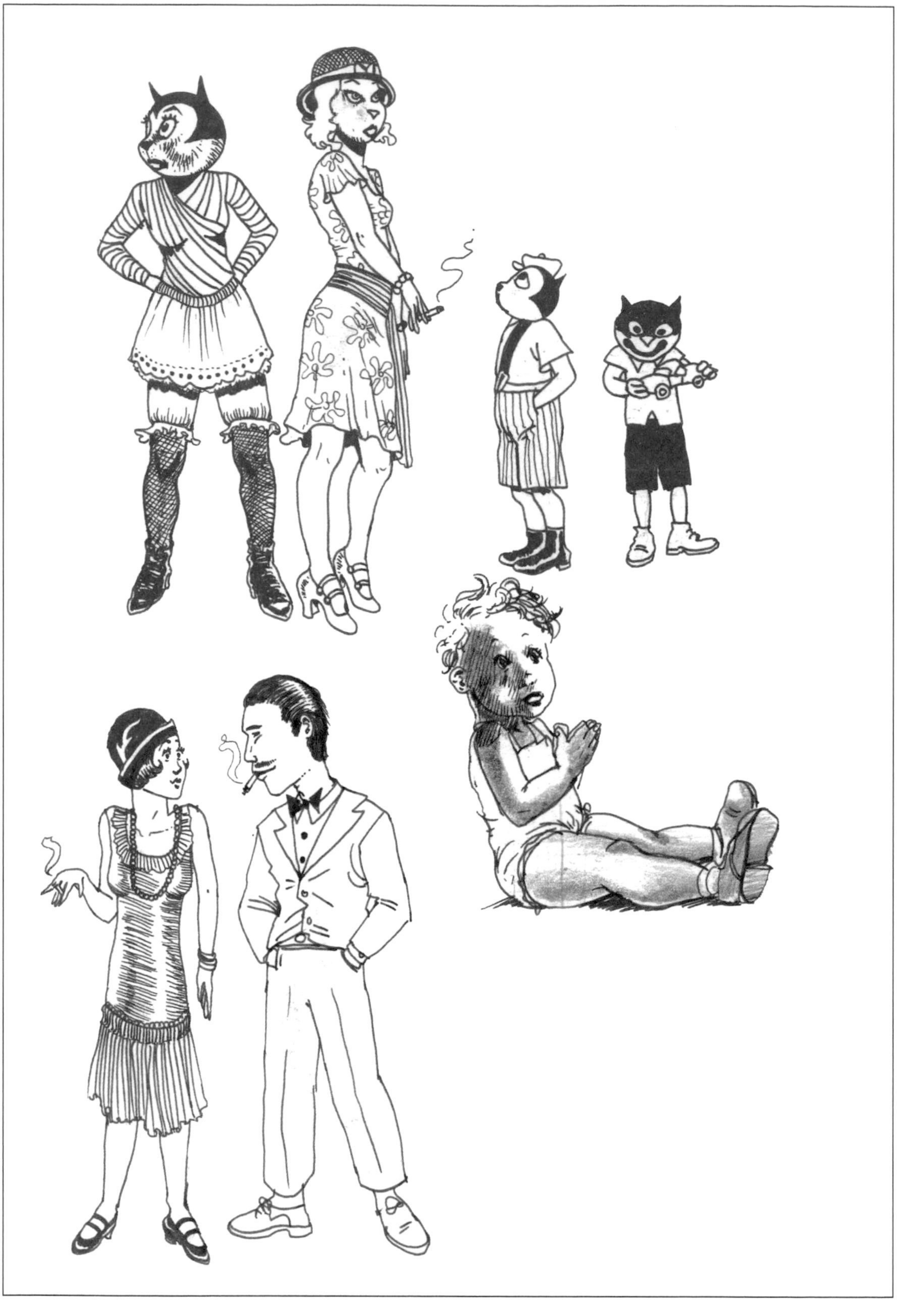

Age 19, Dec., 2000.

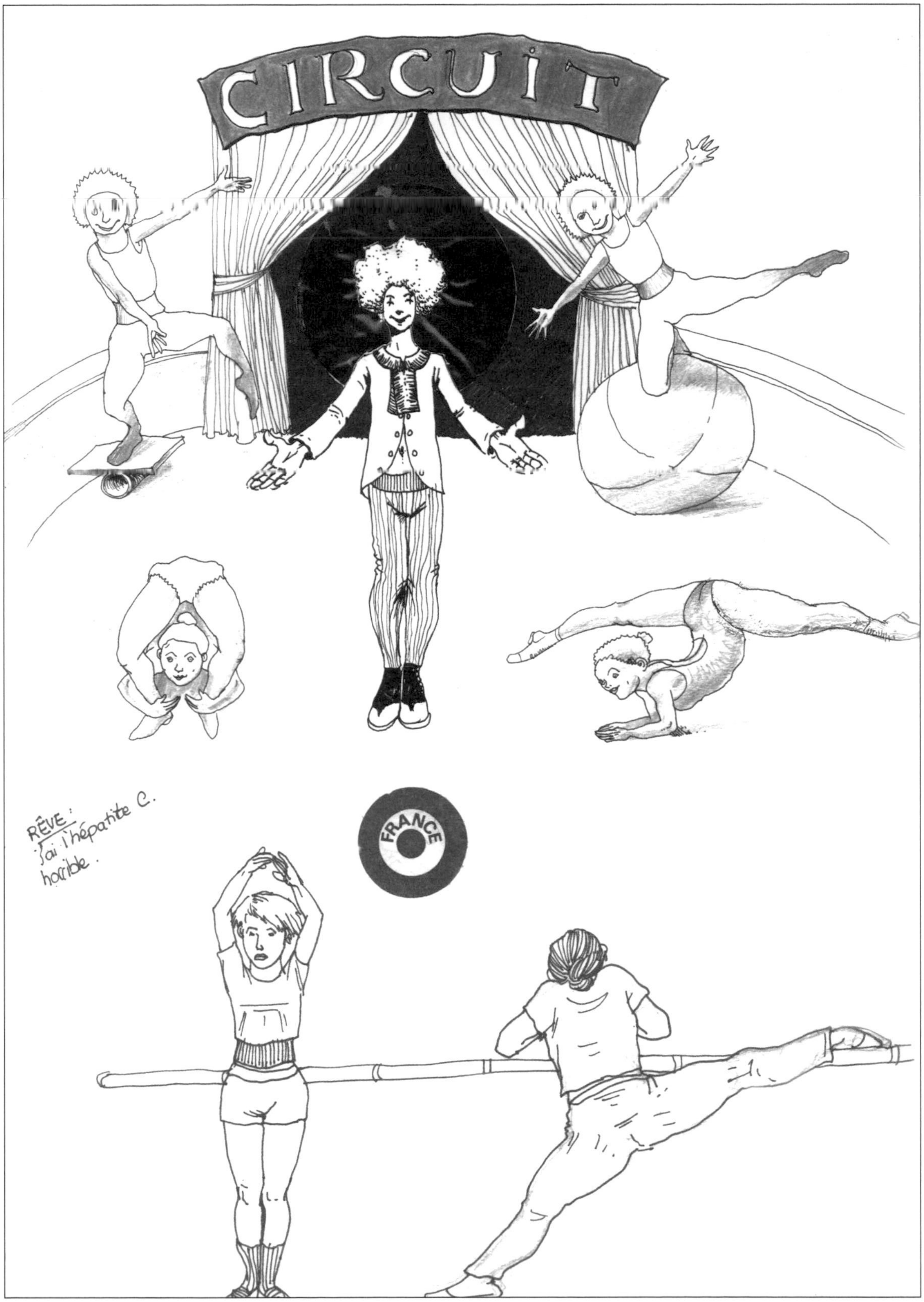
CIRCUIT
RÊVE:
J'ai l'hépatite C.
horrible.
FRANCE

Age 19, Jan., 2001.

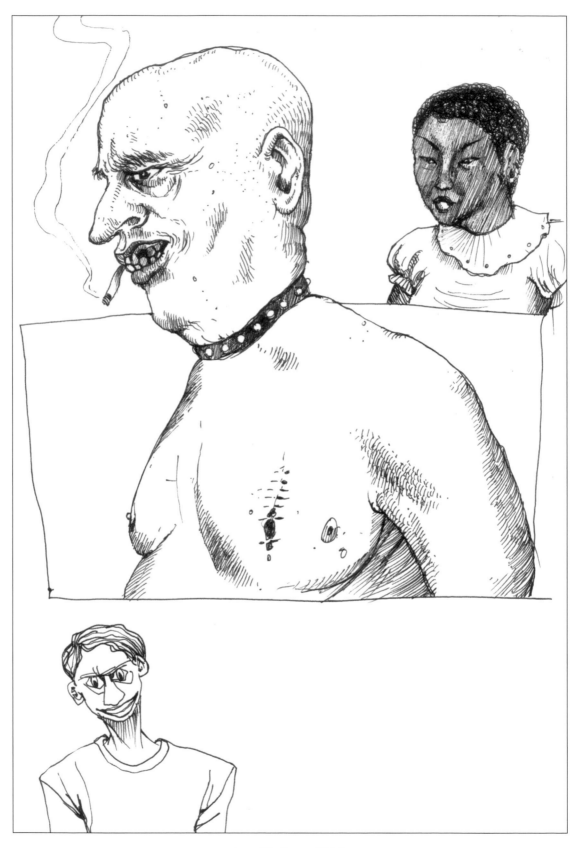

Age 19, June, 2001.

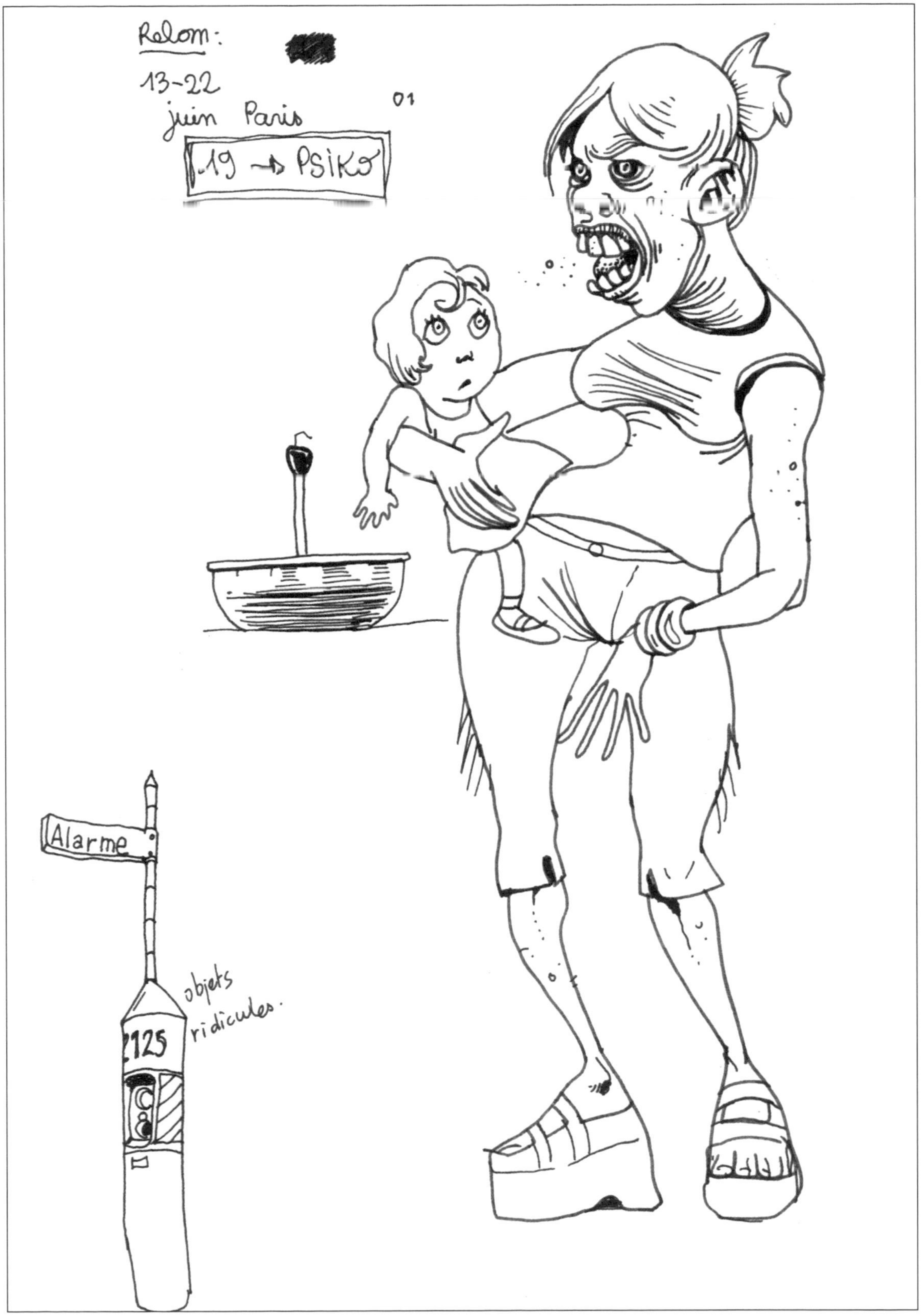
Relom: [redacted]
13-22
juin Paris 01
19 → PSIKO
Alarme
objets ridicules.
2125

Age 19, June, 2001.

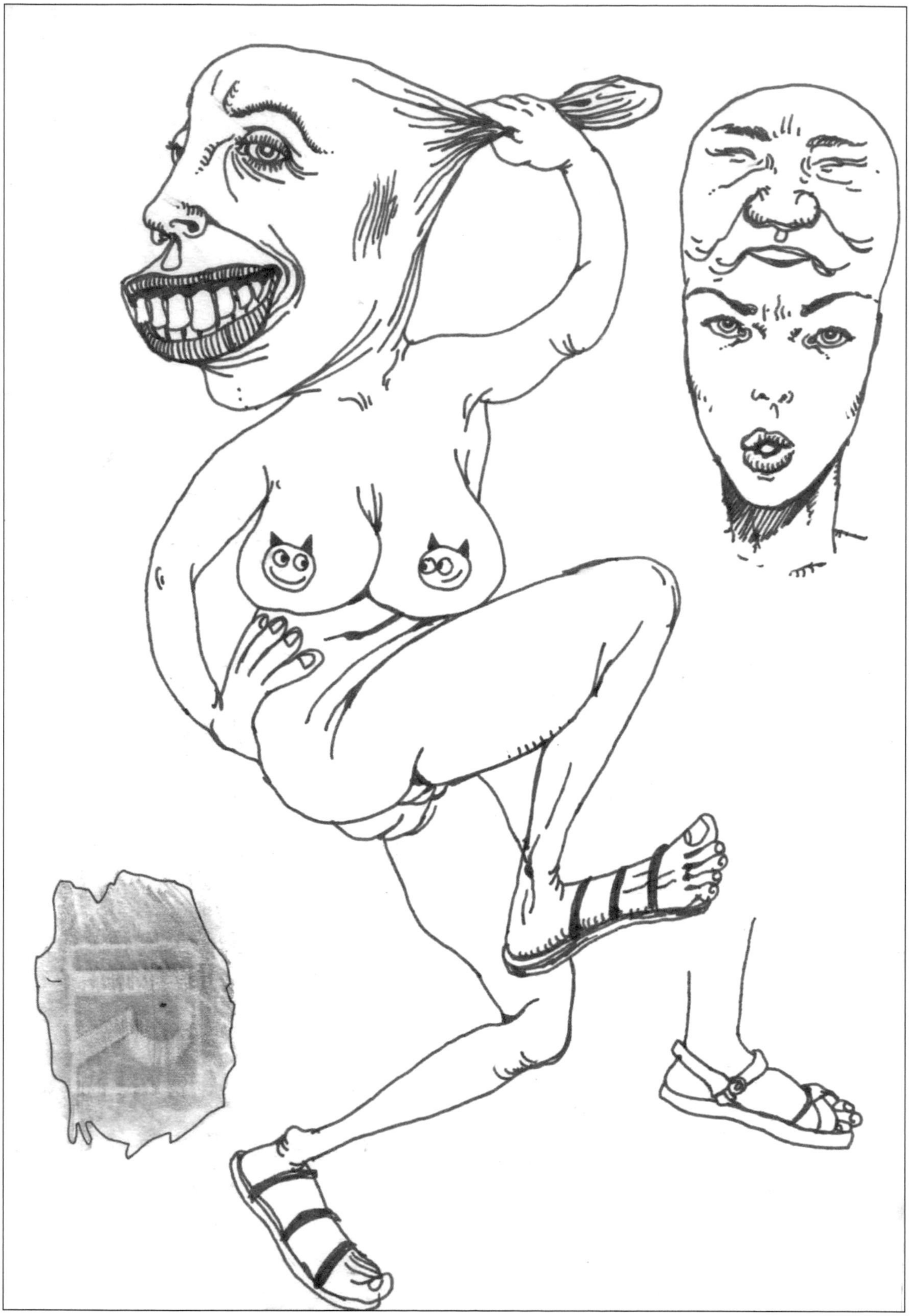

Age 19, July, 2001.

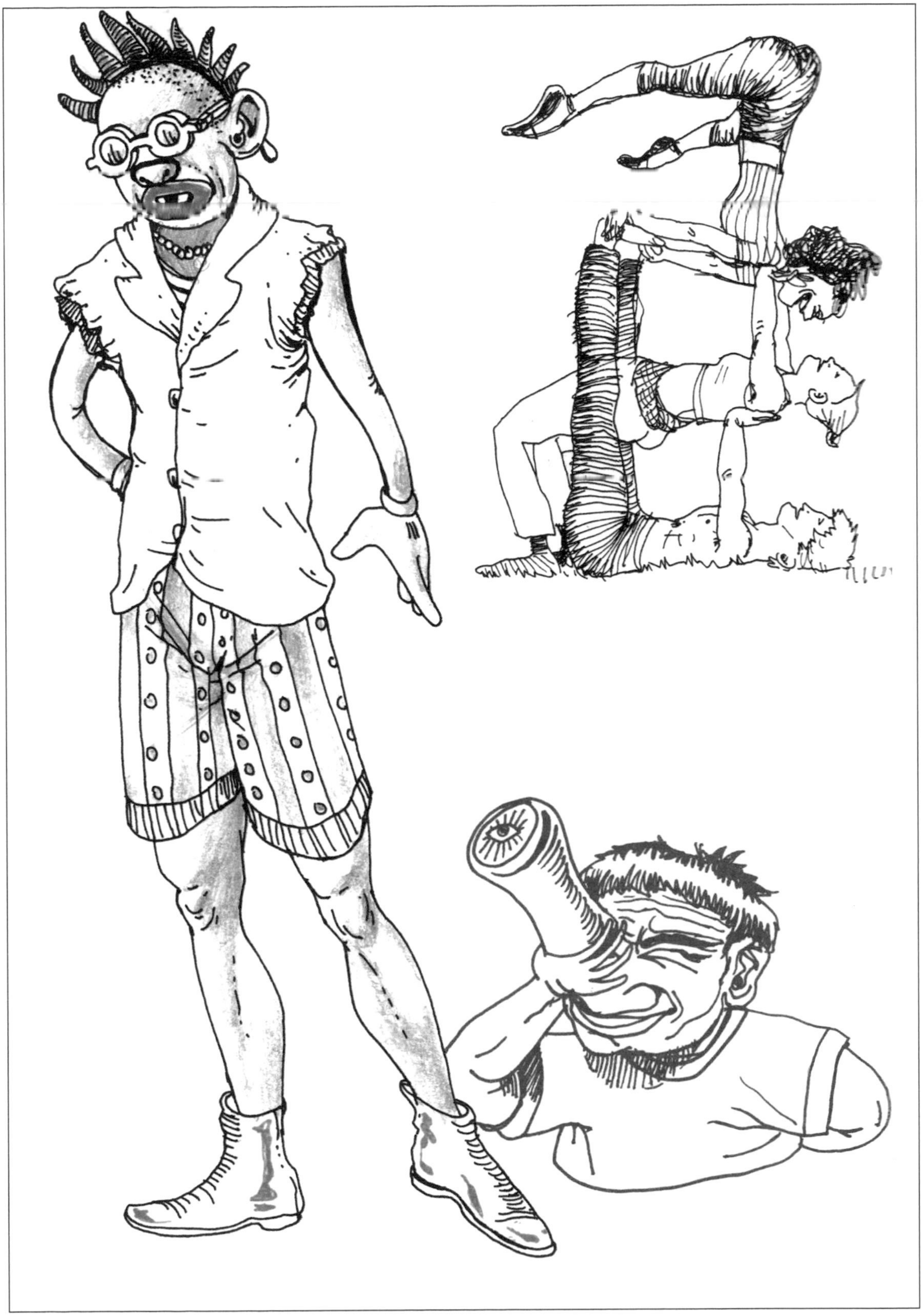

Age 19, July, 2001.

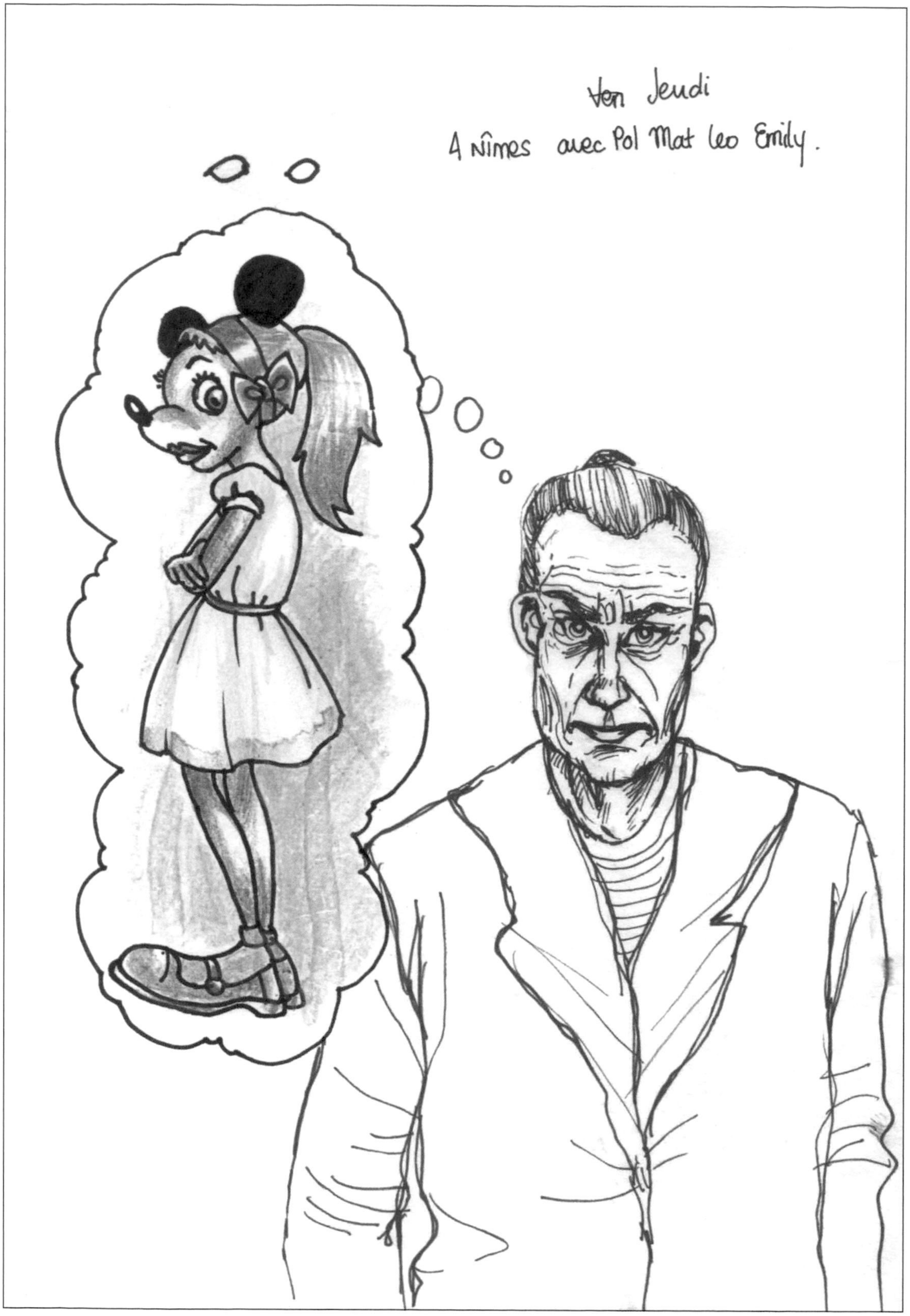
Ven Jeudi
A Nîmes avec Pol Mat Leo Emily.

Age 20, Sept., 2001.

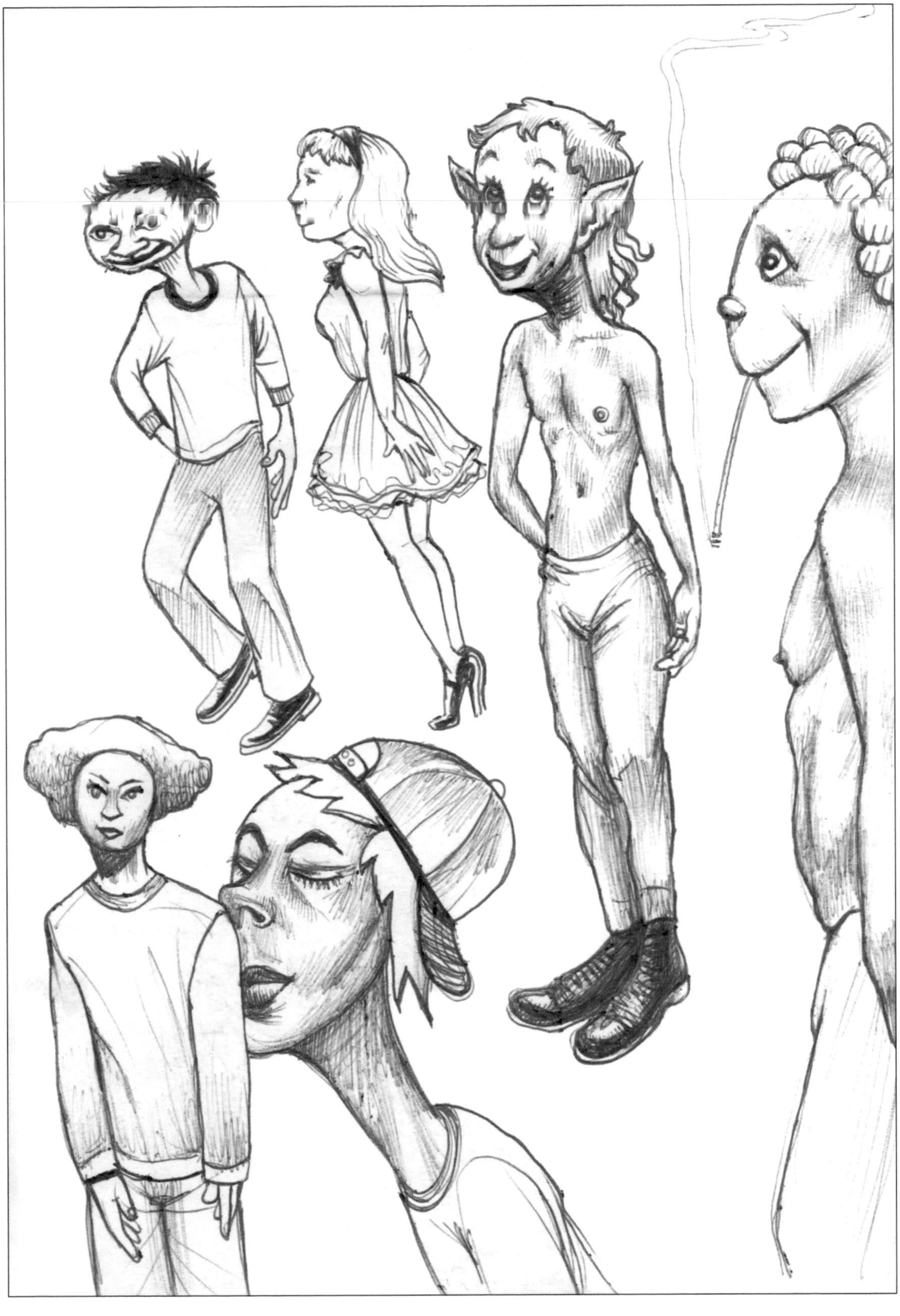

Age 20, Oct., 2001.

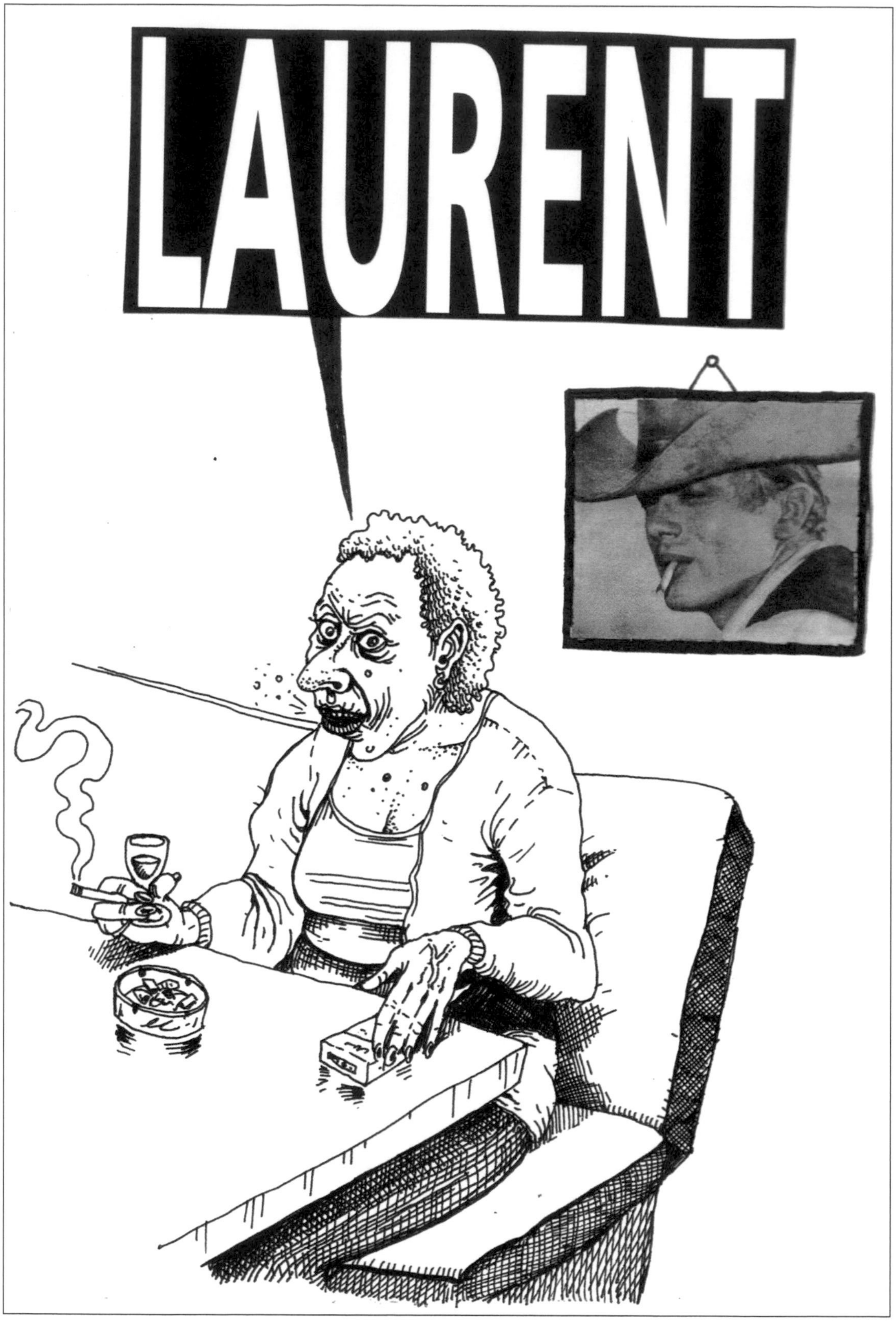
LAURENT

Age 20, Oct., 2001.

Julien. Drawn from life. Age 20, Nov., 2001.

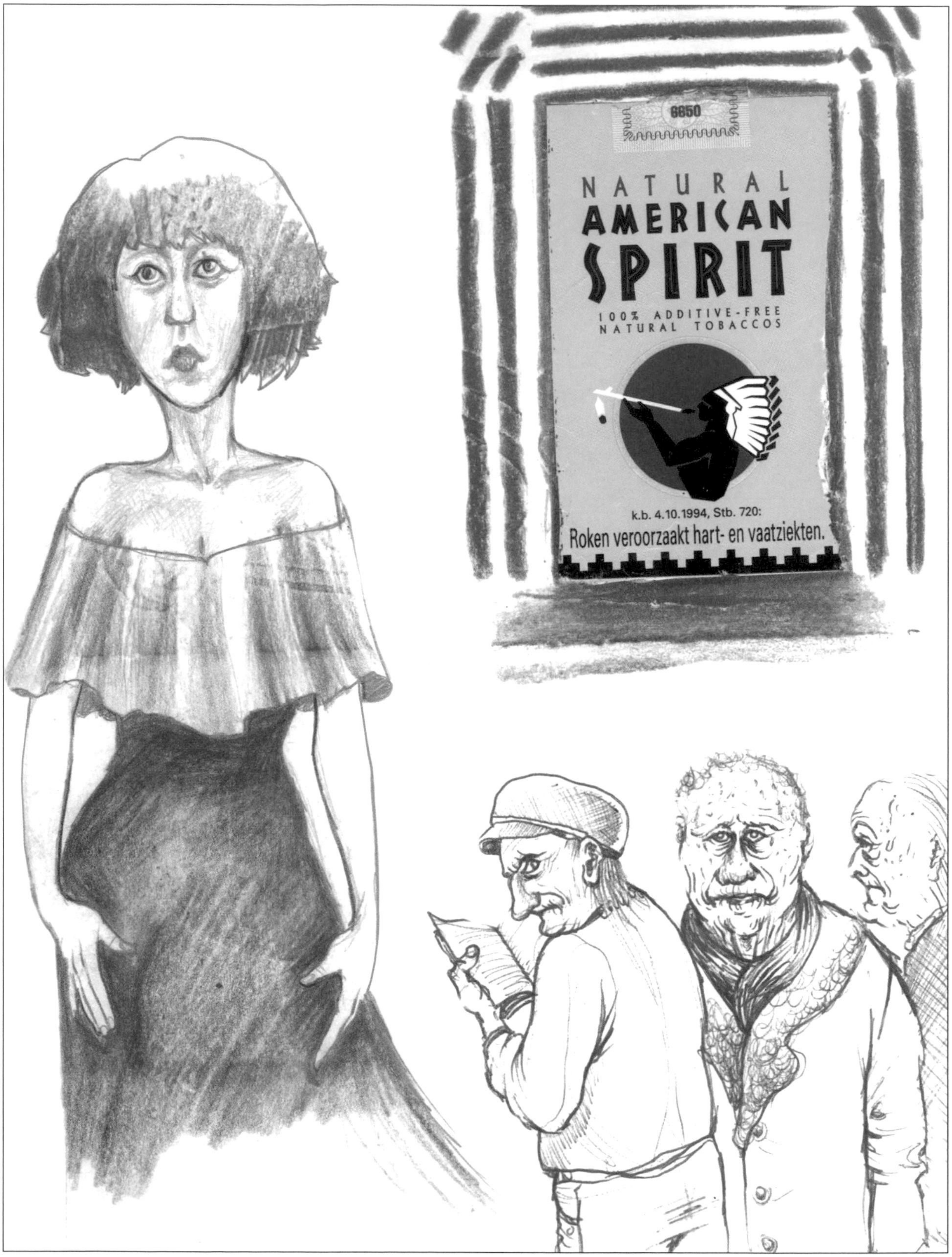
6850
NATURAL
AMERICAN
SPIRIT
100% ADDITIVE-FREE
NATURAL TOBACCOS
k.b. 4.10.1994, Stb. 720:
Roken veroorzaakt hart- en vaatziekten.

Age 20, Nov., 2001.

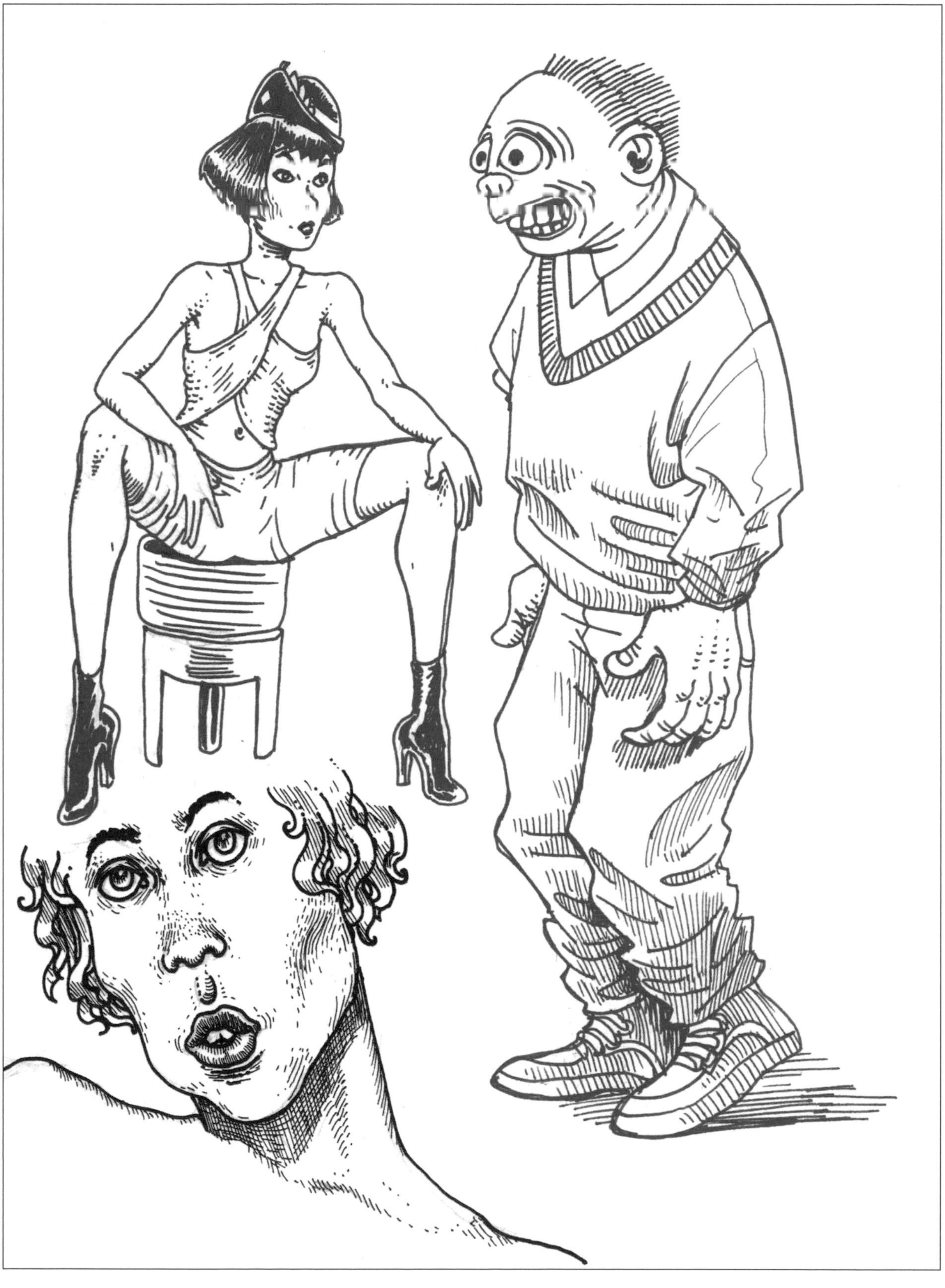

Age 20, Nov., 2001.

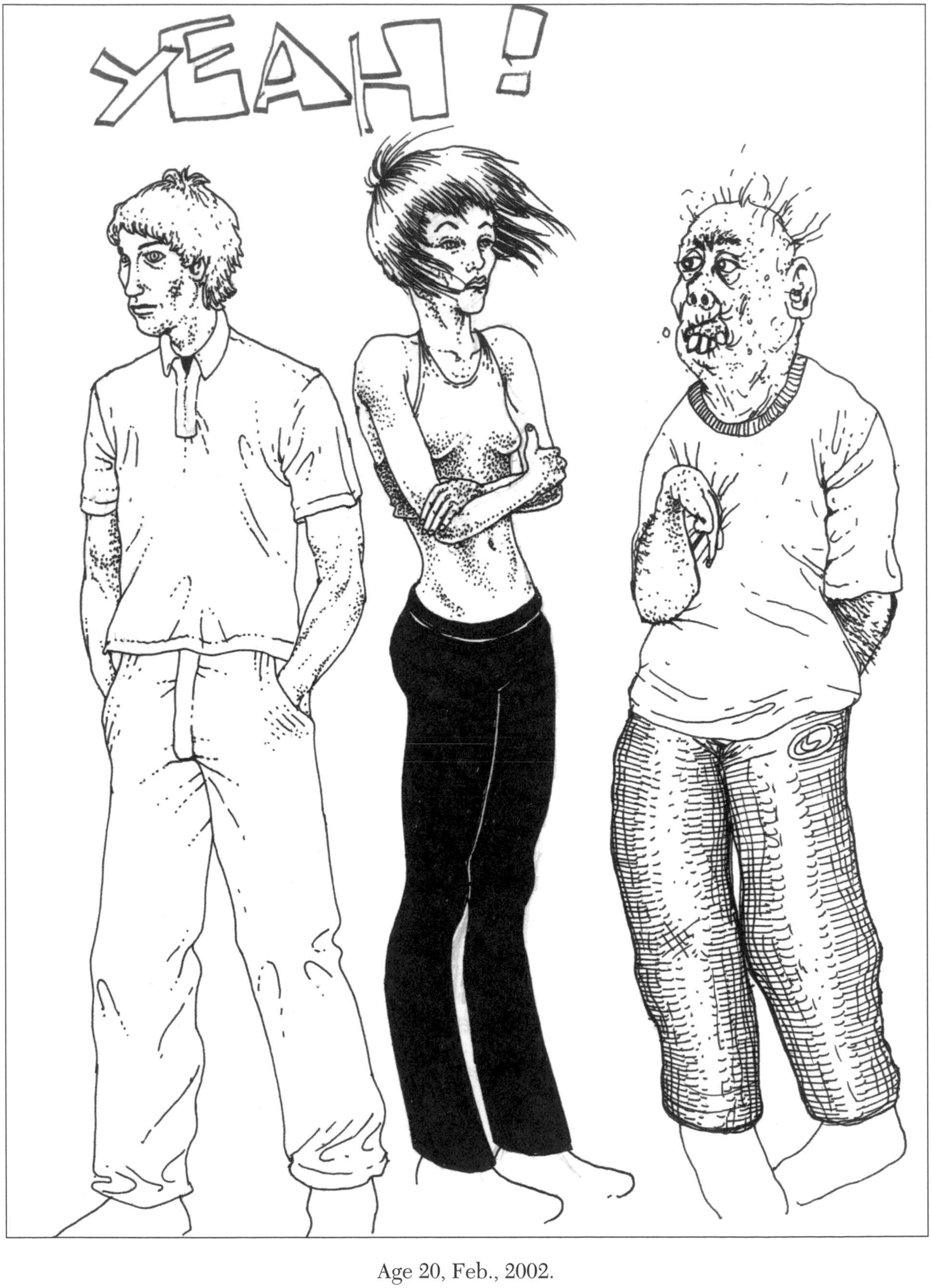
YEAH!

Age 20, Feb., 2002.

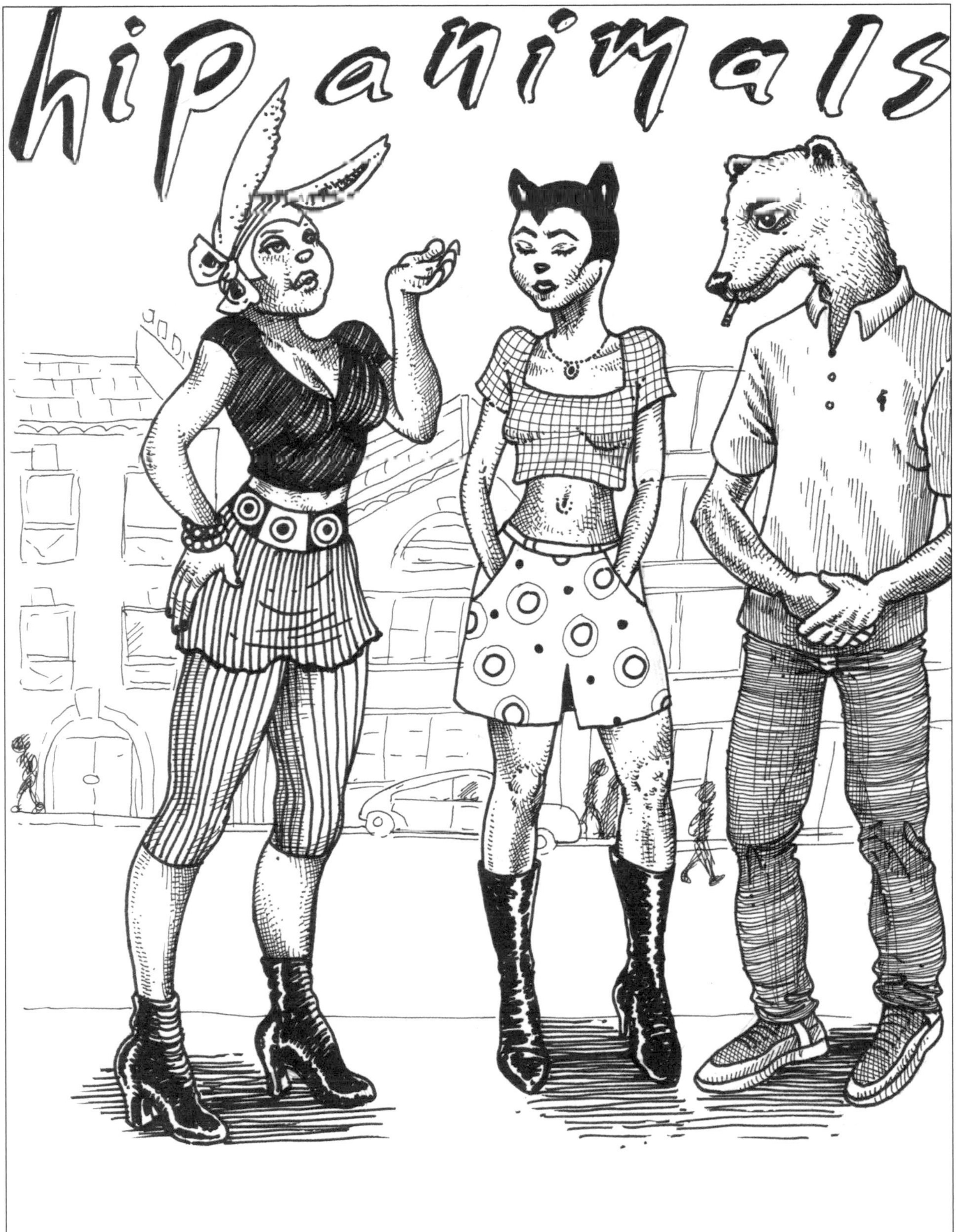
hip animals

Age 20, Feb., 2002.

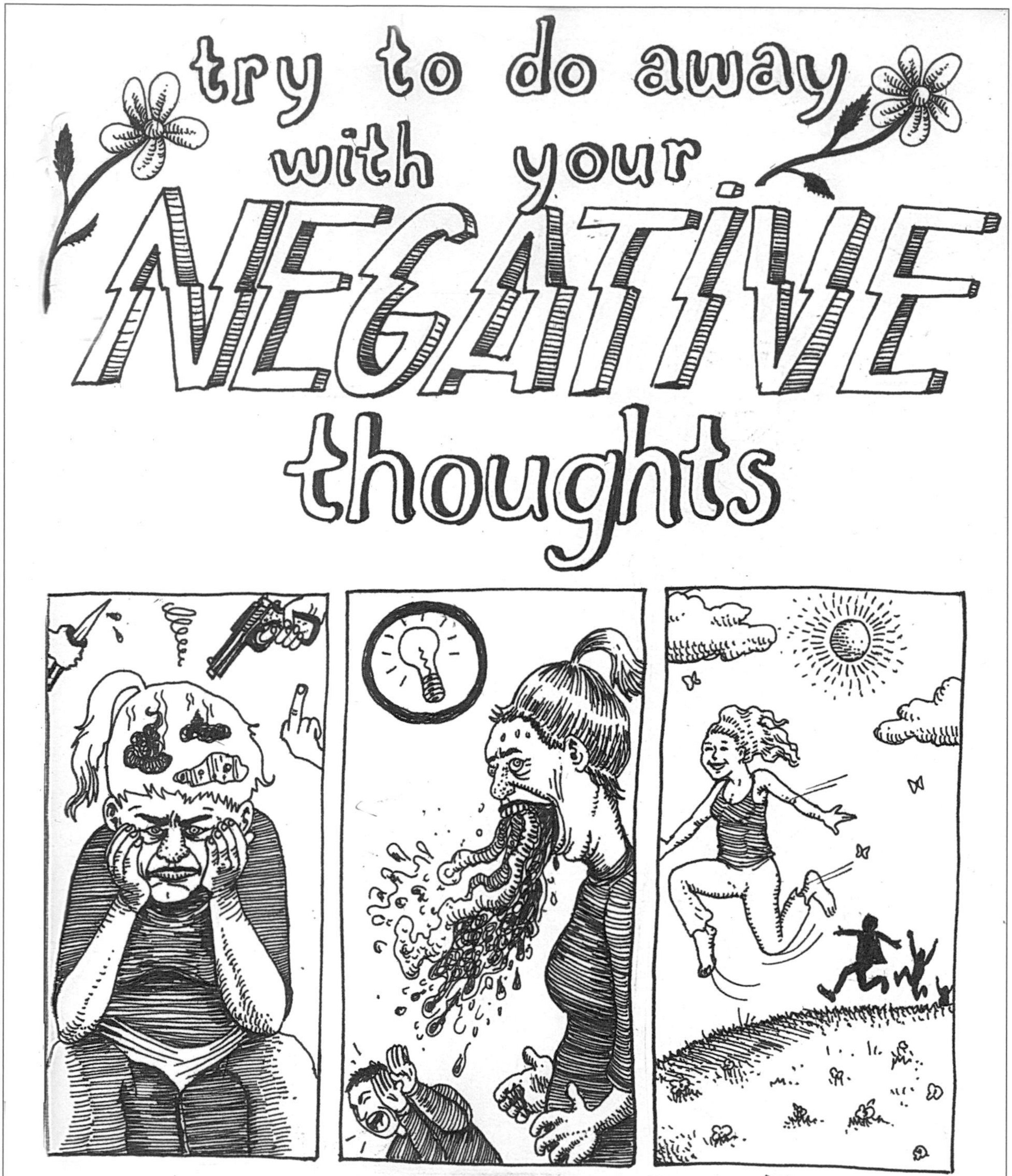
try to do away
with your
NEGATIVE
thoughts
1.
2.
3.

Age 20, Feb., 2002.

LES GUEUX DU XXIe

Age 20, March, 2002.

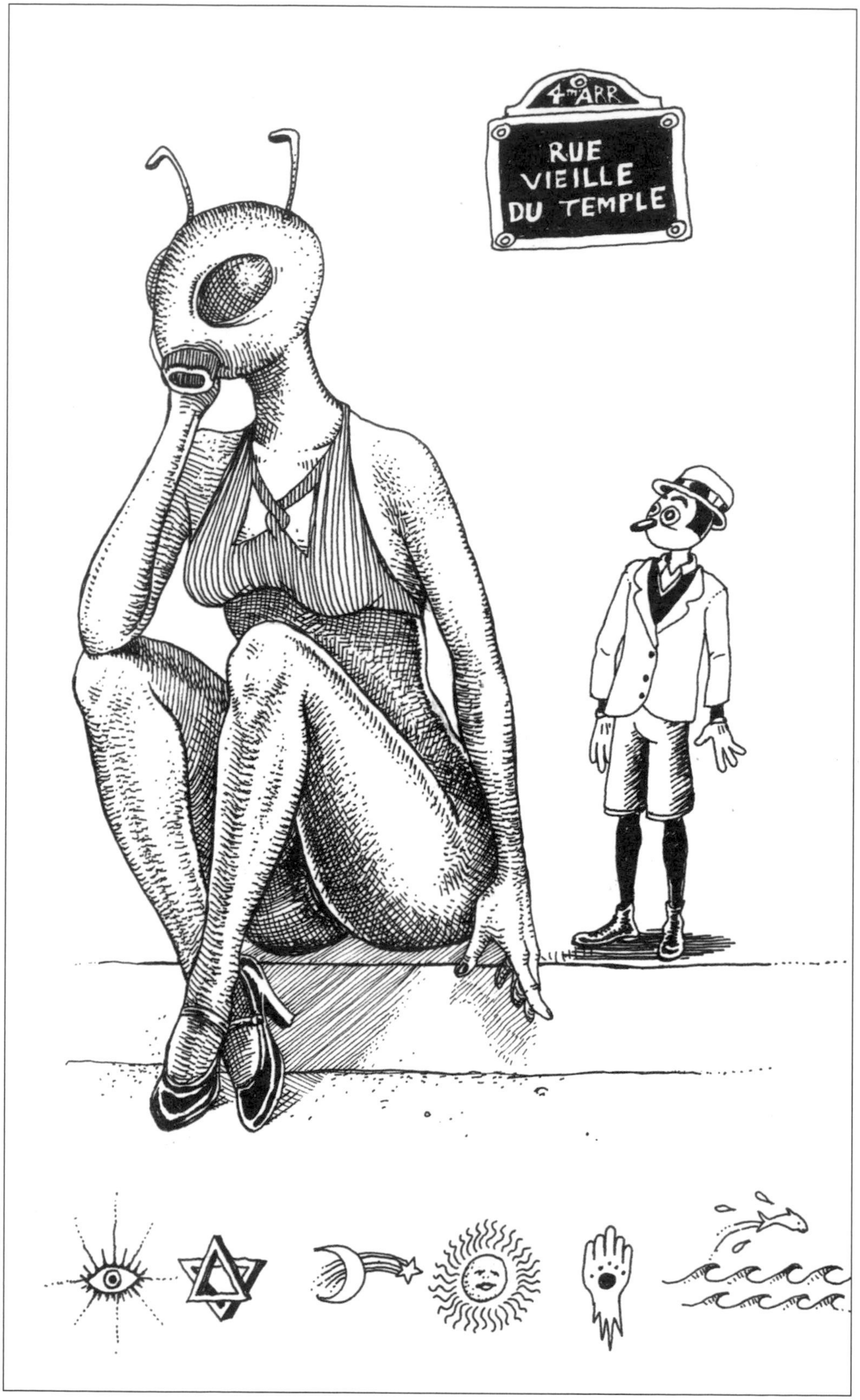
4me ARR
RUE
VIEILLE
DU TEMPLE

Age 20, May, 2002.

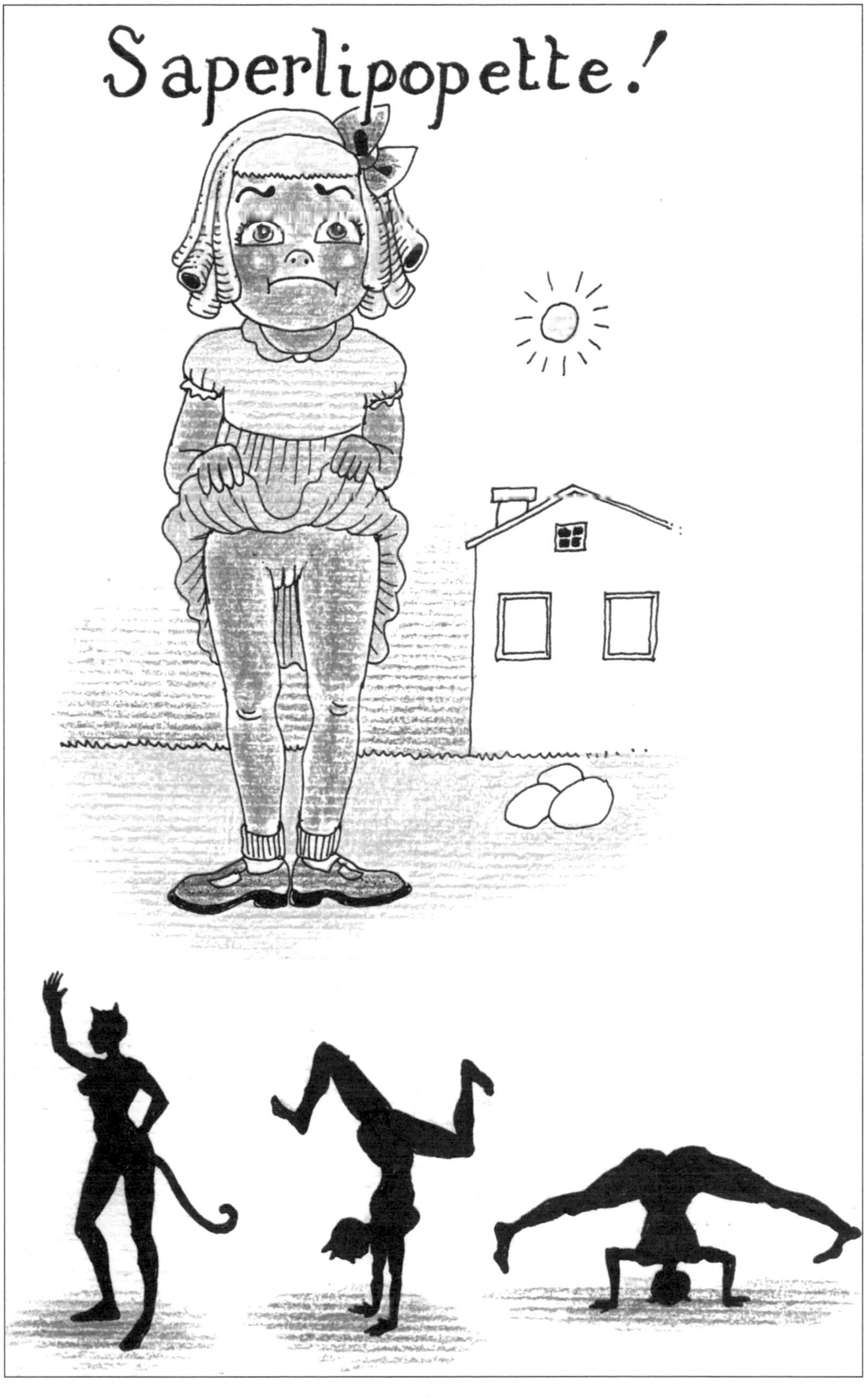
Saperlipopette!

Age 20, May, 2002.

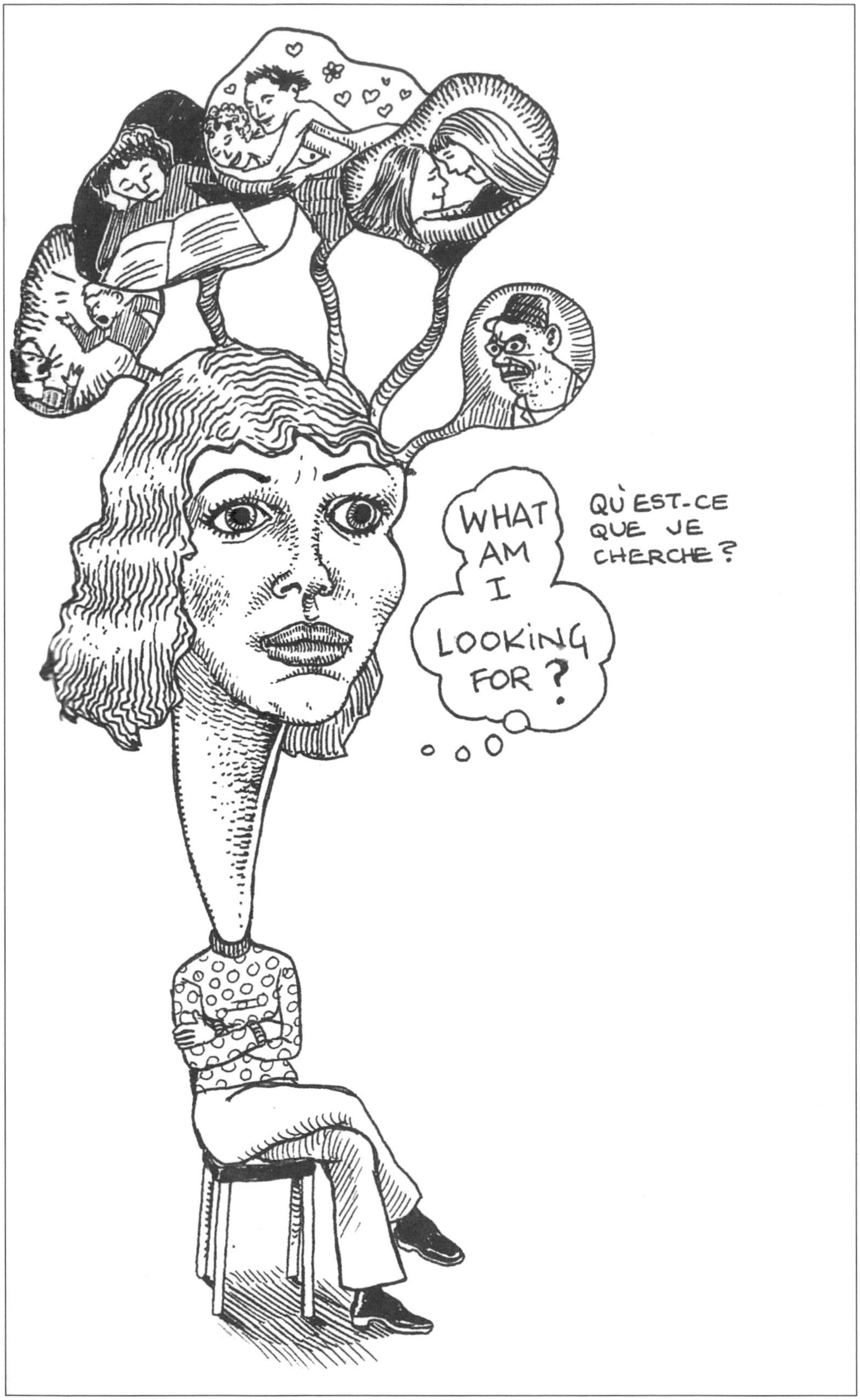
WHAT AM I LOOKING FOR?
QU'EST-CE QUE JE CHERCHE?

Age 20, June, 2002.

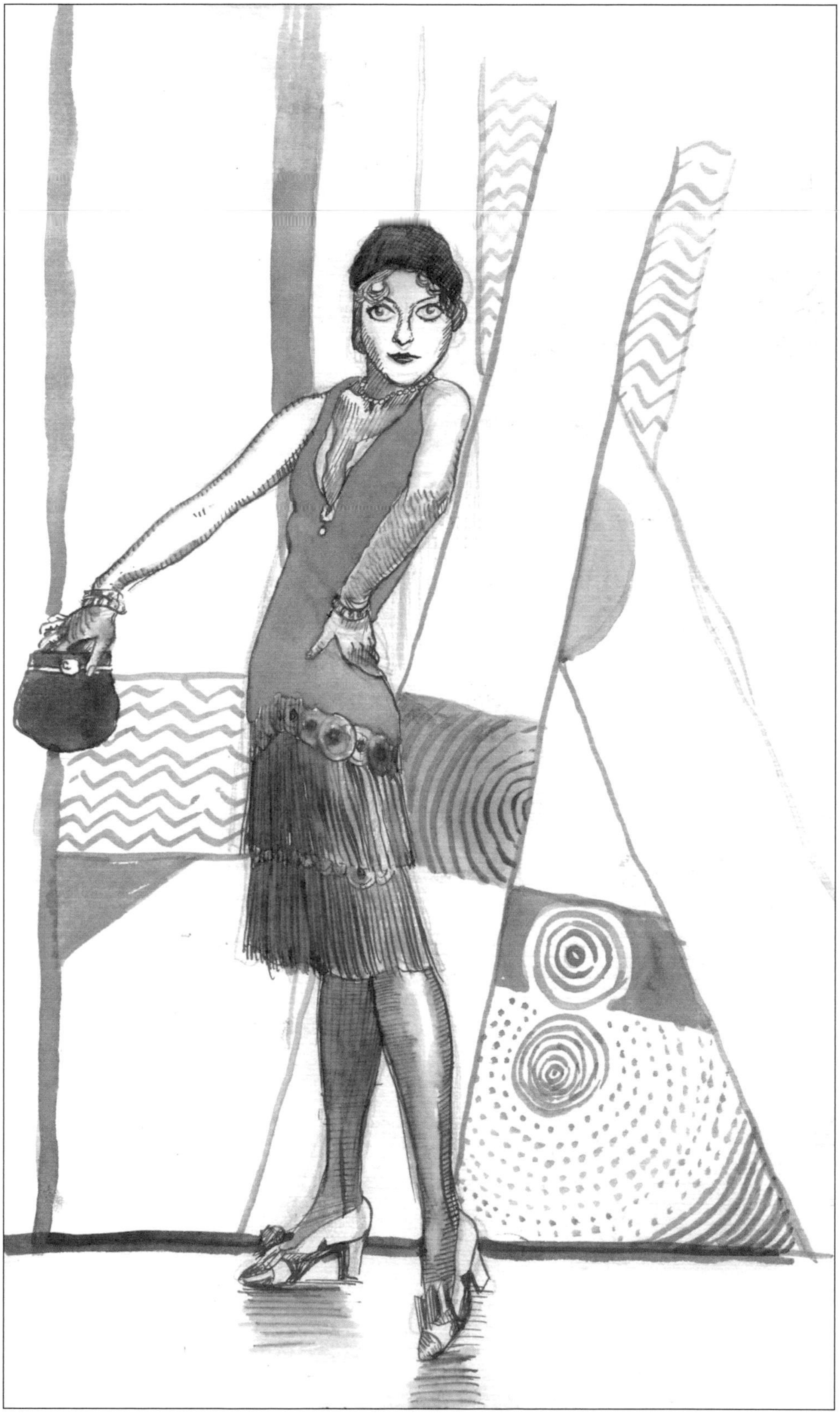

Age 20, Aug., 2002.

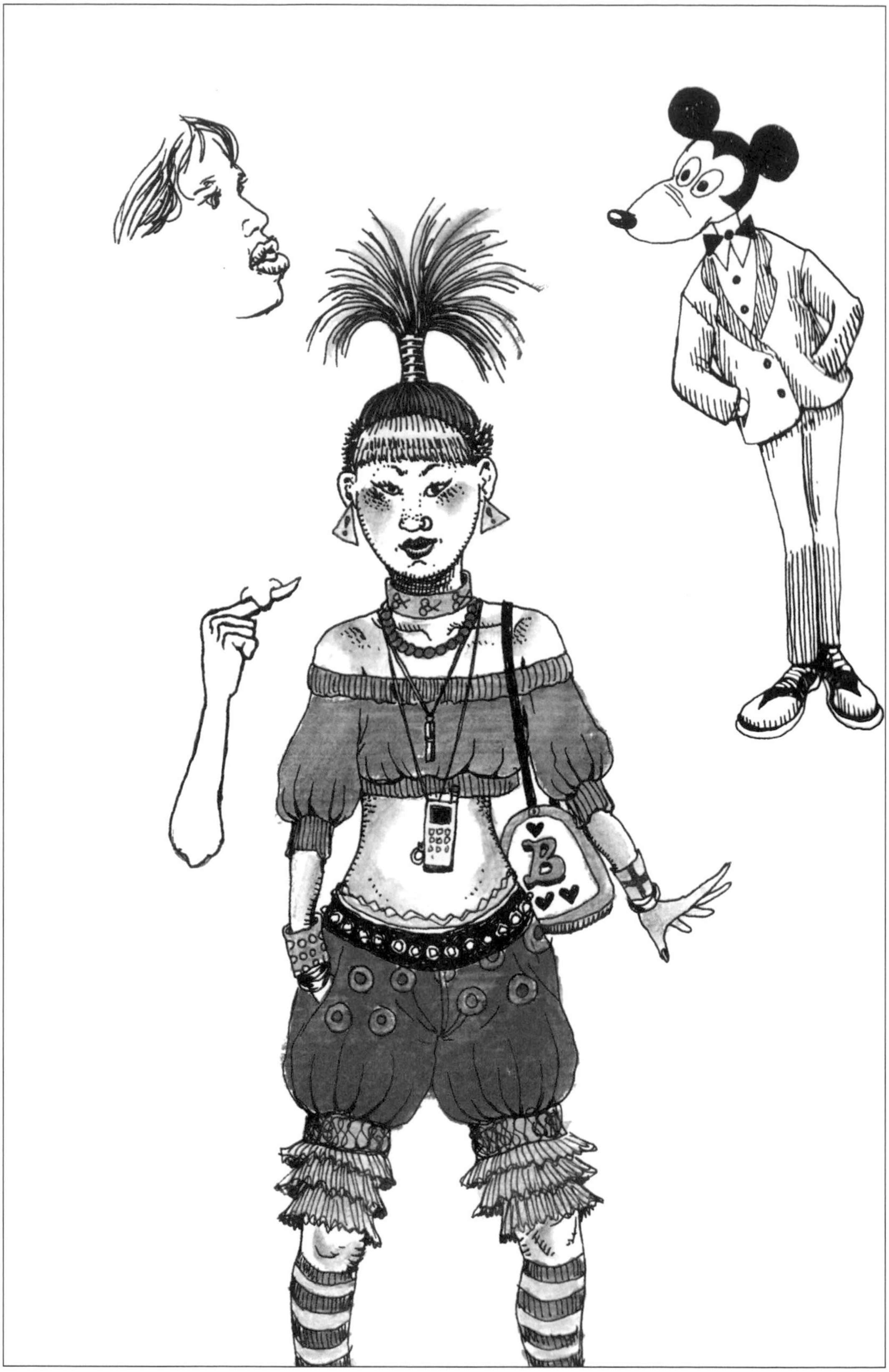

Age 21, Sept., 2002.

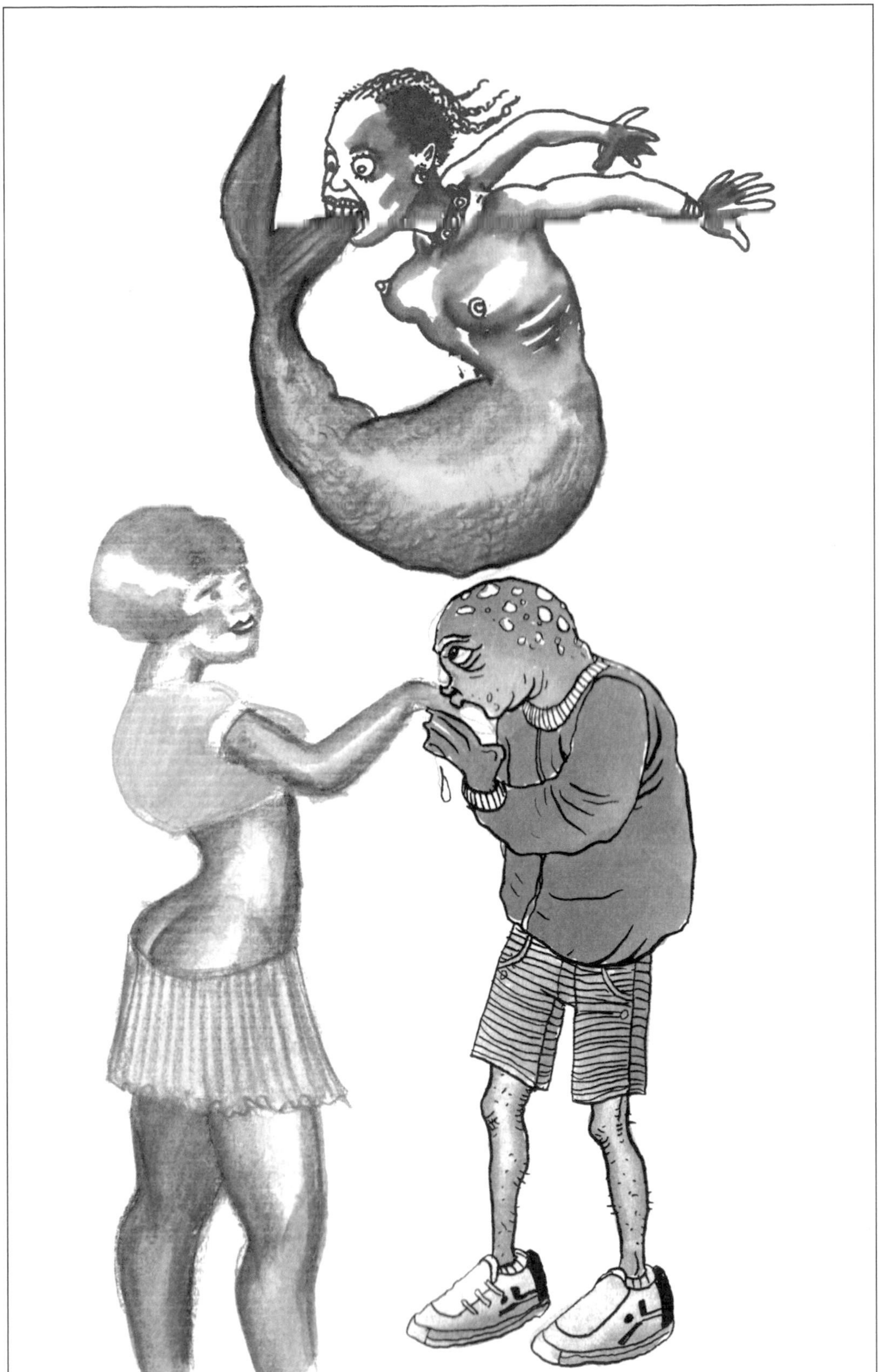

Age 21, Sept., 2002.

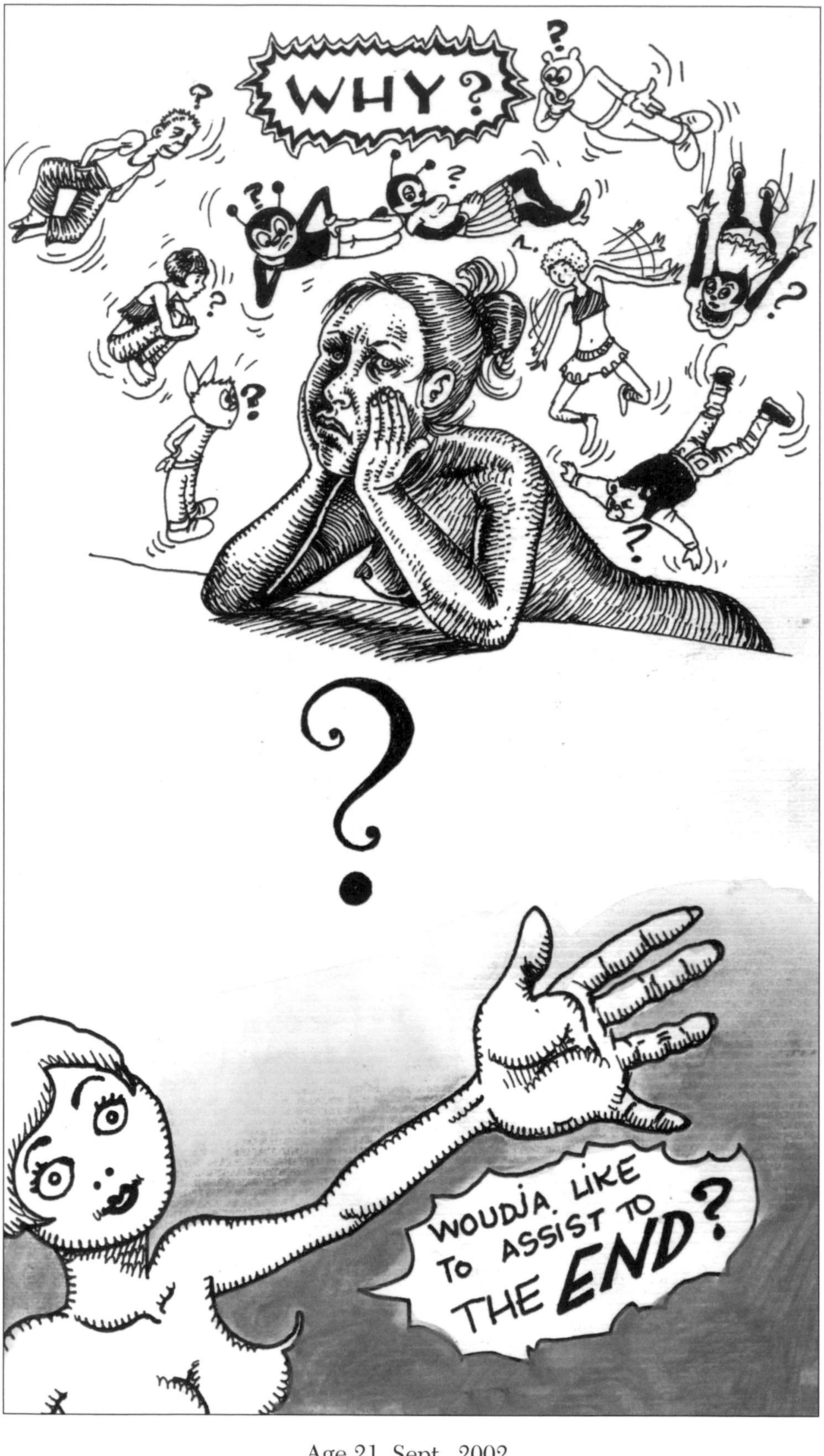
WHY?
WOUDJA LIKE TO ASSIST TO THE END?

Age 21, Sept., 2002.

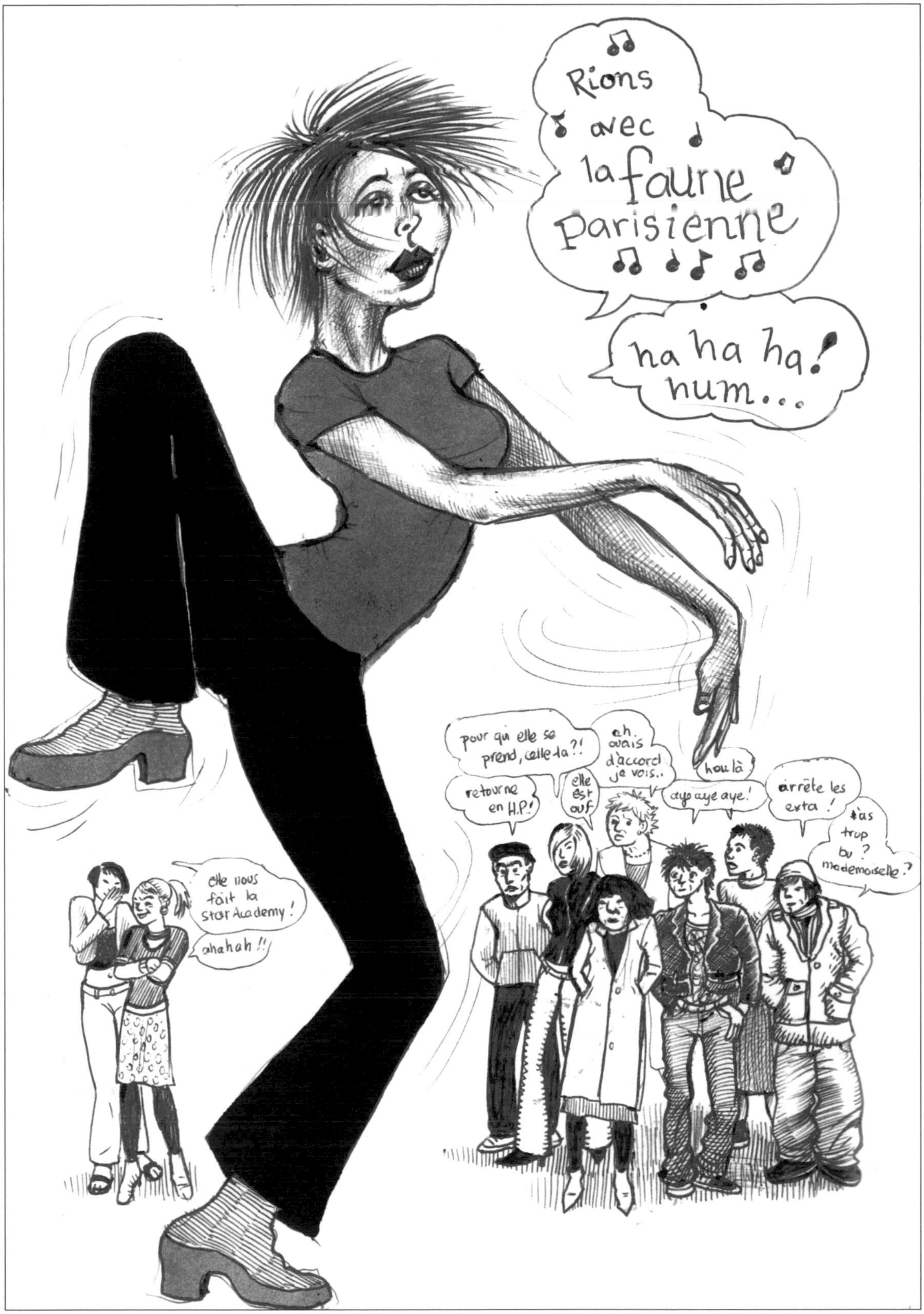
Rions avec la faune parisienne
ha ha ha! hum...
elle nous fait la Star Academy !
ahahah !!
pour qui elle se prend, celle-la ?!
retourne en H.P!
elle est ouf
eh. ouais d'accord je vois..
houlà
aye aye aye!
arrête les exta !
t'as trop bu ? mademoiselle ?

Age 21, Nov., 2002.

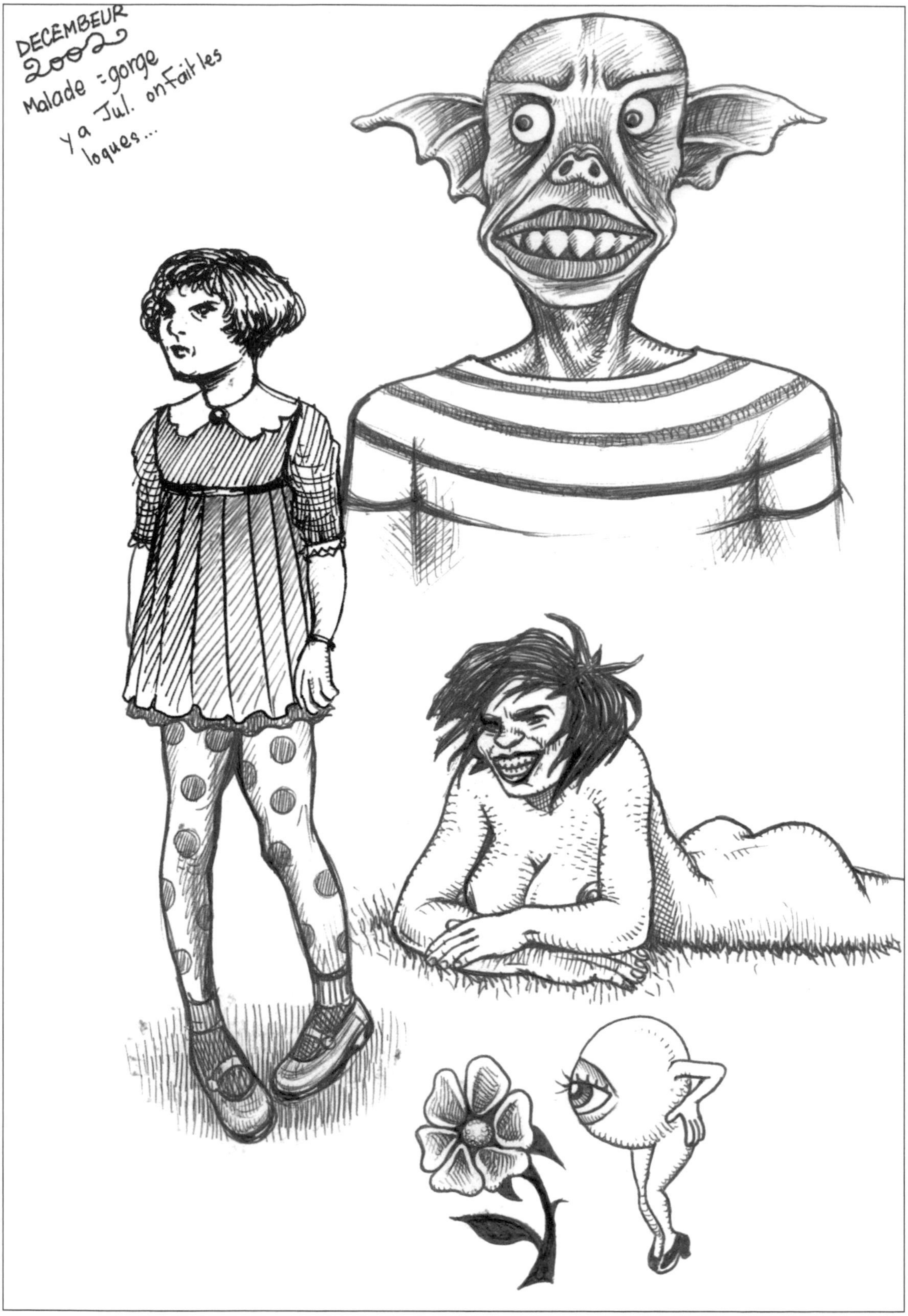
DECEMBEUR
2002
Malade =gorge
y a Jul. on fait les
loques...

Age 21, Dec., 2002.

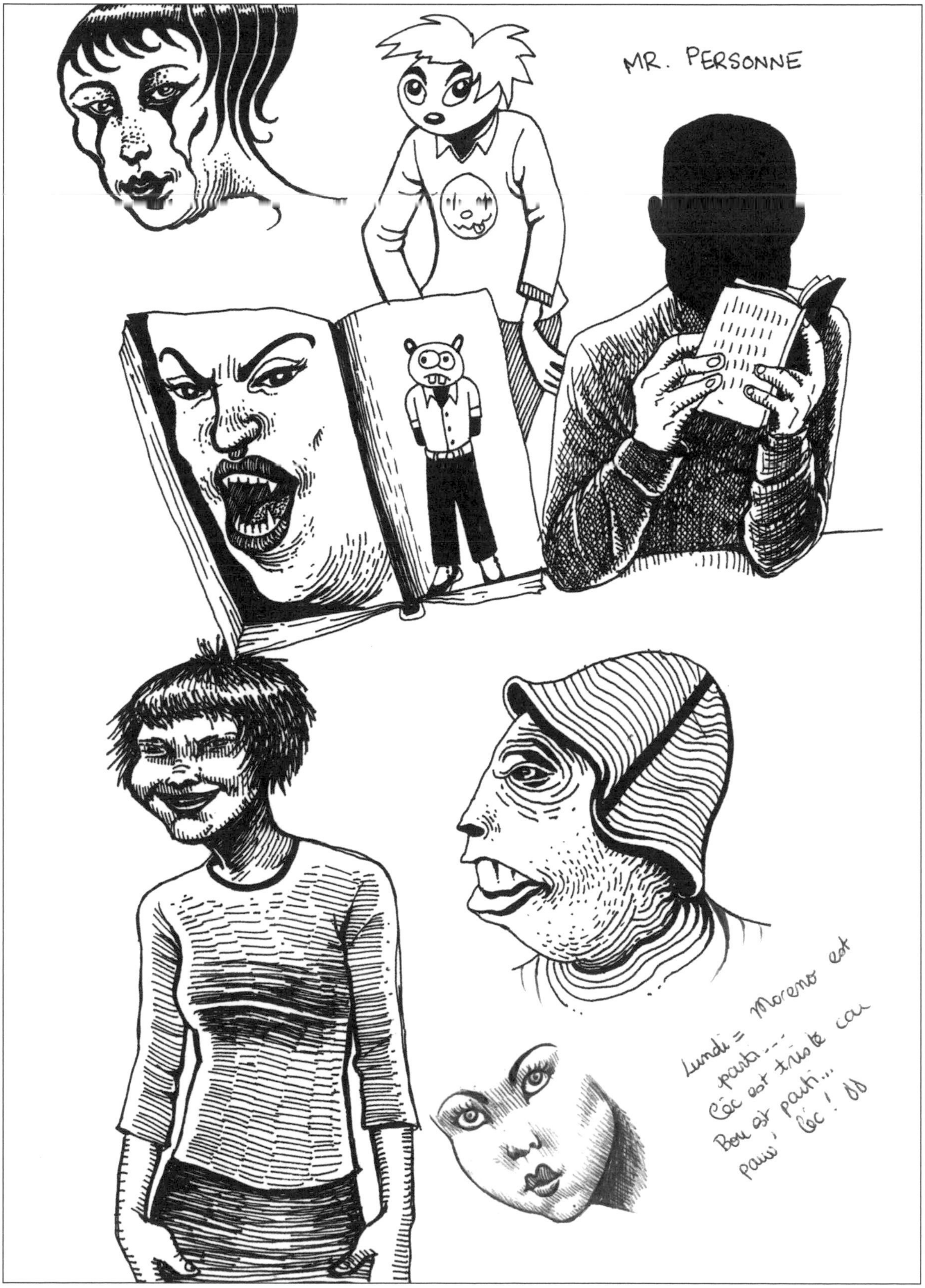
MR. PERSONNE
Lundi = Moreno est
parti...
Céc est triste car
Ben est parti...
pauv' Céc!

Age 21, Dec., 2002.

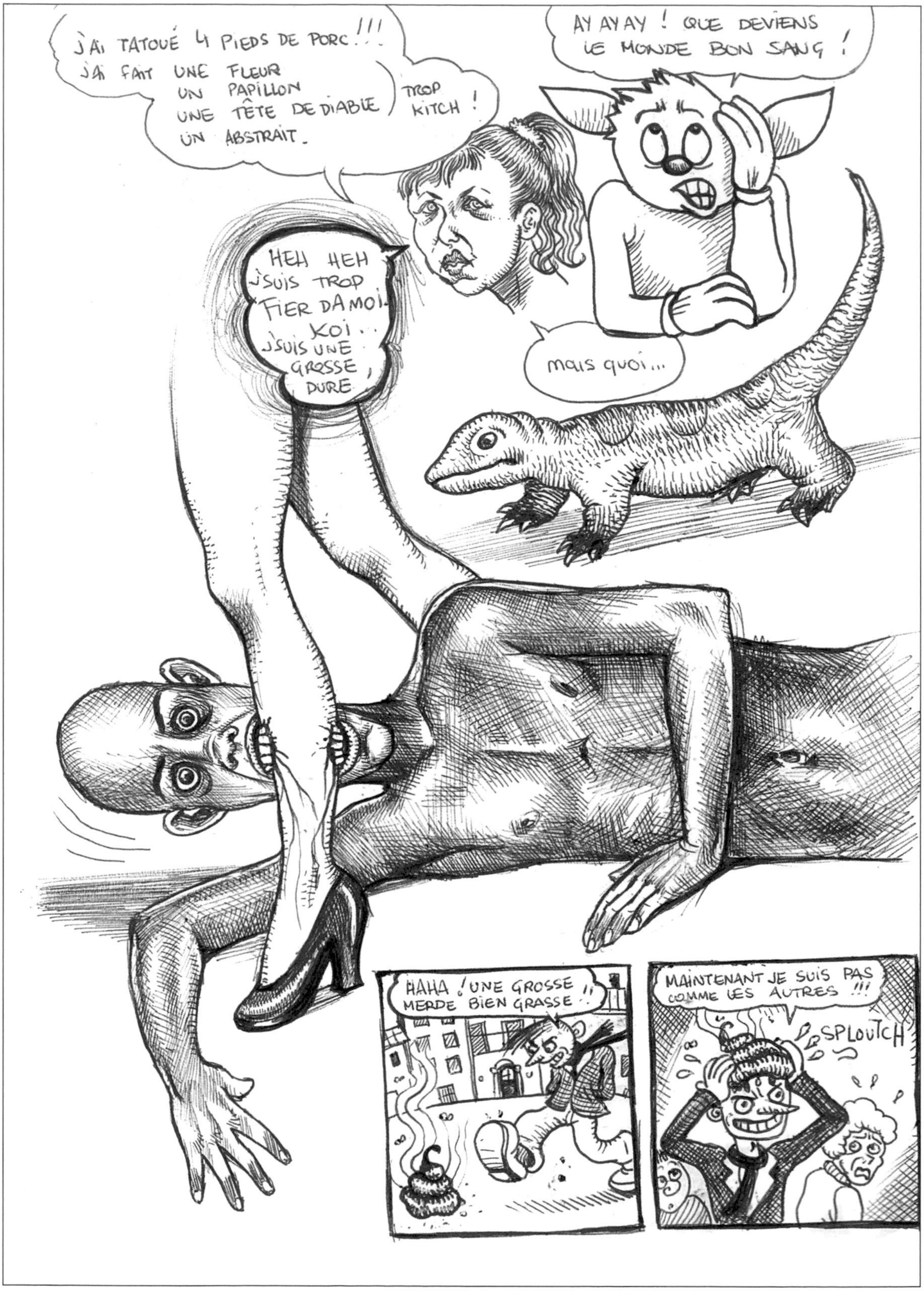
J'AI TATOUÉ 4 PIEDS DE PORC !!!
J'AI FAIT UNE FLEUR
UN PAPILLON
UNE TÊTE DE DIABLE
UN ABSTRAIT.
TROP KITCH !
AY AY AY ! QUE DEVIENS LE MONDE BON SANG !
HEH HEH J'SUIS TROP FIER DA MOI KOI... J'SUIS UNE GROSSE DURE.
mais quoi...
HAHA ! UNE GROSSE MERDE BIEN GRASSE !!
MAINTENANT JE SUIS PAS COMME LES AUTRES !!!
SPLOUTCH

Age 21, Dec., 2002.

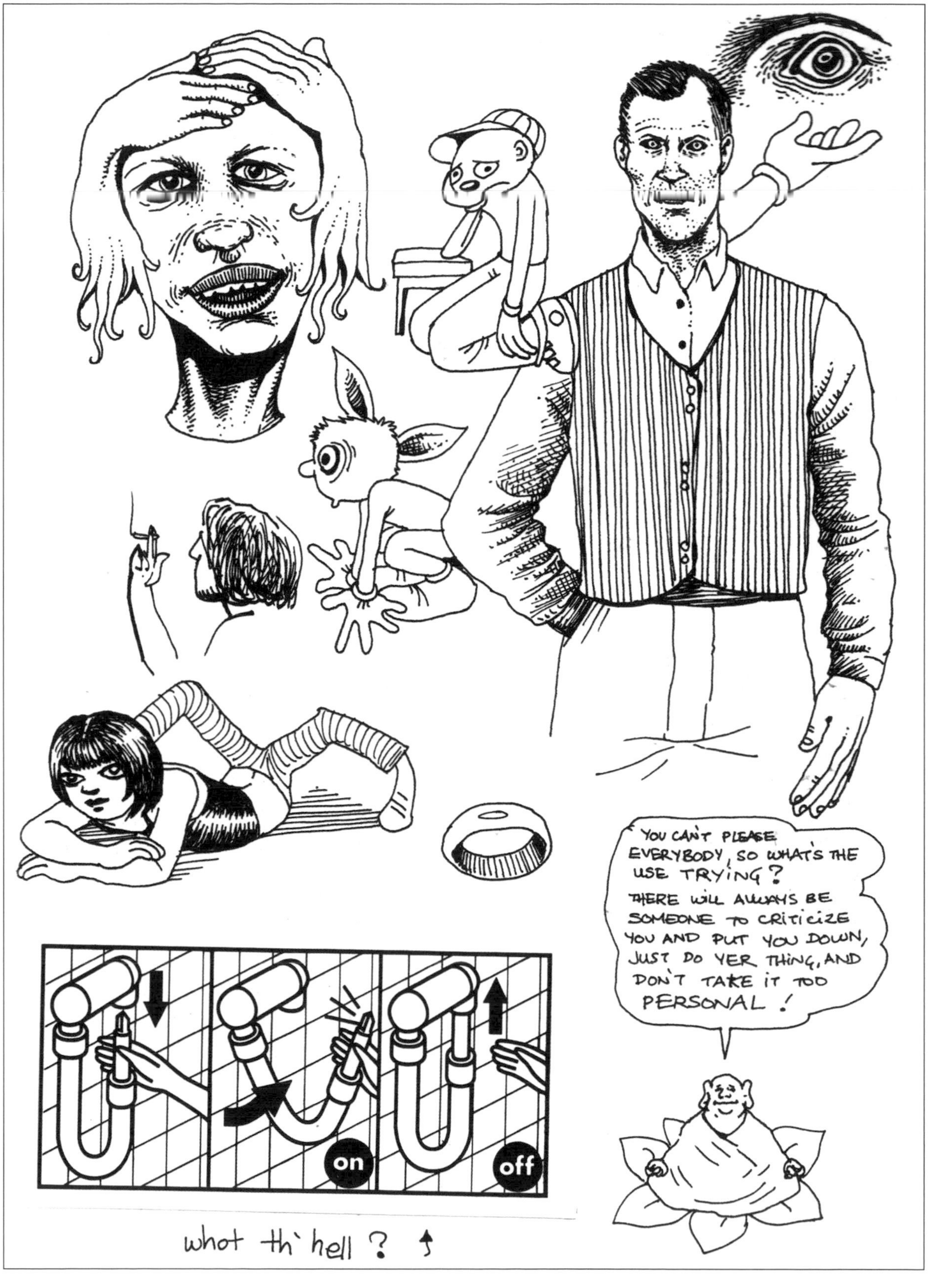
YOU CAN'T PLEASE EVERYBODY, SO WHAT'S THE USE TRYING?
THERE WILL ALWAYS BE SOMEONE TO CRITICIZE YOU AND PUT YOU DOWN, JUST DO YER THING, AND DON'T TAKE IT TOO PERSONAL!
on
off
whot th' hell ?

Age 21, Dec., 2002.

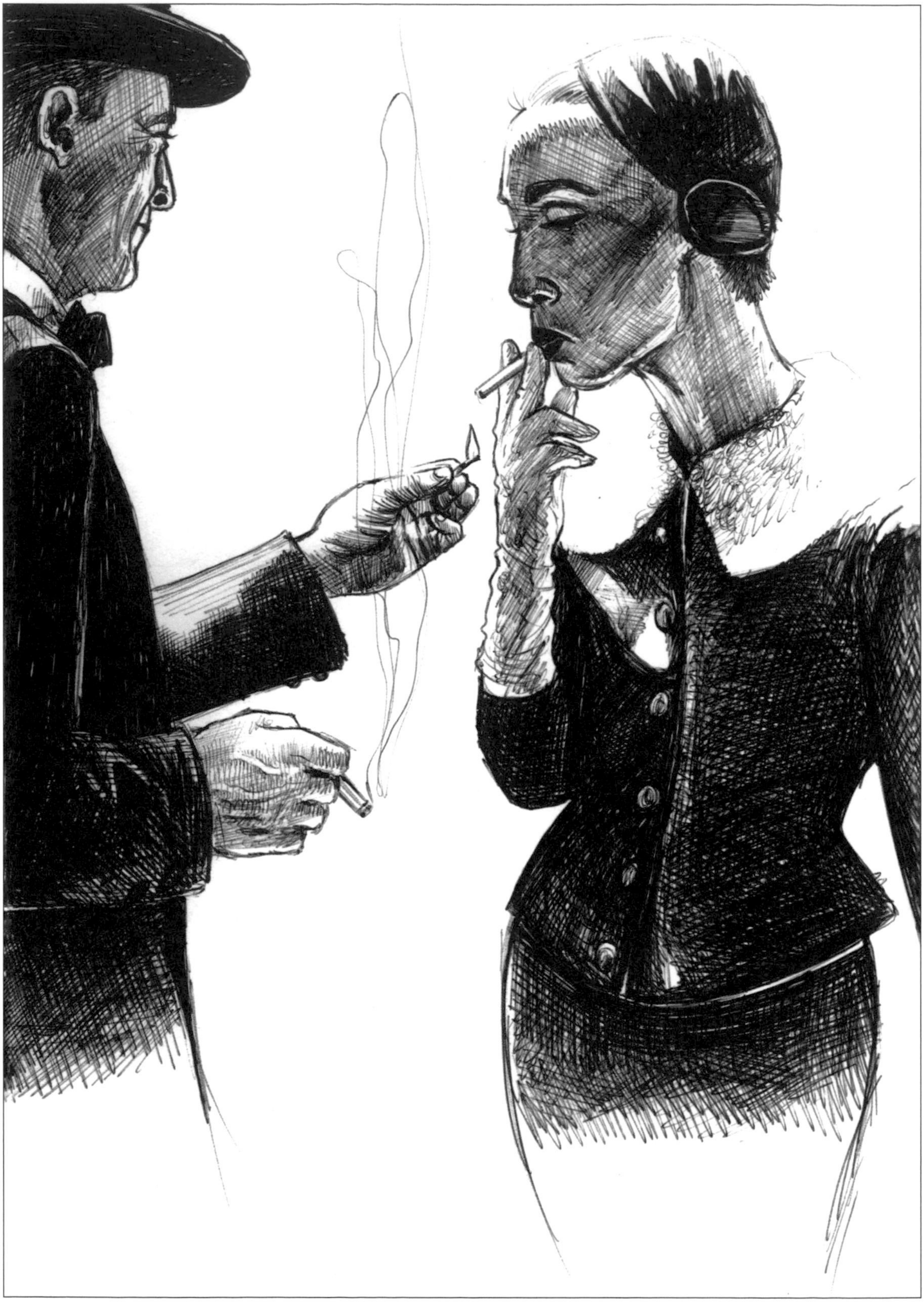

Age 21, Feb., 2003.

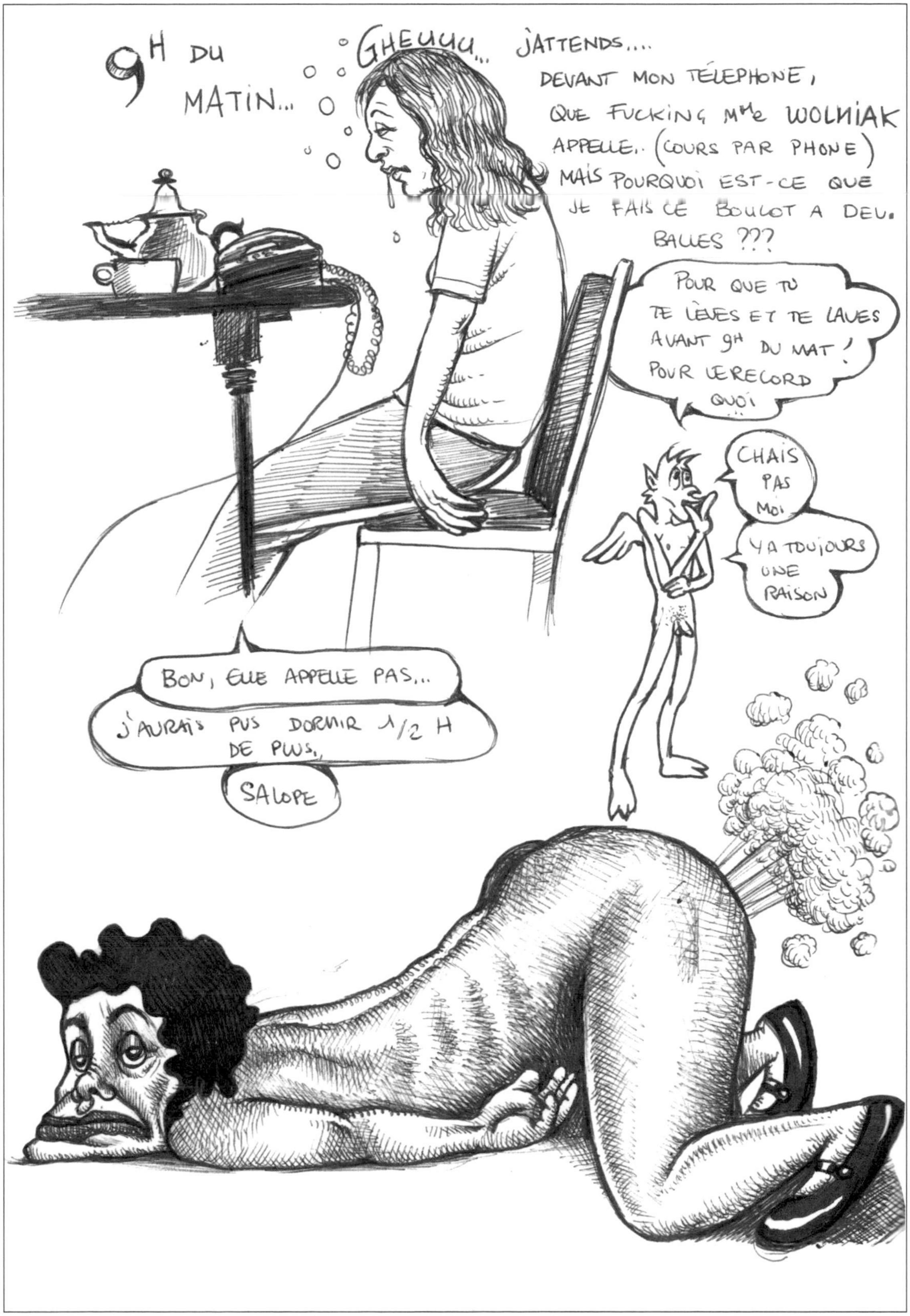
9H DU MATIN...
GHEUUU... J'ATTENDS.... DEVANT MON TÉLEPHONE, QUE FUCKING Mme WOLNIAK APPELLE.. (COURS PAR PHONE) MAIS POURQUOI EST-CE QUE JE FAIS CE BOULOT A DEU. BALLES ???
POUR QUE TU TE LÈVES ET TE LAVES AVANT 9H DU MAT! POUR LE RECORD QUOI...
CHAIS PAS MOI
YA TOUJOURS UNE RAISON
BON, ELLE APPELLE PAS...
J'AURAIS PUS DORMIR 1/2 H DE PLUS,
SALOPE

Age 21, April, 2003.

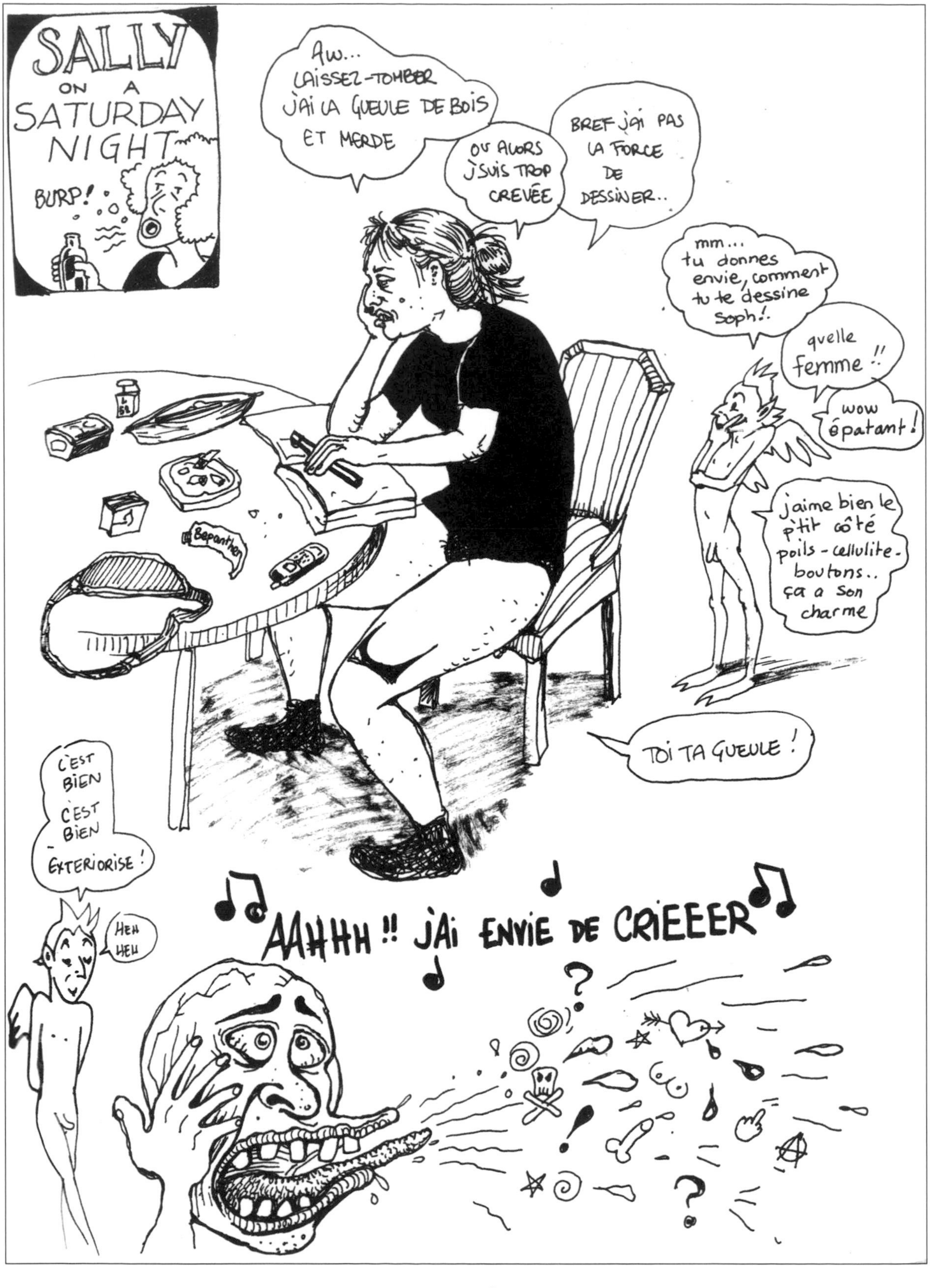
SALLY ON A SATURDAY NIGHT
BURP!
Aw... LAISSEZ-TOMBER J'AI LA GUEULE DE BOIS ET MERDE
OU ALORS J'SUIS TROP CREVÉE
BREF J'AI PAS LA FORCE DE DESSINER..
mm... tu donnes envie, comment tu te dessine Soph!.
quelle femme !!
wow épatant!
j'aime bien le p'tit côté poils-cellulite-boutons.. ça a son charme
Bepanthen
TOI TA GUEULE!
C'EST BIEN C'EST BIEN EXTERIORISE!
HEH HEH
AAHHH!! J'AI ENVIE DE CRIEEER

Age 21, April, 2003.

Last page in a sketchbook. Age 21, April, 2003.

R. Crumb. Drawn from life. Age 21, April, 2003.

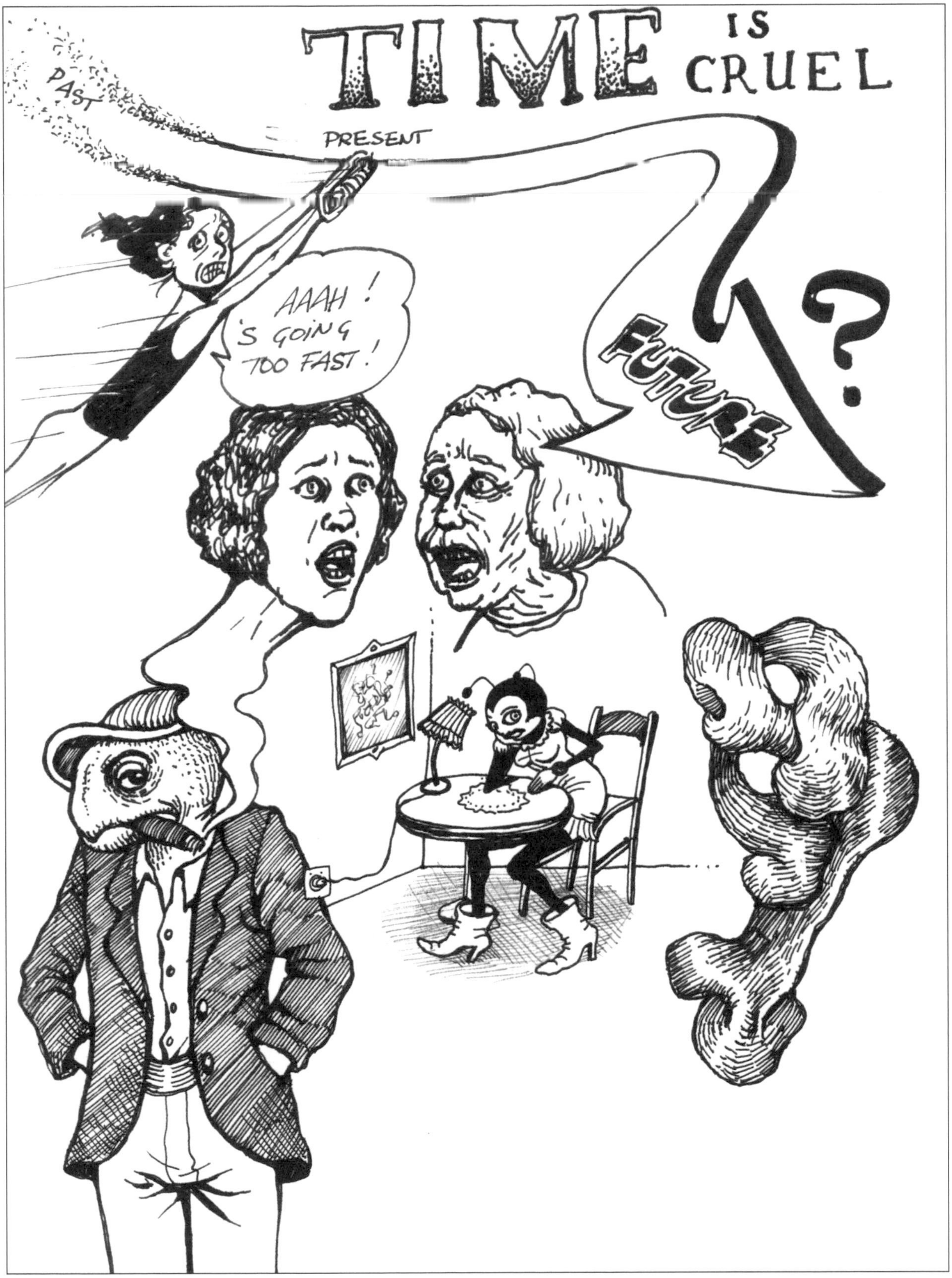
TIME IS CRUEL
PAST
PRESENT
AAAH! 'S GOING TOO FAST!
FUTURE
?

Age 21, mid-2003.

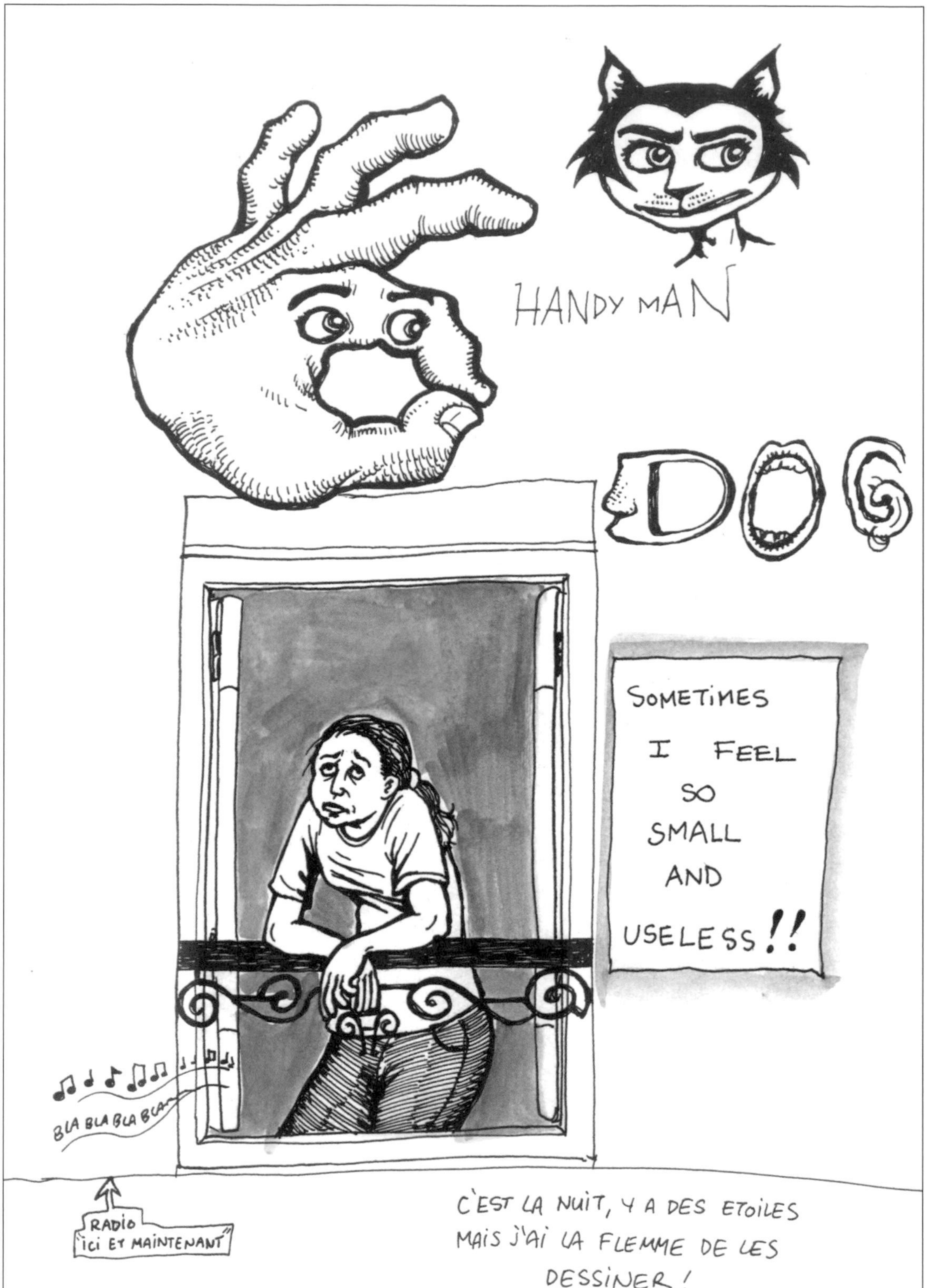
HANDY MAN
DOG
SOMETIMES I FEEL SO SMALL AND USELESS!!
BLA BLA BLA BLA
RADIO "ICI ET MAINTENANT"
C'EST LA NUIT, Y A DES ETOILES MAIS J'AI LA FLEMME DE LES DESSINER!

Age 21, mid-2003.

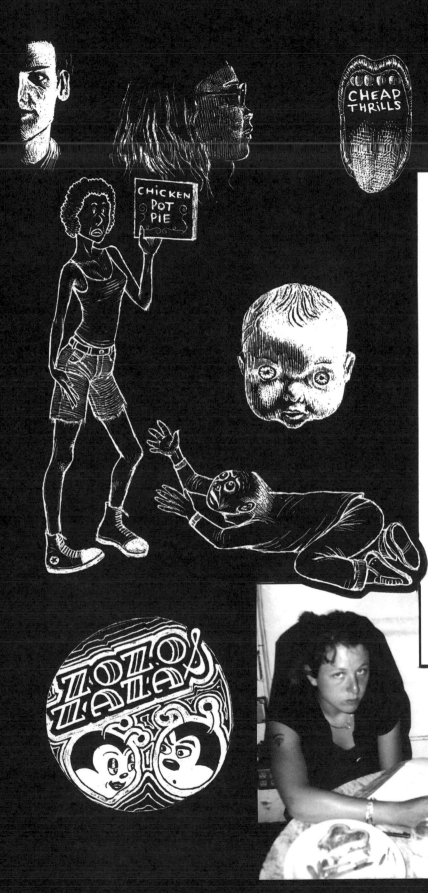

BACK TO THE U.S.A.
2003 TO 2006 / 22 TO 25 YRS OLD

REDISCOVERING MY HOMELAND SOMEHOW LIBERATED ME ON ALL LEVELS, SOLVING CERTAIN IDENTITY ISSUES.

I PUBLISHED SOME MORE AND DREW A LOT, FEELING FREE AND IDENTIFYING SOMEWHAT WITH THE EDGY, OUTSIDER, PUNK YOUTH-CULTURE IN THE BAY AREA AND THEN IN NEW YORK CITY. I EXPLORED AND EXPERIMENTED, LEARNING AND DISCOVERING ALL THE THINGS I HAD MISSED IN FRANCE. I SEE THIS TIME AS A PAGE TURNED AND IT SHOWS IN MY DRAWING AND WRITING.

I APPRENTICED TO BE A TATTOO ARTIST IN BROOKLYN, N.Y., BUT I WAS A LAME STUDENT, AS I WAS HAVING TOO MUCH FUN BREAKING INTO ABANDONDED BUILDINGS, SLEEPING IN PARKS, GETTING FUCKED UP, FALLING IN LOVE, AND GETTING MY HEART BROKE. I WAS WILD, OUT OF CONTROL, IT WAS GREAT!

IN MY SKETCHBOOKS I DREW THE CREEPS AND BUMS, JUNKIES, WING-NUTS, TRAIN-RIDING CRUSTY BRATS, STREET ARTISTS, CRACK WHORES, SQUATTERS AND STRIPPERS. WELL, I TRIED. I FELT QUITE AT HOME, BUT DISILLUSION AND DECREPITUDE SLOWLY REPLACED THE AWE, AND MY THEN LOVE INTEREST (ASS-HOLE) AND I CAUGHT A PLANE BACK TO FRANCE TO "SETTLE DOWN", AFRAID WE'D OTHERWISE SINK WITH THE SHIP. I STILL MISS AND LOVE N.Y.C... IT HAD AN OBVIOUSLY HUGE INFLUENCE ON EVERY ASPECT OF MY BEING.

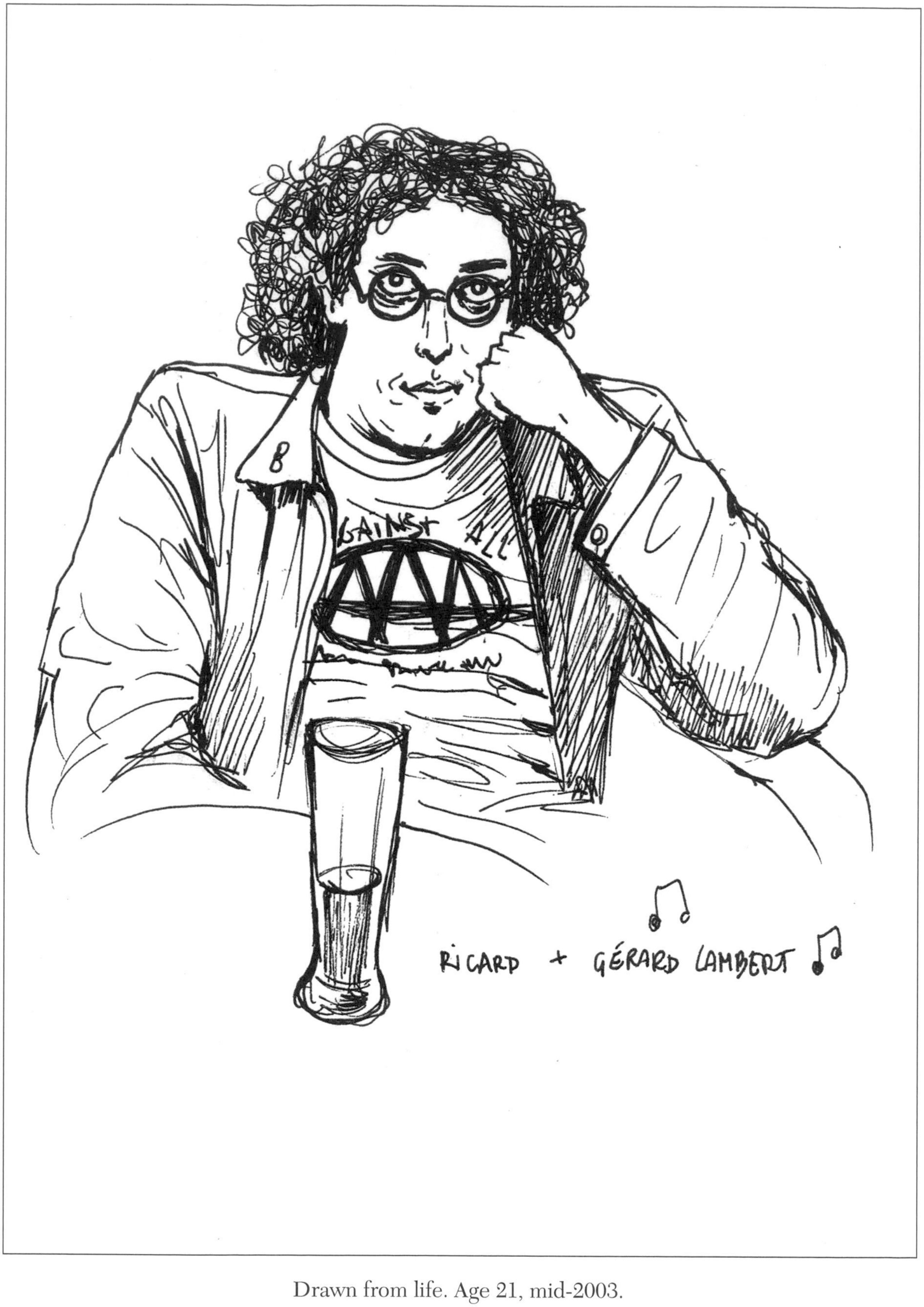
RICARD + GÉRARD LAMBERT

Drawn from life. Age 21, mid-2003.

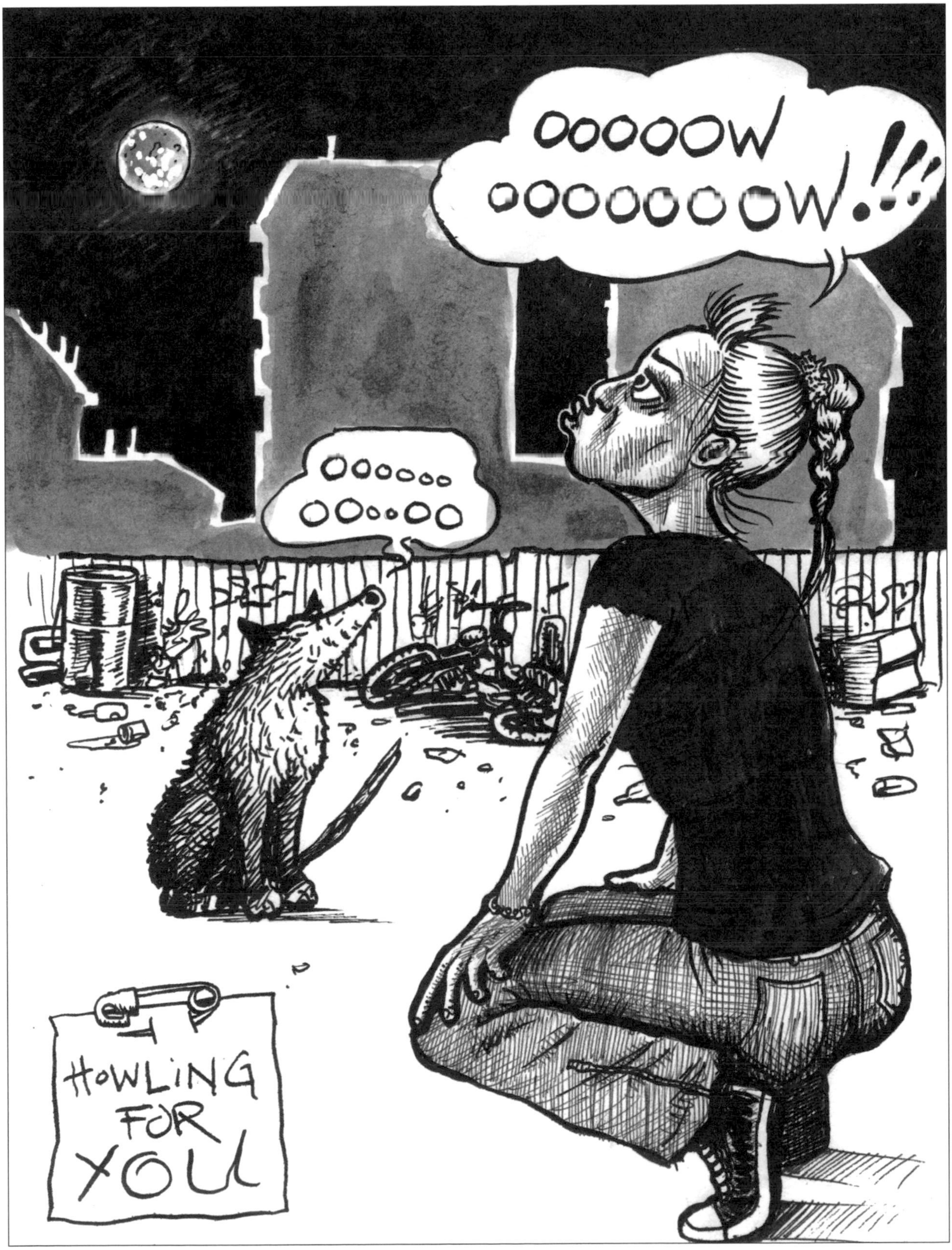
OOOOOW
OOOOOOOOW!!!
OOOOOO
OOOOOO
HOWLING
FOR
YOU

Age 21, mid-2003.

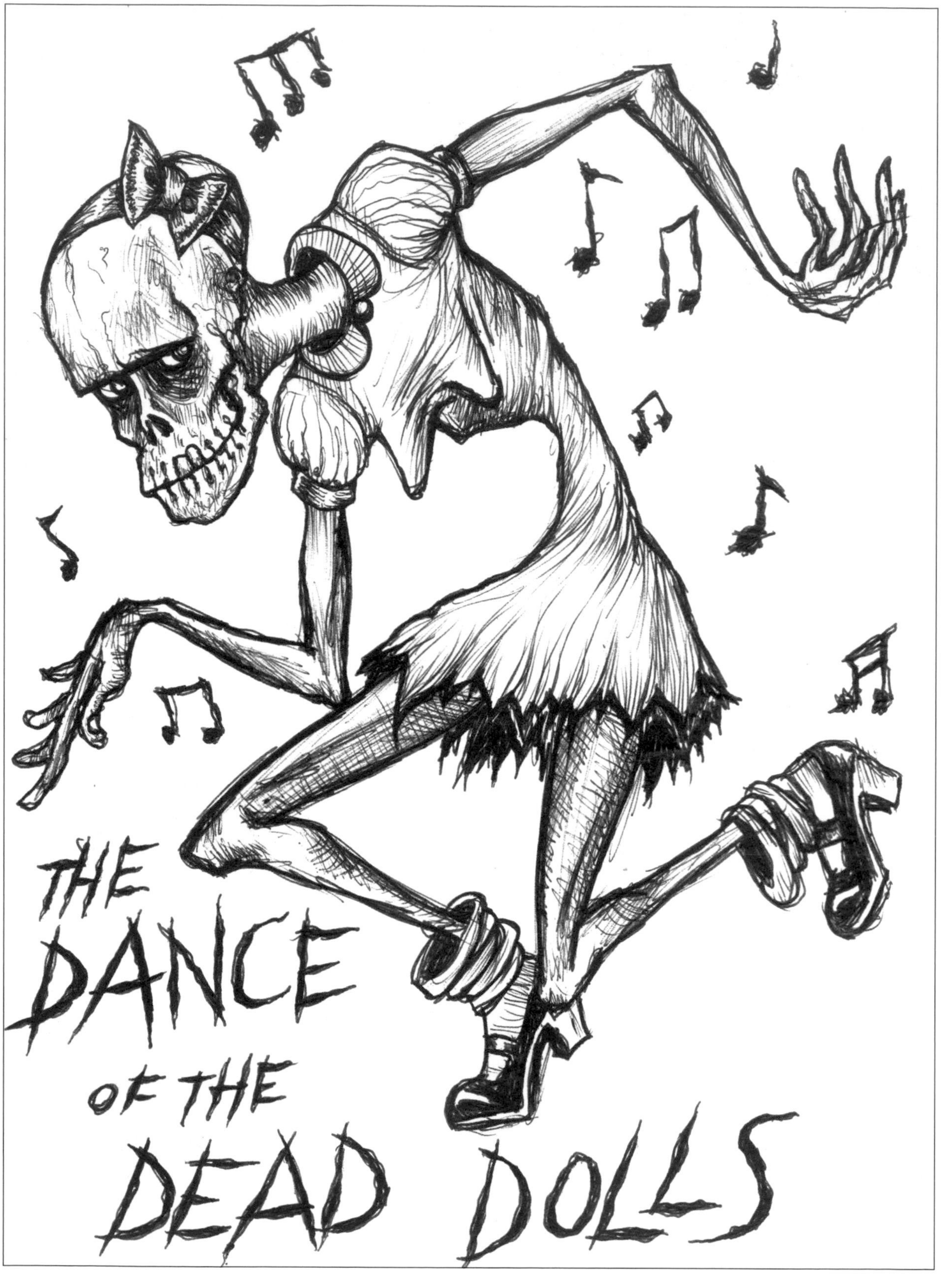
THE
DANCE
OF THE
DEAD DOLLS

Age 21, July, 2003.

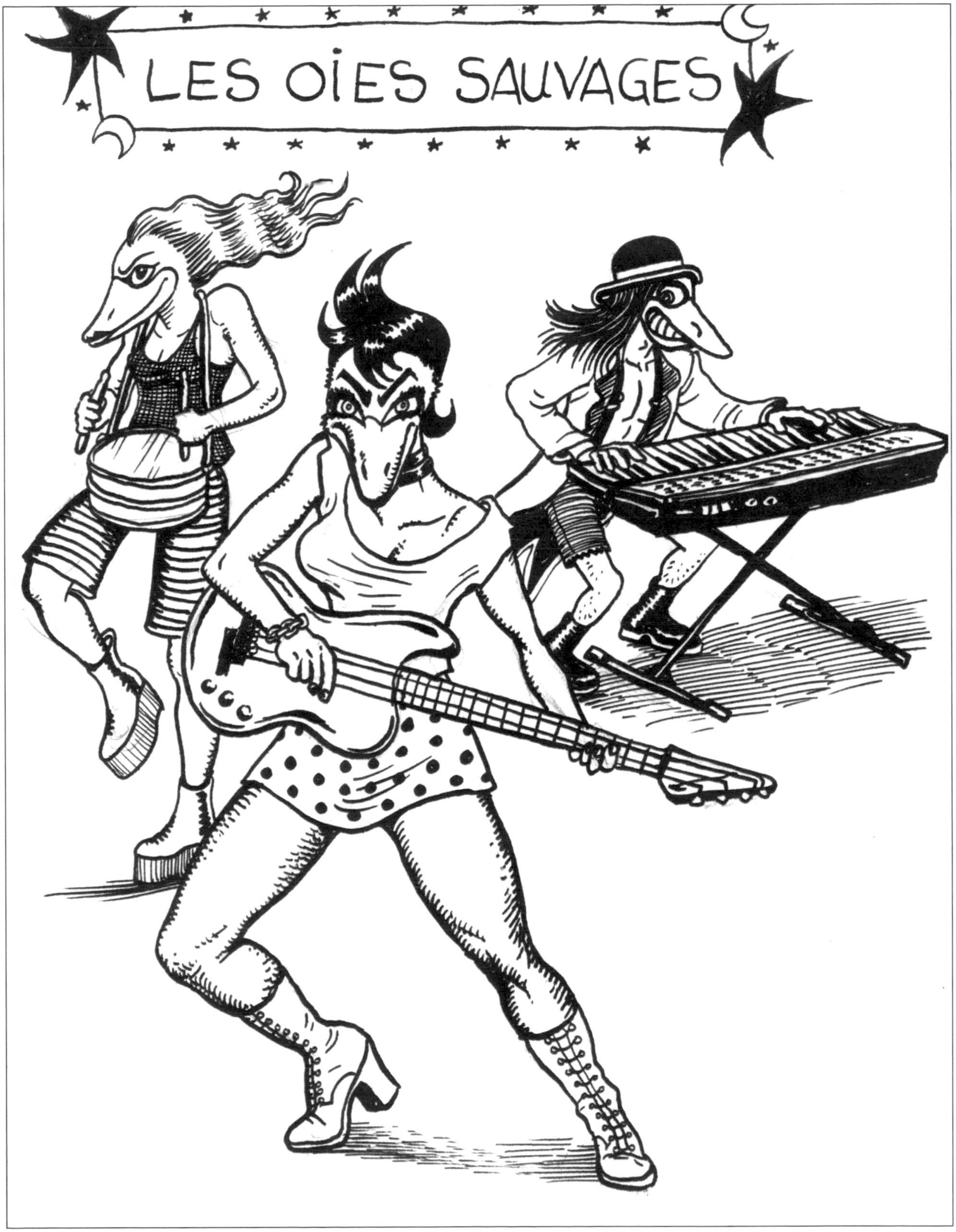
LES OIES SAUVAGES

Age 22, fall, 2003.

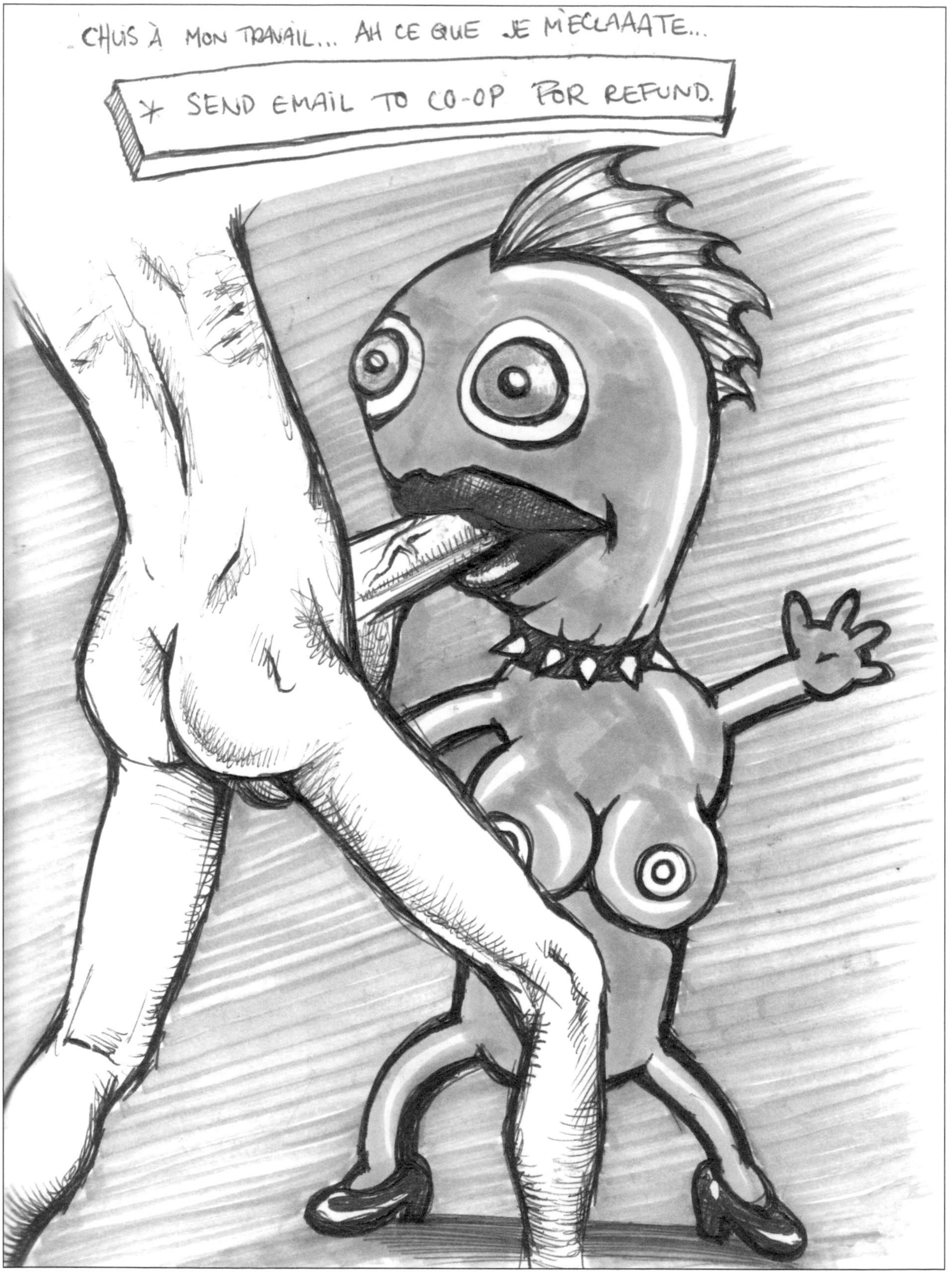
CHUIS À MON TRAVAIL... AH CE QUE JE M'ECLAAATE...
* SEND EMAIL TO CO-OP FOR REFUND.

Age 22, Sept., 2003.

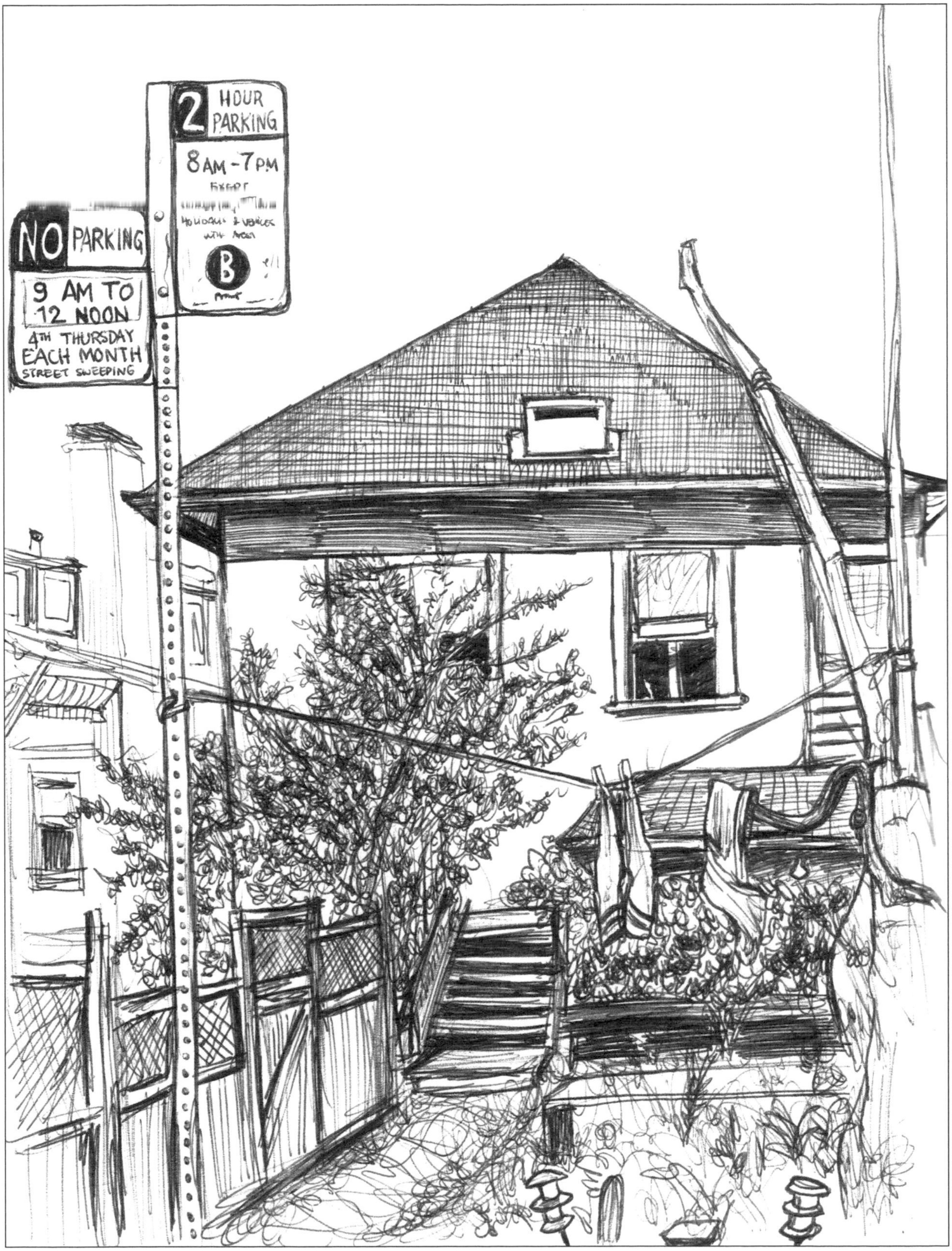
NO PARKING
9 AM TO
12 NOON
4TH THURSDAY
EACH MONTH
STREET SWEEPING
2 HOUR
PARKING
8AM-7PM
B

Age 22, Sept., 2003.

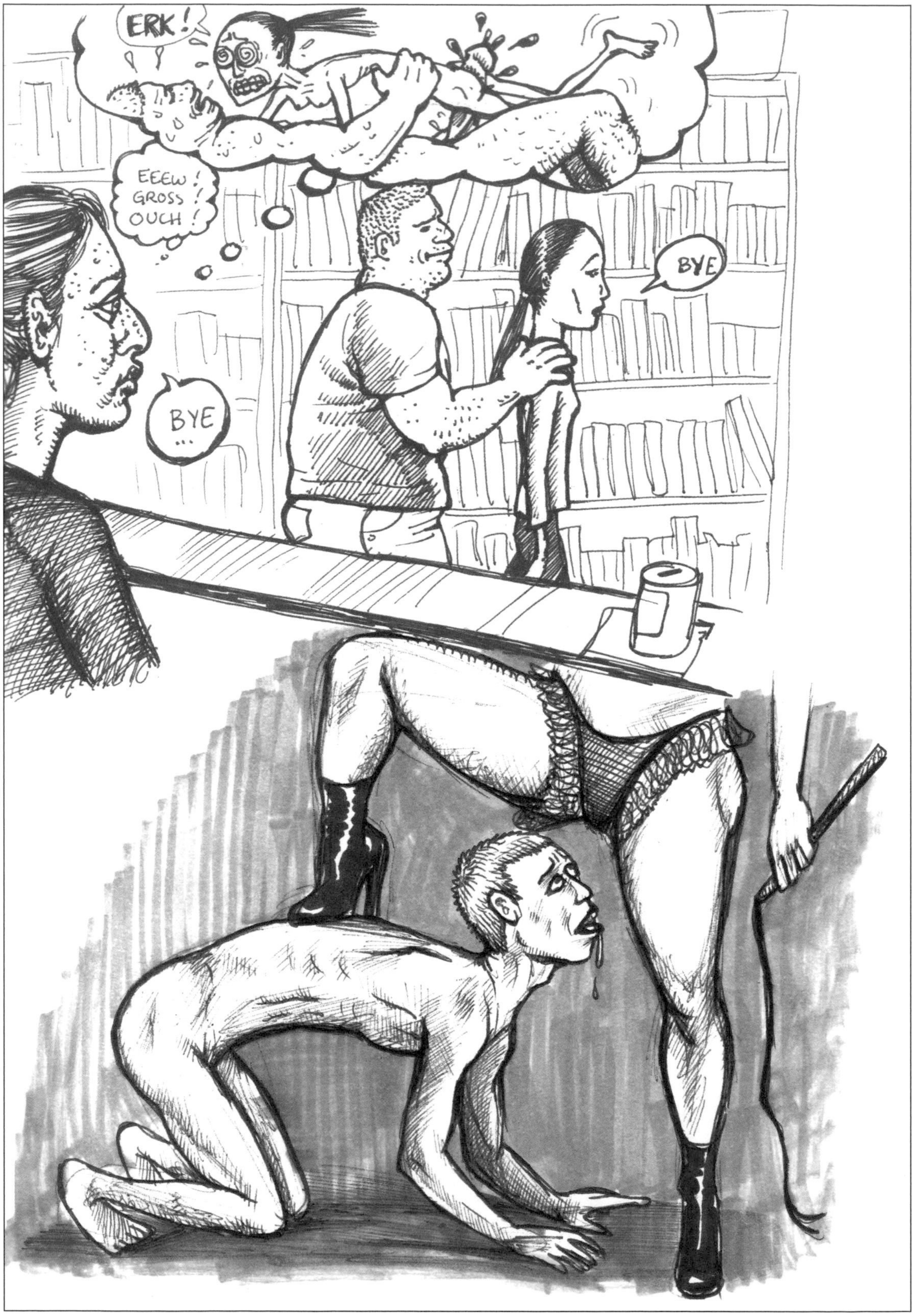
ERK!
EEEW! GROSS! OUCH!
BYE
BYE
...

Age 22, Oct., 2003.

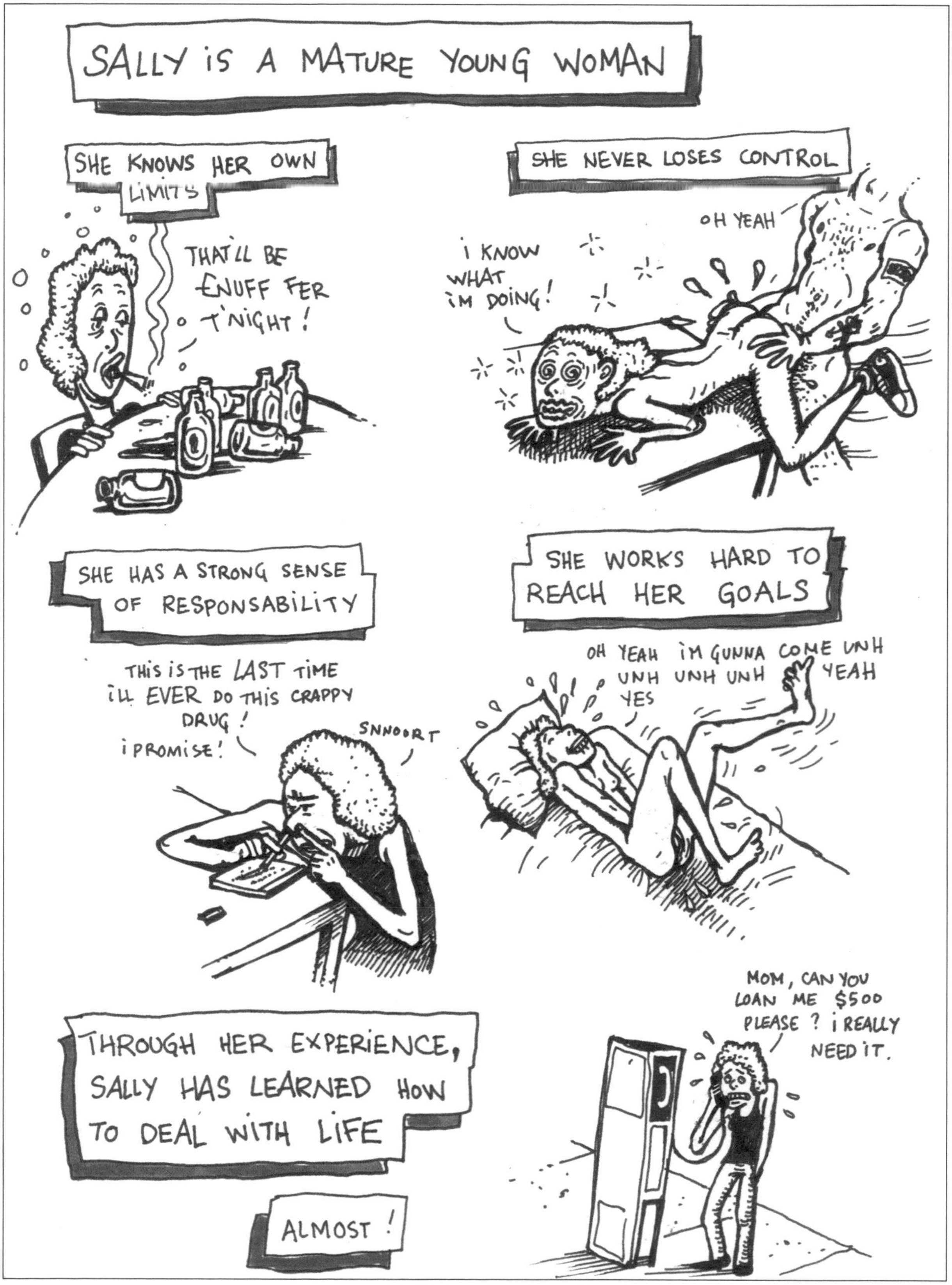
SALLY IS A MATURE YOUNG WOMAN
SHE KNOWS HER OWN LIMITS
THAT'LL BE ENUFF FER T'NIGHT!
SHE NEVER LOSES CONTROL
I KNOW WHAT I'M DOING!
OH YEAH
SHE HAS A STRONG SENSE OF RESPONSABILITY
THIS IS THE LAST TIME I'LL EVER DO THIS CRAPPY DRUG! I PROMISE!
SNNOORT
SHE WORKS HARD TO REACH HER GOALS
OH YEAH I'M GUNNA COME UNH UNH UNH UNH YES YEAH
THROUGH HER EXPERIENCE, SALLY HAS LEARNED HOW TO DEAL WITH LIFE
ALMOST!
MOM, CAN YOU LOAN ME $500 PLEASE? I REALLY NEED IT.

Age 22, Oct., 2003.

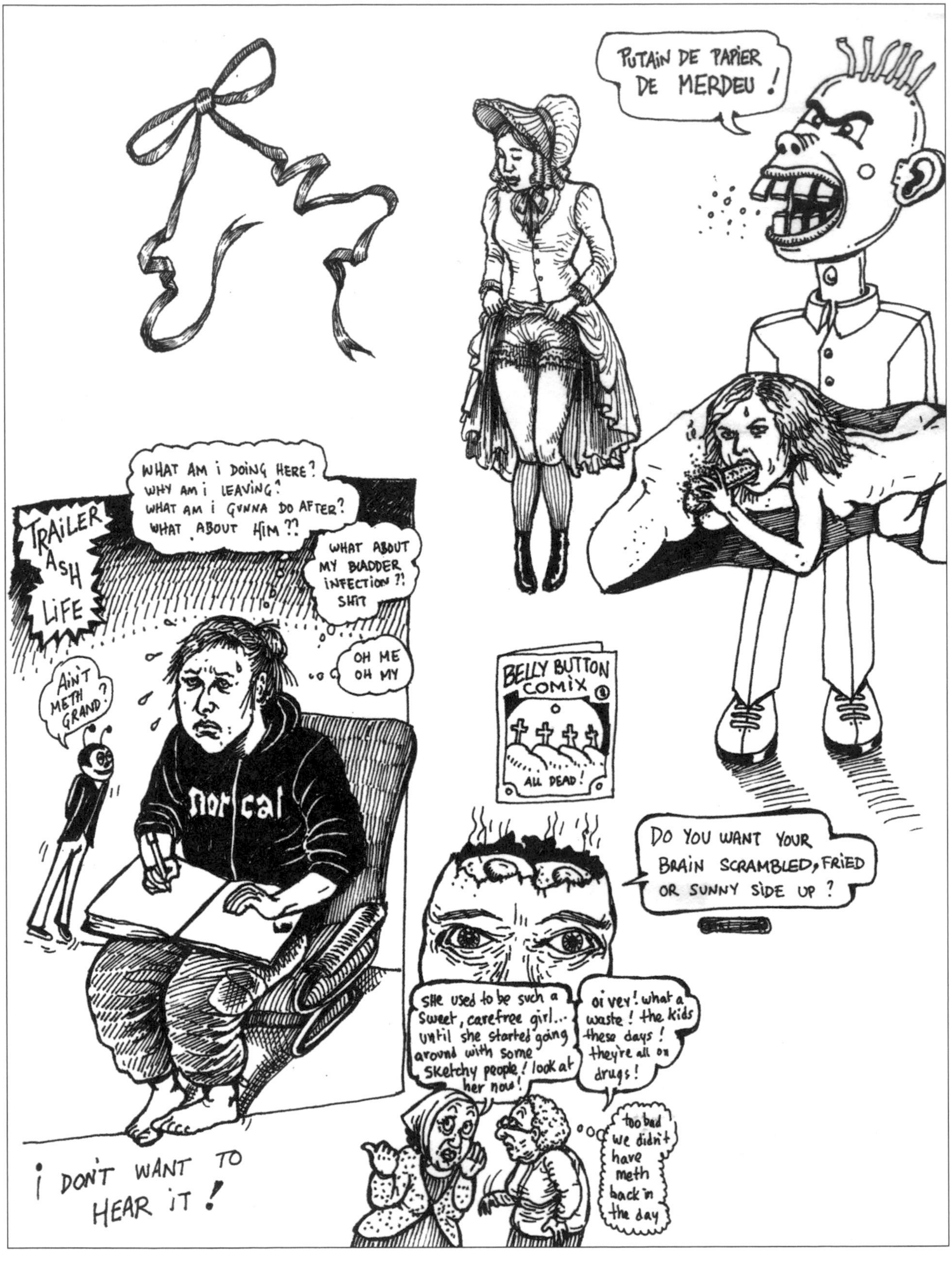
PUTAIN DE PAPIER DE MERDEU !
WHAT AM i DOING HERE? WHY AM i LEAVING? WHAT AM i GUNNA DO AFTER? WHAT ABOUT HIM ??
TRAILER TRASH LIFE
WHAT ABOUT MY BLADDER INFECTION ?! SHIT
OH ME OH MY
AIN'T METH GRAND?
nor cal
BELLY BUTTON COMIX
ALL DEAD!
DO YOU WANT YOUR BRAIN SCRAMBLED, FRIED OR SUNNY SIDE UP ?
SHE used to be such a sweet, carefree girl... until she started going around with some sketchy people! look at her now!
oi vey! what a waste! the kids these days! they're all on drugs!
too bad we didn't have meth back in the day
i DON'T WANT TO HEAR IT !

Age 22, Nov., 2003.

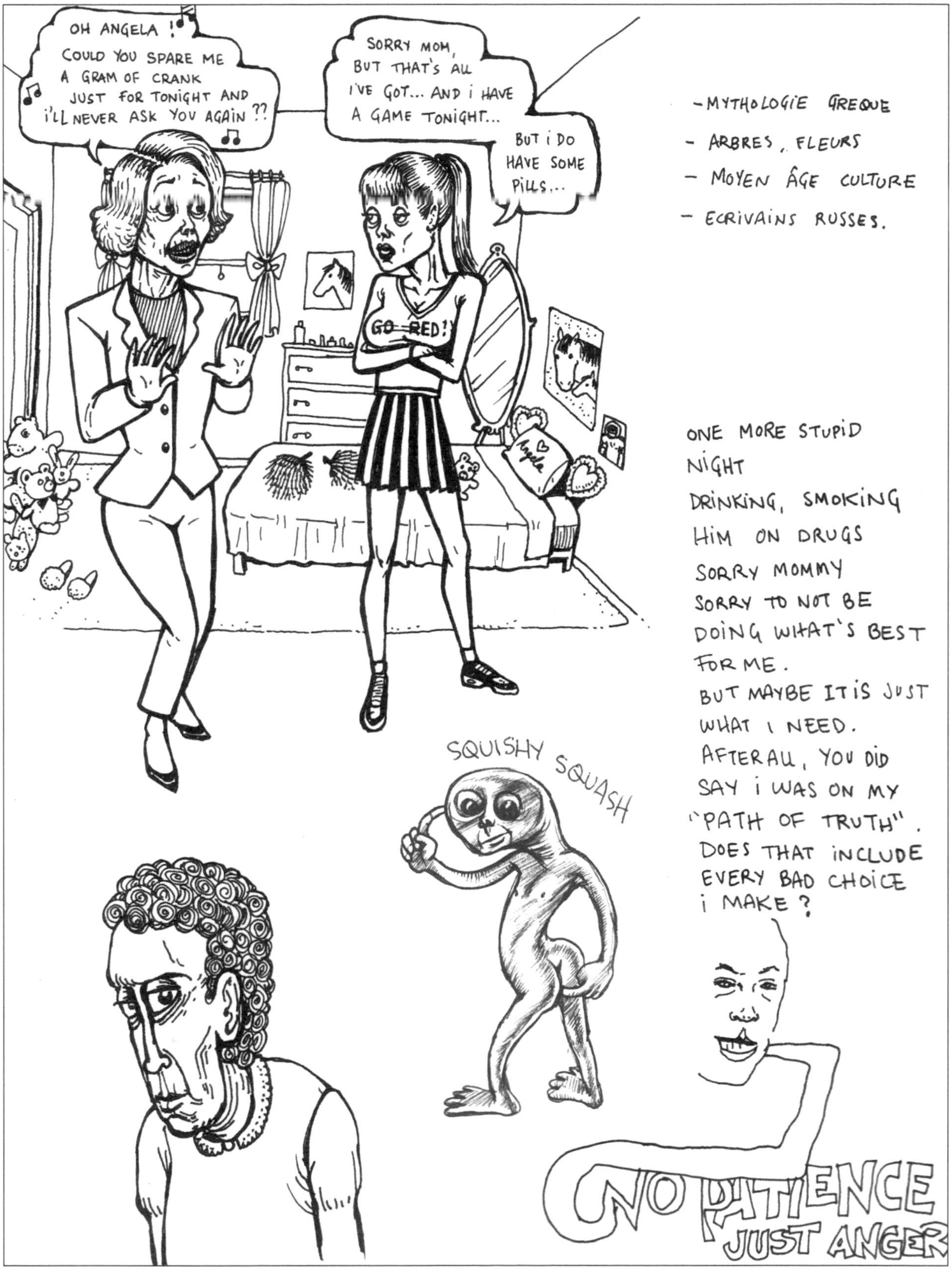
OH ANGELA ! COULD YOU SPARE ME A GRAM OF CRANK JUST FOR TONIGHT AND I'LL NEVER ASK YOU AGAIN ??
SORRY MOM, BUT THAT'S ALL I'VE GOT... AND I HAVE A GAME TONIGHT...
BUT I DO HAVE SOME PILLS...
GO RED!
- MYTHOLOGIE GREQUE
- ARBRES, FLEURS
- MOYEN ÂGE CULTURE
- ECRIVAINS RUSSES.
ONE MORE STUPID NIGHT
DRINKING, SMOKING
HIM ON DRUGS
SORRY MOMMY
SORRY TO NOT BE DOING WHAT'S BEST FOR ME.
BUT MAYBE IT IS JUST WHAT I NEED.
AFTERALL, YOU DID SAY I WAS ON MY "PATH OF TRUTH".
DOES THAT INCLUDE EVERY BAD CHOICE I MAKE?
SQUISHY SQUASH
NO PATIENCE
JUST ANGER

Age 22, Nov., 2003.

Top left: The young R. Crumb. Drawn from a photograph.
Bottom right: Self-portrait. Drawn from mirror. Age 22, Nov., 2003.

Self-portrait. Drawn from mirror. Age 22, late 2003.

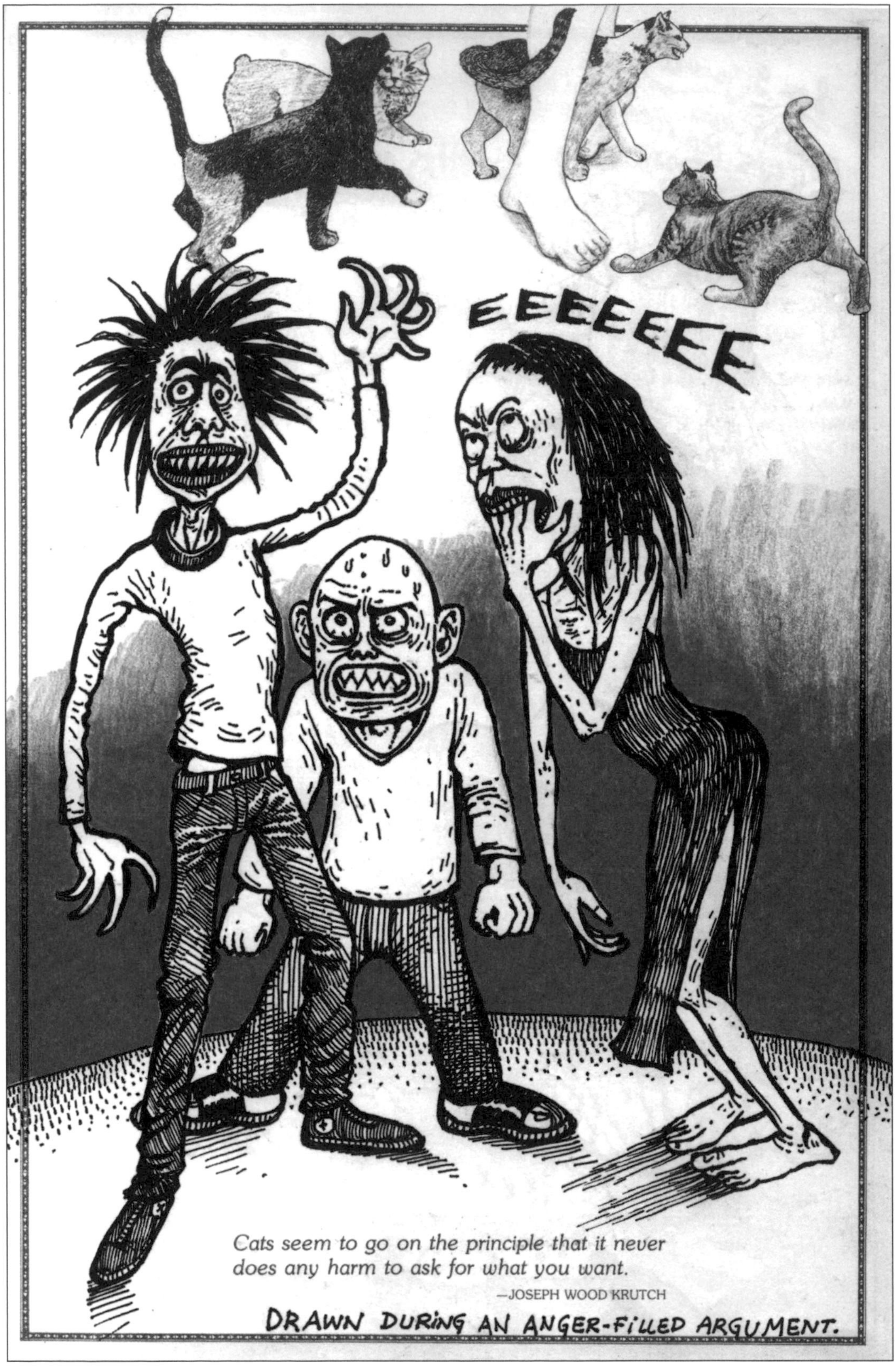
EEEEEEEE
Cats seem to go on the principle that it never does any harm to ask for what you want.
—JOSEPH WOOD KRUTCH
DRAWN DURING AN ANGER-FILLED ARGUMENT.

Age 22, Jan., 2004.

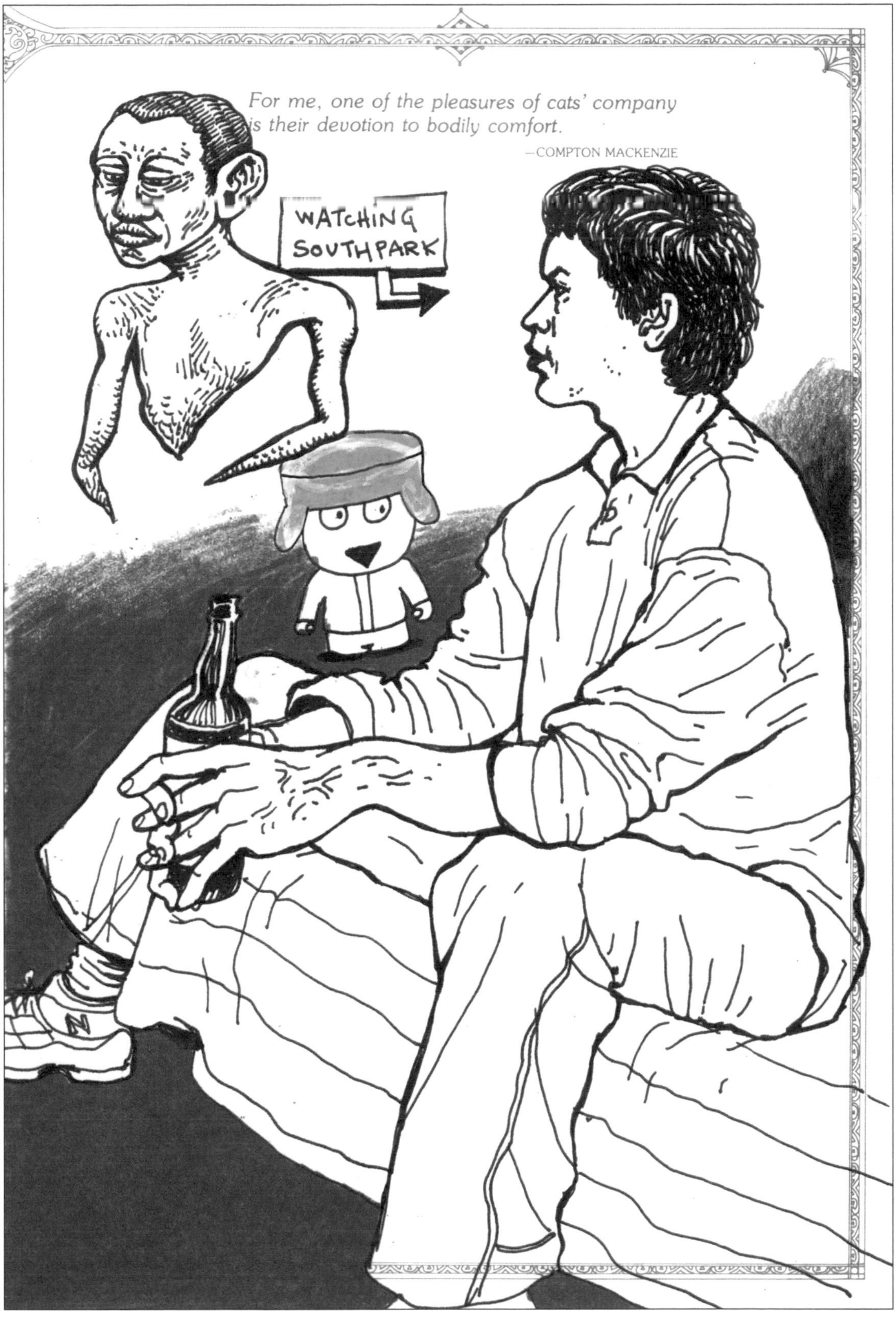
For me, one of the pleasures of cats' company is their devotion to bodily comfort.
—COMPTON MACKENZIE
WATCHING SOUTHPARK

Drawn from life. Age 22, Feb., 2004.

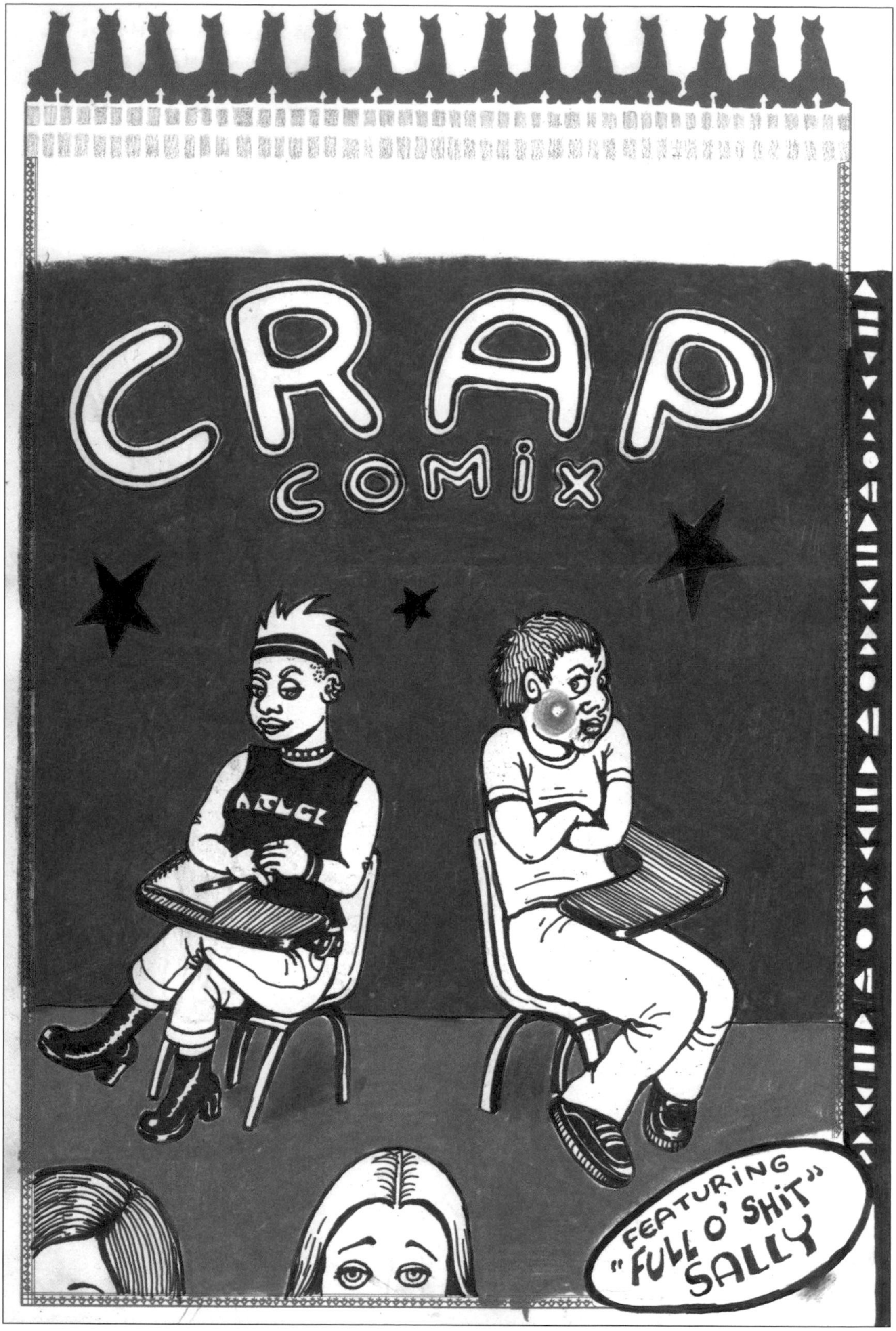
CRAP
COMIX
FEATURING "FULL O' SHIT" SALLY

Age 22, Feb., 2004.

I could half persuade myself that the word felonious
is derived from the feline temper.

—ROBERT SOUTHEY

Drawn from life. Age 22, March, 2004.

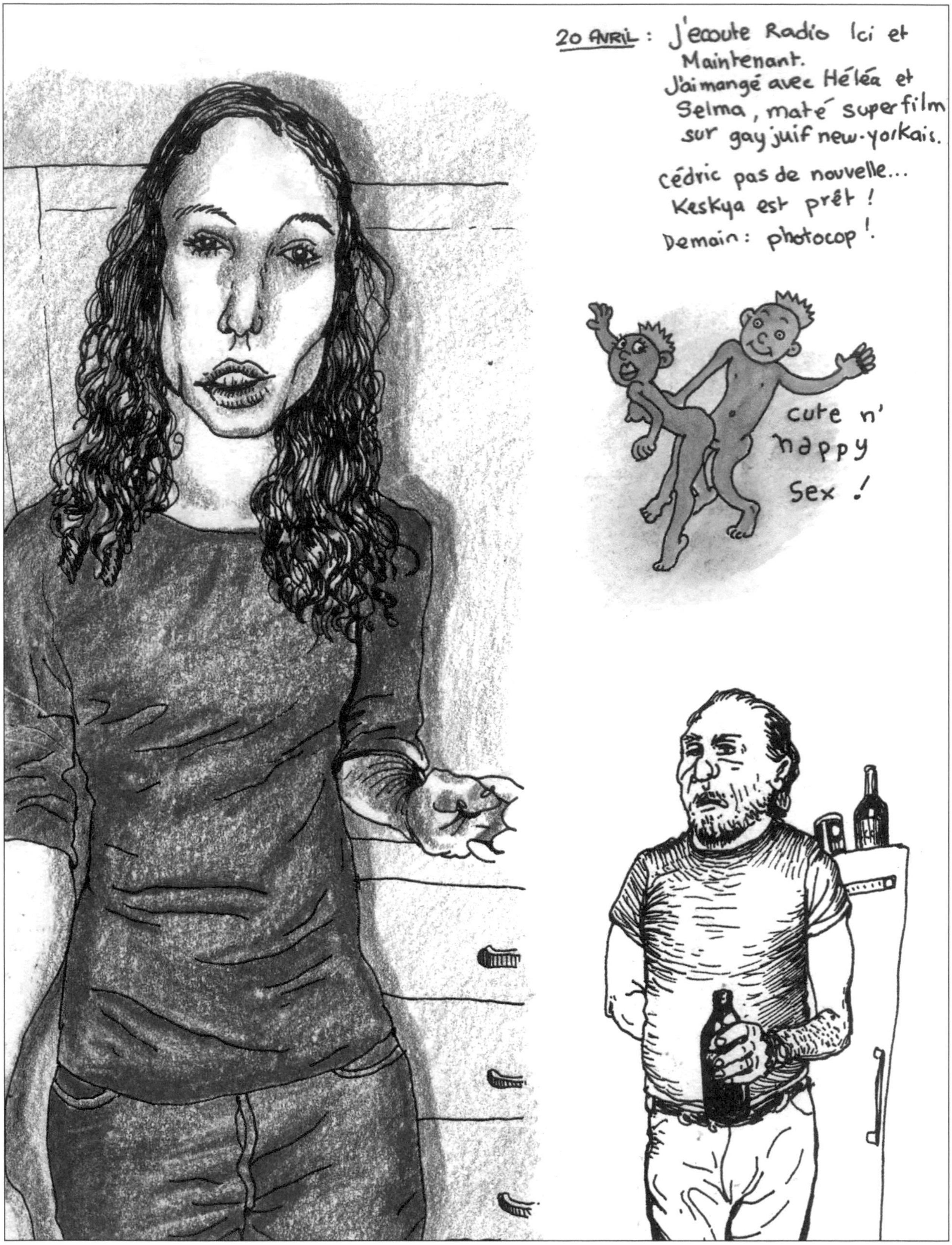
20 AVRIL : J'ecoute Radio Ici et Maintenant.
J'ai mangé avec Héléa et Selma, maté superfilm sur gay juif new-yorkais.
Cédric pas de nouvelle...
Keskya est prêt !
Demain : photocop !
cute n' happy sex !

Age 22, April, 2004.

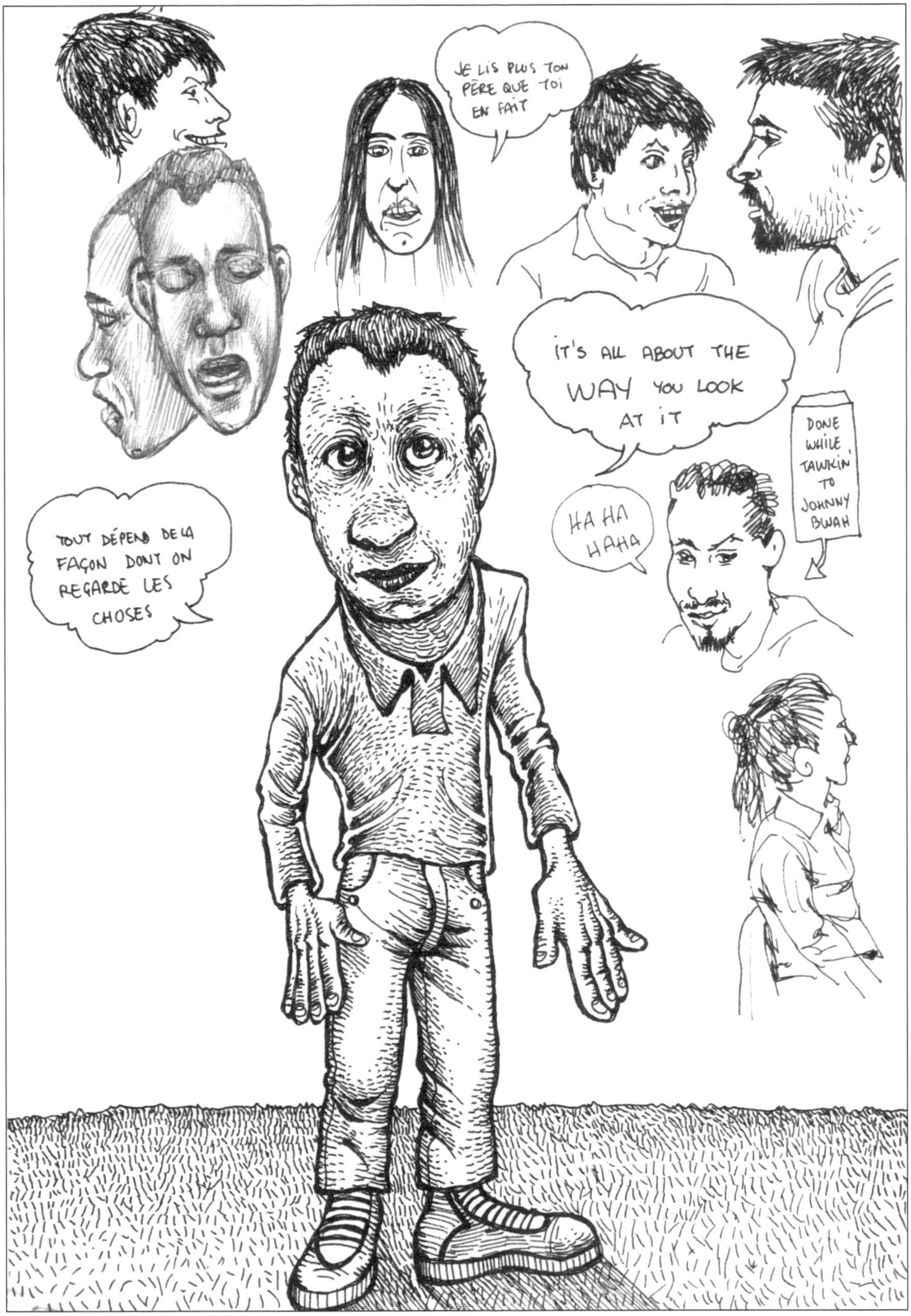
JE LIS PLUS TON PÈRE QUE TOI EN FAIT
IT'S ALL ABOUT THE WAY YOU LOOK AT IT
DONE WHILE TAWKIN' TO JOHNNY BWAH
TOUT DÉPEND DE LA FAÇON DONT ON REGARDE LES CHOSES
HA HA HAHA

Age 22, May, 2004.

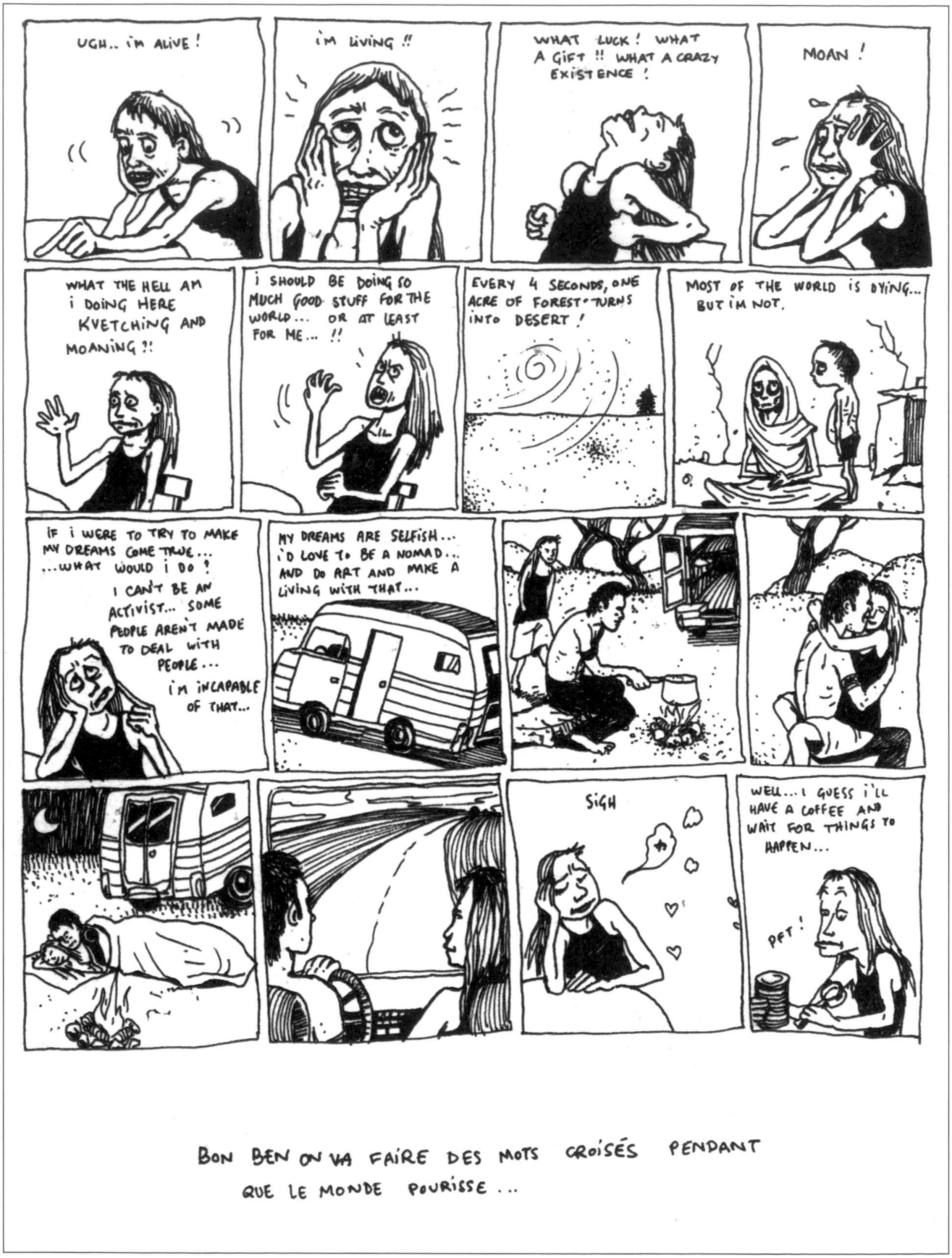
UGH.. I'M ALIVE!
I'M LIVING !!
WHAT LUCK! WHAT A GIFT !! WHAT A CRAZY EXISTENCE !
MOAN !
WHAT THE HELL AM I DOING HERE KVETCHING AND MOANING ?!
I SHOULD BE DOING SO MUCH GOOD STUFF FOR THE WORLD... OR AT LEAST FOR ME... !!
EVERY 4 SECONDS, ONE ACRE OF FOREST TURNS INTO DESERT !
MOST OF THE WORLD IS DYING... BUT I'M NOT.
IF I WERE TO TRY TO MAKE MY DREAMS COME TRUE... ...WHAT WOULD I DO ?
I CAN'T BE AN ACTIVIST... SOME PEOPLE AREN'T MADE TO DEAL WITH PEOPLE...
I'M INCAPABLE OF THAT...
MY DREAMS ARE SELFISH... I'D LOVE TO BE A NOMAD... AND DO ART AND MAKE A LIVING WITH THAT...
SIGH
WELL... I GUESS I'LL HAVE A COFFEE AND WAIT FOR THINGS TO HAPPEN...
PFT!
BON BEN ON VA FAIRE DES MOTS CROISÉS PENDANT QUE LE MONDE POURISSE...

Age 22, May, 2004.

Street in Paris. Drawn from life. Age 22, May, 2004.

Tattoo shop where Sophie worked. Drawn from life. Age 22, 2004.

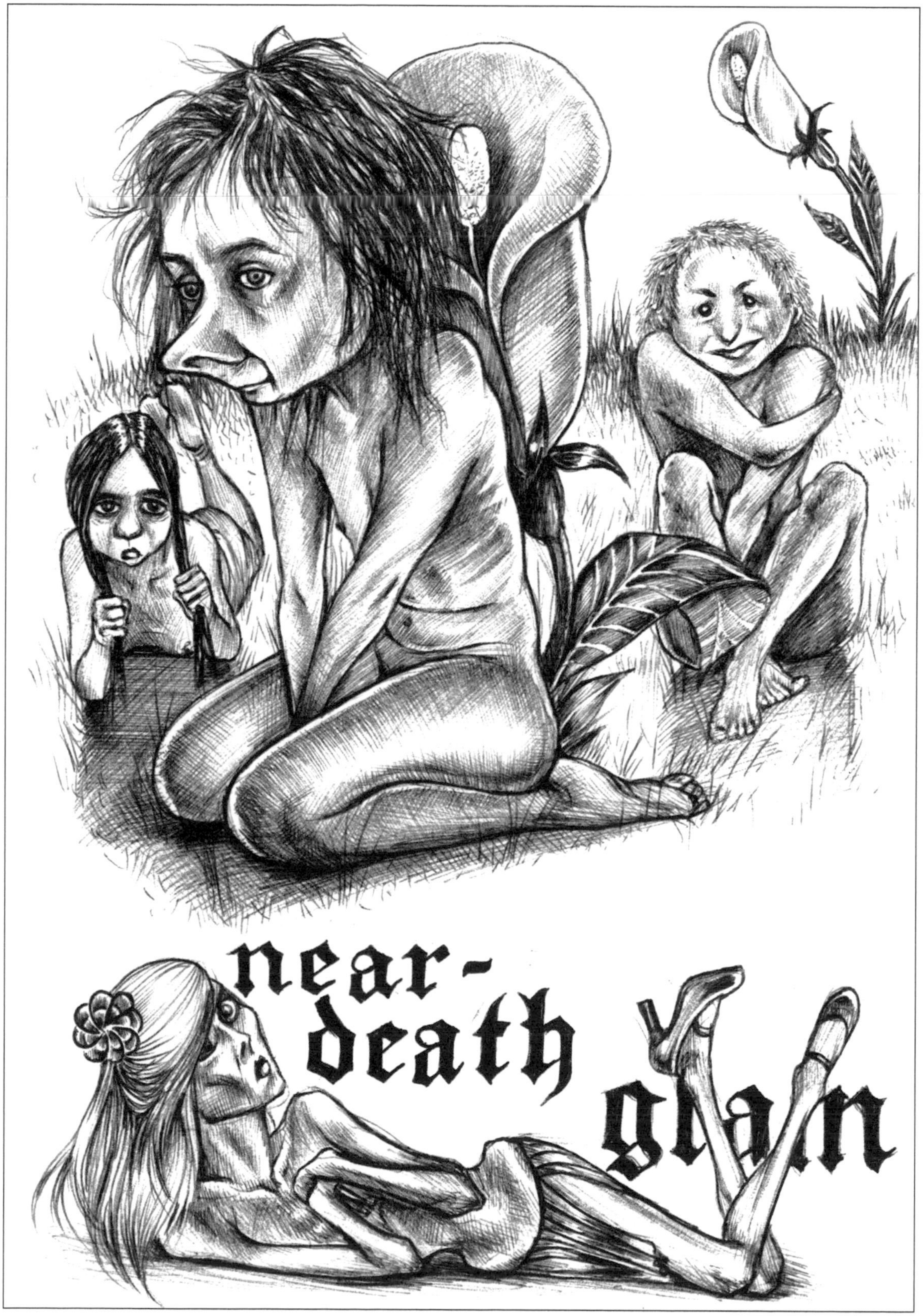
near-
death
glam

Age 22, Aug., 2004.

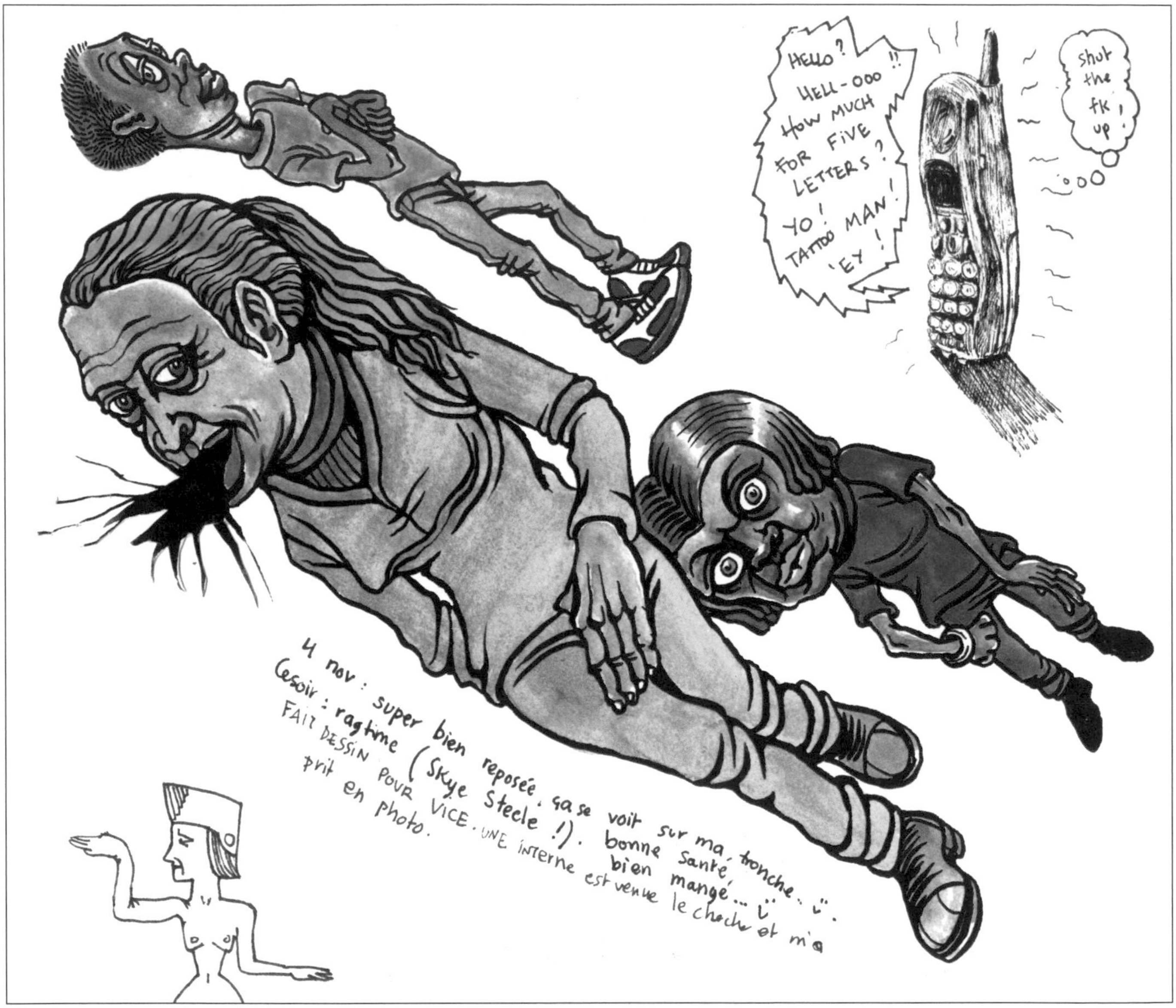
HELLO? HELL-OOO!! HOW MUCH FOR FIVE LETTERS? YO! TATTOO MAN! 'EY!
shut the fk up!
4 nov : super bien reposée, ça se voit sur ma tronche. ;-".
Cesoir : ragtime (Skye Steele !). bonne santé, bien mangé... ;-"
FAIT DESSIN POUR VICE. UNE interne est venue le chercher et m'a prit en photo.

Age 23, Nov., 2004.

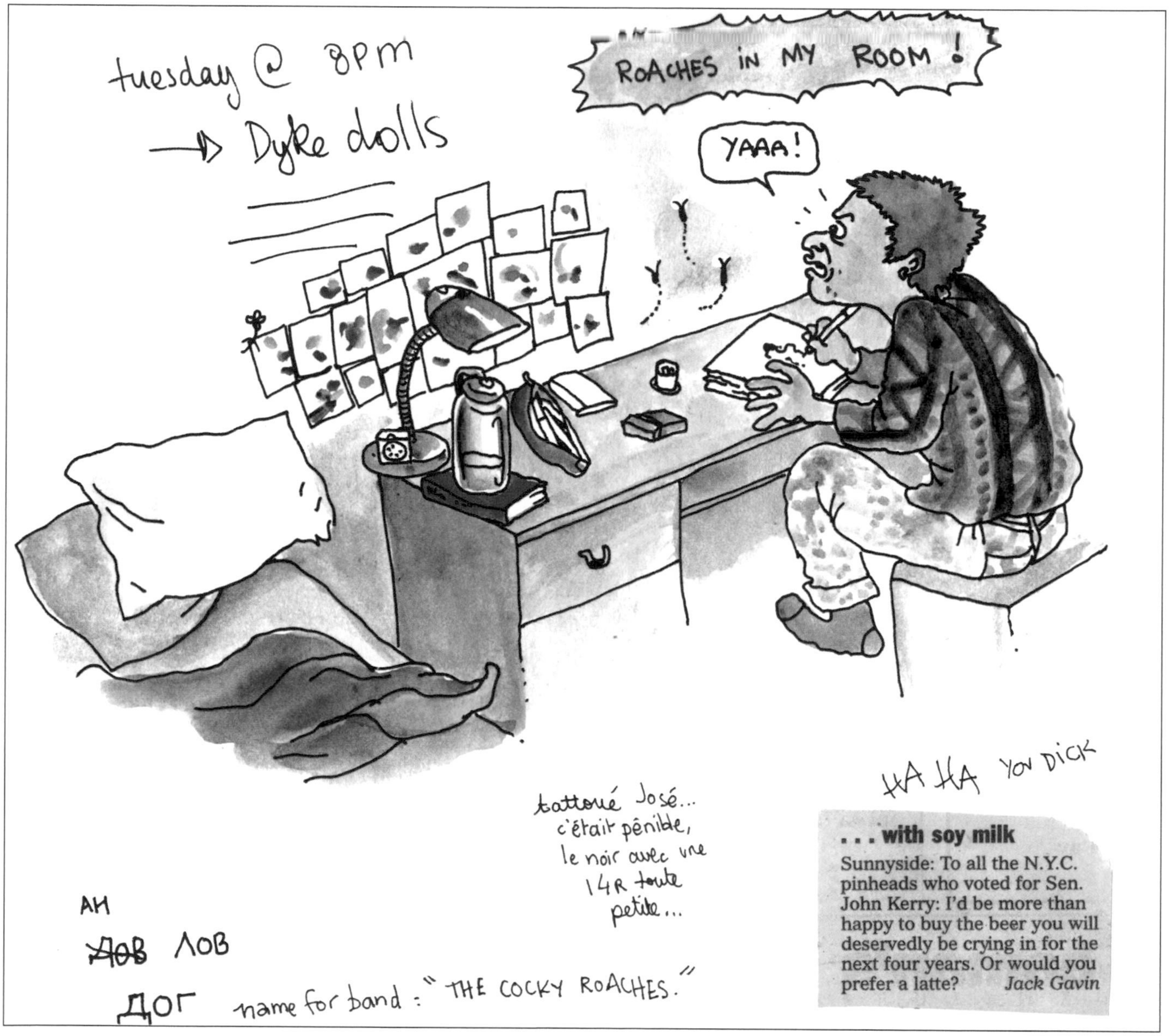
tuesday @ 8PM
→ Dyke dolls
ROACHES IN MY ROOM!
YAAA!
tattoué José... c'était pénible, le noir avec une 14R toute petite...
HA HA YOU DICK
. . . with soy milk
Sunnyside: To all the N.Y.C. pinheads who voted for Sen. John Kerry: I'd be more than happy to buy the beer you will deservedly be crying in for the next four years. Or would you prefer a latte? Jack Gavin
AH
~~ДОВ~~ ЛОВ
ДОГ
name for band: "THE COCKY ROACHES."

Age 23, Nov., 2004.

Mary Pickford, clairvoyant

DONE NOT ON SPEED

Realized it was a girl after.

today walked From Grand St· to 42nd ! (= 60 blocks)
Got a lotta food. Went to "Blue Stockings" and
Saw "Glass" at Union SQ · X-mas
market. There's x-mas shit
everywhere. It's cold...
I can't sleep!
need affection..

got MRR
with Fly's
portrait of MOI

JOHN called this morning and awoke me from a dream about my
parents tripping on mescal (?) in my dad's studio ! I was like
"mom, dad, are you guys tripping ??!"

Drawn from photographs. Age 23, Dec., 2004.

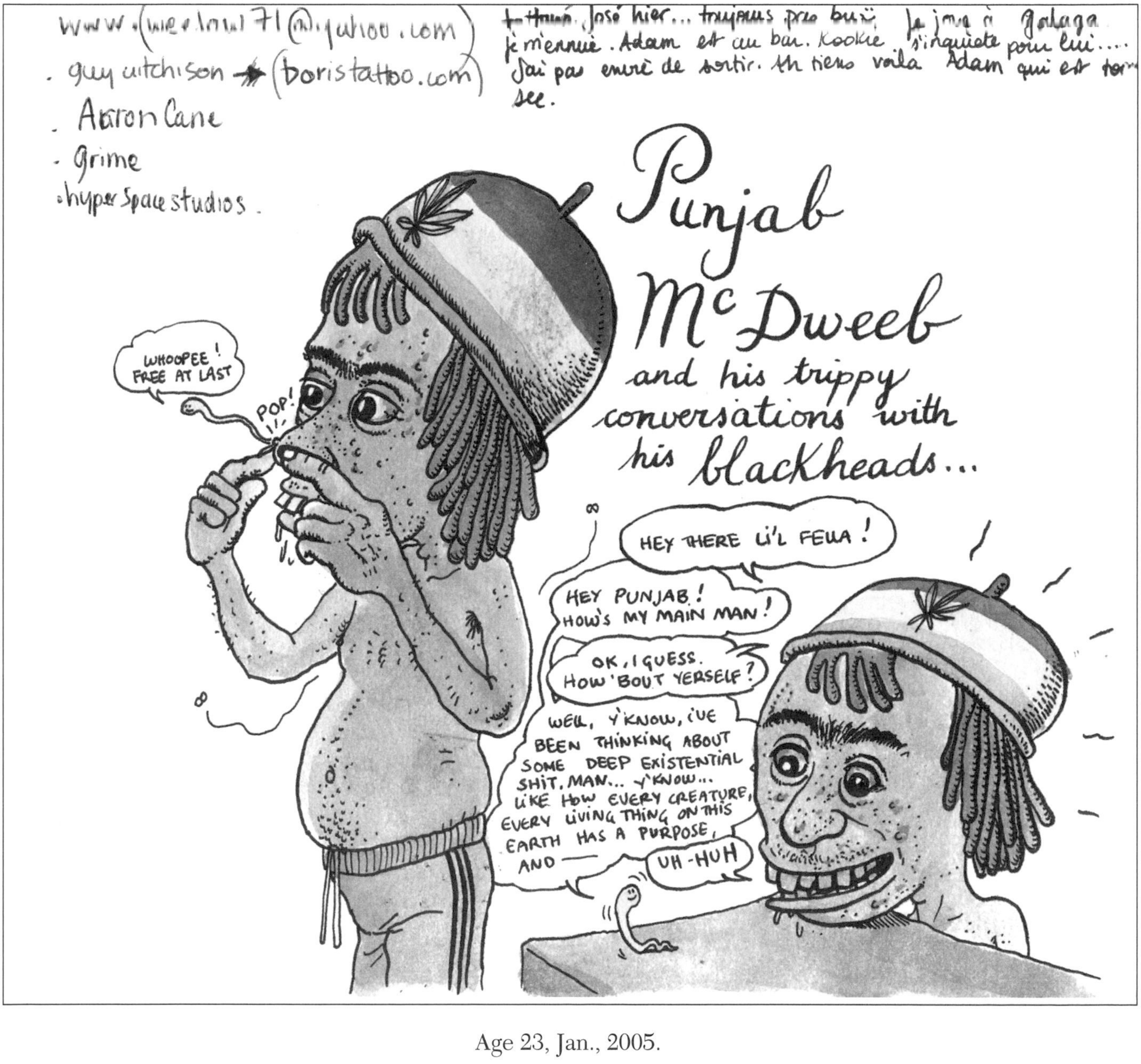
guy aitchison (boristattoo.com)
Aaron Cane
grime
hyper Space studios
Punjab McDweeb and his trippy conversations with his blackheads...
WHOOPEE! FREE AT LAST
POP!
HEY THERE LI'L FELLA!
HEY PUNJAB! HOW'S MY MAIN MAN!
OK, I GUESS. HOW'BOUT YERSELF?
WELL, Y'KNOW, I'VE BEEN THINKING ABOUT SOME DEEP EXISTENTIAL SHIT, MAN... Y'KNOW... LIKE HOW EVERY CREATURE, EVERY LIVING THING ON THIS EARTH HAS A PURPOSE, AND —
UH-HUH

Age 23, Jan., 2005.

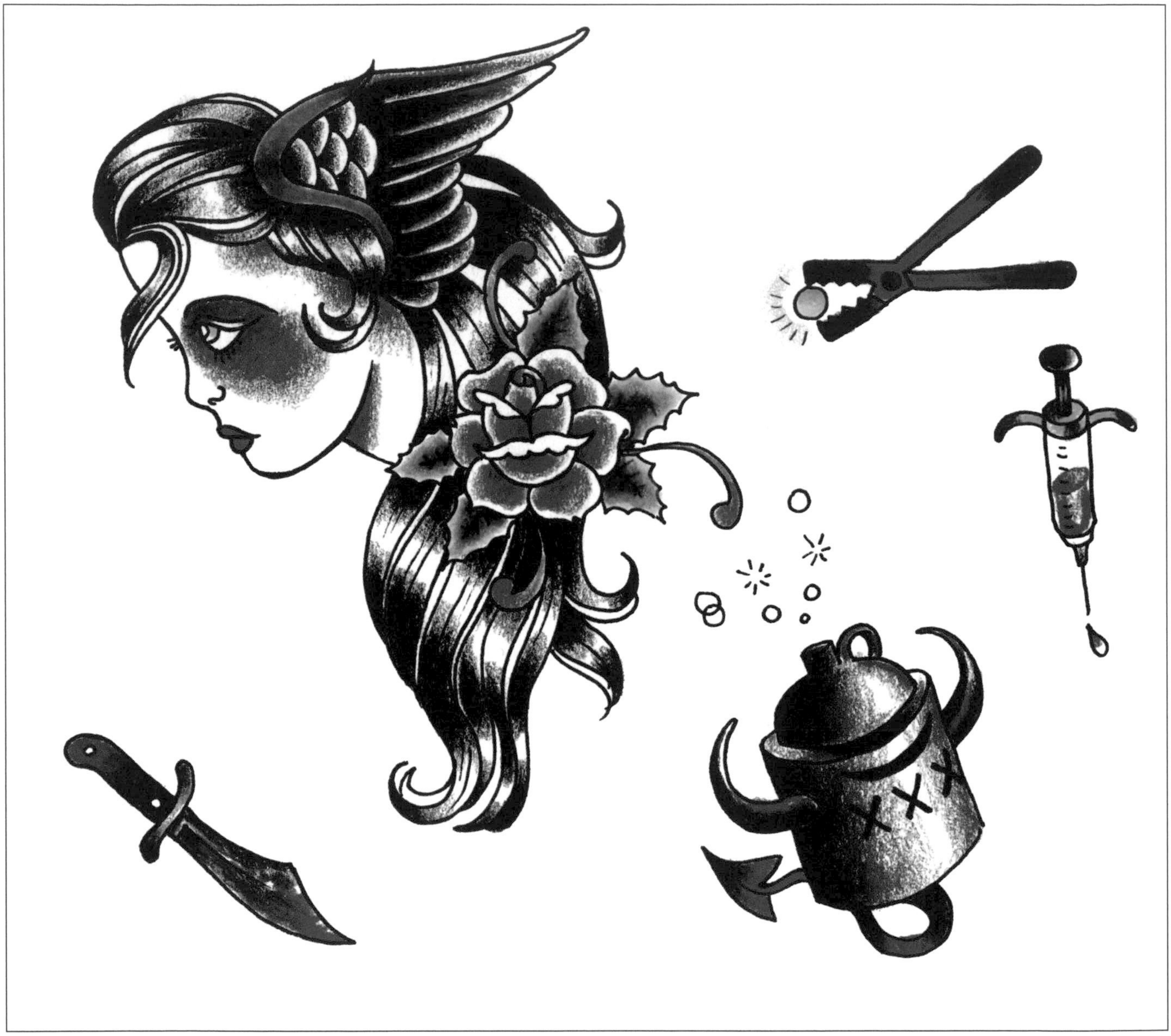

Age 23, Jan., 2005.

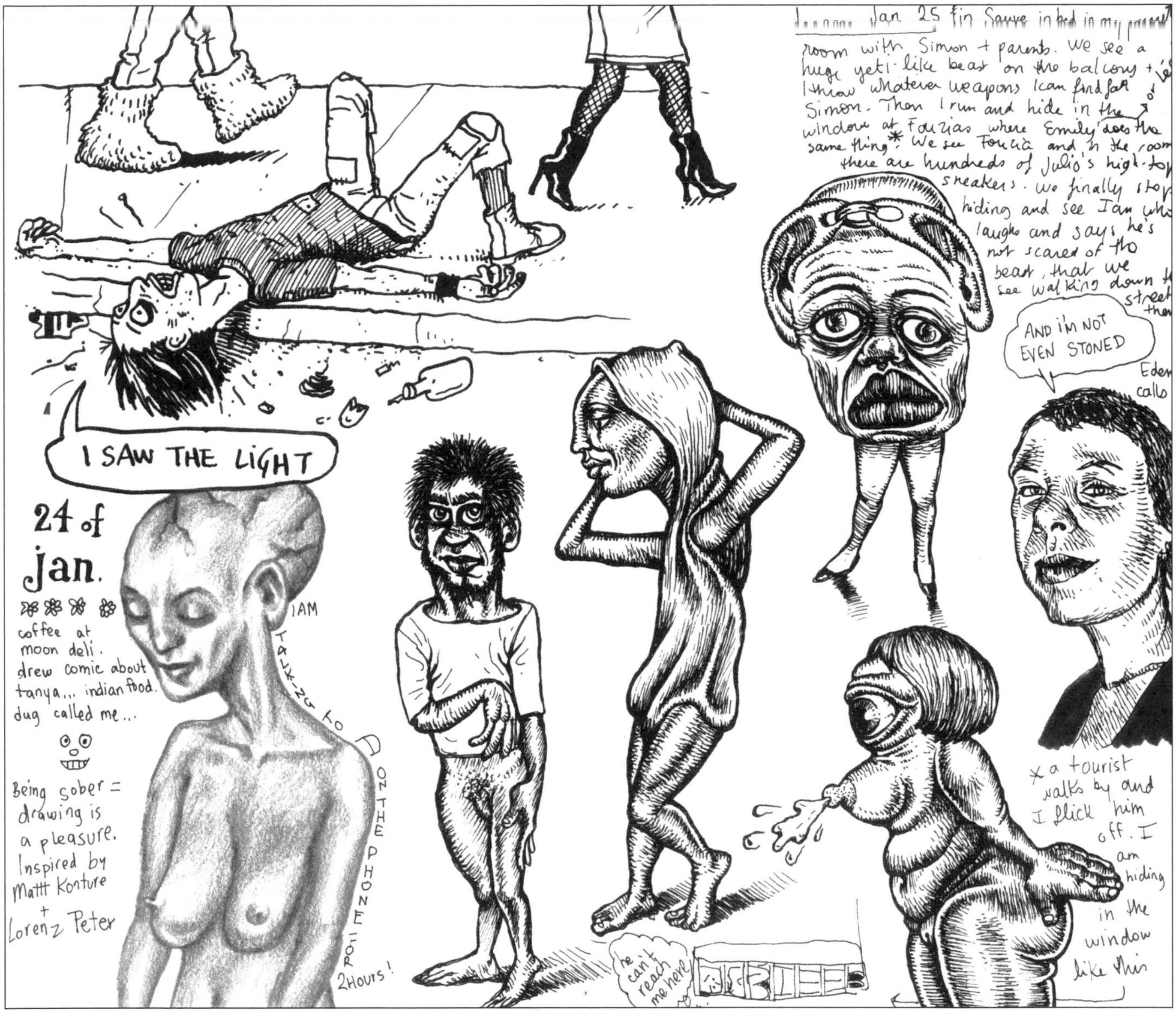
Jan 25
room with Simon + parents. We see a huge yeti-like beast on the balcony + I throw whatever weapons I can find for Simon. Then I run and hide in the window at Fouzias where Emily does the same thing*. We see Fouzia and in the room there are hundreds of Julio's high-top sneakers. We finally stop hiding and see Jan who laughs and says he's not scared of the beast, that we see walking down the street then
AND I'M NOT EVEN STONED
Eden calls
I SAW THE LIGHT
24 of jan.
coffee at moon deli. drew comic about tanya... indian food. dug called me...
Being sober = drawing is a pleasure. Inspired by Matt Konture + Lorenz Peter
I AM TALKING TO ON THE PHONE FOR 2 HOURS!
he can't reach me here
* a tourist walks by and I flick him off. I am hiding in the window like this

Age 23, Jan., 2005.

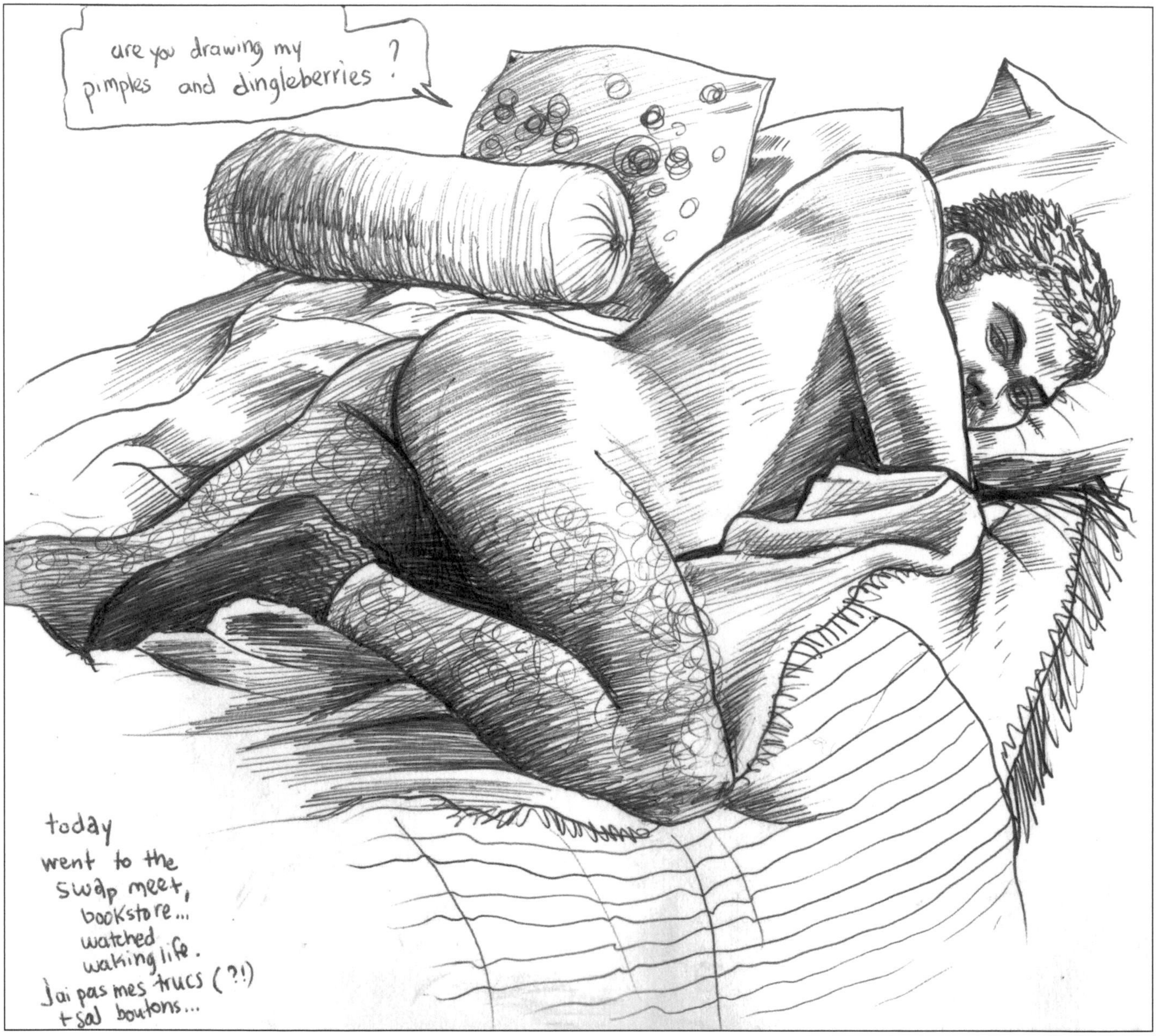
are you drawing my pimples and dingleberries ?
today went to the swap meet, bookstore... watched waking life. Jai pas mes trucs (?!) + sal boutons...

Drawn from life. Age 23, Jan., 2005.

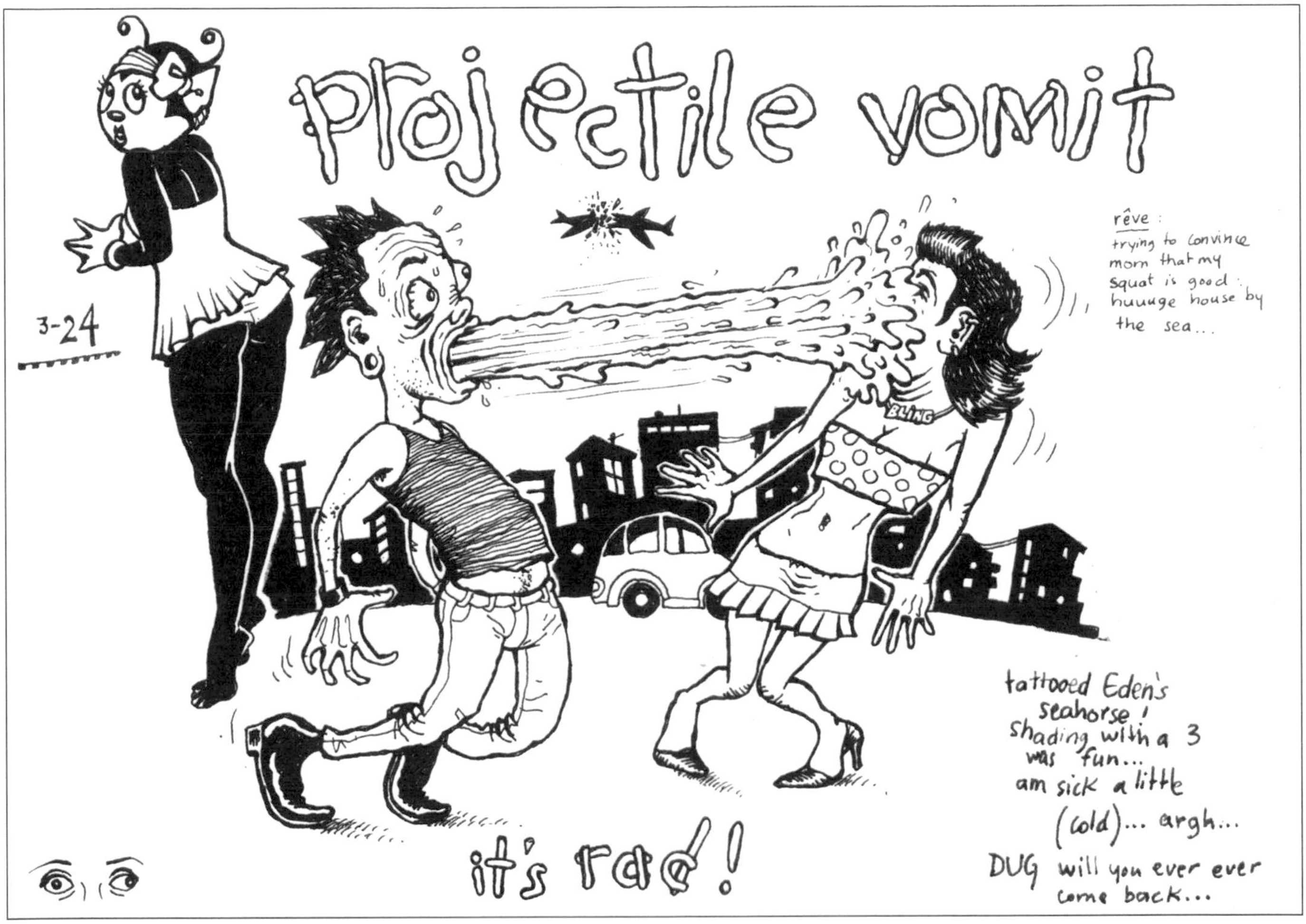
projectile vomit
3-24
rêve:
trying to convince mom that my squat is good: huuuge house by the sea...
BLING
tattooed Eden's seahorse! shading with a 3 was fun...
am sick a little (cold)... argh...
DUG will you ever ever come back...
it's rad!

Age 23, March, 2005.

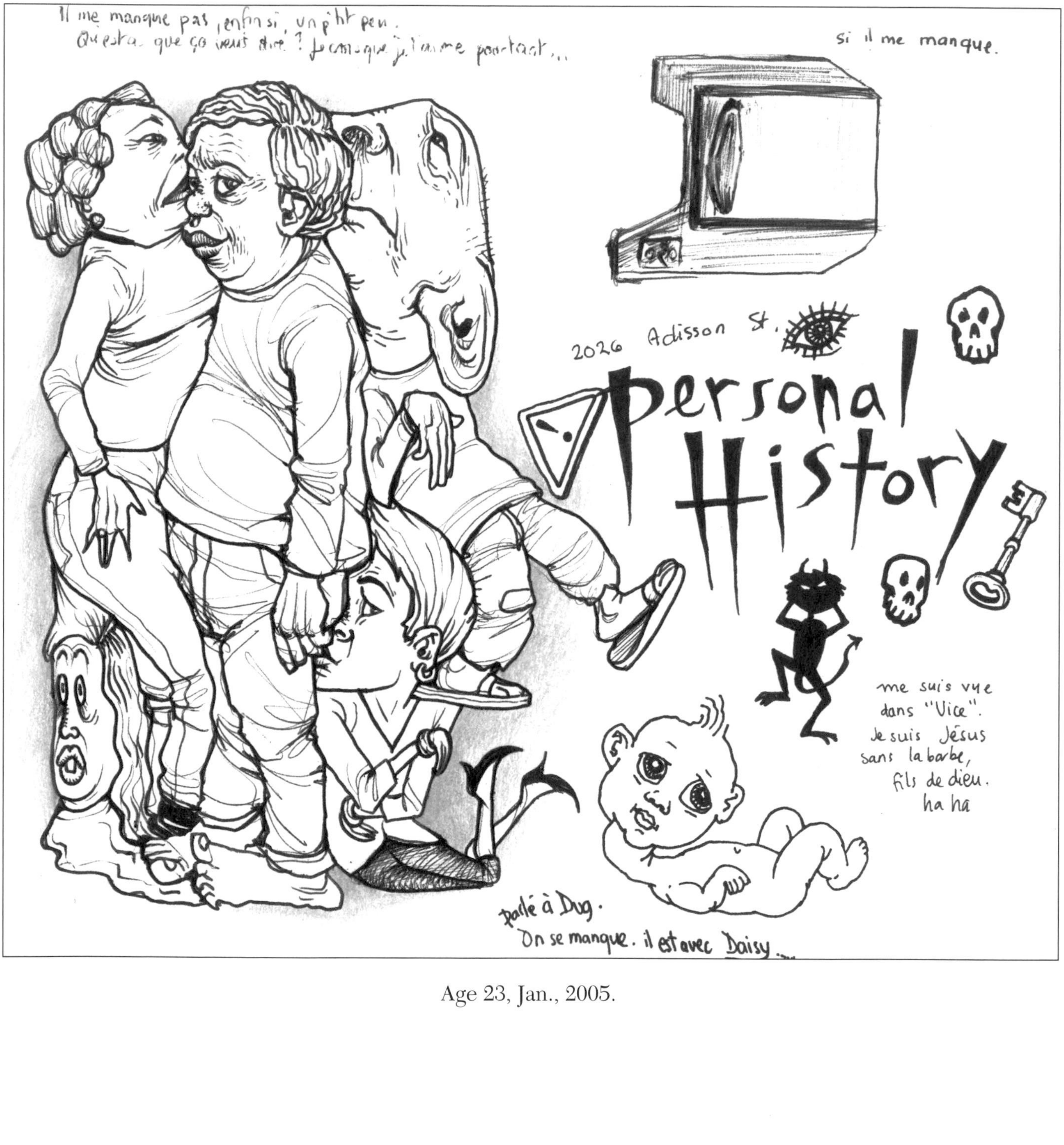
Il me manque pas, enfin si, un p'tit peu.
si il me manque.
2026 Adisson St.
Personal History
me suis vue dans "Vice". Je suis Jésus sans la barbe, fils de dieu. ha ha
parlé à Dug. On se manque. il est avec Daisy...

Age 23, Jan., 2005.

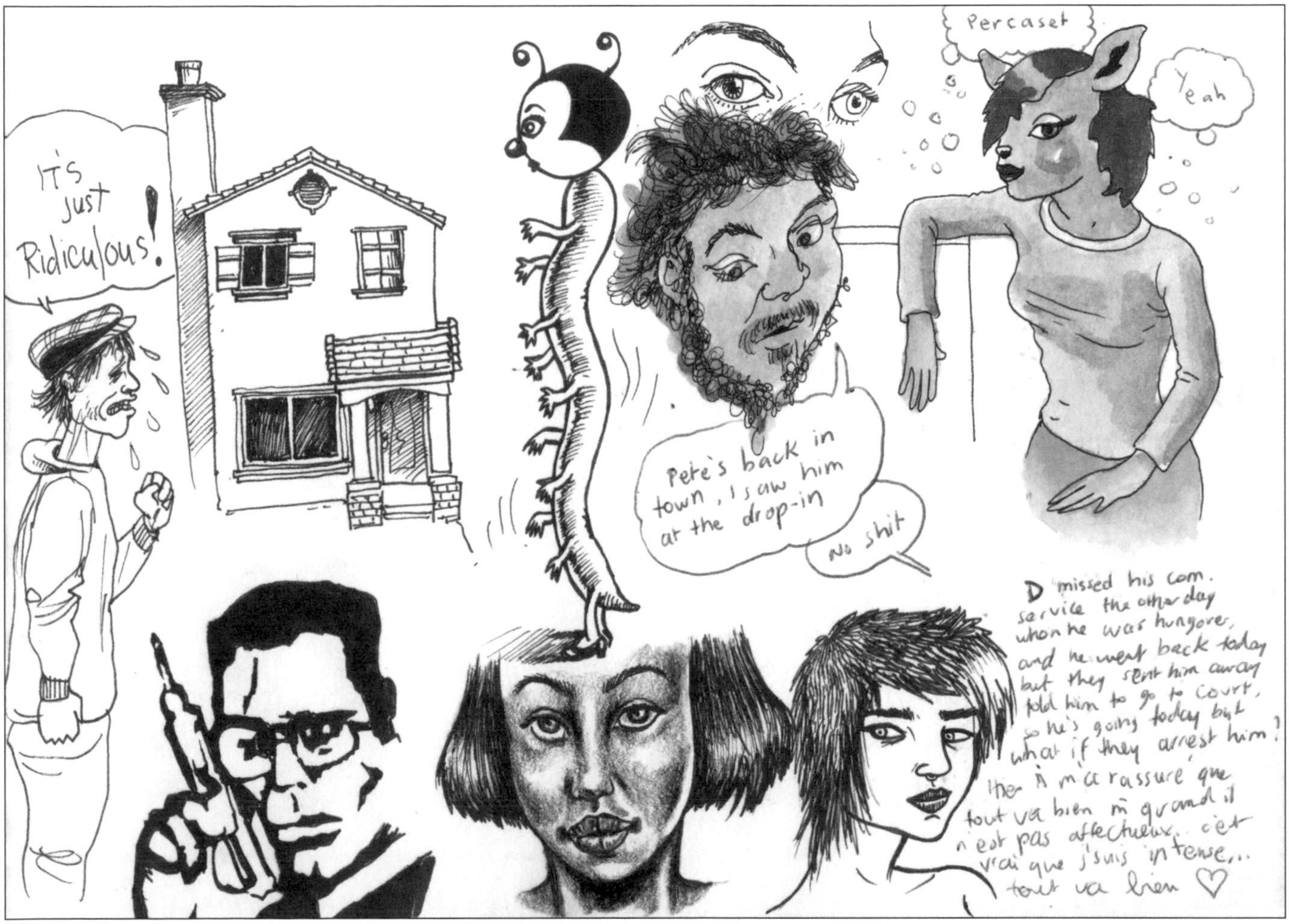

It's just Ridiculous!
Percaset
Yeah
Pete's back in town, I saw him at the drop-in
No shit
D missed his com. service the other day when he was hungover, and he went back today but they sent him away told him to go to court, so he's going today but what if they arrest him?
then A m'a rassuré que tout va bien m quand il n'est pas affectueux. c'et vrai que j'suis intense...
tout va bien ♡

Age 23, April, 2005.

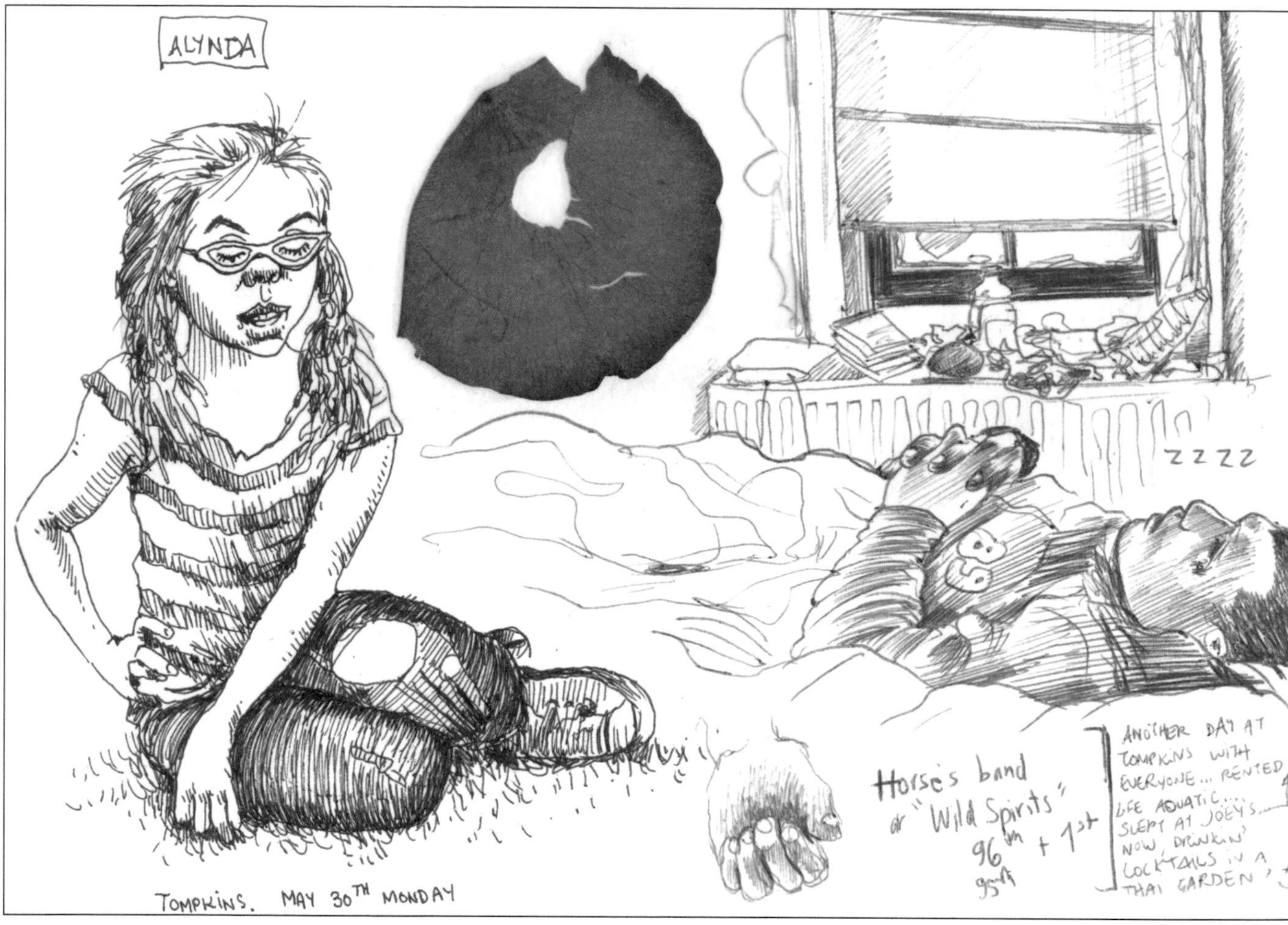
ALYNDA
ZZZZ
Horse's band
or "Wild Spirits"
96th + 1st
ANOTHER DAY AT TOMPKINS WITH EVERYONE... RENTED LIFE AQUATIC.... SLEPT AT JOEY'S.... NOW, DRINKIN' COCKTAILS IN A THAI GARDEN,
TOMPKINS. MAY 30TH MONDAY

Drawn from life. Age 23, May, 2005.

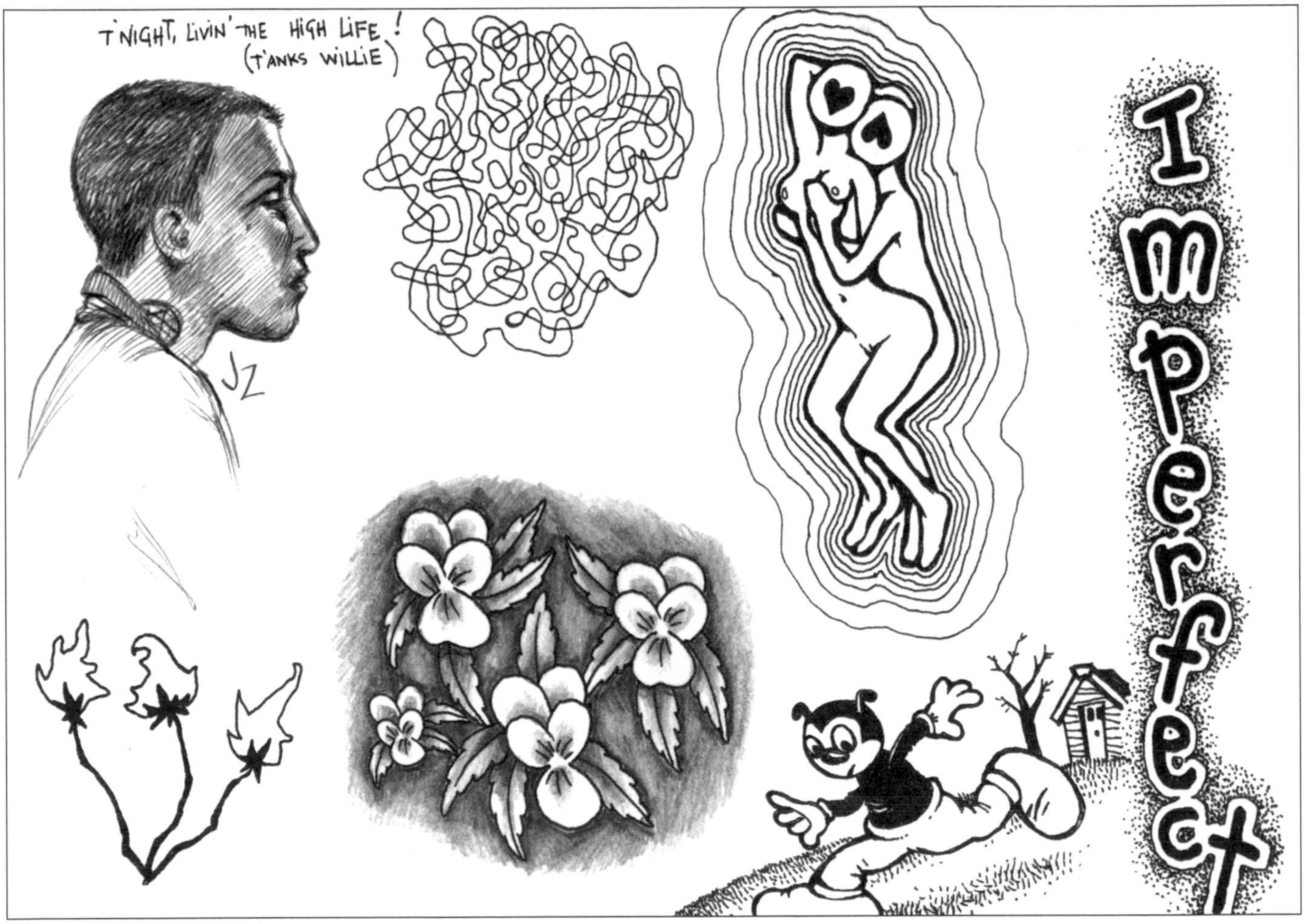
T'NIGHT, LIVIN' THE HIGH LIFE!
(T'ANKS WILLIE)
JZ
Imperfect

Age 23, June, 2005.

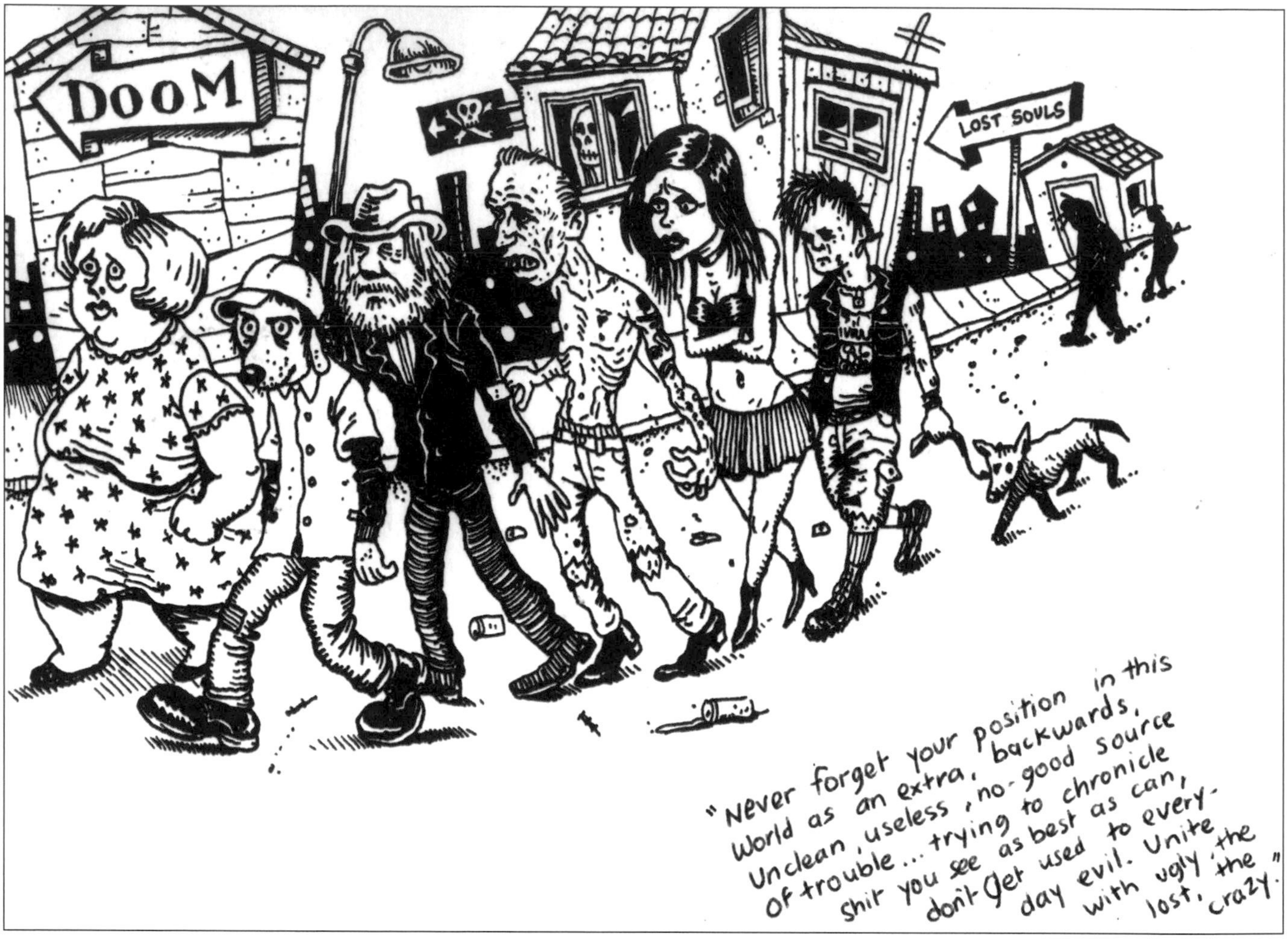
DOOM
LOST SOULS
"Never forget your position in this world as an extra, backwards, unclean, useless, no-good source of trouble... trying to chronicle shit you see as best as can, don't get used to every-day evil. Unite with ugly, the lost, the crazy."

Age 23, July, 2005.

13 Juillet
DUG est revenu
avec CHLOE...
il m'aime...
sais pas quoi penser...
regardé film avec Joey...
shiffelHPS, zines
hier regardé Latcho Drom...
ça a commencé a chauffer
(à poil nous 2) mais il pouvait
pas car il avait pris de l'héro
car il a raté sa dose de
methadone...
Tatoué Zach aussi...
j'ai trop envie de Joey...
on s'aime BEAUCOUP...
ma mère veut que j'aille
en France en sept...
Dug veut voyager...
il m'a dit qu'il faut
que je lui dise que c'est
fini pour de bon pour
qu'il "move on"
mais je peux pas...
je devrais sans
doute mais
est-ce vraiment
fini entre nous?
argh...
TETH
(number 9)
9 in
sanskrit
Junky
survey
Monday,
1pm!

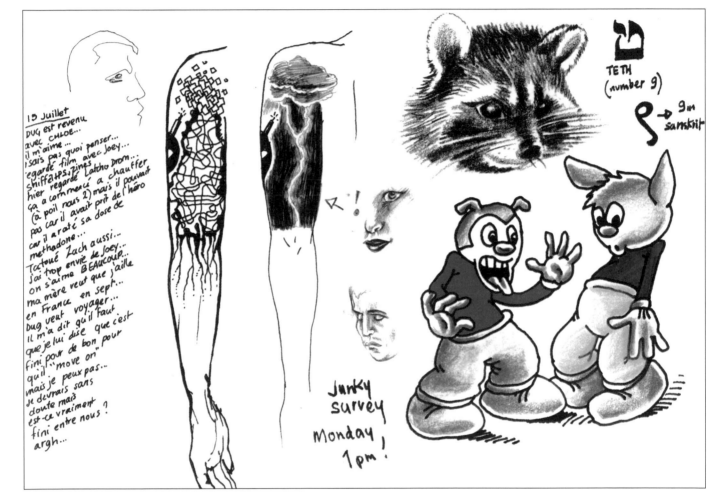

Age 23, July, 2005.

Drawn from life. Age 23, July, 2005.

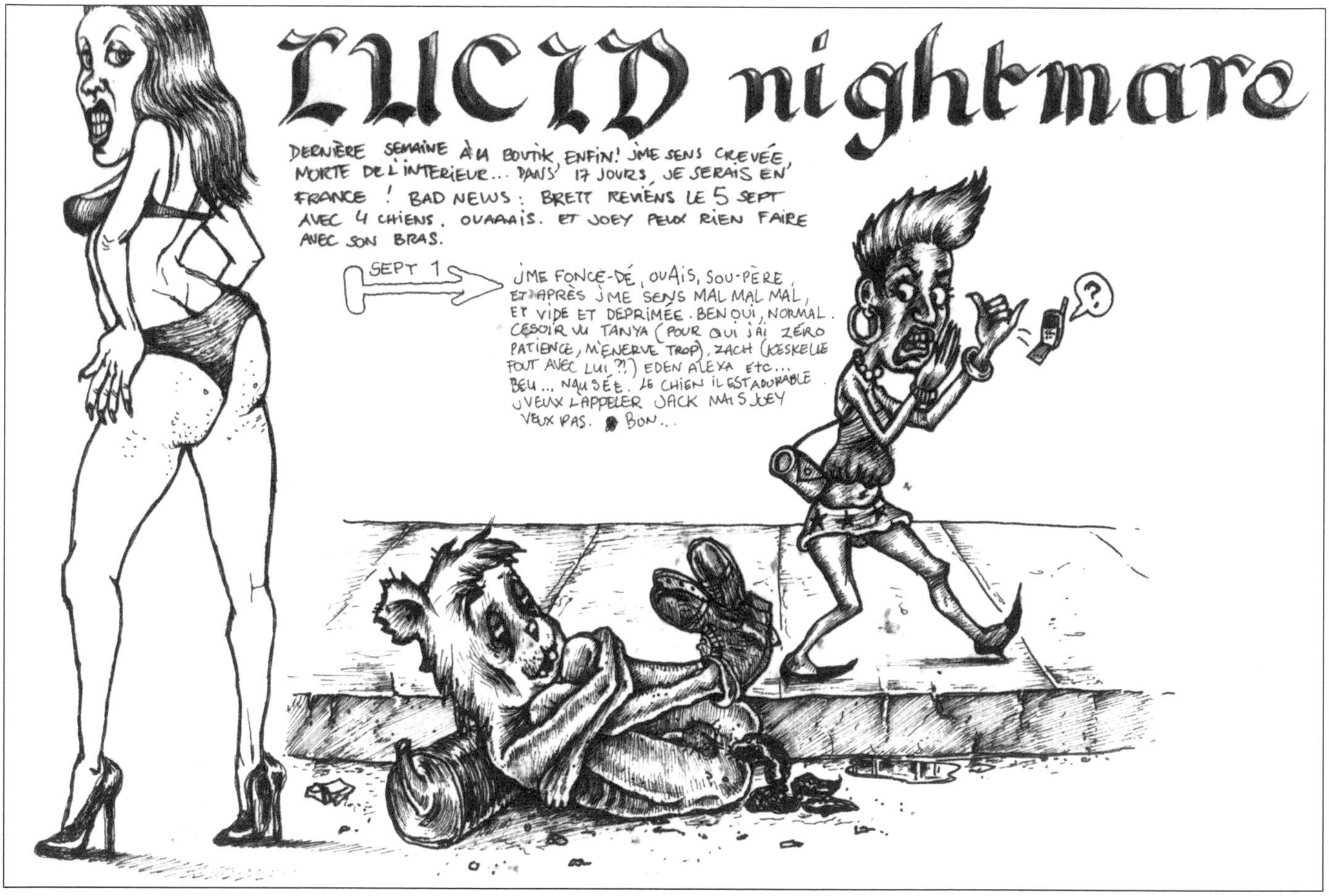
LUCID nightmare
DERNIÈRE SEMAINE À LA BOUTIK, ENFIN! JME SENS CREVÉE, MORTE DE L'INTERIEUR... DANS' 17 JOURS, JE SERAIS EN' FRANCE! BAD NEWS: BRETT REVIÉNS LE 5 SEPT AVEC 4 CHIENS. OUAAAIS. ET JOEY PEUX RIEN FAIRE AVEC SON BRAS.
SEPT 1
JME FONCE-DÉ, OUAIS, SOU-PÈRE, ET APRÈS JME SENS MAL MAL MAL, ET VIDE ET DEPRIMÉE. BEN OUI, NORMAL. CESOIR VU TANYA (POUR QUI J'AI ZÉRO PATIENCE, M'ENERVE TROP), ZACH (KESKELLE FOUT AVEC LUI ?!) EDEN ALEXA ETC... BEU... NAUSÉE. LE CHIEN IL EST ADORABLE. JVEUX L'APPELER JACK MAIS JOEY VEUX PAS. BON...
?

Age 23, Aug.–Sept., 2005.

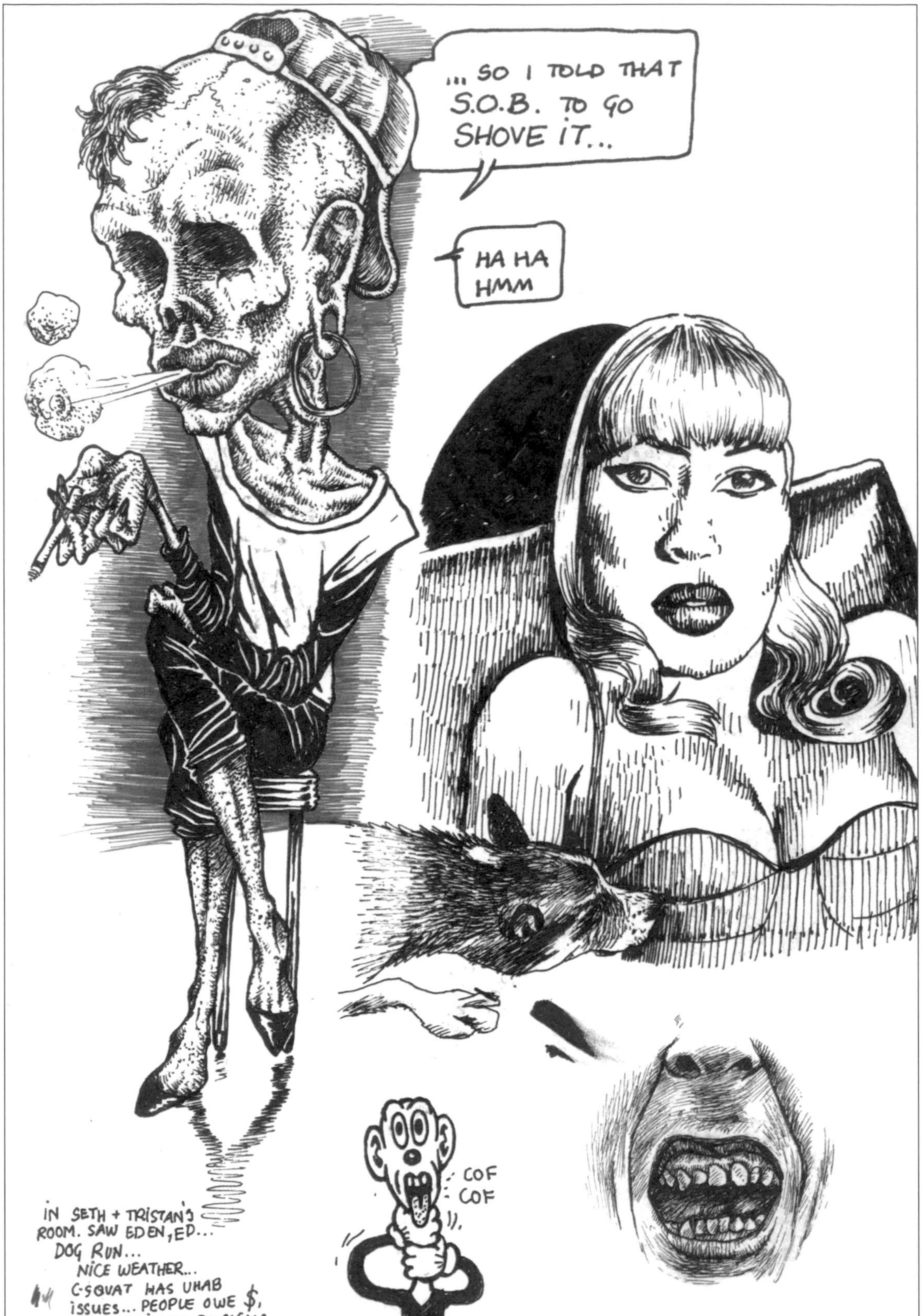
... SO I TOLD THAT S.O.B. TO GO SHOVE IT...
HA HA HMM
COF COF
IN SETH + TRISTAN'S ROOM. SAW EDEN, ED... DOG RUN... NICE WEATHER... C-SQUAT HAS UHAB ISSUES... PEOPLE OWE $, HAVE ATTITUDE PROBLEMS...

Age 24, Oct., 2005.

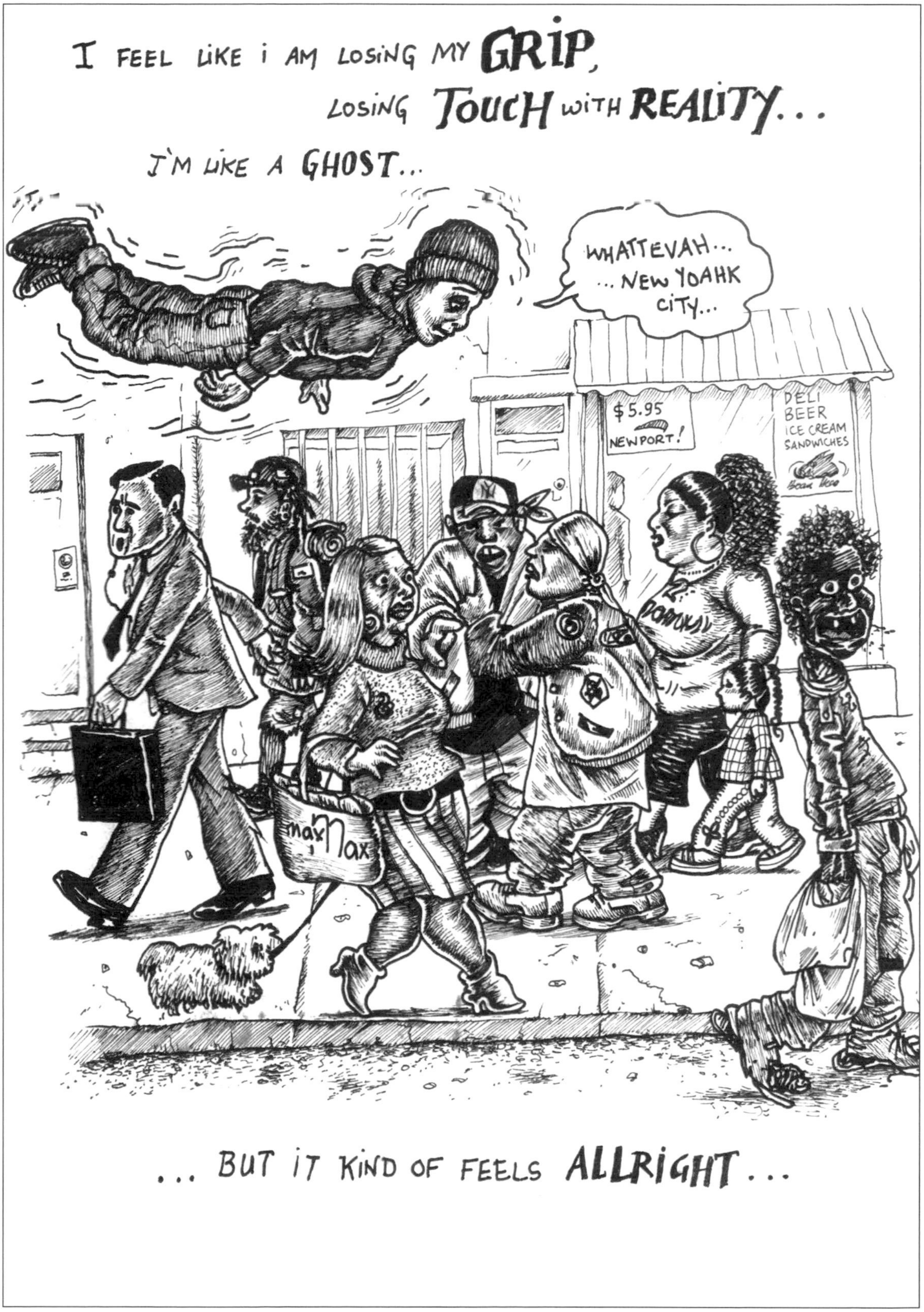
I FEEL LIKE I AM LOSING MY GRIP,
LOSING TOUCH WITH REALITY...
I'M LIKE A GHOST...
WHATTEVAH...
... NEW YOAHK CITY...
$5.95 NEWPORT!
DELI
BEER
ICE CREAM
SANDWICHES
maxNax
... BUT IT KIND OF FEELS ALLRIGHT...

Age 24, fall, 2005.

the ZZZ page ...

Drawn from life. Age 24, Nov., 2005.

!xotenusiusej!

TODAY, i PINCHED COUGH DROPS & LIP BALM

Age 24, Dec., 2005.

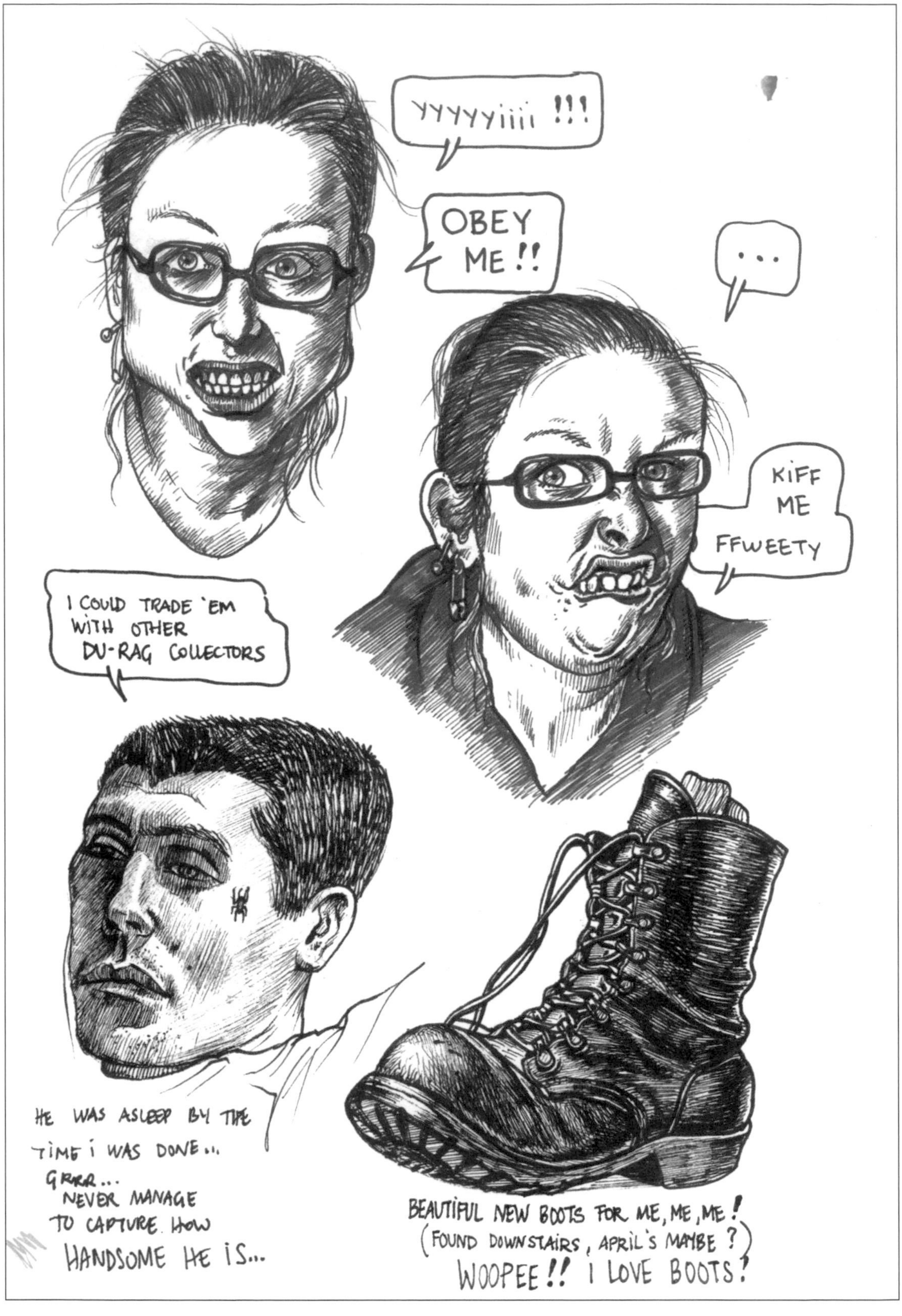
YYYYYiiii !!!
OBEY ME!!
...
KIFF ME FFWEETY
I COULD TRADE 'EM WITH OTHER DU-RAG COLLECTORS
HE WAS ASLEEP BY THE TIME I WAS DONE... GRRR... NEVER MANAGE TO CAPTURE HOW HANDSOME HE IS...
BEAUTIFUL NEW BOOTS FOR ME, ME, ME!
(FOUND DOWNSTAIRS, APRIL'S MAYBE?)
WOOPEE!! I LOVE BOOTS!

Drawn from life. Age 24, Jan., 2006.

Top and bottom left: Drawn from life. Age 24, Jan., 2006.

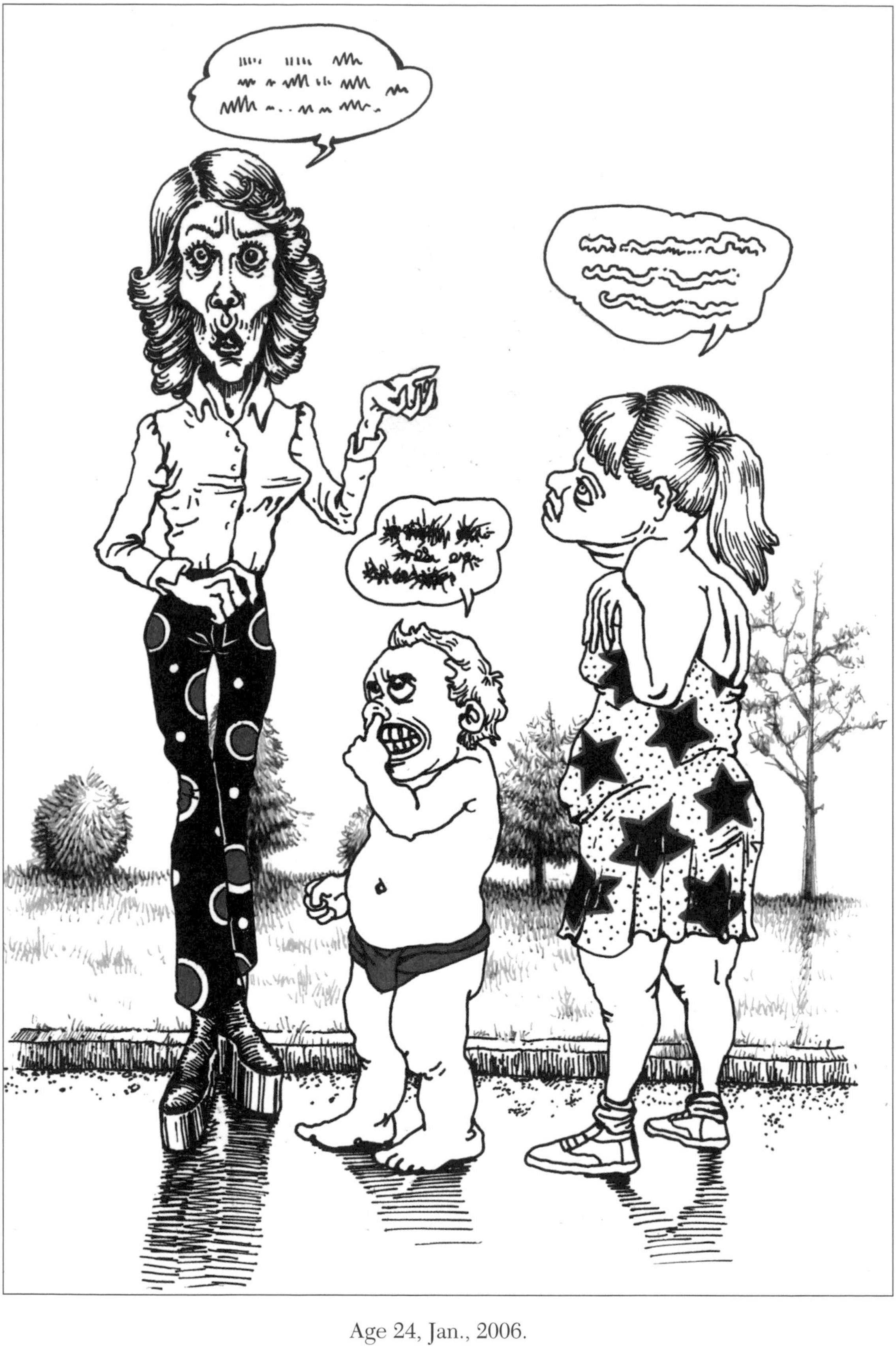

Age 24, Jan., 2006.

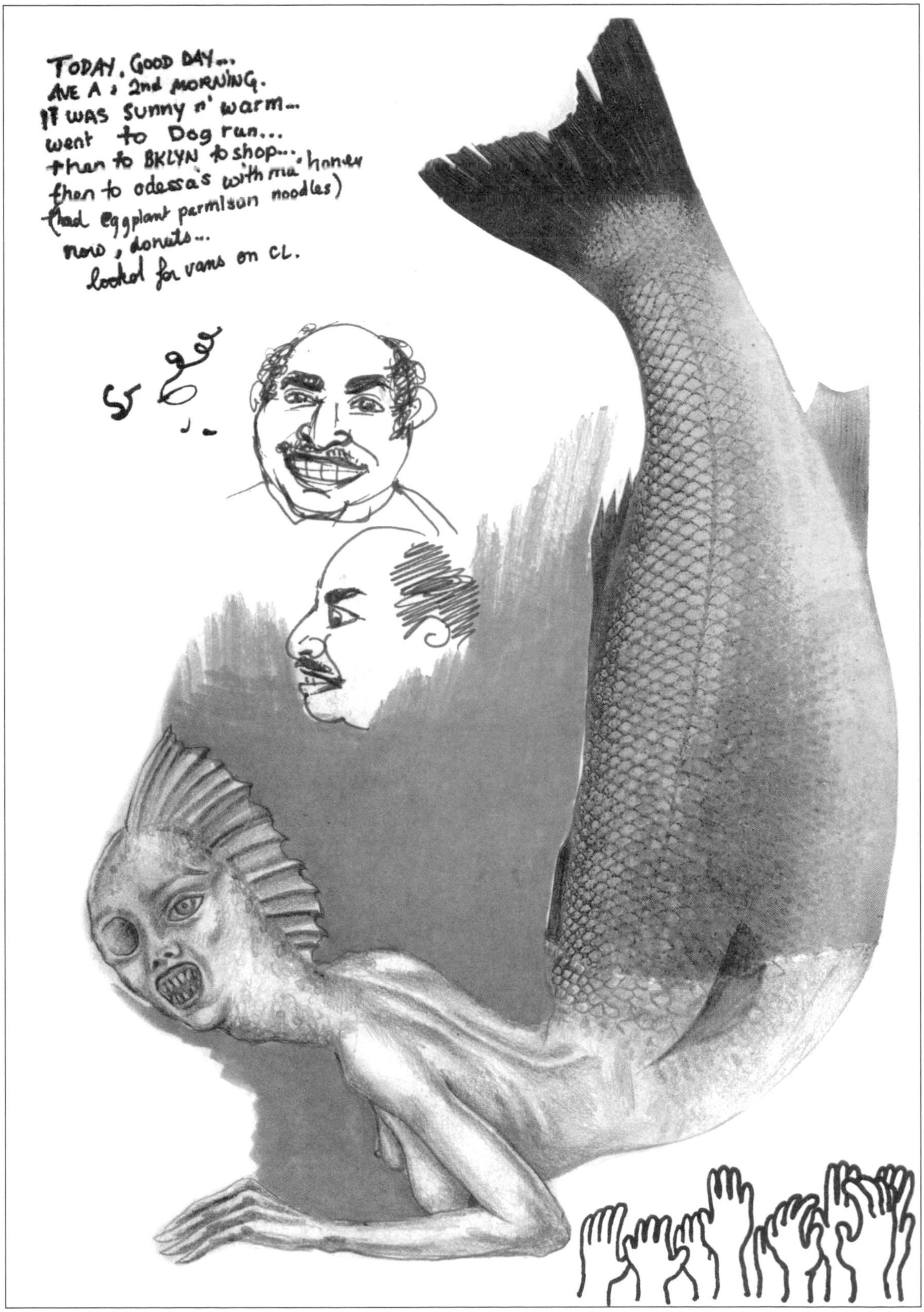
TODAY, GOOD DAY...
AVE A ; 2nd MORNING.
IT WAS Sunny n' warm...
went to Dog run...
then to BKLYN to shop...
then to odessa's with ma' honey
(had eggplant parmison noodles)
now, donuts...
looked for vans on CL.

Age 24, Feb., 2006.

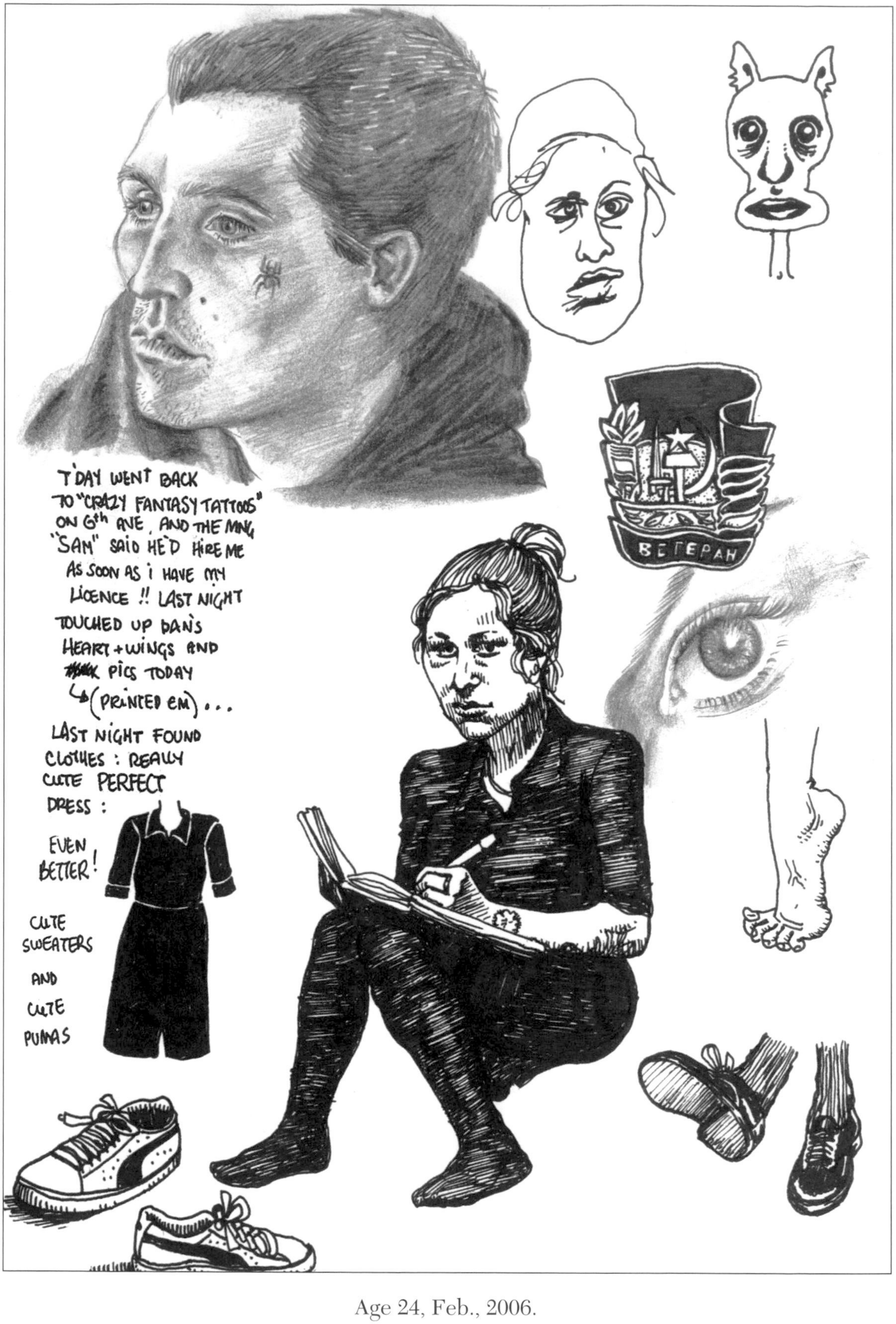
ВЕТЕРАН
T'DAY WENT BACK TO "CRAZY FANTASY TATTOOS" ON 6th AVE, AND THE MNG, "SAM" SAID HE'D HIRE ME AS SOON AS I HAVE MY LICENCE !! LAST NIGHT TOUCHED UP DAN'S HEART + WINGS AND PICS TODAY
(PRINTED EM) . . .
LAST NIGHT FOUND CLOTHES : REALLY CUTE PERFECT DRESS :
EVEN BETTER !
CUTE SWEATERS
AND
CUTE PUMAS

Age 24, Feb., 2006.

ENCORE CHERCHÉ VAN SUR CL...
Y A DES OCAZ...
VU IMAGES DE EUGENE. C'EST BEAU.
ON A QU'UNE ENVIE C'EST ÊTRE LA BAS
AU PRINTEMPS, A VISITER TOUTE LA CÔTE
NORD·EST, CAMPER, SE BAIGNER, TROUVER
UNE P'TITE MAISONÉTTE DANS LA CAMPAGNE
PRÈS D'EUGENE... LE PARADIS... DOUCHE,
CUISINE, ESPACE DESSIN, JARDIN
POUR CHIEN... AAAH... J'AI HATE!!

Age 24, Feb., 2006.

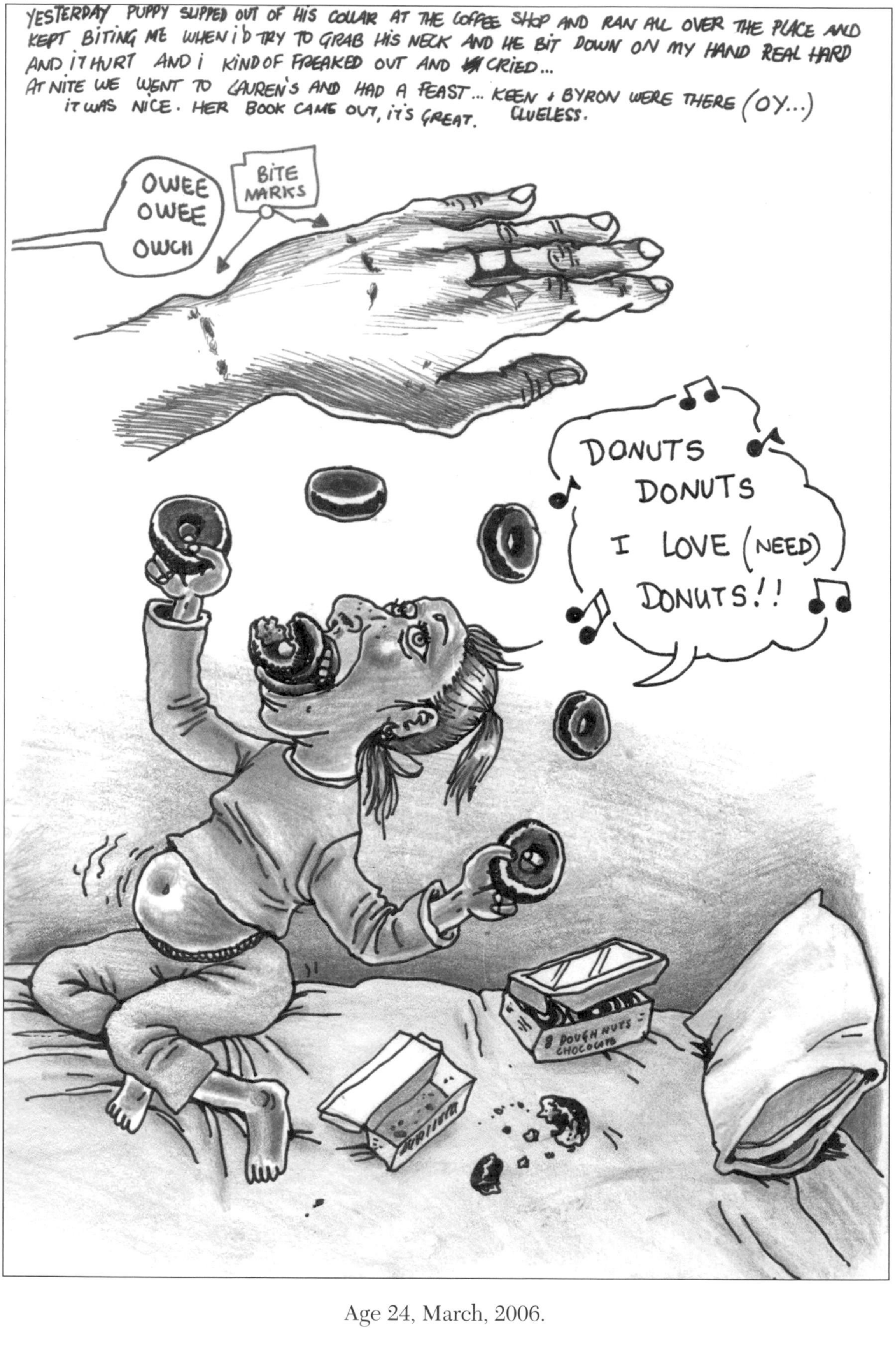
YESTERDAY PUPPY SLIPPED OUT OF HIS COLLAR AT THE COFFEE SHOP AND RAN ALL OVER THE PLACE AND KEPT BITING ME WHEN i'D TRY TO GRAB HIS NECK AND HE BIT DOWN ON MY HAND REAL HARD AND iT HURT AND i KIND OF FREAKED OUT AND CRIED...
AT NITE WE WENT TO LAUREN'S AND HAD A FEAST... KEEN + BYRON WERE THERE (OY...)
iT WAS NICE. HER BOOK CAME OUT, iT'S GREAT. CLUELESS.
OWEE OWEE OWCH
BITE MARKS
DONUTS DONUTS I LOVE (NEED) DONUTS!!
8 DOUGH NUTS CHOCOLATE

Age 24, March, 2006.

To all the P.C., health-crazed, low-carb, Madonna moms; the more you run around being perfect, the more your kids will become your worst night-mare !! And you know what? They're right and you are all psycho bitches !!

Age 24, April, 2006.

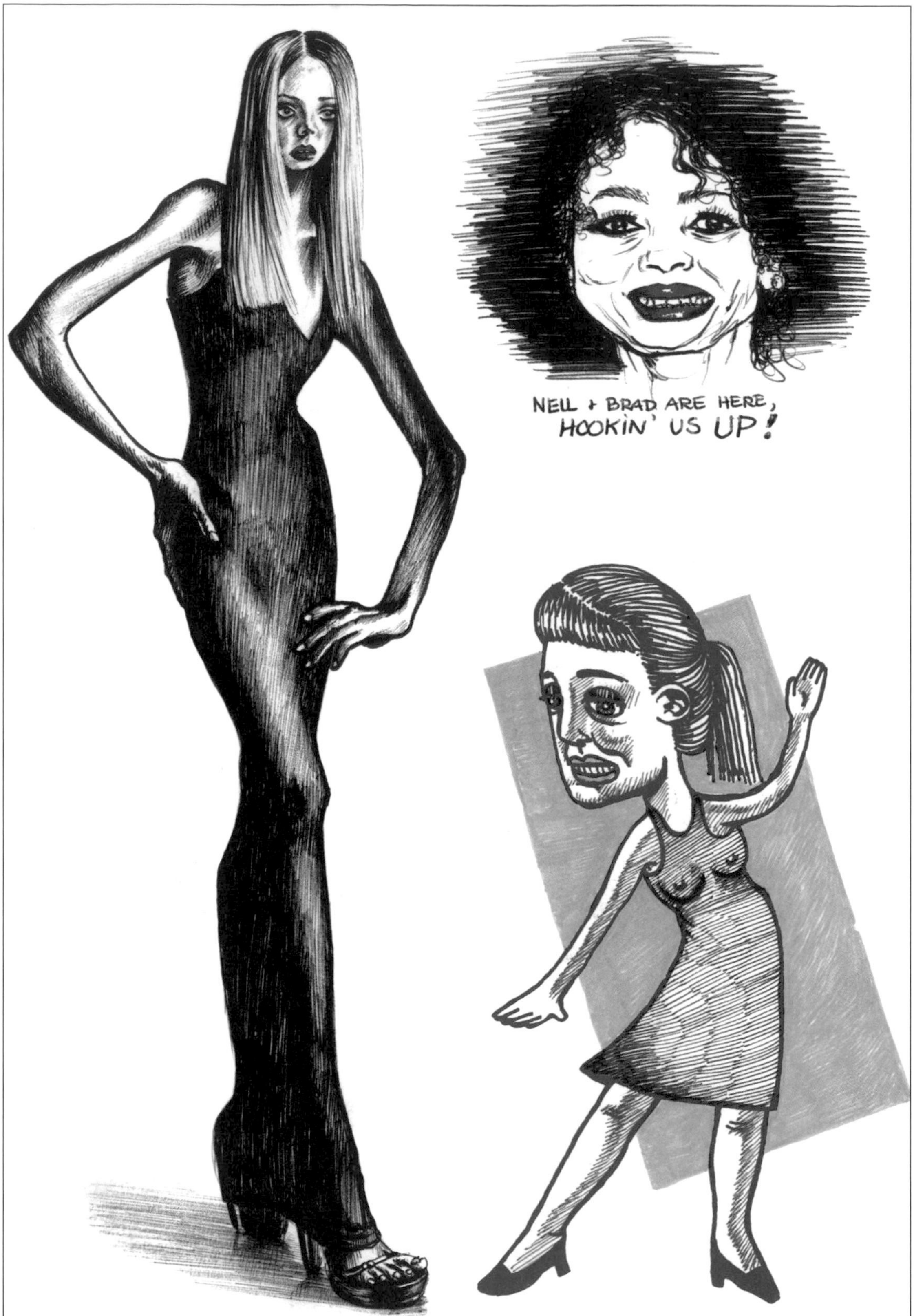
NELL + BRAD ARE HERE,
HOOKIN' US UP!

Age 24, May, 2006.

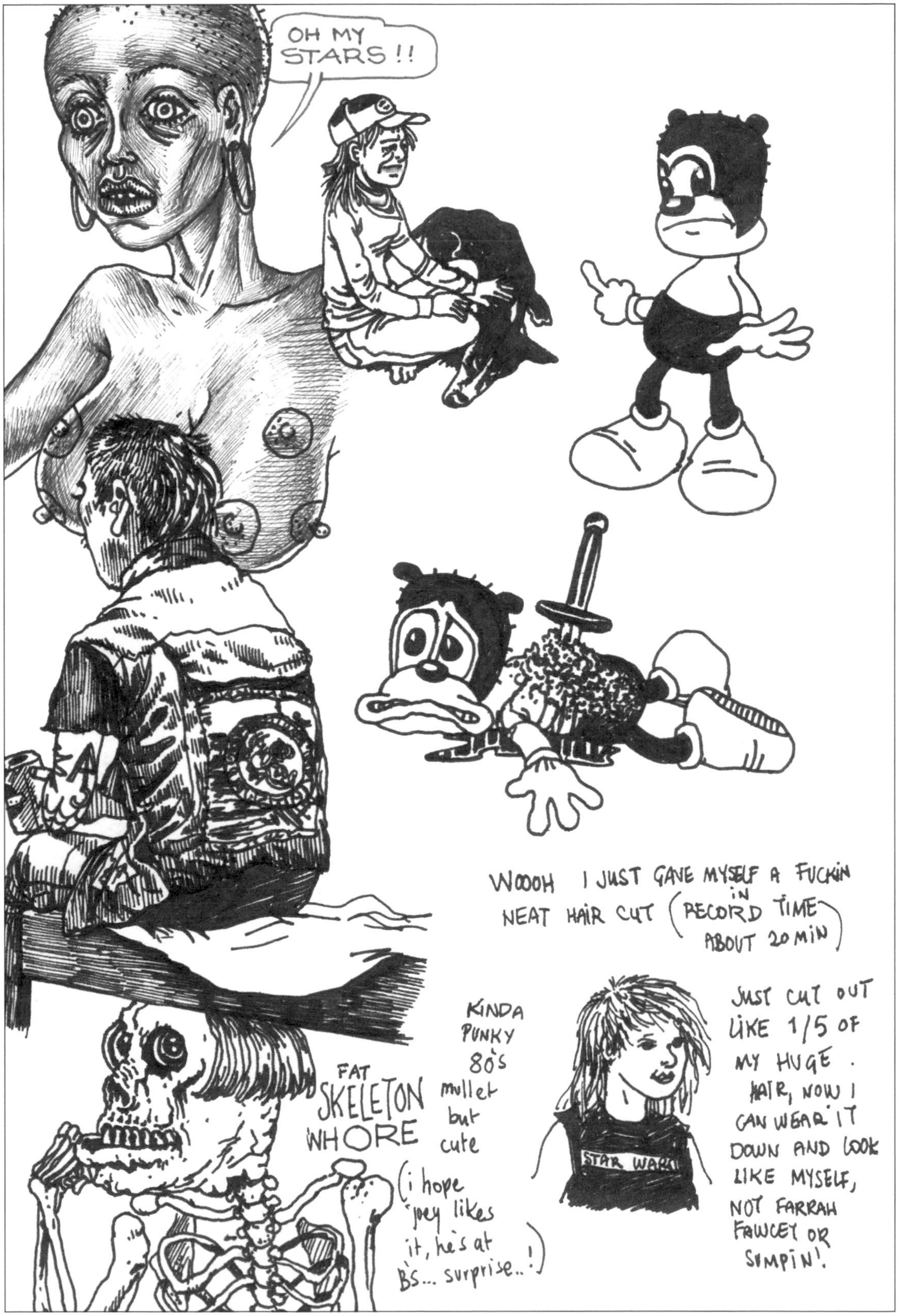
OH MY STARS!!
WOOOH I JUST GAVE MYSELF A FUCKIN NEAT HAIR CUT (IN RECORD TIME ABOUT 20 MIN)
KINDA PUNKY 80's mullet but cute
FAT SKELETON WHORE
(i hope joey likes it, he's at BS... surprise..!)
JUST CUT OUT LIKE 1/5 OF MY HUGE. HAIR, NOW I CAN WEAR IT DOWN AND LOOK LIKE MYSELF, NOT FARRAH FAWCET OR SUMPIN'.
STAR WARS

Age 24, May, 2006.

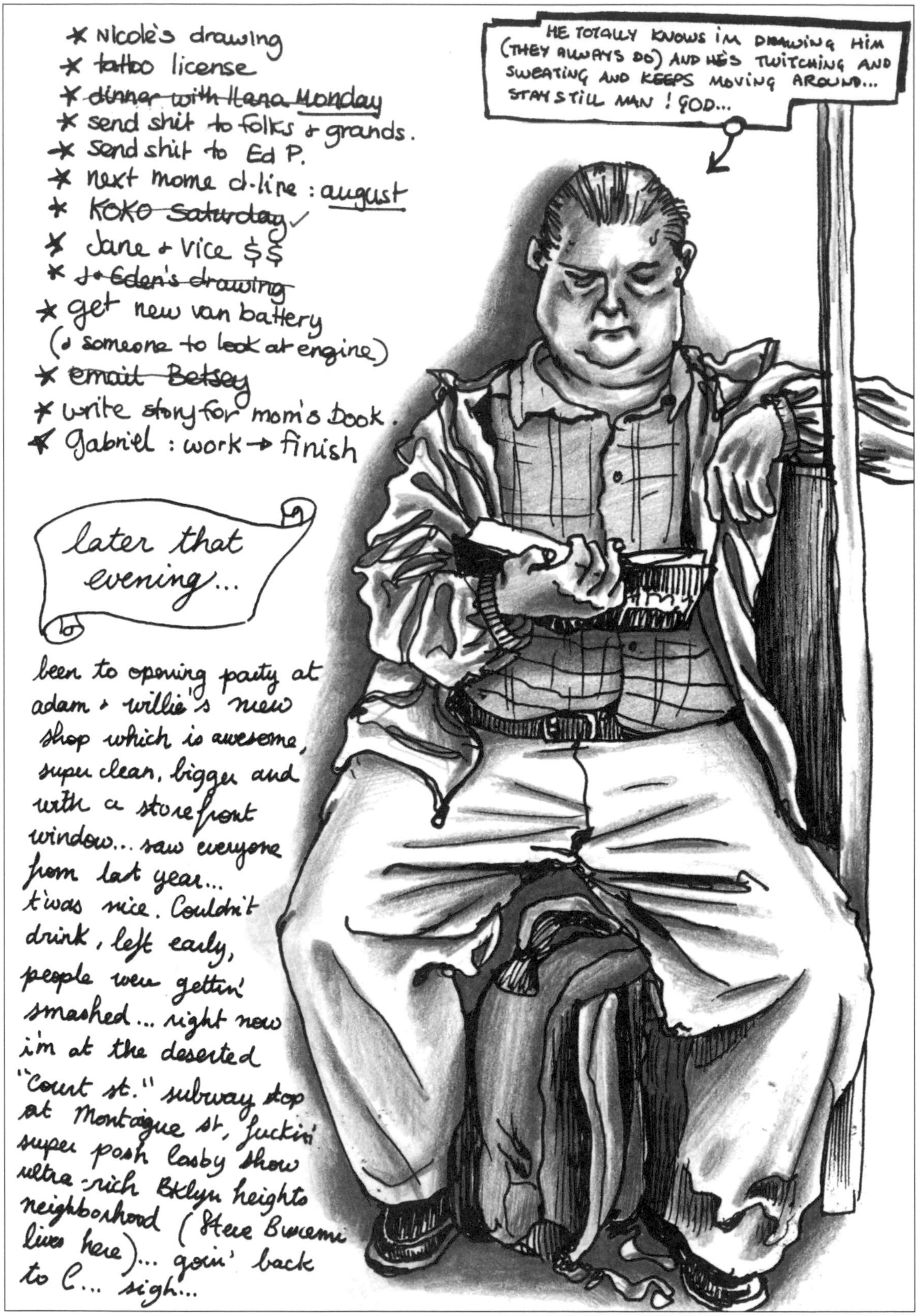

Drawn from life. Age 24, May, 2006.

GROWIN' UP, SETTLIN' DOWN
2006 TO 2010 / 25 TO 28 YRS OLD

I AM STILL PAYING THE PRICE FOR MY ROWDY TIMES IN THE STATES; I GOT PULLED UNDER BY A MEAN CURRENT, BUT I HAD REASONS TO STAY ALIVE AND I COULD SAY I'M OUT OF TROUBLE NOW.

GOING THROUGH ALL THOSE OLD DRAWINGS AND WORDS COULD MAKE ME SICK TO MY STOMACH OR SEND A SHIVER THROUGH ME, RELIVING THOSE DAYS WITH THE PEOPLE AND PLACES THAT FILLED THEM... I DO THINK THEY MAKE SOME INTERESTING PAGES TO LOOK AT FROM AN OUTSIDE POINT OF VIEW.

IN MY CURRENT SITUATION, FINALLY SETTLED DOWN AFTER A FEW YEARS OF DARKNESS AND STRUGGLE, SET UP NICE AND COZY WITH A GOOD MAN AND OUR BABY, I FEEL NO RESTLESSNESS, NO BOREDOM. THE PROSPECT OF CALM, QUIET DAYS WITH TIME TO READ, WRITE AND DRAW IS ALL I ASK.

I HAVE LET GO OF ALL THAT PRESSURE OF LIVING UP TO AND BEING COMPARED TO "THE LEGEND". I DON'T EVEN REALLY EXPECT MUCH FROM MYSELF ART-WISE, MAYBE A FEW DRAWINGS... BAH.

I FIGURE IF I CAN PUT ALL THE ABNORMALITY, PERVERSION AND ZANINESS ONTO PAPER AND STILL MANAGE TO BE A PARTIALLY NORMAL MOTHER TO MY KIDS, I WILL HAVE DONE ALL RIGHT. ♡

BORN INTO THIS.

Born into this.

"Born into this."

"D'AILLEURS, POUR LA SÉANCE PHOTO, SON AGENT NOUS A PRÉVENUS : CÉCILE DEVRA S'ABSENTER PENDANT LE SHOOT POUR ALLAITER."

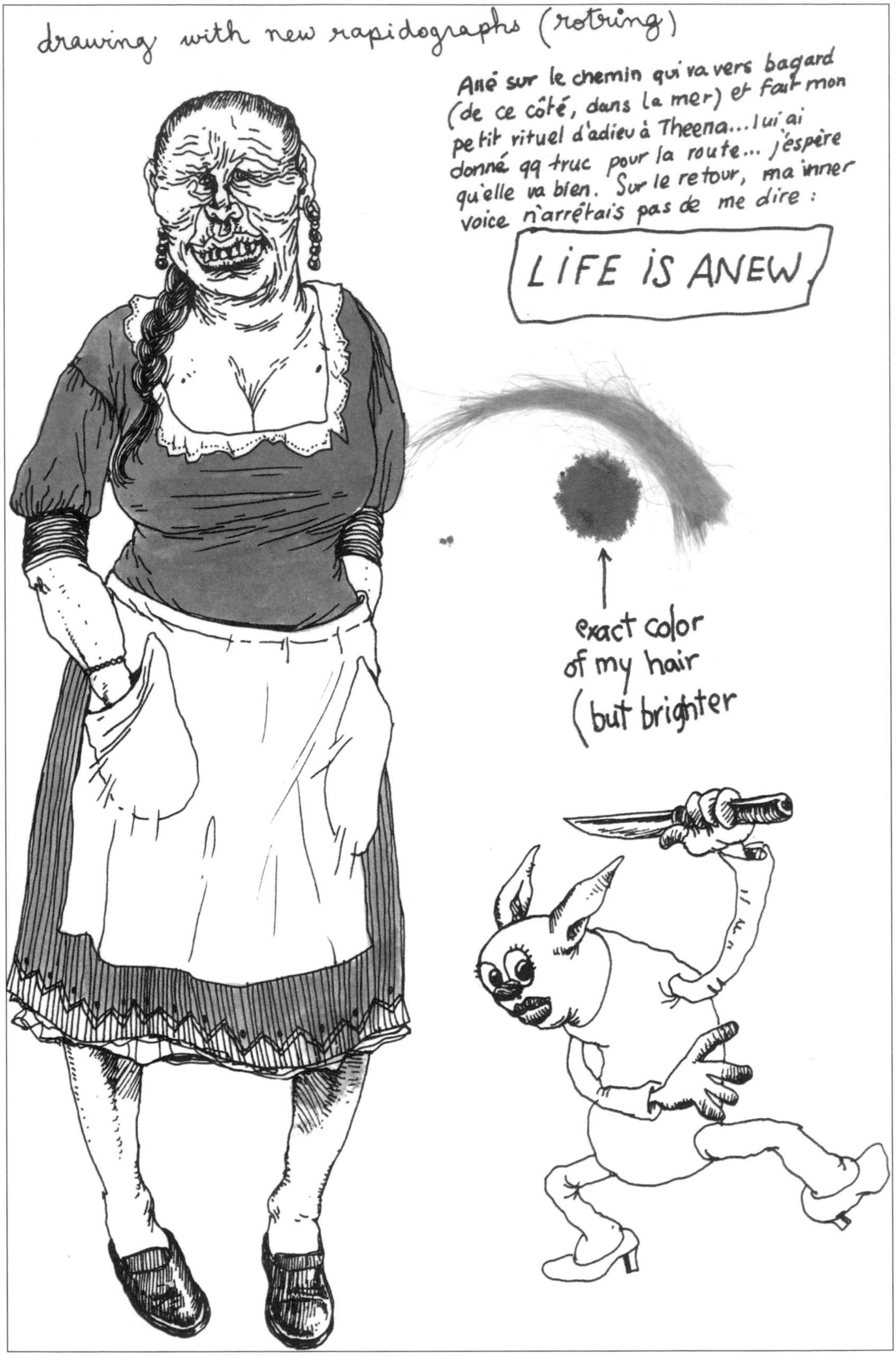
drawing with new rapidographs (rotring)
Allé sur le chemin qui va vers bagard (de ce côté, dans la mer) et fait mon petit rituel d'adieu à Theena... lui ai donné qq truc pour la route... j'espère qu'elle va bien. Sur le retour, ma inner voice n'arrêtais pas de me dire :
LIFE IS ANEW
exact color of my hair
(but brighter

Age 24, Aug., 2006.

Drawn from life. Age 24, Sept., 2006.

le doudou est rentré ! youpi -tralala !

Drawn from life. Age 25, Oct., 2006.

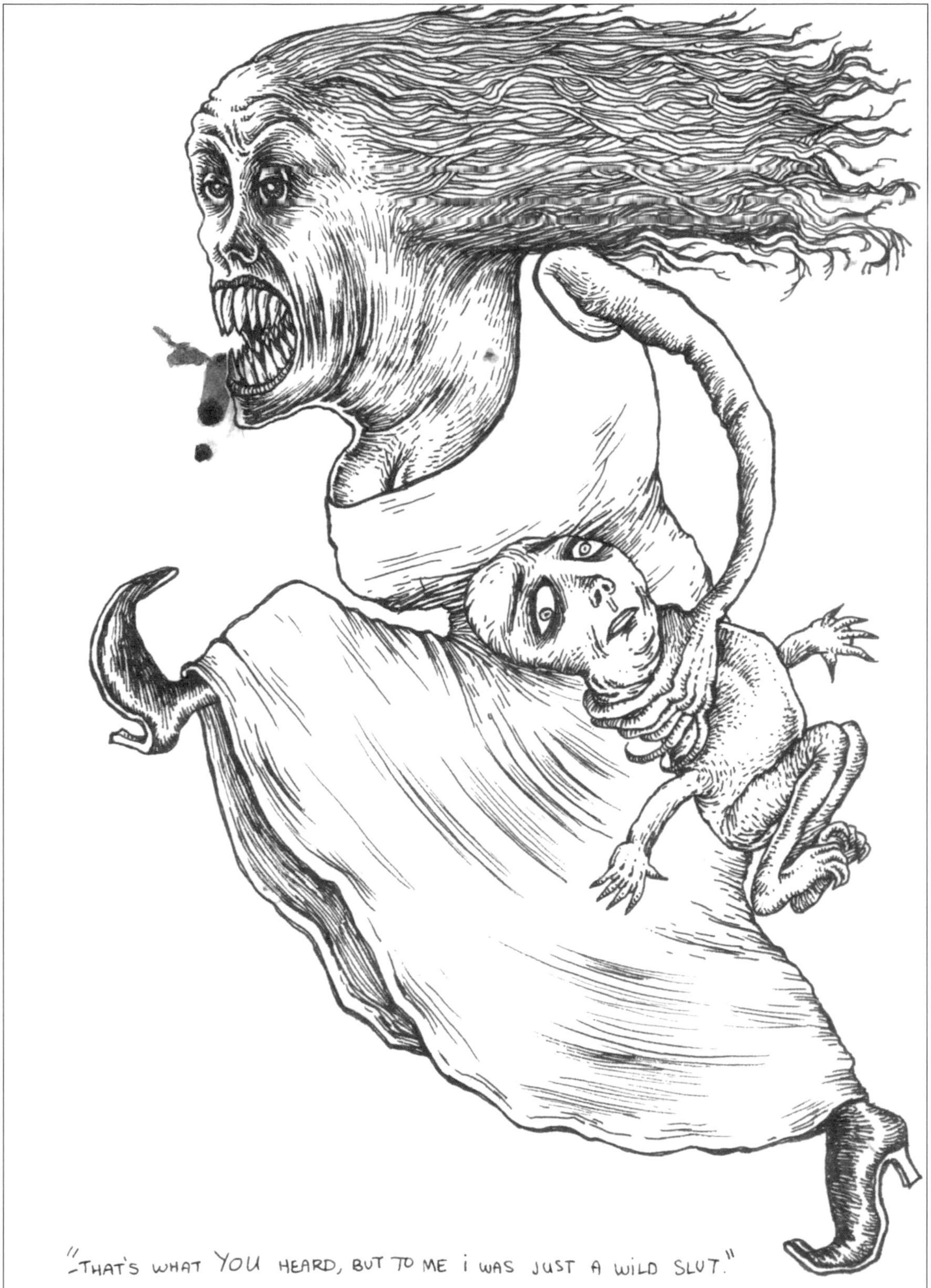
"-THAT'S WHAT YOU HEARD, BUT TO ME i WAS JUST A WILD SLUT."
-BETSY AT THE TOUR, OCT 15 '06

Age 25, Oct., 2006.

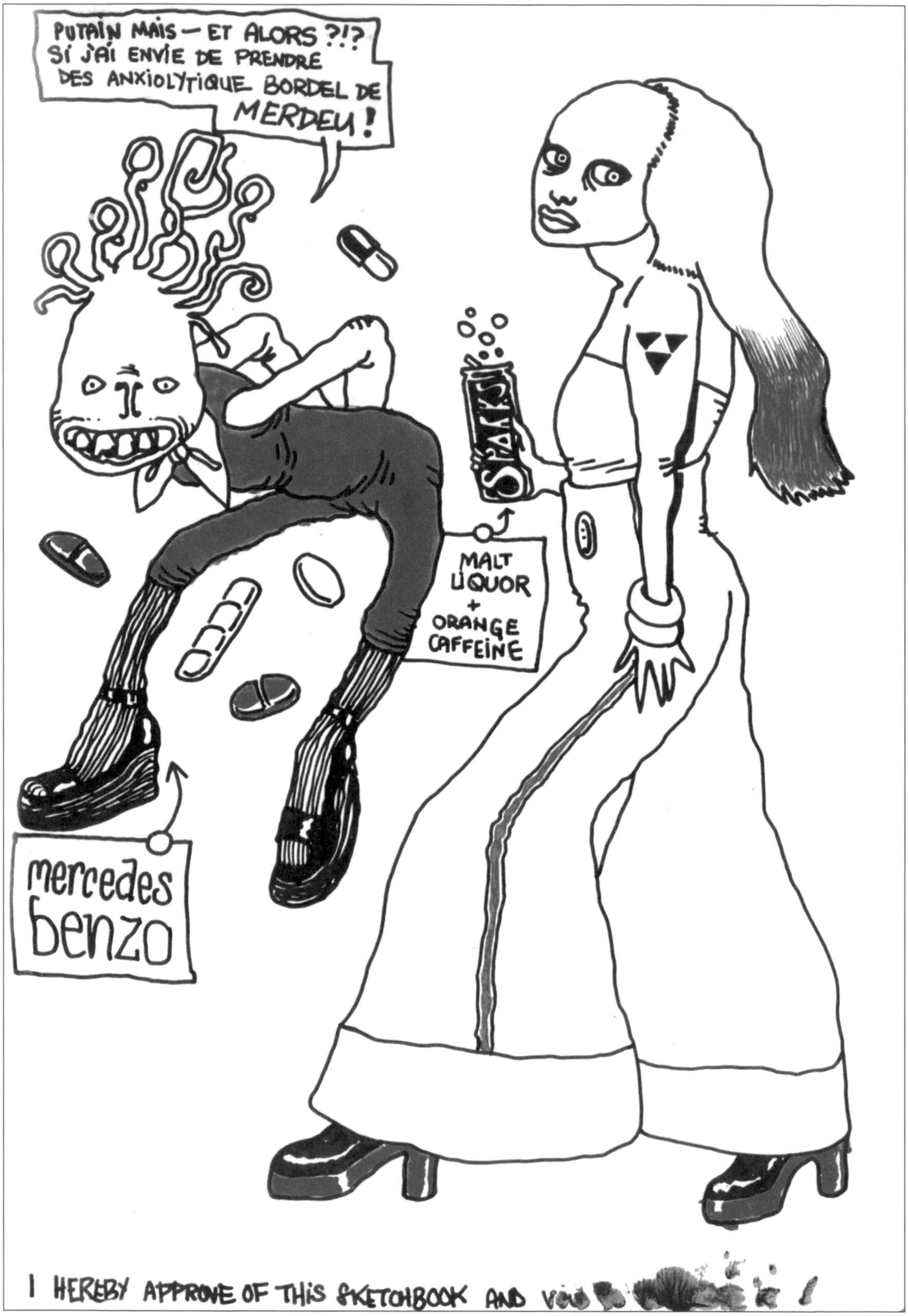
PUTAIN MAIS — ET ALORS ?!?
SI J'AI ENVIE DE PRENDRE DES ANXIOLYTIQUE BORDEL DE MERDEU!
SPARKS
MALT LIQUOR + ORANGE CAFFEINE
mercedes benzo
I HEREBY APPROVE OF THIS SKETCHBOOK AND

Age 25, Nov., 2006.

there are garlands of lights, santas and
x-mas trees all over the village!

Age 25, Dec., 2006.

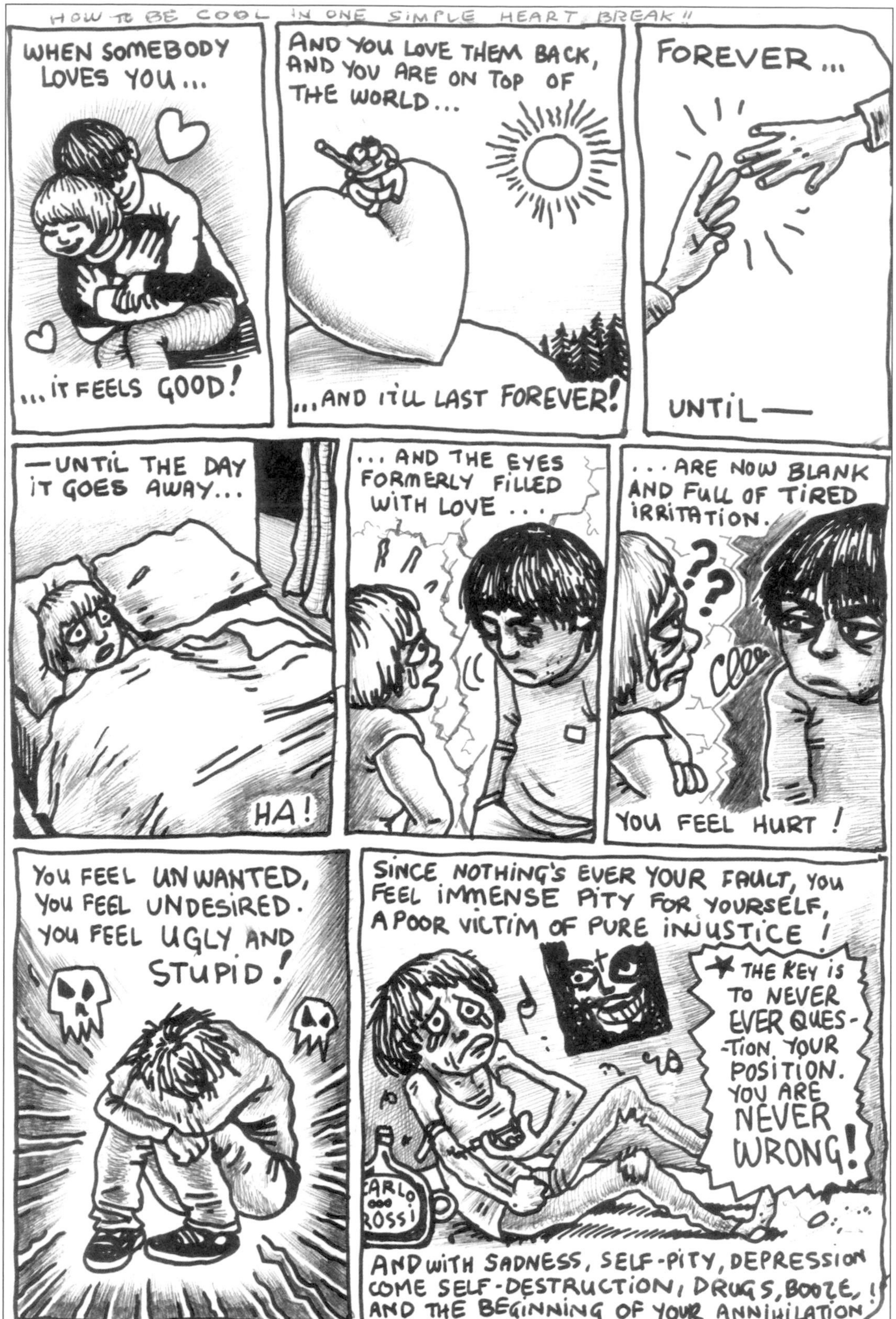
HOW TO BE COOL IN ONE SIMPLE HEART BREAK!!
WHEN SOMEBODY LOVES YOU...
...IT FEELS GOOD!
AND YOU LOVE THEM BACK, AND YOU ARE ON TOP OF THE WORLD...
...AND IT'LL LAST FOREVER!
FOREVER...
UNTIL—
—UNTIL THE DAY IT GOES AWAY...
HA!
...AND THE EYES FORMERLY FILLED WITH LOVE...
...ARE NOW BLANK AND FULL OF TIRED IRRITATION.
YOU FEEL HURT!
YOU FEEL UNWANTED, YOU FEEL UNDESIRED. YOU FEEL UGLY AND STUPID!
SINCE NOTHING'S EVER YOUR FAULT, YOU FEEL IMMENSE PITY FOR YOURSELF, A POOR VICTIM OF PURE INJUSTICE!
* THE KEY IS TO NEVER EVER QUES-TION YOUR POSITION. YOU ARE NEVER WRONG!
CARLO ROSSI
AND WITH SADNESS, SELF-PITY, DEPRESSION COME SELF-DESTRUCTION, DRUGS, BOOZE, AND THE BEGINNING OF YOUR ANNIHILATION!
Age 25, Feb., 2007.

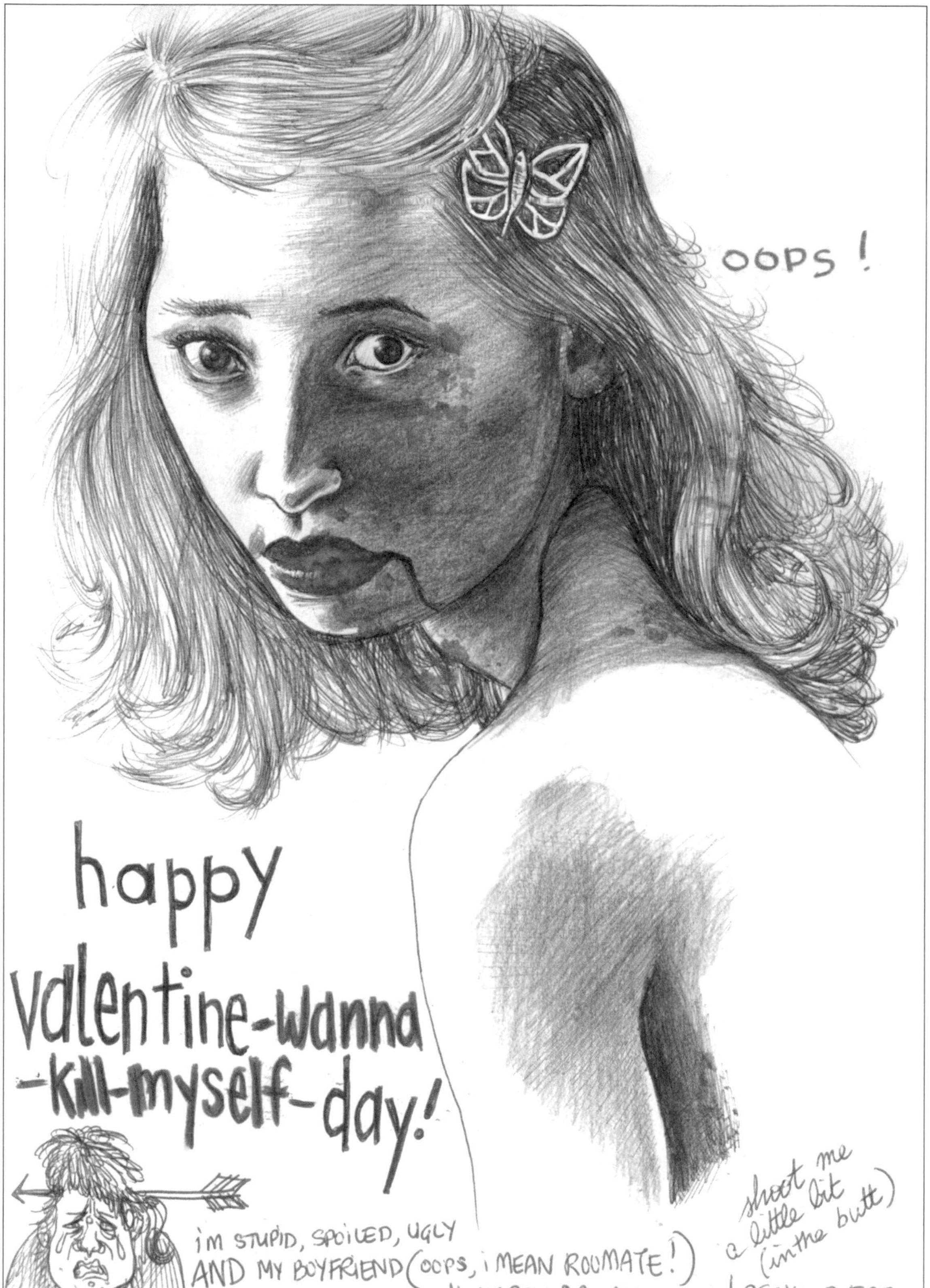
OOPS!
happy valentine-wanna-kill-myself-day!
im STUPID, SPOILED, UGLY
AND MY BOYFRIEND (OOPS, i MEAN ROOMATE!)
HAS NO DESIRE FOR ME !! HAPPY ♥ DAY, DEAR! PS=YOUR FAT
shoot me a little bit (in the butt)

Age 25, Feb., 2007.

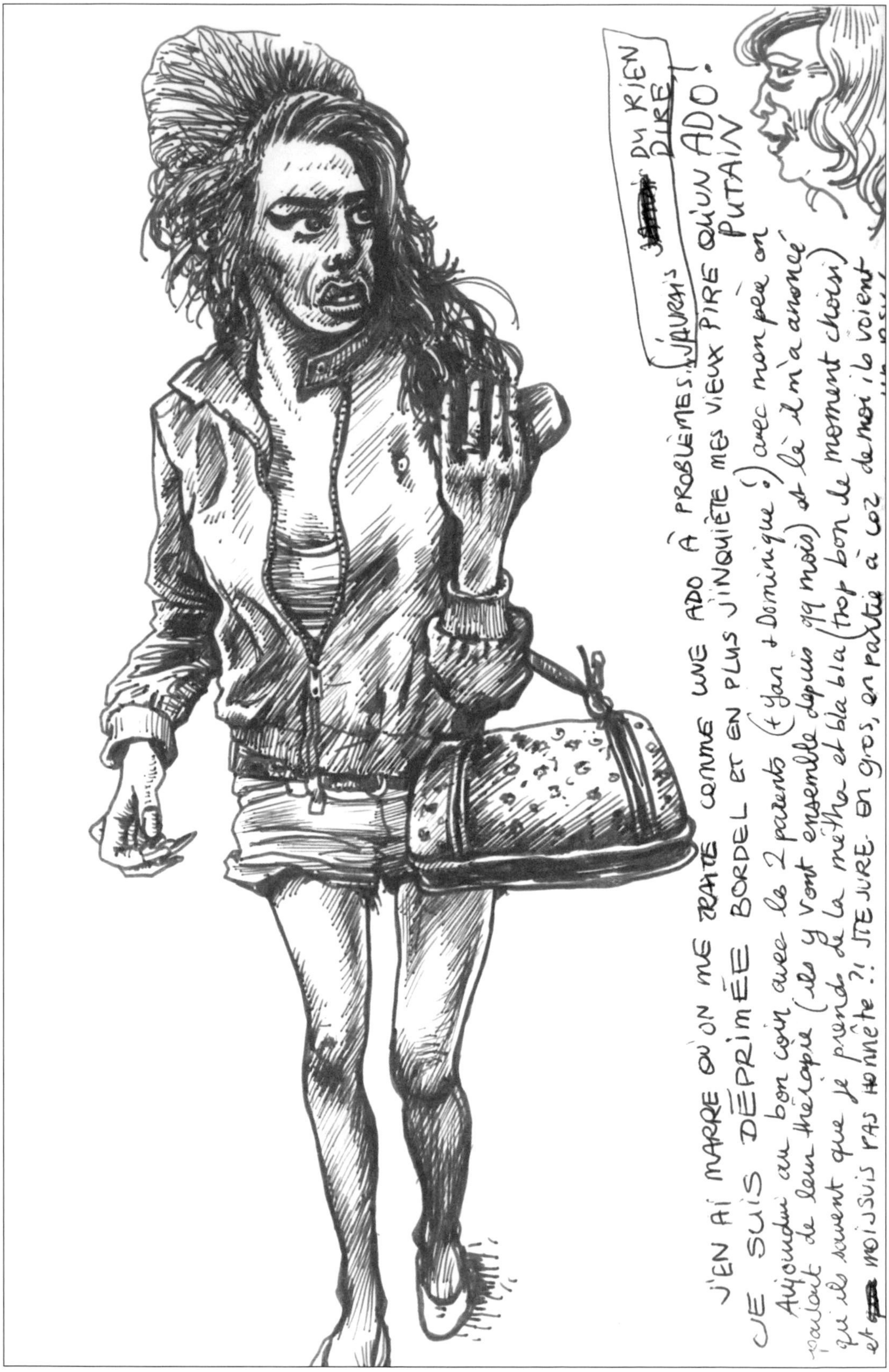
J'EN AI MARRE QU'ON ME TRAITE COMME UNE ADO À PROBLÈMES... J'AURAIS DU RIEN DIRE !
JE SUIS DÉPRIMÉE BORDEL ET EN PLUS J'INQUIÈTE MES VIEUX PIRE QU'UN ADO ! PUTAIN
Aujourdui au bon coin avec les 2 parents (+ Yan + Dominique !) avec mon père on
parlait de leur thérapie (ils y vont ensemble depuis qq mois) et là il m'a anoncé
qu'ils savent que je prends de la métha et bla bla (trop bon le moment choisi)
et MOI J'SUIS PAS HONNÊTE ?! J'TE JURE. En gros, en partie à coz de moi ils voient

Age 26, Sept., 2007.

APRÈS, Ernest leur a vivement dit DE PARTIR PASKILS SONT RESTÉS trop LONGTEMPS (en partie PASQUE JE LES AI DESSINÉ) ET IL VOULAIENT QU'ILS SE CASSENT! ILS ÉTAIENT VENU ACHETER DE LA BIÈRE.

29/09/07

Drawn from life. Age 26, Sept., 2007.

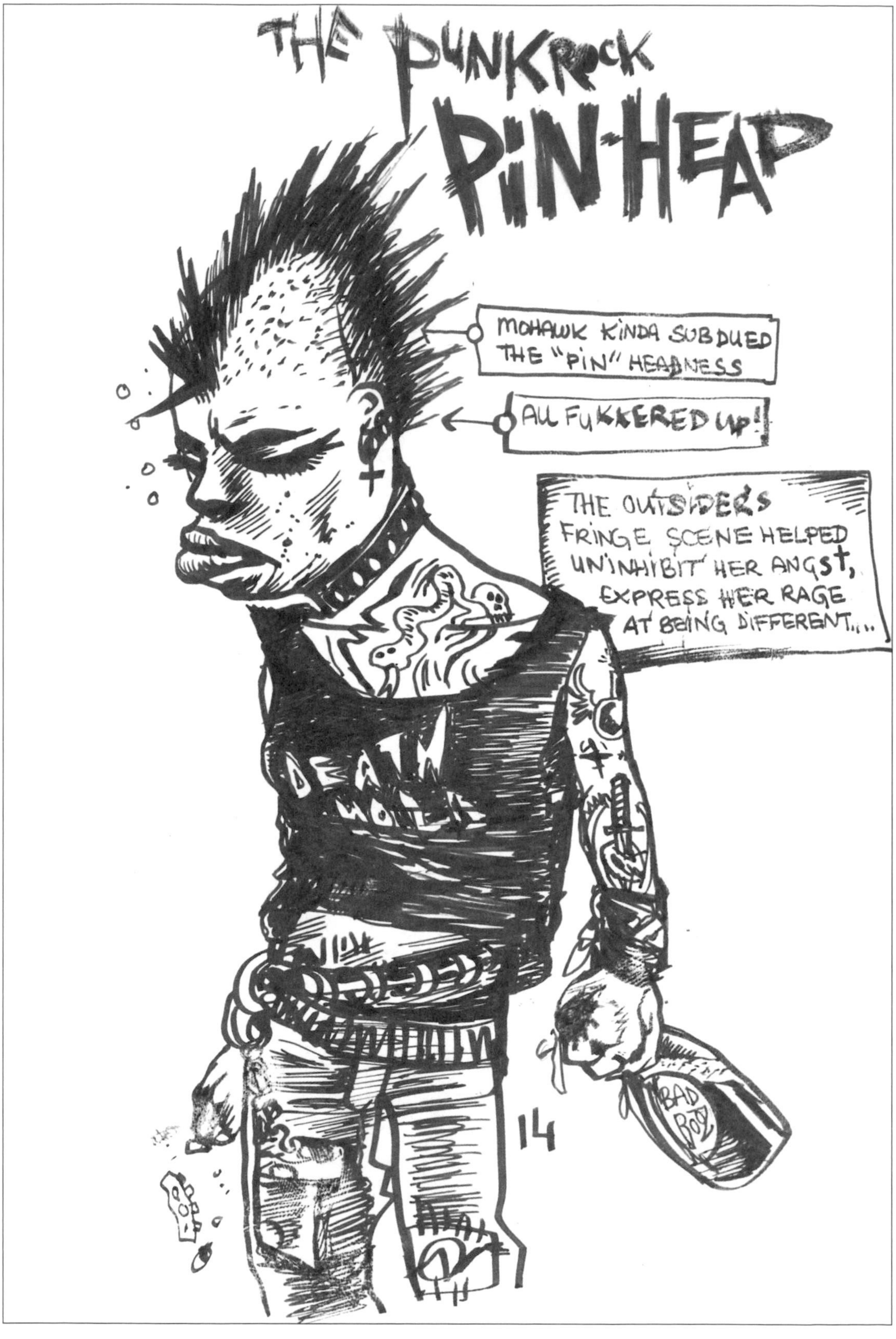
THE PUNKROCK
PIN-HEAD
MOHAWK KINDA SUBDUED THE "PIN" HEADNESS
ALL FUKKERED UP!
THE OUTSIDERS FRINGE SCENE HELPED UN'INHIBIT' HER ANGST, EXPRESS HER RAGE AT BEING DIFFERENT.....
14
BAD BOY

Age 26, Oct., 2007.

Aline. Drawn from life. Age 26, Dec., 2007.

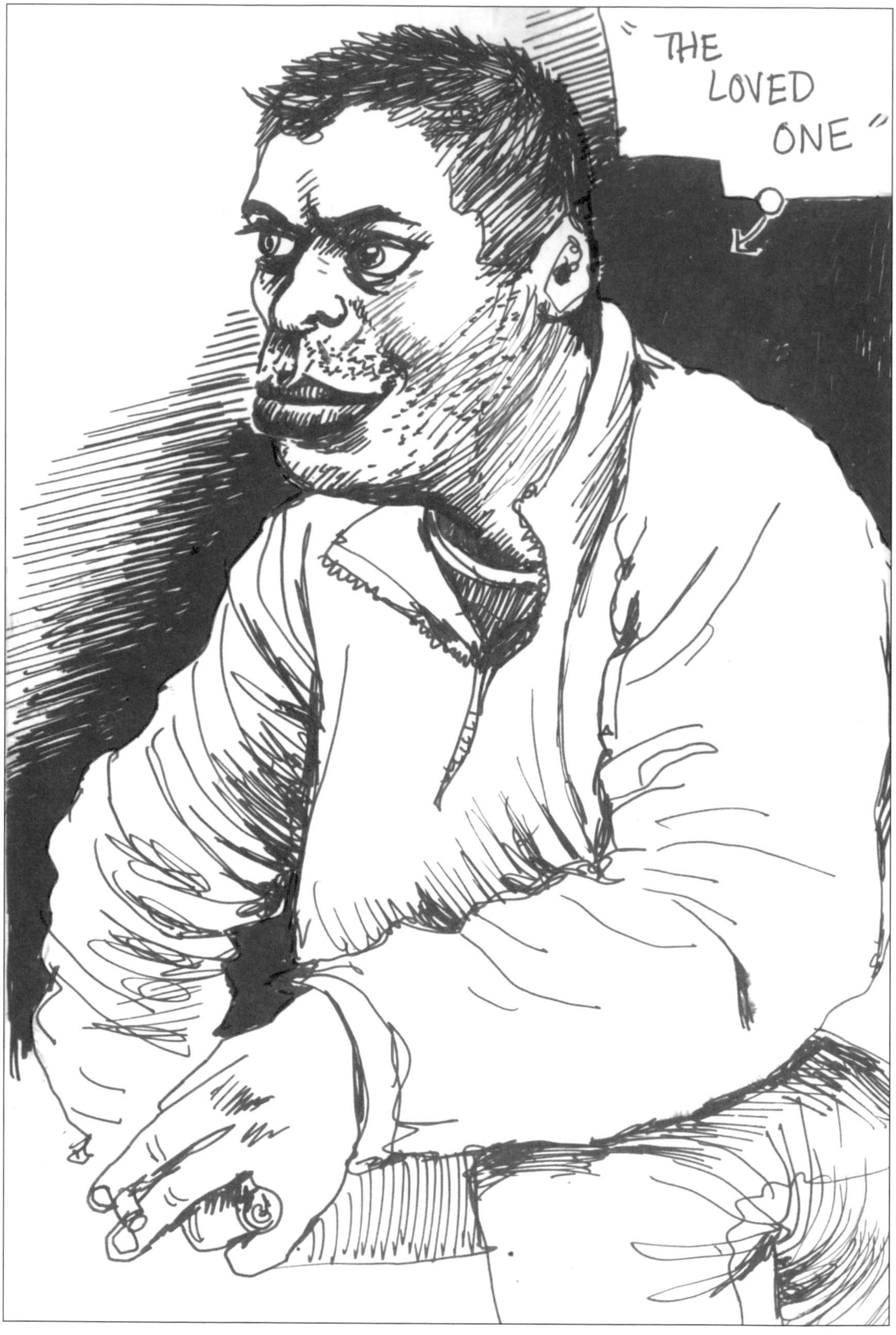
"THE LOVED ONE"

Drawn from life. Age 26, Jan., 2008.

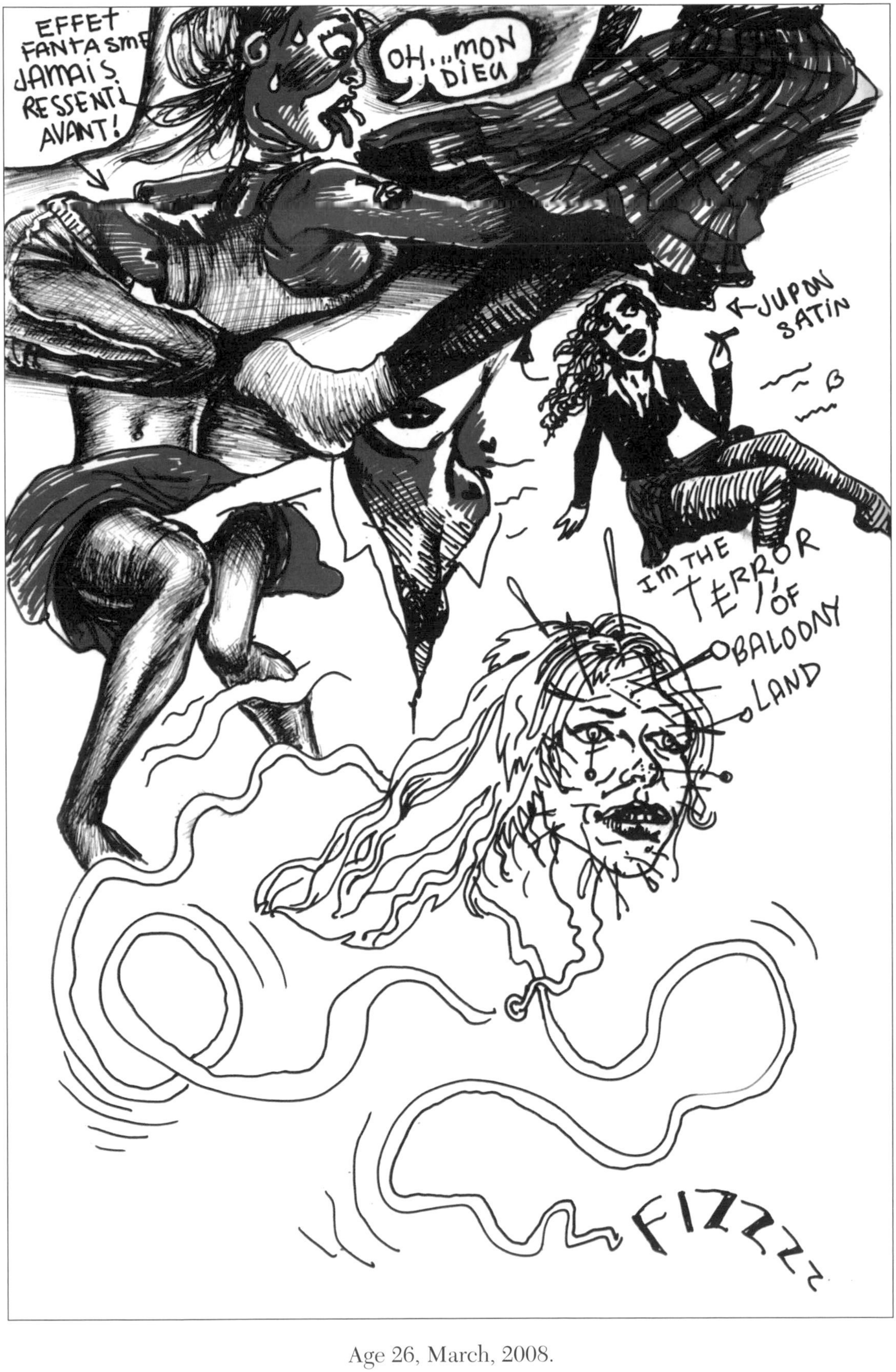
EFFET FANTASME JAMAIS RESSENTI AVANT!
OH...MON DIEU
JUPON SATIN
I'M THE TERROR OF BALOONY LAND
FIZZZZ

Age 26, March, 2008.

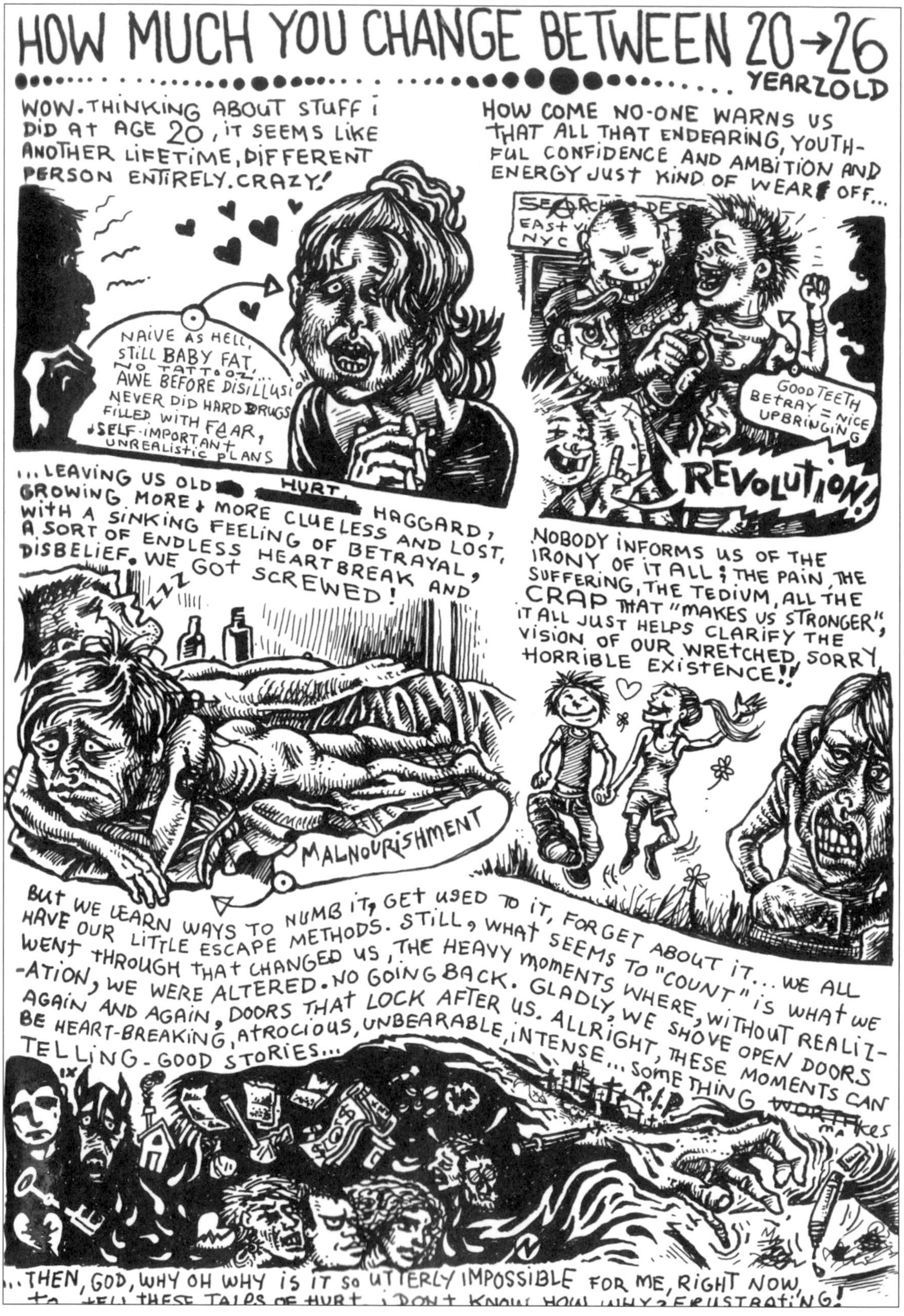
HOW MUCH YOU CHANGE BETWEEN 20→26 YEARZOLD
WOW. THINKING ABOUT STUFF I DID AT AGE 20, IT SEEMS LIKE ANOTHER LIFETIME, DIFFERENT PERSON ENTIRELY. CRAZY!
NAIVE AS HELL, STILL BABY FAT, NO TATTOOZ... AWE BEFORE DISILLUSION NEVER DID HARD DRUGS FILLED WITH FEAR, SELF-IMPORTANT UNREALISTIC PLANS
HOW COME NO-ONE WARNS US THAT ALL THAT ENDEARING, YOUTHFUL CONFIDENCE AND AMBITION AND ENERGY JUST KIND OF WEARS OFF...
EAST V NYC
GOOD TEETH BETRAY = NICE UPBRINGING
REVOLUTION!
...LEAVING US OLD [redacted] HURT, GROWING MORE & MORE CLUELESS AND LOST, HAGGARD, WITH A SINKING FEELING OF BETRAYAL, A SORT OF ENDLESS HEARTBREAK AND DISBELIEF. WE GOT SCREWED!
ZZZ
MALNOURISHMENT
NOBODY INFORMS US OF THE IRONY OF IT ALL; THE PAIN, THE SUFFERING, THE TEDIUM, ALL THE CRAP THAT "MAKES US STRONGER", IT ALL JUST HELPS CLARIFY THE VISION OF OUR WRETCHED, SORRY, HORRIBLE EXISTENCE!!
BUT WE LEARN WAYS TO NUMB IT, GET USED TO IT, FORGET ABOUT IT... WE ALL HAVE OUR LITTLE ESCAPE METHODS. STILL, WHAT SEEMS TO "COUNT" IS WHAT WE WENT THROUGH THAT CHANGED US, THE HEAVY MOMENTS WHERE, WITHOUT REALIZ-ATION, WE WERE ALTERED. NO GOING BACK. GLADLY, WE SHOVE OPEN DOORS AGAIN AND AGAIN, DOORS THAT LOCK AFTER US. ALLRIGHT, THESE MOMENTS CAN BE HEART-BREAKING, ATROCIOUS, UNBEARABLE, INTENSE... SOMETHING WORTH makes TELLING - GOOD STORIES...
R.I.P.
...THEN, GOD, WHY OH WHY IS IT SO UTTERLY IMPOSSIBLE FOR ME, RIGHT NOW, TO TELL THESE TALES OF HURT. I DON'T KNOW HOW, WHY? FRUSTRATING!

Age 26, April, 2008.

Drawn from life. Age 26, Sept., 2008.

Drawn from life. Age 26, Sept., 2008.

Drawn from life. Age 26, Sept., 2008.

le 15-09-08

Drawn from life. Age 26, Sept., 2008.

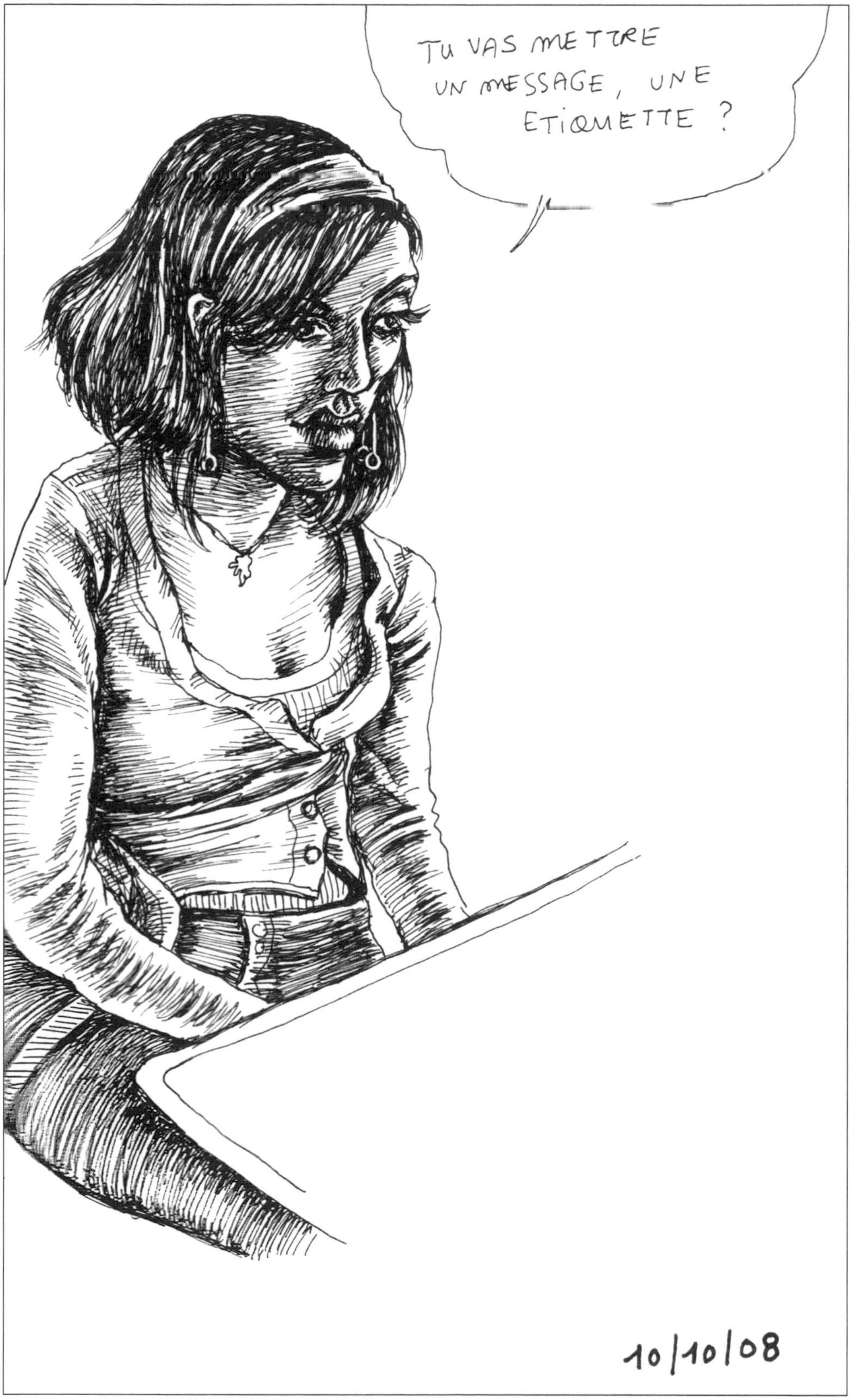
TU VAS METTRE UN MESSAGE, UNE ETIQUETTE ?
10/10/08

Drawn from life. Age 27, Oct., 2008.

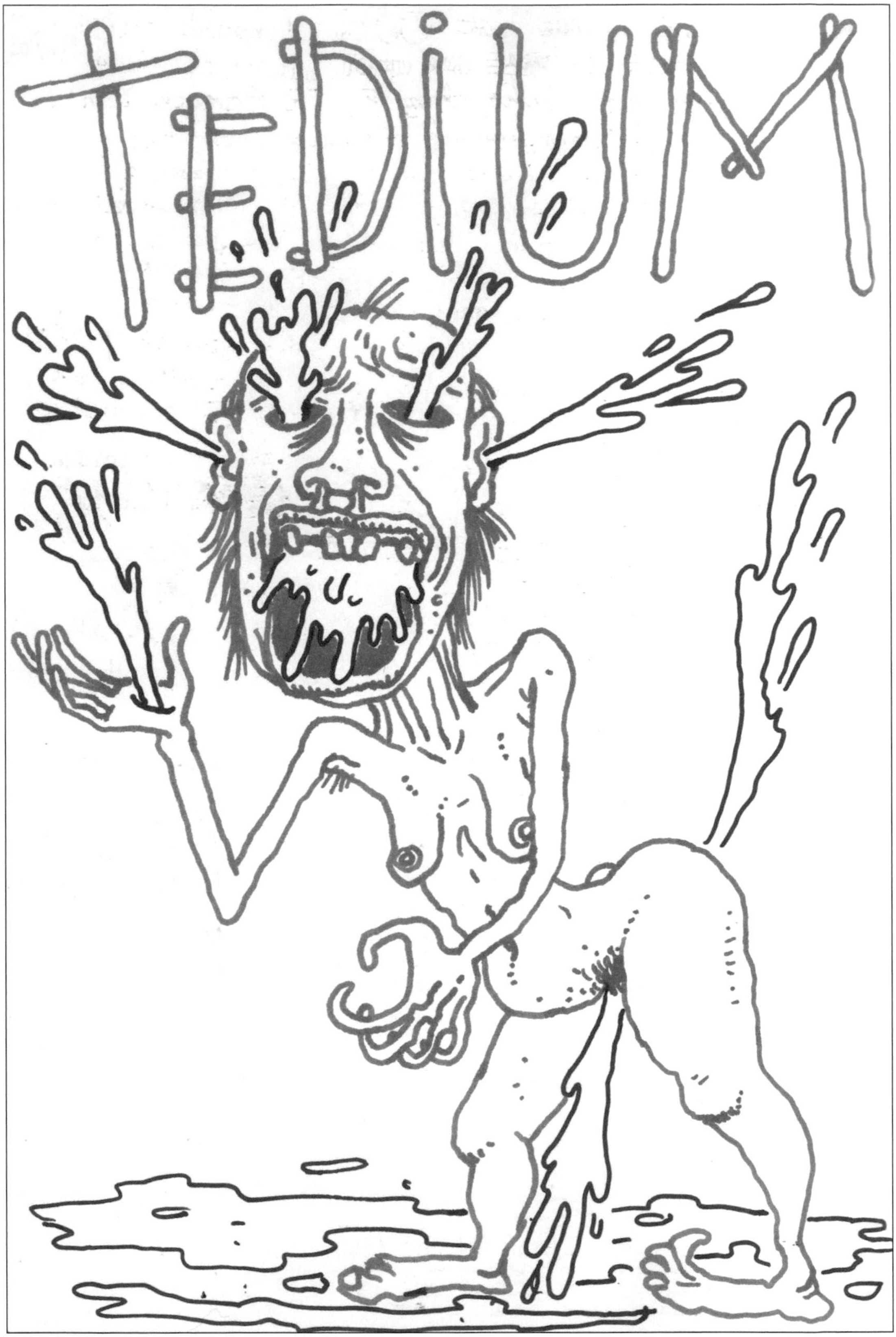
TEDIUM

Age 27, Nov., 2008.

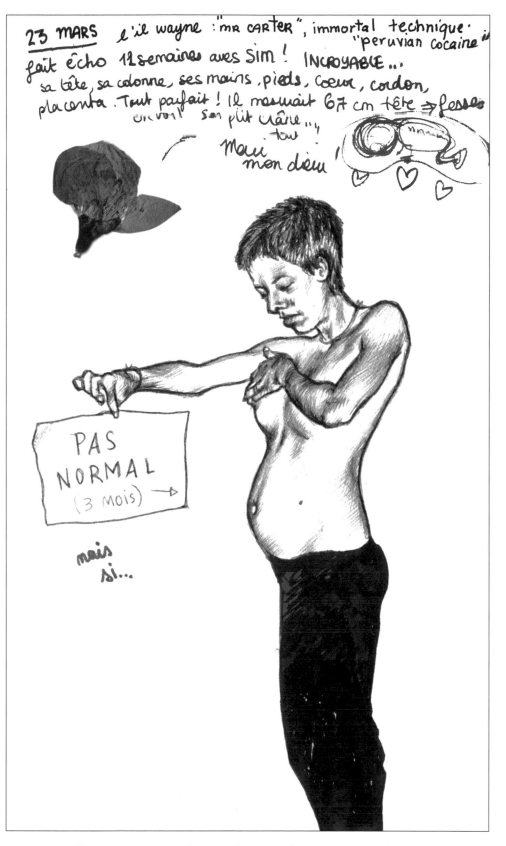

Self-portrait. Drawn from a photograph. Age 27, March, 2009.

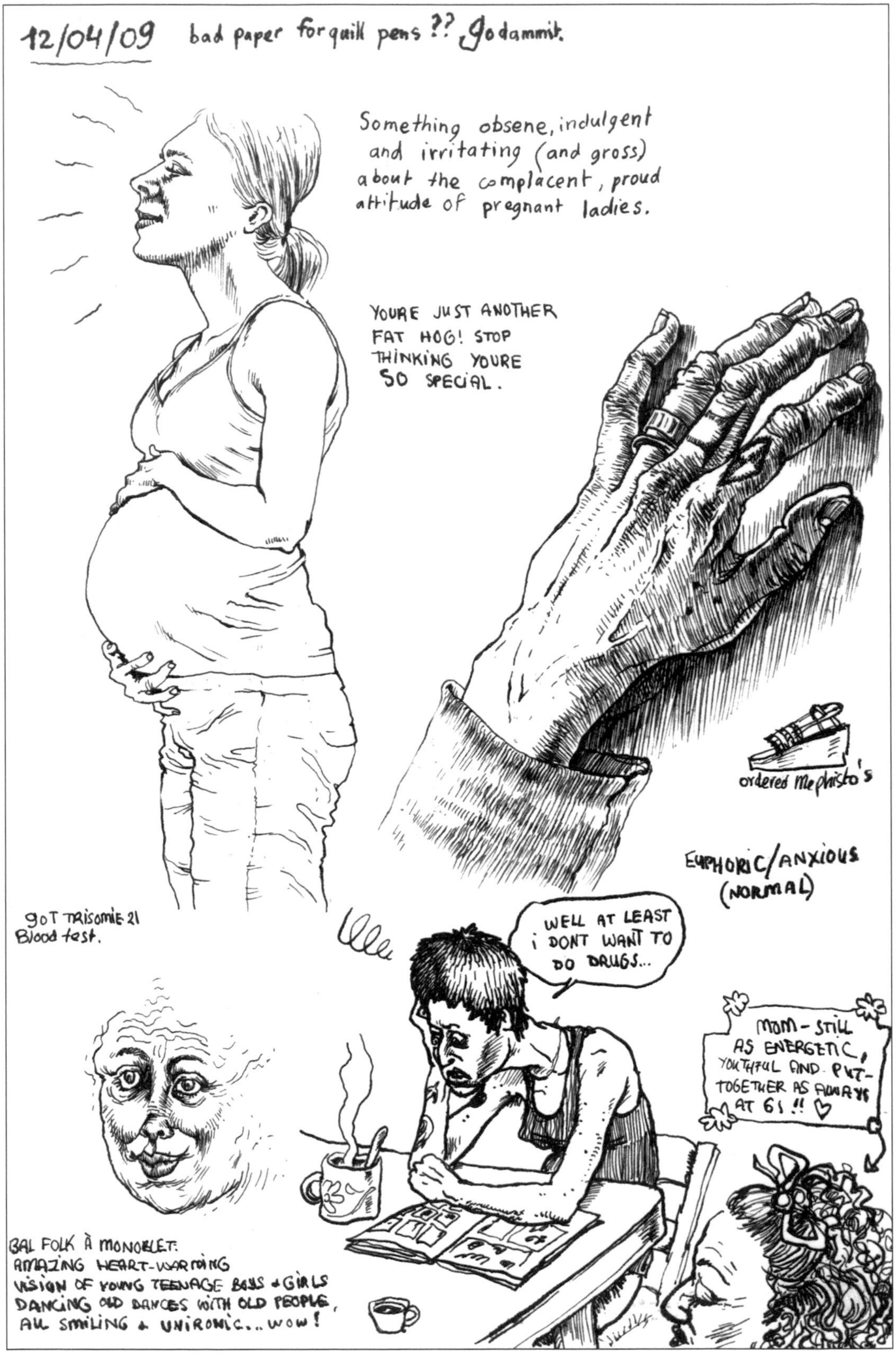
12/04/09 bad paper for quill pens ?? godammit.
Something obsene, indulgent and irritating (and gross) about the complacent, proud attitude of pregnant ladies.
YOURE JUST ANOTHER FAT HOG! STOP THINKING YOURE SO SPECIAL.
ordered Mephisto's
EUPHORIC/ANXIOUS (NORMAL)
got TRISOMIE 21 Blood test.
WELL AT LEAST i DONT WANT TO DO DRUGS...
MOM - STILL AS ENERGETIC, YOUTHFUL AND PUT-TOGETHER AS ALWAYS AT 61 !!
BAL FOLK À MONOBLET: AMAZING HEART-WARMING VISION OF YOUNG TEENAGE BOYS + GIRLS DANCING OLD DANCES WITH OLD PEOPLE, ALL SMILING + UNIRONIC... WOW!

Age 27, April, 2009.

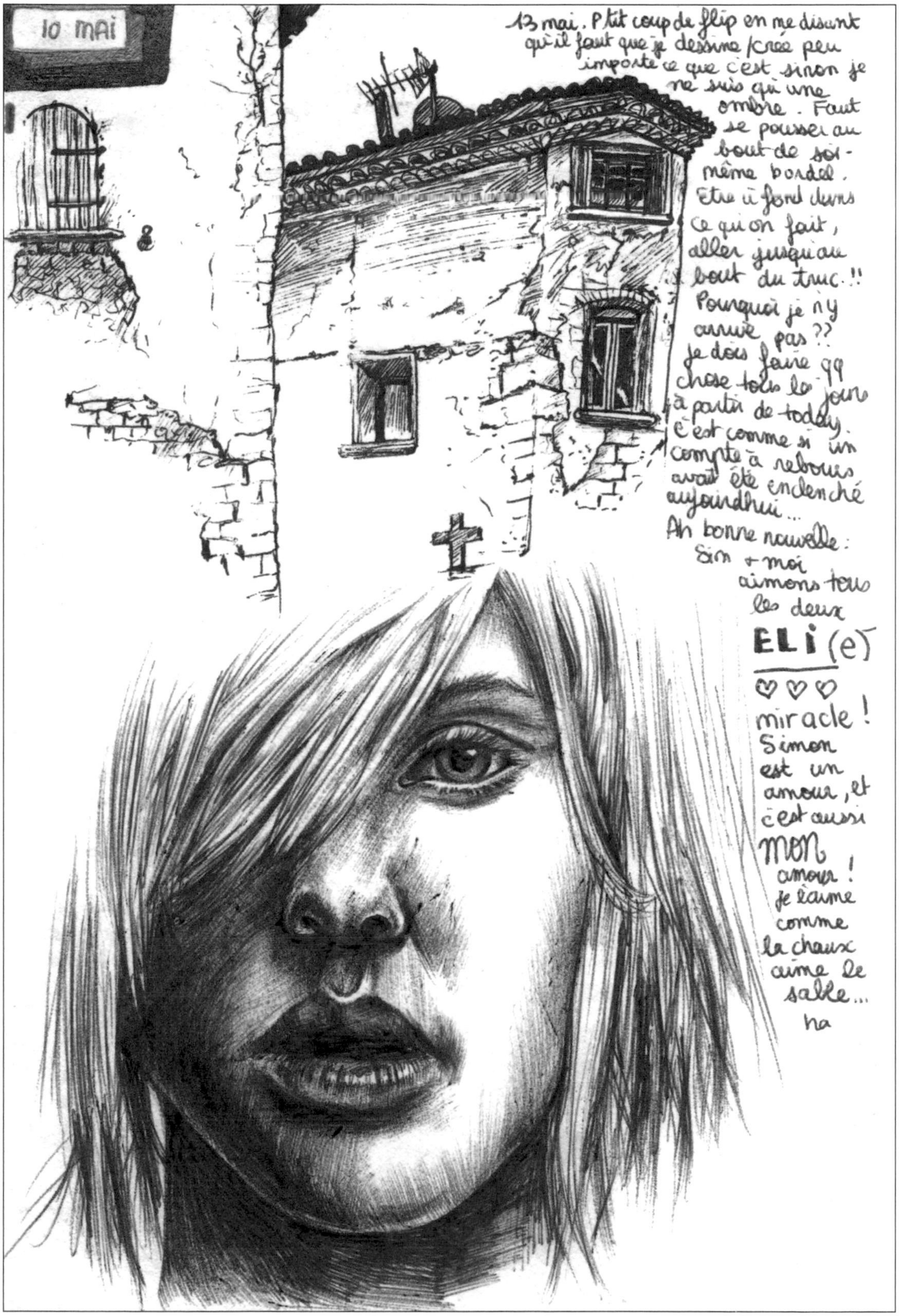
10 MAI
13 mai. P'tit coup de flip en me disant qu'il faut que je dessine/crée peu importe ce que c'est sinon je ne suis qu'une ombre. Faut se pousser au bout de soi-même bordel. Etre à fond dans ce qu'on fait, aller jusqu'au bout du truc.!! Pourquoi je n'y arrive pas?? je dois faire qq chose tous les jours à partir de today. C'est comme si un compte à rebours avait été enclenché aujourd'hui...
Ah bonne nouvelle: Sim + moi aimons tous les deux
ELI(e)
♡♡♡
miracle! Simon est un amour, et c'est aussi MON amour! je l'aime comme la chaux aime le sable... ha

Age 27, May, 2009.

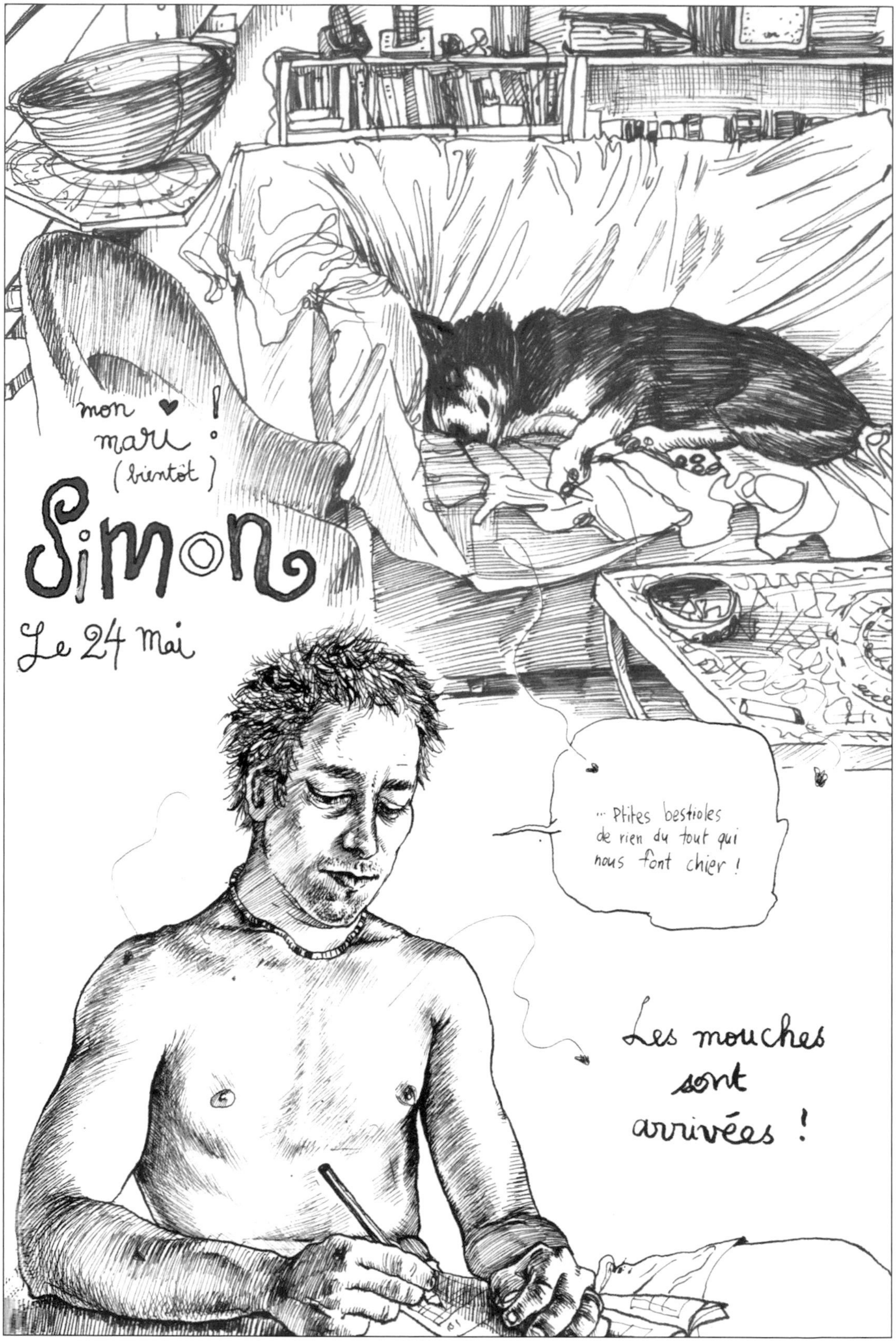
mon ♥ mari ! (bientôt)
Simon
Le 24 mai
... Ptites bestioles de rien du tout qui nous font chier !
Les mouches sont arrivées !

Drawn from life. Age 27, May, 2009.

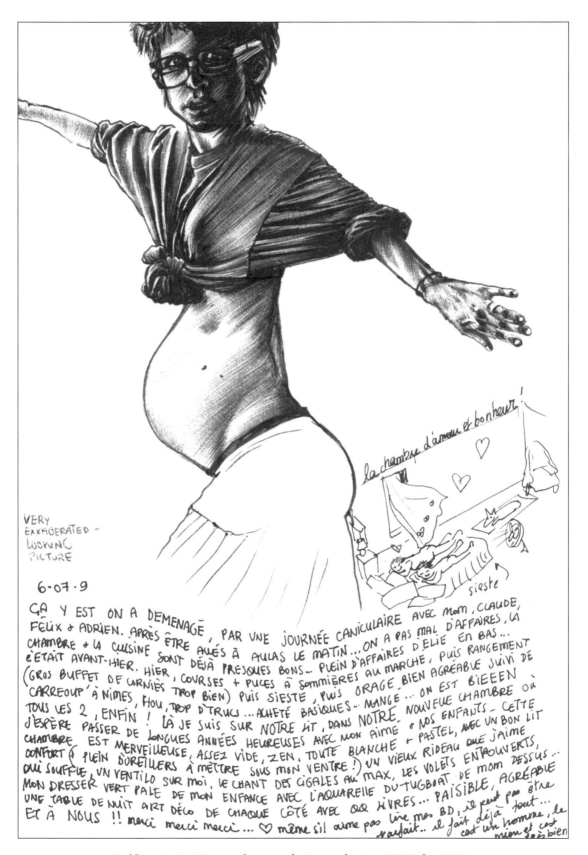

Self-portrait. Drawn from a photograph. Age 27, July, 2009.

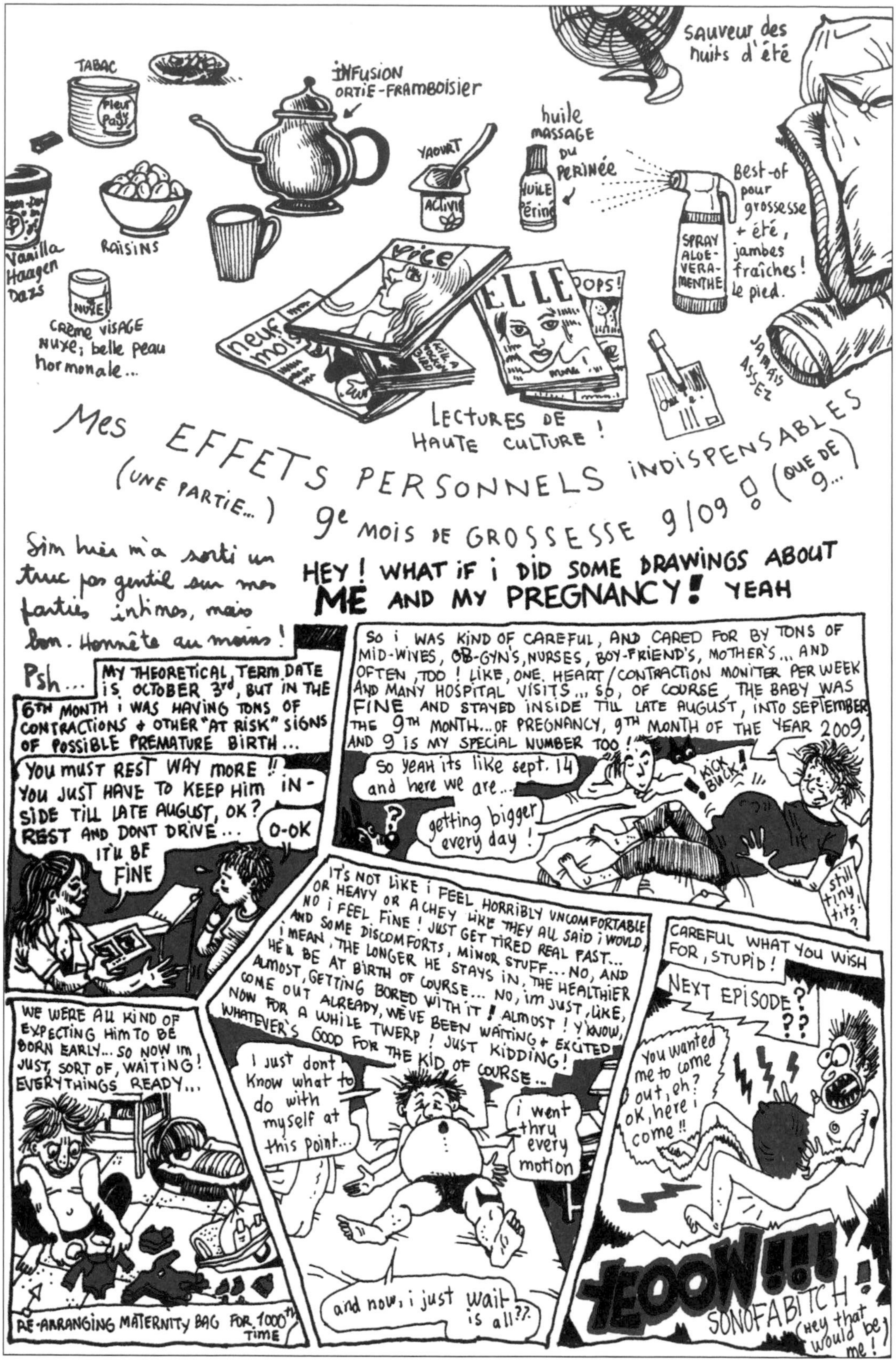
sauveur des nuits d'été
TABAC
INFUSION ORTIE-FRAMBOISIER
huile massage du PERINÉE
YAOURT
ACTIVIA
HUILE Périné
Best-of pour grossesse + été, jambes fraîches! le pied.
SPRAY ALOE-VERA-MENTHE
Vanilla Haagen Dazs
RAISINS
NUXE
Crème visage Nuxe; belle peau hormonale...
VICE
ELLE
OOPS!
neuf mois
LECTURES DE HAUTE CULTURE!
JAMAIS ASSEZ
MES EFFETS PERSONNELS INDISPENSABLES (UNE PARTIE...)
9e MOIS DE GROSSESSE 9/09 (QUE DE 9...)
Sim lui m'a sorti un truc pas gentil sur mes parties intimes, mais bon. Honnête au moins!
Psh...
HEY! WHAT IF I DID SOME DRAWINGS ABOUT ME AND MY PREGNANCY! YEAH
MY THEORETICAL TERM DATE IS OCTOBER 3rd, BUT IN THE 6TH MONTH I WAS HAVING TONS OF CONTRACTIONS & OTHER "AT RISK" SIGNS OF POSSIBLE PREMATURE BIRTH...
YOU MUST REST WAY MORE!! YOU JUST HAVE TO KEEP HIM INSIDE TILL LATE AUGUST, OK? REST AND DONT DRIVE... IT'LL BE FINE
O-OK
SO I WAS KIND OF CAREFUL, AND CARED FOR BY TONS OF MID-WIVES, OB-GYN'S, NURSES, BOY-FRIEND'S, MOTHER'S... AND OFTEN, TOO! LIKE, ONE HEART/CONTRACTION MONITER PER WEEK AND MANY HOSPITAL VISITS... SO, OF COURSE, THE BABY WAS FINE AND STAYED INSIDE TILL LATE AUGUST, INTO SEPTEMBER THE 9TH MONTH... OF PREGNANCY, 9TH MONTH OF THE YEAR 2009, AND 9 IS MY SPECIAL NUMBER TOO!
So yeah its like sept. 14 and here we are...
KICK BACK!
getting bigger every day!
still tiny tits!?
IT'S NOT LIKE I FEEL HORRIBLY UNCOMFORTABLE OR HEAVY OR ACHEY LIKE THEY ALL SAID I WOULD, NO I FEEL FINE! JUST GET TIRED REAL FAST... AND SOME DISCOMFORTS, MINOR STUFF... NO, AND I MEAN, THE LONGER HE STAYS IN, THE HEALTHIER HE'LL BE AT BIRTH OF COURSE... NO, IM JUST, LIKE, ALMOST, GETTING BORED WITH IT! ALMOST! Y'KNOW, COME OUT ALREADY, WE'VE BEEN WAITING & EXCITED NOW FOR A WHILE TWERP! JUST KIDDING! WHATEVER'S GOOD FOR THE KID OF COURSE...
CAREFUL WHAT YOU WISH FOR, STUPID!
NEXT EPISODE???
WE WERE ALL KIND OF EXPECTING HIM TO BE BORN EARLY... SO NOW IM JUST, SORT OF, WAITING! EVERYTHINGS READY...
RE-ARRANGING MATERNITY BAG FOR 1000th TIME
I just dont know what to do with myself at this point...
i went thru every motion
and now, i just wait is all??
You wanted me to come out, eh? ok, here i come!!
YEOOW!!!!
SONOFABITCH! (hey that would be me!)

Age 28, Sept., 2009.

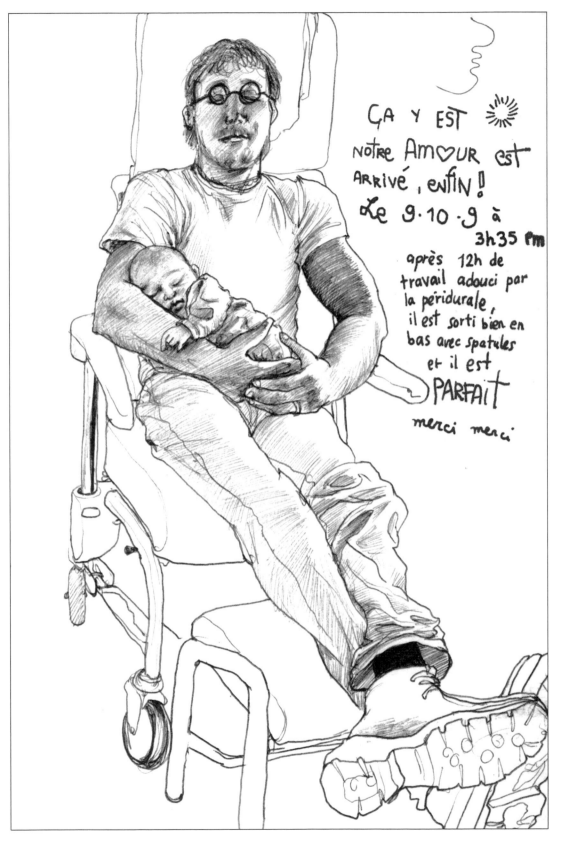

Simon asleep at the hospital, holding his and Sophie's newborn baby son, Elie.
Drawn from life. Age 28, Oct., 2009.

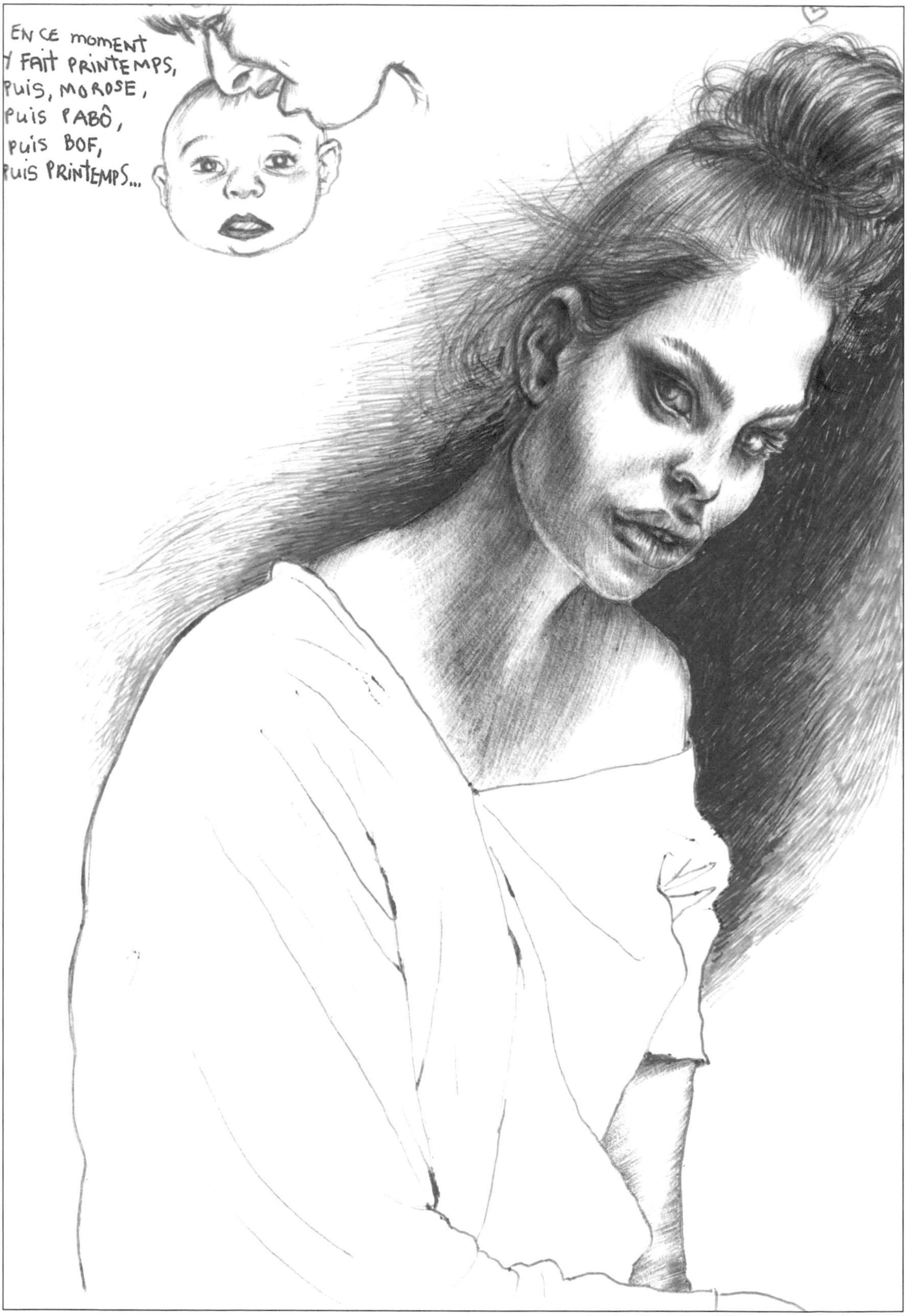
EN CE moment
Y FAIT PRINTEMPS,
PUIS, MOROSE,
PUIS PABÔ,
PUIS BOF,
PUIS PRINTEMPS...

Age 28, March, 2010.

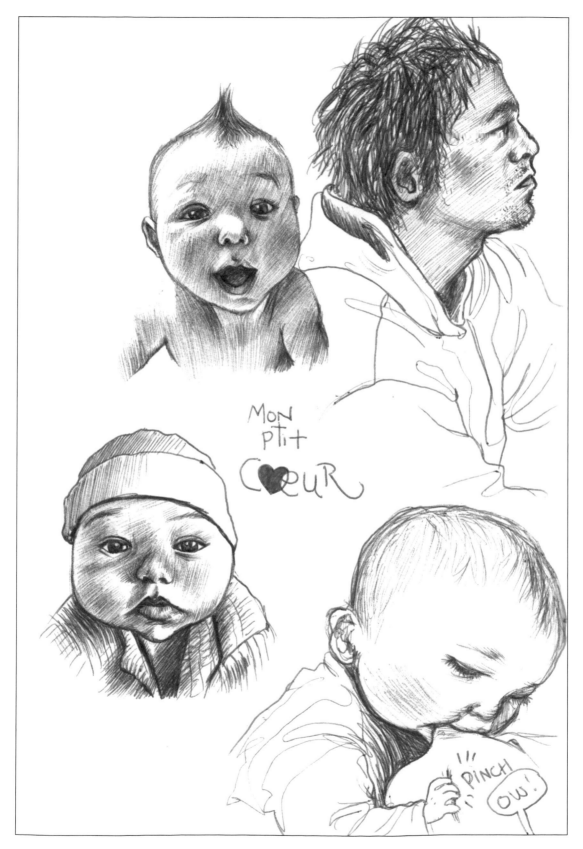

Sophie's baby, Eli, and husband, Simon. Drawn from photographs and from life.
Age 28, March, 2010.

FOUND PARIS RUE DES CASCADES . 5 MAI 2004 "Alex"

GRAY FOR STREET ART